WALKING FR JERUSALEM: MY LIFE IN THE WORLDWIDE CHURCH OF GOD

BY COY REECE HOLLEY

[PROLOGUE:] "The Ravensbruck Prayer"

"…Peace be to men who are of bad will, and may an end be put to all vengeance and to all talk about punishment and chastisement. The cruelties mock all norms and principles, they are beyond all limits of human understanding and there are many martyrs. Therefore, God does not weigh their sufferings on the scales of your justice, so that you would demand a cruel account, but rather let it be valid in a different way. Rather, write in favor of all executioners, traitors, and spies, and all bad men, and credit to them all the courage and strength of soul of the others…

"…All the good should count and not the evil. And for the memories of our enemies, we should no longer remain their victims, no longer their nightmare and their shuddering ghosts, but rather their help, so that they may cease their fury. That is the only thing that is asked of them, and that we, after it is all over, may be able to live as humans among humans, and that there may be peace again, on this poor earth for the men of good will and that this peace may come also to the others." [Excerpt from "By The Waters Of Babylon", p. 223; Warner Books, Inc. (New York City), Nelson Demille, © 1978]

[Author's Personal Addenum Prayer: May the above be quickly and speedily done even so in these very days through Yeshua Ha'Meshiach/the Lord Jesus Christ…Amen.]

[INTRODUCTION:] Why Am I Even Walking In The First Place?

It seems after all these years that in one way or the other I've spent a good amount of my time walking in some form both physically and spiritually. Some of the time it was because I wanted to just get away from the house. But mostly it was due to financial reasons because it was the ONLY way I could get to where I needed to go.

Most people in today's society can not even fathom or understand what I just said. "YOU MEAN YOU DON'T HAVE A CAR? WHY???? Well, don't you have a driver's license?" I most certainly do—I've had one ever since I was a junior in high school. I've kept one up for years now. Besides, it's hard to cash a check or do much else these days without one. "Then why don't you have one?" One of my most standard responses tends to be—"...no dinero, no automobile." (Doesn't that strangely seem too much like the truth to you or not?)

What's even more interesting is this—that where I live in West Texas, it almost seems to be a MANDATORY constitutional requirement that you must have something of your own to drive. And if—oh, gasp, the horror of such a thought—it's basically a bleeped if you do and bleeped if you don't dilemma that seems next to impossible to overcome. And, oh—by the way, forget about having a realistic shot at most jobs around here in West Texas if you don't have a car—ESPECIALLY if you want a GOOD job WITH BENEFITS!

In a place that I bet most city slickers couldn't survive two minutes, this is also where the nearest airports are at least an hour to an hour-and-a-half away; Amtrak doesn't even know that we exist (or at least that's what it seems like—because you have to go an eight-hour drive to Fort Worth just to catch it); and all Greyhound buses only run north or south twice a day at best [and guess what—if you want to get anywhere else they may run, you will have to go through either Lubbock, Big Spring, or (most of the time) Amarillo].

And in Plainview where I currently reside, forget completely about subways or city buses. There is one rural transportation service, of course—but it only runs on weekdays, requires at least a one-day advance notice to even get on the list, and will cost you about the price of an arm AND a leg just for a one-way trip out of town. [Plus...FYI--they tend to give more preference to Medicaid patients with doctor's appointments rather than working stiffs like me due to one reason--our benevolent federal government pays this same transportation service a whopping $125 for every Medicaid patient...while working folks like myself who only pay a dollar per ride and/or use a punch card good for 20 rides are sometimes forced to be on the shorter end of the stick.] So if there has been an ideal description of someone who has been forced to literally "walk by faith", don't be too surprised if you keep seeing my picture on potential candidate posters for the title during the next round of elections.

Obviously, there have been various advantages and disadvantages as well as highs and lows during the many times I've walked on various journeys in my life. Not all of those were always on foot—some did involve vehicles and various other modes of transportation at various times. There have been many who have at various points of my life provided rides and other things that I've needed along the way. Some of them are no longer with us—and whom I may never see again until the Savior comes back and His Kingdom's finally established on this earth.

One of those is a lady whose picture on her funeral bulletin reminded me as I originally wrote this of someone that was a part of some of those journeys for a number of years who died in 2010. Some I only got to meet one time at life's most critical junctures. Others I've had the privilege of establishing long-term relationships that have lasted for years and still continue even to this very day. Either way, at those times I've needed them most, they've helped add more fuel to my fire to continue on the roads I've needed to travel for Him.

And what are some of those roads I've had to walk down? The soles of the many pairs of shoes I've worn throughout the years could tell a lot of stories and tales much better than I even could. They could first tell you some of the things I had to endure while growing up—of life as a son of a single mother whose dad left both of them just a few months before that son was even born, of various bullies, heartache, rejections, of going to both my junior and senior proms alone, and how even as I felt like Norm Peterson on "Cheers" that I could still feel somewhat like a social outcast in my own high school.

Other pairs could tell you what it was like for me during my college years—yes, the good AND the bad AND even (gasp!) the ugly. They could tell you of fun times I had (or some at least on the surface appeared to be), of lessons learned, and some interesting experiences I went through and different people I had the chance to meet.

One or two of those same pairs could also tell you of a summer in Western Maryland that would prove to be one of my own lynchpin experiences that would forever change the way I saw my world. That included occasions that forced me out of my West Texas comfort zone and see some places throughout this nation of ours that wouldn't have been otherwise able to see in several lifetimes.

The dress shoes and boots in particular could reveal more specific details of my life (pre- AND post-split) as a member of the Worldwide Church of God (now known as Grace Communion International). Those dress shoes and boots could really tell you some of the stories from my vantage point that many in orthodox Christianity once regarded as a "cult"—but to which I can now more proudly say is instead "the church that changed". The dress shoes and boots will especially help me set the record straight about a movement that some still call "Armstrongism"— and why in the world I would have desired to be a part of a church like this in the first place (let alone still maintain my membership even after these many years and the sort of "trail of tears" I had to personally go through in the process).

Also, while we're in the shoe closet, I might as well show you the shoes I wore during my time in Albuquerque—and in which I sadly had to also wear when I had to personally go through my "Siberian Exile/Great Tribulation" period. They would still tell you the sad stories of the trials I suffered during that time and of what happens when it seems everything in life is literally crashing down around you. How does one keep their sanity, faith, and even their life intact in the midst of what seems to be the modern equivalent of financial and other forms of slavery? You'll find out as we go along. Also, they'll teach you personally about how you should act when it seems everything you once relied upon is gone and about what is truly important when it's said and done.

But let me also, though, show you some shoes from much happier times after that when I was finally able to move to Plainview. A couple of those pairs will tell you how those years all began for me. Others will tell you of other special trips I made along the way—one of those in particular which eventually led to how I received "...the baptism of the Holy Spirit". Others will go more into detail about some walks in faith I've literally taken on His behalf that have led to immense blessings that I could not contain or imagine. There's even a brand-new pair I've never worn that will help me talk about some things on my heart and mind that I feel He may desire for me to share with the world involving a vision for the future that the Universal Body of Christ should consider adopting as well as perspectives and viewpoints on current trends and issues that face our world today.

A brief proviso I must add, though, before I go too much further...I will very much promise you that there WILL be more than enough things that I will say in the upcoming pages that may be EXTREMELY controversial in one form or the other—especially when it comes to topics such as those of a political nature; spiritual gifts, or observance of Biblical customs, traditions, and holidays. Save yourself the trouble of sending me the e-mails, etc. if your hope is to try to one way or the other "get me back into the fold" of what YOU perceive as your appropriate denominational tradition—because this homey DON'T play that game. I instead challenge you to read the Word for yourself, check out everything said here against, and talk to Him about it. If you don't agree with it, then I right now allow you the liberty of eating the meat and spitting out the bones and trashing them into File 13.

Now with that little bit of business taken care of, let's check out two more pairs of shoes in the shoe closet I haven't shown you yet. One of those is in a size that only the Master Himself can wear and in which I save for His exclusive use anytime He wishes to come alongside me on the journey I'm taking. And the final pair is for someone that the Lord Himself told me to buy for. Guess what? It just happens to be in YOUR shoe size. And have I truly got a deal for you today! They're yours to keep under one condition—that you accept my invitation to go along with me on a sort of guided tour of my own life that will be the contents of the remainder of this book. Does that sound like a plan to you? Wanna join me? OK!!! Go ahead and pick up those shoes and try them on—'cause we're fixing to leave pretty soon.

First, while you're putting those shoes on, let me go ahead and fill you in on the general game plan for this trip we're fixing to take. Our starting point will be in Lockney where for me it all began. When we get there, I'll take you through a pretty lengthy tour around town for at least the first part of this book. After that, we'll proceed from there and I'll let you know where we're going to next. Deal?

Oh, yeah—you're saying that you didn't know you were going and forgot to pack? That's alright—I've already got you covered there. And besides—didn't the Master Himself say to His disciples before He sent them out (Matt. 10:9 & 10, NLT): "…Don't take any money in your money belts—no gold, silver, or even copper coins. Don't carry a traveler's bag with a change of clothes and sandals or even a walking stick. Don't hesitate to accept hospitality, because those who work deserve to be fed."

And, oh—The Master called me before you came and said that He'd join us later and catch up with us along the way. I told Him to make sure he stops by here first to pick up His shoes whenever He gets ready to meet us. He's already got the key to this place anyway—so hopefully we'll see him somewhere down the road as we travel along. OK—help yourself to something to drink from the fridge while I wrap up some final details first….

[AUTHOR'S SPECIAL DEDICATIONS:] This book is dedicated to the following—

> **In memory of (but NOT in worship to) former WCG/GCI Pastor Generals Herbert W. Armstrong and Joseph W. Tkach, Sr....**
> **In memory of (as well as in honor of) all past, present, and former members of WCG/GCI—both to those no longer with us as well as those that are still pressing on in some form (…for those who couldn't quite make it to help tell the full story, let mine substitute as their voice for part of theirs)...**
> **AND…others in the Universal Body of Christ (regardless of denomination, personal background, etc.)—You're the reason I'm still walking today not only for myself, but for a number of others as well so that their own stories can now also be told to the world and be as accurately and fairly presented as much as is realistically possible.**

For those that now don't have a voice, now comes from it my own obligation to write to speak for them.

This author especially wishes to formally thank members of the Plainview, Texas Witness Writers chapter of the North Texas Christian Writers Group for their honest and sometimes brutal critiques of various parts of this books as well as several special friends and other supporters who have specifically requested to remain anonymous, but who nevertheless were crucial to the development of this project.

All digital camera photography was done by the original author of this work...

We've got a long road to travel and not a lot of time or space to do it in—you ready to go? Let's get out of Dodge, shall we? Even now, as we're leaving the city limits...

We see this very informative sign up ahead:

TXDOT should have added another thing to this sign—

        NEW JERUSALEM   ??????

HAVE A GREAT TRIP! Let's go—I promise you it'll be a great walk indeed!

[Chapter 1: (Lockney--Part I) W. Wilson St.—Being Raised As A "Black Sheep"]

Well—we've finally managed to go down US 70 and get closer to Lockney where our journey through my life begins. As we're coming into town, we see Farm To Market Road 97 branching off and calling us to go to Flomot on our left. But we'll resist that call and instead continue here on 70 for a few more blocks past what used to be the old railroad tracks and also what is one of the maintenance department buildings of the city of Lockney.

At the next crossover, we'll then take a left, then once we see Spruce Street take an immediate right. We'll continue east on Spruce for a couple of blocks, then turn right on Sixth. Our first tour stop will be near where Sixth and Wilson Streets mutually dead end with each other. You'll see a couple of houses down on the left the very small one-bedroom, one-bath rent house that Mother and I stayed in during most of my childhood years. On the steps next to the back door on the east side next to the storm cellar will be the spot that I'll start talking to you about what I can remember about my formative years and formally introduce you to my mother who was primarily responsible for my raising.

My grandparents, Granvel and Jo Webb, were originally both born and raised in North Texas in the community of Pike about 30 miles drive from McKinney and the northern part of the Dallas/Fort Worth area and within 2 hours drive of the Sherman/Denison area south of the Red River and the Texas/Oklahoma state line. My grandmother's father and family during her youth ran a general merchantile store for the folks in the local area while my granddad and his family were very active farmers of cotton, corn, and other crops. Both of my grandparents were very highly influenced by this strong work ethic. My granddad due to economic conditions at the time between the time of the Great Depression and the start of WWII never got past the sixth grade in school because he had to help his family out in the fields. "Papa" (as I would later call him) was eventually drafted during WWII to serve in the US Army as a truck driver in a tank battalion that fought in southern Germany and France.

After the war was over and Papa came back home, my grandmother was very young when my mother, Lynda, was born. I'm not sure of the exact circumstances involved at the time, but it turns out that my granddad was actually Mother's stepdad due to the fact that my grandparents didn't actually get married until Mother was five years old. After my grandparents married, their union would eventually produce three more offspring: Rubie (the next eldest daughter), Randy, and Arlene (the youngest).

Sometime in 1950 or 1951, my grandparents moved the family to our current home here in West Texas where my granddad took a job with what was then called Acco Seed at their production facility north of the community of Aiken where he served as a grain manager for nearly 30 years until his retirement around 1980. My grandmother meanwhile worked as a sales clerk in several stores and dry cleaners' establishments in the Plainview area and developed a reputation for being an excellent seamstress who was highly in demand amongst the locals. The family for a number of years lived in a company-owned house a couple of miles south of the Aiken production facility before my grandparents eventually bought the house in Lockney after most of the kids were grown--where my grandmother still makes her residence to this day.

The rest of my mother's siblings did manage to at least graduate from high school and get some sort of college education—with both Rubie and Arlene both having attended West Texas State University in Canyon, TX. My uncle Randy decided to go into the field of auto mechanics where he eventually worked in a number of car dealerships and repair garages before eventually opening his own very busy and thriving auto repair shop in Plainview.

My aunt Rubie first started in teaching before eventually moving on to follow in similar footsteps to my grandmother in working for several Plainview area ladies' clothing stores. She eventually married Jimmy Wardlow, a lineman with Southwestern Public Service (SPS—now called Xcel Energy) for around 40 years before he eventually retired. Both Rubie and Jimmy lived in Plainview for a number of years before making their vacation home on Lake Kemp near Seymour their permanent residence—where they still call home to this day.

Arlene, meanwhile, took her own different path working as a bookkeeper for a feedlot near Littlefield and has continued working in similar capacities since. Arlene still maintains her current home in Littlefield where she at various times through the years has played the parent to several very active dogs (thankfully, only one each at a time).

And then last, but not least in this immediate family portrait is where Mother and I come in. To give you a bit more background about the relationship between my mother and myself, I first need to let you know that one song that Mother and I always seemed to relate to most while I was growing up was the John Anderson song "Black Sheep In The Family":

[John Anderson - Black Sheep (WITH LYRICS), From The Album "Greatest Hits"; 1985]

"...Little sister married a banker, yeah--/he owns a country club/He bought her a big ol' racing horse and a funny lookin' little dog He buys her big rings and diamonds and a brand new Japanese yacht/They like to get together and talk about all the things they've got/But they never mention me/I'm the black sheep of the family...

"...Yeah I drive me a big ol' semi truck/I'm makin' payments on a two room shack/ My wife--she waits on tables and at night she rubs my back/And I tell her what my papa said to my mama when he got off a highball train/Wake me up early, be good to my dogs/And teach my children to pray..."

My mother didn't necessarily drive a semi-truck—but she didn't exactly have the greatest of starts neither as far as her overall life was concerned. She herself was a high school dropout (FYI—she did eventually get her GED many years later) who made her living for a number of years as a waitress and/or short order cook in various restaurants and cafes in the Plainview/Lockney area. In her twenties, my mother met and eventually married the man who would become my father, James Reece Holley. But Mr. Holley didn't stay for too long in his marriage to Mother and eventually abandoned her with myself still in the womb just a few months before I was born in 1968 never to be seen again (and in whom I never even got to meet or have any recollection or memory of). There were only two things my father left behind as a sum total of his legacy to me: my middle name and an old ratty briefcase he left behind with my mother. And so my life as a son of a single mother inauspiciously started.

There were several things that stand out in my mind about my early childhood years. One of them was a picture of myself as a baby (according to my mother) in which I was actually drinking Dr. Pepper from my baby bottle. Why at the time—I don't honestly know. But I do know why I still to this day have a fondness and preference for DP and tend to be reluctant to drink anything else if DP is otherwise available to me on the table.

Another early memory I have was when I was three years old. At that time, I started having a number of problems with allergies—especially in regards to eczema and other skin problems throughout my body. This required my mother to take me to a dermatologist in Lubbock for special skin treatments (usually including ultraviolet light treatments in which I basically had to take off my clothes and endure what was the placement of this special light similar to what folks in tanning booths now do to themselves these days).

On one of these doctor's appointments, I remember myself getting into the elevator of the building this doctor's office was in—and afterward got lost and stuck in it not knowing what to do for awhile. Eventually I think I found one of my aunts who had went with myself and Mother for that particular doctor's visit.

Allergies, asthma, and doctor's visits were a pretty common theme for me during these early years. I remember a lot of times having to endure such things as being forced to avoid certain foods (such as eggs, milk, and wheat) and certain medicines. My doctors even told my mother that I could never do any work related to agriculture due to my allergies to certain agricultural chemicals.

You didn't have to tell me twice usually about my allergies and asthma problems after the cotton harvest took place and ginning season started. When the gin smoke started (usually sometime between Halloween and Christmas each year), so did the humidifier in our house. It was a real struggle to breathe for me—especially when our small town has several gins operating all at once. I had to use a bunch of medicine including such things as cough syrup (one of them in particular looked like a horrible shade of green and tasted even worse than that) and even an inhaler that I had to use for a while.

Just as remarkable about my allergy and asthma problems were the medications I could NOT take. This point was especially brought home one day during the summer when I was in third grade. I had went from the house and walked a few blocks away to the tennis court that was right by the junior high school. After I had hung out for a bit at the tennis courts, I was on my way back home when I was confronted about a couple of blocks from the house by a barking Chihuahua that wasn't on a leash. At the sight and sound of this dog, I got scared and started running. Bad move—I found out later—for the chihuahua started chasing me while I was running away from him in a panic. The dog eventually caught up with me and bit me in the leg. In tears and sheer terror, I somehow made it back to the house where my mother eventually had to take me to the emergency room at the Central Plains Hospital (now Covenant Hospital) in Plainview.

With the pain from the dog bite and the bandages and wrappings still evident, I saw the doctors being forced to take different measures with me than was usually done due to what I later found out was my allergy to the medication used for tetanus shots (which involved—guess what—my allergy to eggs). According to the doctors, the use of a tetanus shot could possibly cause me to have convulsions and eventually die. (That was NOT a pleasant prospect to hear about in the least.) Let's say that I tended to maintain a healthy fear of dogs (especially Chihuahuas) immediately afterwards.

But my allergy to tetanus medications weren't the only reason why dogs and other pets were a major concern to me during my youth. One of the absolute worst allergies to me above all was the violent ones I had to both cats AND dogs. This was especially self-evident if I was indoors with them. I'd be sneezing, wheezing, and no telling what else even if a dog or cat wasn't physically present due to the dander and other stuff they might leave behind. It was even worse if I didn't either have my medication or some Dr. Pepper or something caffeinated to relax my breathing. The main key, though, most of the time was usually my need to maintain my ability to breathe. If I was outside with those same pets, it could be a totally different story (unless the grass and other pollens got me first).

None of this, though, deterred the rest of my family from keeping pets in their house—not in the least. When I was younger, for instance—my grandparents had this old Chihuahua named Tiny who came with them from their old house near Aiken. Tiny eventually lived to a ripe old dog's age of 30 before he died and was buried in my grandparents' backyard. Afterwards, my grandparents at various intervals always managed to keep a dog of some kind (as well as the rest of my immediate relatives). We were definitely a big dog family overall (even though neither Mother nor I could keep one for ourselves as a real pet).

Mother as a single parent did her absolute best to raise me as best to raise me as best as she could trying to be both mom and dad to me. I'd definitely remember the many times we'd go out here in this very backyard in the summer (even with a bunch of weeds in the back and the clothesline and my old swingset sometimes in the way) and play catch—myself in my baseball glove and her with her softball glove and wearing one of her caps. No telling also the number of times inside this house we'd play lots of board, dice, and card games like Skip Bo, Monopoly,

Happy Days, and especially Yahtzee. (Our games, FYI, definitely got really competitive.)

When my mother used to work for Pinner's Drive-In on the east side of town close to the football field and the city swimming pool, there were times I had to stay inside the drive-in while my mother helped take orders from customers or cooked burgers, fries, steak finger baskets, and the like. One of the two drive-up windows nearest the intersection of FM Roads 97 and 378 (which wasn't too far from the eastern city limits) was close to the ice cream freezer where the Pinners used to serve various ice cream treats to customers (in which I obviously liked the ice cream cones that were a rare treat for me when I was allowed by my mother to have one). But I in particular remember the times when there was extra that she would bring in a big mess of both French fries and onion rings cooked together. That was a special time indeed when Mother was able to bring that home from work.

Other times I had to be babysat by either my grandmother or by Mr. and Mrs. W.L. Carthel's daughter, Shari. I remember spending a good deal of time at the Carthels' house watching TV after school and/or in the summer when Mother had to work over at Pinner's. But Shari at times was a very interesting character of a young lady and babysitter. The politically correct crowd these days wouldn't have condoned some of her personal babysitting methods towards me—but Shari was quite insistent at times that I learned how to fight and stand up for myself. I was usually pretty reluctant to heed this unique instructional curriculum—but Shari wouldn't take no for an answer. I have a feeling that if this had occurred in today's more challenging parental training climate, Child Protective Services would have probably been all over both Mother and Shari in a heartbeat. But thankfully, those were different times when strict discipline was not only still considered necessary, but also a good hallmark of a well-behaved child.

I also fondly remember a couple of truck drivers who were for a while some of Mother's closest friends, Sam and Rose Cherry and their two teenage sons. Rose in particular definitely had what we would call today a smoking addiction. Rose and Mother would also play no telling how many games of Skip-Bo and Yahtzee with all of us kids at each other's houses. One time, we all even got in Sam and Rose's pickup for a weekend trip to Six Flags in Arlington (in the Dallas/Fort Worth area) in which Sam, Rose, and Mother were in the front and myself and the two sons in the back of the pickup (which was covered by a camper on top of it). All of us, I think, stayed in one room at a motel near Loop 12 during our time there.

Back here closer to home in this very neighborhood, I grew up in what was definitely a place where most of us at least knew each other to some degree. Next door to me on the right was a younger guy named Jeff Webb (no relation) who had a sandbox made out of an old tire outside his family's mobile home. Jeff's dad worked for the local office of SPS as a lineman very much like my Uncle Jimmy did.

At times, Jeff and/or I would go play with Amy Nance (who was a year younger than me) at the two-story house just a half-block from here. She and her folks (Peggy and Joe) had a good tree swing that all of us kids used to swing as high as possible into the sky. I also remember at times going back and forth in her house and playing with Amy and the dolls she had. Also for a little while, Cassie Probasco and her mom lived in a trailer home across the street from the Nances. I remember a time or two when Cassie used to have a trampoline in which all of us kids bounced up and down on for fun. Our neighborhood lineup also included the Marrs next door to the Probascos who ran an insulation company even as Mrs. Marr herself was the biology teacher at Lockney High.

On the other side of Fifth Street was where my mother's landlord and storm cellar owner, Mr. Leach, lived. Mr. Leach had a two-car garage with an old car that he never hardly drove and especially had a real penchant and love for drinking beer. When his relatives came over for a special dinner, there would always be smoke coming from his BBQ grill from the stuff they'd be cooking. Mother and I, though, usually didn't get a chance to taste their stuff. Just as well anyway—considering how loud Mr. Leach's drinking buddies might get in the garage when they were drinking.

Across the street from Mr. Leach, an elderly couple named the Reeves maintained their little abode. At various times throughout my childhood years (especially when my mother couldn't work as a waitress anymore due to a knee injury she got playing softball), the Reeves were one of several families that my mother would clean houses for around town to get some extra money to help pay our bills. The best thing for Mother about this particular work arrangement? She didn't have to use any gas to go to work over there.

Next door to the Reeves and across the street from us were Rudy and Wanda Zachary. Rudy owned the main barber shop for the men in Lockney—and I was one of those local kids who was taken by their parents to Rudy's Barber Shop downtown for the necessary rite of passage to receive one of Rudy's haircuts. Mine due to my allergies was usually a buzz cut—although a Mohawk cut was also available as an alternative style (which Rudy at times would tease me about).

Filling out our Wilson Street neighborhood map were the two small rent houses that had their share of various unknown Hispanic family tenants that we usually didn't have too much contact with. And next door to the Webb's house on Sixth Street for a number of years was Ray Rollings, the milkman who worked for Bell Dairy. It was always a sight to see his milk truck parked in the back of his driveway. (And the ice cream sandwiches I got to occasionally buy from him thanks to money Mother might have on hand to give me weren't bad either.)

Mother first owned an old '59 four-door Ford Fairlane in which I would remember going with her to the movies at the old Seale Drive-In Theater west of town. I still remember listening to the intercom speaker that you could attach to your car to listen to the sound of the movie. Also, I remember the concession stand that was behind us where Mother might get popcorn and drinks (and where, if necessary, we could also use the bathroom facilities as well). I also remember the sight of the swing sets that were closer to the movie screen near the front entrances and how you could see the lights and hear the sounds of the theatre even as you go out the exit and back onto the highway going into town.

I didn't always have the greatest assortment of friends growing up during my school years. That usually showed in the fact that it was a rare sight for me to not at least have one bully of some kind who would taunt me and cause any time on the school playground to be a lonely, haunting nightmare. When I wasn't being chased by bullies, I was usually having problems of some kind involving asthma that required me to spend plenty of time sick in Nurse Ulmer's office. I also had to spend several sessions as well with the mother of one of my fellow students who happened to work for the school as a speech therapist.

Therefore, I tended to be more into my studies than most of the other students--and especially into books. I recall a number of times when my mother and I would go to a combination service station/general store owned by Mary Hutton. Not only do I remember how very dark and cluttered the Hutton's store usually was, but also the number of comic books that Mother wound up buying for me to satisfy my voracious appetite for reading.

Part of the reason why I didn't always seem to fit in with my peers might have had something to do with how slow I tended to be during PE and athletic activities. Due in part to myself being overweight—if I ever had to do laps on a track or wind sprints or anything of the sort, I always seemed to be lagging up the rear with one other guy who was in similar condition. I always seemed to get called "Fatso" or other horrible nickname. It's amazing to me how transparently cruel and insincere kids can be to others that don't necessarily fit the molds they establish themselves. (I guess some things never change indeed.)

One of the biggest culprits of this throughout the majority of my school years was a fellow classmate who. mostly through words, but also sometimes through actions, caused me to be in constant terror of him. He seemed convinced at times that he thought one of his biggest missions in life was to make mine as miserable as possible. His house just also happened to be across the street from the high school—so obviously in light of this, I usually steered as far away from it as much as I could.

One big example in my memory that stands out about how extremely sensitive to teasing I was at that time was one time in the sixth grade when he and several others in my class pushed my buttons to the point where I actually called him the biggest six-word phrase of profanity that I'd ever called anyone in my life. Doing that to this day is still one of my biggest lowlights and regrets.

This along with a number of other emotional problems where I literally acted in junior high like a two-year-old with temper tantrums among other things eventually forced Mother to also have to take me to Amarillo to go to see a psychiatrist, Dr. Erickson, for reasons I wasn't exactly aware of at the time. I apparently acted to the point where Mother had to actually leave me at the Kilgore Psychiatric Hospital for about a month. It was to me one of the worst times of my school years because I was homesick and I didn't want to be there at all.

I still remember the area of Amarillo the hospital was at near the Discovery Center and a lake near the Texas Tech Health Sciences Center campus and the High Plains Baptist Hospital (now called Baptist/St. Anthony's) where we would go for outside activities. I also remember the strict diet I got put on (maybe because of my weight—I don't know) and where I always seemed to get Diet Dr. Pepper (which I wasn't always too fond of because it seemed like a tasteless, non-sugary imitation of what was to me the REAL thing).

I don't think that I was ever able to fully get across the point to both Mother and even Dr. Erickson that as long as I had bullies continually taunting me and calling me bad names that I couldn't help or be responsible for my actions or behavior around other classmates. Even after I came back from Amarillo, nothing ever really seemed to change that fact either. As long as these bullies kept up this abuse, it was very hard for me to avoid trouble anywhere near their presence.

The ironic thing, though, about this is that I wound up going through the very same Boy Scout troop for a couple of years that this particular bully and a number of other local boys around my age were also a part of. Sadly, this was where I was also introduced to what peer pressure really was. I also wish I could say that my personal experience in Scouting was a useful one for myself as a growing boy— but a few other experiences unfortunately proved to be otherwise. (No offense to the BSA meant by this, of course—it was just the particular folks of this Scout troop I was in—that was all.)

A couple of Scouting experiences particularly stand out head and shoulders above it all. One of them was when we went on a trip to Lake Greenbelt near Clarendon. During the campout near the lake, the rest of the boys decided to initiate me into the joys of "snipe hunting". The rest of the troop one night gave me a bucket and then proceeded to instruct me on exactly what I should do in case I might happen to encounter a "snipe". Not knowing obviously what a "snipe" was in the first place, I naively took them at their word. They then went on their way further down the road while I awaited for this strange creature to show up, ready in a crouched position with hands on my knees ready to strike at any moment.

I stayed in this position for quite a while as I wondered why in the bleep I hadn't seen a "snipe" yet. All of a sudden in front of me (not realizing that it was actually the rest of the troop playing the role of the "snipes" in this little drama), I heard screams worse than banshees shouting—"…WE ARE THE SNIPES! WE ARE THE SNIPES!"—and other similar stuff. At the sheer sound of it, I fled in terror back towards the campsite—just about ready to do a little tattletale act to the Scoutmaster. But nothing ever happened from it.

Another similar Scouting trip to Roaring Springs was the opportunity that this guy and some of my other fellow Scouts first introduced me to what they thought were the joys of dipping snuff. I remember all of us sitting in the back of one of our Scoutmaster's pickups on the way down there when they gave me a little

21

instruction on how to properly use Skoal and Copenhagen. I think I probably swallowed a pinch or two before I got the hang of it.

That started my regretful period of use of this snuff stuff in an attempt to try to fit in with the rest of my peers. This habit continued for about a year or two during the rest of my infamous time with this Scout troop until my dermatologist eventually laid down the law and told me not to do it anymore. This and also realizing my selfishness in asking Mother to take some of her very already hard-to-come by financial resources as well as my problems with allergies and asthma proved to be the biggest encouragements to quit what was really a gross habit in retrospect before the addiction got too much worse. It was one of many personal lessons I was forced to learn throughout the rest of my years that just because the band and drums were marching in lockstep with each other didn't necessarily mean that YOU had to either.

But there were also some good things I did try to do in the summers and after school. I wasn't always a big sports guy, but I did like it when we played baseball in the summer. I was in it from Pee Wee League all the way up to 14/15-year-old Babe Ruth play. We didn't necessarily have an officially recognized Babe Ruth league program, but those of us still playing at the 14/15-year-old level did get to play teams from other area towns such as Petersburg, Idalou, Floydada, Roosevelt, Lorenzo, and New Deal.

I always played in right field or in some other outfield position. I didn't do too well on catching or anything else—but I did like it when I occasionally got to hit a single like Pete Rose did (which for me was rare and far between). Sadly, our high school at the time was too small to field a UIL-level competitive baseball team. But if I had been able to have baseball as one of the choices of a sport I would have liked to play, baseball would have definitely been it for me.

Since I couldn't go work in the cotton fields like most of my other peers, I wound up doing things such as selling greeting cards and wrapping paper door-to-door to have enough money to get certain prizes that I wanted. I even wound up for a little while maintaining a steady route of customers selling a newspaper called Grit as well around town (with Mother's help, of course) to try to get a few extra shekels in my pocket.

I even got involved in 4-H for a while. Obviously because of financial and medical reasons, I didn't get to show livestock. But I did get to do a few things such as archery, something called a "home demonstration project" (which was the 4-H operative term at the time for public speaking), and even cooking. I did get to win a few ribbons at the county level for the cooking—thanks in part to a family recipe for a fruit salad-like concoction called "Watergate salad" that basically consisted of Cool Whip, pistachio pudding, pineapple chunks, and maraschino cherries mixed together in a bowl and then chilled in the fridge overnight before serving.

And of course, throughout a good bit of my school years, I even found out how fickle infatuation was between myself and the opposite sex. One very humorous example actually involved three separate occasions in junior high where three different girls (not all at the same time, of course) claimed to have a crush on me one day only to turn around the next day that they were out of love with me. Oh, young puppy love—how temporary it can surely be.

However, these things usually didn't faze me as much. Why? Because I had much bigger game in mind—and I was truly smitten by this young lady. From about the fifth grade all the way until I was a junior in high school when I finally saw the writing on the wall and gave up, I held on like a bulldog to my almost borderline obsession with her. Who was this object of my continuing desires and affections? None other than Heather Holt...

My infatuation with and deep physical attraction to Heather really took off after a Royal Ambassadors' trip to Waco where she came with her parents, Kenneth and Jackie Lou. (Kenneth was, FYI, one of the leaders of our RAs group at our church. He for a number of years operated a cotton farm before eventually becoming a Farm Bureau agent while Jackie Lou worked as a secretary in the superintendant's office. Something about her more than any other girl around me attracted me to her more than I could ever say to her face. Unfortunately, she didn't quite return my affections in similar fashion towards me—and she always seemed to be interested in someone else. But that didn't necessarily stop my attempts to try to convince her otherwise. I tried cards, gifts, poetry—but the answer was usually no.

I even heard that she had broken up with a junior high boyfriend. After hearing this, I even went so far as to get HIS blessing to try to take his place. He graciously consented to my request. However, Heather DIDN'T acknowledge even this attempt at her affections and stood her ground. I even remember one time on her birthday managing to get our local florist with money I had earned from my sales stuff one red rose and even a ring with her birthstone on it. She even turned THAT down (graciously and appreciately, though—at least).

But there was one memory of her that kept hope springing eternal burning in my heart for a while that she would eventually change her mind and see the light. It was at a junior high dance where the two of us danced together as close as we ever did in our years being around each other. It was a song by country artist Kenny Rogers called "Lady":

"...Lady, I'm your knight in shining armor and I love you
You have made me what I am and I am yours
My love, there's so many ways I want to say I love you
Let me hold you in my arms forever more..."

When the song got to the chorus, I started singing it to here as we held each other on the dance floor. When the song was over with and I escorted her back to her seat, I whispered in her ear these words—"It just felt so natural being out here with you." Never again, though, was I able to recapture that sense of presence that I personally felt being next to her at that time. But that never stopped me from trying until as a junior I began to finally see that it was a lost cause and finally gave up.

During this time, the seeds of what would eventually become my burgeoning interest in music also began to grow. But they started off pretty inauspiciously at first. When fifth grade rolled around (which was usually the time where we students were finally allowed by the school district to get involved in band) and it was time to start band, I told my mother and the rest of the folks that I wanted to play the drums.

But we couldn't afford drums or anything like that on our own. Instead, my grandparents had an old saxophone that both Uncle Randy and Aunt Arlene had played themselves when they were in school. So my mother and grandparents laid down the law—either I take their sax and learn to play it OR I couldn't be in band—period. From it began my own personal musical journey that lasted for many years afterwards.

As I sit here on this front sidewalk to my old house, it's obvious how many childhood memories start flooding my mind. But many years later as I write this, I'm also just as mindful of just how pivotal my own mother had in shaping the life I now lead today. This chapter's even harder to write now more than ever for several reasons. I didn't know now over 30 years later the number of things that my mother would be forced to throughout the years due to both stupid stuff at times I would do in which I still reap the consequences of even today as well as other circumstances neither of us could ever hope to control.

It's natural in whatever field of endeavor people may pursue that folks might want to find some outlet to acknowledge the valuable contributions their parents make into their childrens' lives. The biggest problem for me personally, though, is where exactly to put my own personal tribute to my own mother. What further complicates and compounds the problem for me is that as I write this at what is now chronologically the midpoint of my life I have personally seen Mother as through so many medical and financial trials. This lady who for about all of my life has been one of my biggest bulwarks has by now almost died twice and is now spending the rest of her remaining days of her life in a nursing home. It's even more challenging for me to write this stuff because I don't even know how much longer she has left to live. And I'm even more scared and hesitant to write this because I'm very concerned that by writing these things I'm also most certainly signing her death warrant.

My flesh doesn't want to do that! I haven't yet at this time been able to find the woman that I still believe my God would have for me to take as my future wife. I'd at least love to see Mother live long enough to be there for my wedding day to my future bride. I'd like for Mother to at least live long enough to see for all the years of pain and heartache that she went through to raise me that I at least was blessed by my God to have her personally witness me finally truly be a reasonable success at something in life that would truly make a difference and impact on others. Only then after all that has happened to her would I be willing to allow my Lord to finally dismiss her in peace. And when that day finally arrives (which I know now will most certainly need to come), it will regardless still be a very hard pill for me to swallow. After all, I'm only losing the lady that has served as both my mom AND dad, right?

The day when I'm finally forced to let her go will surely be one of the hardest challenges I will ever face in my life. And for now, I'm still asking God right now for a few specific things to happen about the eventual time of Mother's passing—because Baby Black Sheep will surely miss Mama Black Sheep when it's time for her to move on.

What are those things I'm asking the Lord to do for her concerning her passing? First, I'm asking that it not happen prematurely due to the plans of the Adversary and his devices—but instead that it would occur in a time of peace at both Mother's and my God's choosing. Second, that it not happen until she at least has finally been able to see some of the sweet and most pleasant things that I still yet expect to happen to me in my life. And when it is finally time for my God to dismiss her in peace that I will have been by that time more than emotionally and other ways have already been more than fully prepared for this to happen. For when Mother finally goes, it will definitely be a double-whammy Hiroshima-type bomb that only my God and His Holy Spirit Themselves can help me personally recover from the immediate fallout and aftermath that will surely follow.

So maybe after all, the best lesson we all can glean from this might be that sometimes the best time to give an appropriate tribute to someone is when they're still around to hear it. Therefore, this seems to be the first major item of personal business that I need to take care of before we do anything else on this walking tour of my life's journey.

And maybe the best way for now to give that tribute to Mama Black Sheep——Mother--might be this...that no matter what else is written throughout the rest of this book, if you've got to know why I continue my walk through life like I do, one of the fastest ways to find out the answers to some of your questions is to first ask the lady who was there herself when I first originally physically walked my very first steps. Ask the lady who changed the water in my humidifier when I couldn't sleep at night because of the gin smoke outside. Consider the woman who changed my diapers or who as a single parent worked long hours on her feet flipping burgers at Pinner's or cleaning houses just to keep the bills paid or make the sacrifices necessary around Christmas time or my birthday to make sure I had something close to what I might have wanted or needed.

If you wonder why I might make such a big effort to get a funny Mother's Day card or even give Mother something for her birthday even though I still don't observe Christmas anymore, consider all the numerous things she's done for me personally over her lifetime—and then from there, you'll finally know. And like it or not, when Mama Black Sheep passes on, her only baby black sheep will probably miss here more than you'll ever know.

[Chapter 2:] [Lockney (Part II—Main Street)] How I Began To Listen To Mr. Armstrong

Our tour of Lockney wouldn't be entirely complete without an exploration of my personal religious roots—and especially what originally got me interested in listening to Herbert W. Armstrong and "The World Tomorrow". So in order to continue this tour, we will need to first go from the small rent house that my mother and I lived throughout most of my childhood, take a left on Fifth Street in between where our landlord Mr. Leach and the Marrs lived, then turn right at Pat Adams' old house and go several blocks until you get to Main Street. If you turned right on Main, you could find the former Webster's Service Station, the old location of J&K Insurance, and at the end of Main where it intersects with Sherbet Street Davis Lumber Company with a couple of cotton gins in the nearby vicinity.

But instead, we'll be turning left on Main where on the west side of the street you will see a row of houses for about two blocks until you get to the Methodist Church with the funeral home across the street. On the east side as you continue north on Main, you'll find the Main Street Church of Christ on one block—and then at the intersection of Main and Poplar right by the old Baccus Motor Co. building the main focus of this chapter—the First Baptist Church of Lockney where my mother and I went to church throughout most of my youth. "Now wait a minute!", you say. "What does this have to do with Mr. Armstrong?" Stay with me—and I'll show you.

My family through the generations in East Texas and even prior to my grandfather's move to West Texas has been pretty much evangelical Protestant in nature to some degree. I actually had an uncle who at one time was a Missionary Baptist music minister in a church in Ardmore, OK and another uncle who was a Primitive Baptist preacher. (FYI on Primitive Baptists—I was forced to go with my family to one of these services in Plainview—most likely when that uncle happened to be in town for some sort of special meeting they were having at the time. The long and short of it? Let's say that all the hymns that were sung were done a capella—and I didn't remember too much else about it otherwise.)

Some in my family have been (and still are) dyed-in-the-wool Church of Christ. But as far as my own immediate family was concerned, all of our religious upbringing was primarily Southern Baptist. My grandparents would go several miles away to attend the Baptist church in Aiken way out in the country where my grandmother served for many years as a Sunday School teacher and my granddad as the Building Fund treasurer. My mother, though, usually preferred to stay in town to go to church right here at FBC-Lockney.

As was typical amongst most Baptist kids, I went through most of the elementary grade departments and even throughout most of my time in high school at that church. I was a part of Royal Ambassadors (RAs) [the Southern Baptist church equivalent of Boy Scouts] where I took part in a number of games (football and otherwise) that would be played on the church lawn. [That was—when I wasn't otherwise affected by my persistent problems with asthma and allergies—and also that I was overweight and probably didn't do very well in the area of sports activities as others would.} I also recall the Pinewood Derby races that were a part of it (and the derby care that I probably didn't do too good of a job on—and which I got plenty of help on. It was all brown paint...I mean, dark brown...]

Several men that led our RA groups and who even served as some of our church deacons at the time included Claude Stallings, Don Vernon (who sadly died way too early of a rare disease some time during my school years), Kenneth Holt (whose daughter I told you about in the last chapter), and Lawson Rowell.

Not having a daddy around was definitely a real disadvantage during my youth in many ways—so it was a real blessing to especially have the example of a Godly male role model Lawson Rowell was to me personally. He and his parents operated Rowell's Variety Store that was located right across the street from Jackson Tire Company and also by the one and only stop light in Lockney at the time. I remember the many times when I would go into Rowell's (both with my mother and also on my own) seeing that front counter full of candy and other merchandise and especially of Lawson at the old-fashioned cash register ringing up a sale...and even giving me his advice when I'd ask him a question about matters of life and the various situations of life that would face a young man like myself.

There were also several youth ministers who worked at FBC-Lockney that did provide an interesting memory to two. One of them was a Randall Stotts who was originally from Tahoka. I remember in particular one thing about Randall and some other stuff that I can recall about these youth pastors. First was Randall's long-time relationship since childhood with former gospel singer and now Texas Country artist Daron Norwood. I also remember a number of overnight church lock-ins our youth group used to have—especially when the lights in church would be completely turned off and we'd play "hide-and-seek" all through the church facilities. (One time, one of those youth pastors named Mitch Wilson even took us to s similar church lock-in in Ropesville in which I have a very faint memory of that church building as I write this.)

There was another youth pastor named Bro. David (I'm not able to recall exactly what his last name right now) also did similar things with us as our youth minister. But one thing that especially was memorable in retrospect about his tenure at FBC-Lockney was when he did a series of what I think were what we called "Training Union" lessons (usually special classes before our church's Sunday night service) where we talked about some things about what churches and religious groups that Baptists at the time very much considered "cults" that our youth should stay away from. Even as I heard the teaching of this material and gave lip service to it, little did I know how much some of this would eventually foreshadow a majority of the rest of my life that was to come.

You see—I went through my youth doing what most Baptist kids did. I would find myself "walking down the aisle" during the invitation part of a church service, shaking hands with the pastor and making what was called my "decision for Christ" and even being baptized by the pastor when I was a kid. I just did what everyone else did—but inside, I was really in my heart a sort of "Holy Joe" hypocrite who at best was just simply going through the motions. That would change one night with an incident involving my mother that would shake what I though and perceived was my personal faith in Him to the very core.

After my mother due to her knee injury and various other medical problems began to arise in her life prevented her from working actively as a waitress anymore, we as a single-parent family were forced to live on many forms of public assistance as well as what other housekeeping jobs she was able to pick up for extra money. Mother also eventually started working for her church as a part-time nursery worker for a while.

One night after some sort of church business meeting, though, we came home from church. I found here crying and asked her what was wrong. She told me that the Nursery Committee for reasons unknown to her said that they were firing her. I later found out that the possible reasons for my mother's termination may have involved church politics by some influential people in the church at the time who may have been angling to get someone else there a job at the expense of my mother. [Special NOTE: I am NOT implicating ANYONE in saying this—in fact, I very full well know that I may not have gotten all the facts of the situation and that

I can be very much wrong in saying what was just said there. To anyone that is possibly offended by such statements, please take this as my deepest apologies.] After this incident occurred, I could see that this would put my mother in a real financial bind…so Mother was naturally distraught over this sudden turn of events—and the road to disillusionment with my Southern Baptist church would begin.

After this incident happened, it was around the latter part of my junior high years and even into my freshman year in high school when during the summer and also weekends I started watching late at night what a very unique religious program that was broadcasting on the newest independent TV station in Lubbock called KJTV-34. The program was by an iconoclastic preacher out of California named Dr. Eugene Scott. To say that Dr. Scott's program was unique and different is to say the least a massive understatement. Dr. Scott had some very unique penchants and an egotistical, no-nonsense, "get-out-of-my-face" approach to delivering the Biblical truths he espoused (that is—on those rare occasions on his program where he allowed himself to do so). Most of the time, Dr. Scott would be constantly using fundraising tactics that would make most of today's televangelists blush with shame. Dr. Scott loved hats (and wore a multitude of them as it suited him), duck-billed slippers, and playing ad infinitum a video of a certain men's gospel quartet singing "I Wanna Know" to the point of insanity.

So WHY in the world would I even tolerate this—much less obsess over this program? Because on the few occasions Dr. Scott did actually teach on his program, he actually dared to talk about topics such as the Egyptian pyramids and the Lost Ten Tribes that I definitely didn't hear in my Southern Baptist church. And Dr. Scott furthermore challenged you to check it and study the thing for yourself if you didn't see it—or much less agree with it. Dr. Scott didn't pull any punches about what he believed about the Word of God. And furthermore—he did it in a way that made sense. If you wish to know how captivated I was by Dr. Scott's program, here's one example to demonstrate. One time, Mother actually chewed me out and got on my case for not turning off the TV before I went to sleep because she wound having to do it for me. I'd be up sometimes until 2 or 3 AM just watching Dr. Scott and his antics—wondering what he'd do next—even to the point of falling asleep to the test picture on TV.

During this period of time, I happened to be sick one Sunday morning and wound up staying home from church. For the first time, I saw a program called

"The World Tomorrow" on another one of our Lubbock area TV stations that was hosted by an elderly gentlemen with gray hair that I would later know as Herbert W. Armstrong. I forgot what the specific program at the time was about (most likely something dealing with world events of some kind—but the program was at least compelling enough for me to write the Worldwide Church of God's headquarters in Pasadena, CA for further literature. As I requested more and more literature and even enrolled in WCG's Correspondence Course, I started learning even more things that I felt my own church wasn't teaching me—such as what the 10 Commandments and Old Testament were really about, what the "World Tomorrow" would look like, and other WCG doctrines of the time…I ate those up like the greatest thing since sliced bread.

At one point, I even requested contact and wrote the nearest local WCG pastor at the time, David Dobson, about certain questions I had and the unique situation I was in since I was still a minor under my mother's and grandparents' immediate authority. Even what was some wise advice Mr. Dobson wrote me at the time to basically stay where I was until I graduated high school still didn't completely temper my desire to start going to WCG services. I admit that I even entertained a fantasy or two of joining the Army Reserve just so that I would have an excuse to go to Lubbock for services. [Good thing I didn't, though—considering that I would later fail a tryout for the Marine Corps Band—plus the fact that I would find out about years later that I wouldn't have at the time be able to be BOTH an active WCG member AND a part of the military. I even years later had to go so far as to actually declare conscientious objector status from the military due to religious reasons.]

I admit—I really tried to keep this quiet from my mother and family (but now in retrospect wonder if they actually knew much more about what I was doing than I thought). But there are two distinct memories about my initial contacts with WCG that are interesting to note. The first was a time or two when I actually slipped in a couple of WCG booklets to one of our youth groups at church. Another time was actually when our high school band was on the bus heading to a football game. Along with the band uniforms and stuff we took for the ball game, I also took a few WCG booklets and brochures with me for something to read during the long bus rides back and forth between home and where we were having the ballgame. I happened to be reading a brochure on God's design for marriage and sex when of all people Heather (yes, the very same young lady I referred to earlier in this chapter who I had a massive crush on) asked me what I was reading. When I told her it was about sex and marriage and showed the booklet cover to her, she asked me if she could take a look at it. I let her—and after a quick look at the booklet, she gave it back to me without saying very much. I think those immediately around me might have snickered a little bit in hearing that the book was about sex, but then reacted the same way Heather did after a little while.

My interest in WCG during the remainder of my high school years continually increased—but I was at the time constrained to continue going to my mother's church as long as I was a minor and not allowed to make my own decisions. But in my heart, I knew that I was on the path of completely leaving the Southern Baptist roots –even to the point that I felt I was chafing at the neck from obeying things that I no longer held to be true. And I vowed that at the first chance I would get to be free and independent that I would act on those desires and get out of that Southern Baptist church once and for all and instead start going to WCG services. But there was one problem at the time with that—I wasn't 18 yet…and there was still a long time left to go until graduation and time to go to college when I would be finally able to make that choice for myself.

["Walking…" Chapter 3:] [Lockney—Part III (Lockney High School)—The Long Wait Until Graduation]

Now that I formally introduced you to what originally got me listening to Mr. Armstrong and "The World Tomorrow" broadcast in the first place, we can now go on to our next Lockney tour stop just a few blocks up the street from here at First Baptist.

Continuing west here on Poplar Street, we'll pass First Methodist immediately on our right and the funeral home and Schacht's Flowers on the left. After passing about three more blocks of primarily houses, we'll eventually find ourselves at the intersection/four-way stop of Fourth and Poplar. At the southwest corner will be the backdrop that I'll use to tell you a little bit about some of what I did during my high school years until the time finally came for me to be on my own for the first time. As we begin this session sitting on the front steps of Lockney High, I need to first ask you to join me in turning our mutual attention to a couple of things in the nearby vicinity.

The first one is right across the street at what was once called the Longhorn Inn. The Inn was operated during the majority of my junior high and high school years by Violet Cooper during the school year when she wasn't running the city swimming pool. For most of the students here that could afford lunch here and didn't want to eat the free lunch in the school cafeteria at the elementary school, the Longhorn Inn was the place to be during lunch. And the crowds during lunch breaks proved it—for the place was usually packed.

If you didn't have money on your person and your parents had a current charge account, it was even better than you thought. As most any LHS student at the time could attest, hamburgers, cheeseburgers, and other standard fast-food fare were obviously far more preferable to what the cafeteria offered. No telling how many times I had ordered various items on the menu there—whether it was a Coke, candy, you name it…I probably ate or tasted most (if not all) of the items on the menu at least once or twice EACH over a period of years. Remembering the smell of chili cooking and burgers, hot dogs, and twin cronies on the grill definitely brings back some of the smells of my youth. And all of that plus your friends and other classmates you could usually find at one time or another all in one place…

The other things that we need to turn our attention to just happen to be right beside us here on these front steps. That's my personal copy of the LHS school annuals starting from 1983 until I graduated in 1986. Feel free to flip through these with me and see for yourself just how bad I looked in those pictures that had been taken of me down through those years…LOL…

I could spend the time here about what you see here in these yearbooks—but I think that as you go through them, you'll probably find as I have that these yearbooks tell a good part of what needs to be told about my time as an LHS alum. But at the end of this, I will give you nevertheless a quick written summary of all my high school achievements to make sure that my personal historical record is complete.

Outside of what is presented in these annuals, there's basically a few more major things that I will need to spend the rest of the chapter on that you probably wouldn't necessarily see by just looking at these things at a glance.

First, I do need to tell you that as I finally went up the grades in the Lockney ISD, my mother and I also wound up making a change in our physical location as well. As Mother's health began to deteriorate to the point where she couldn't physically keep up with the demands of housekeeping and the various other odd jobs she did around town, we moved from the Wilson Street house that we had lived in for most of my childhood to another house next door to my grandparents across town during the summer right before my freshman year started here.

At the time due to some personal situations he faced, my Uncle Randy also wound up staying in one of the rooms in my grandparents' house. When I was about 14, Randy took on the responsibility of being my first driver's ed instructor. I remember the two of us going down the dirt roads west of town in an old beat up Chevy pickup truck that he'd literally taken from scratch and restored with his own two hands.

For probably a couple of years or so until I finally went through the official driver's ed course offered at school, Randy very patiently (and even exasperatingly at times to his chagrin) graciously took me through the finer points and paces of how to drive.

Randy's particular individualized course curriculum didn't just end there. With him being an auto mechanic by trade, it was expected and even mandatory that I go through what amounted to be his unique version of an additional basic auto mechanics course. I wasn't necessarily too thrilled about that part because I wasn't necessarily the type (and probably still am not) that really wanted to do things such as change tires and oil or even figure out the difference between a crescent wrench and a ratchet or a socket or a whatchamacallit thing. I just wanted to learn to drive and leave it at that.

But I wasn't given that option by Randy or any of the rest of the family for that matter. I'm glad now in retrospect they didn't. Even though I'm still to this day in my family the most mechanically challenged of the whole bunch, I am quite grateful nonetheless to Randy, Papa, and the rest of the family for continuing to drill in me the importance of being as wise as possible in maintaining the cars I've been privilege to drive over the years. Knowing there's a lot of people out there that couldn't find a dipstick if their life depended on it, it's been great at times when I've needed it most to at least have some small idea of how to do a few basic car maintenance things such as keeping fluid levels in the radiator in proper check and they arise and deal with them appropriately. I still, though, haven't been perfect to this day in this department—but I definitely owe my uncle a major debt of gratitude in attempting to steer me in the right way.

While we're still dealing in the automotive department, I also owe an even greater debt of gratitude to Mother for putting one major rule on me as far as driving her car was concerned. She probably had to put this condition on me primarily due to our financial situation. But doing that also had an unintended positive consequence on me personally by scaring the bejeevers out of me in being as safe of a driver as was possible. In fact, this stroke of brilliance and example on her part was so great that if I even had to opportunity to raise kids of my own around the time they might hit driving age, I think that I might actually place a similar type of restriction on them as well. Granted, it's a pretty draconian rule in nature. But maybe other parents that would like to save money on their car insurance and other expenses might do well to heed Mother's very wise example.

Her rule was simple—if I got even ONE ticket or ended up in ONE accident due to my stupidity (or any other possible reason)—bye, bye, car...PERIOD...end of discussion with no appeals allowed or granted whatsoever. Scary—but thankfully, it worked for the most part. There was one time during my high school years while driving Mother's old 1974 Ford Pinto two-door hatchback where I did happen to get stopped by a state trooper right as I literally had already turned into our home driveway—with his lights flashing behind me. But thankfully, I got away that time with a warning. Other than that during these high school years, tickets and accidents were pretty rare and/or non-existent with me. (Of course, I really didn't get the privilege of driving the car too much until I was a senior. Mother probably drove me a lot more to most of the stuff I went to in high school anyway.)

The rest of my high school experience could be divided up in two main sections in which I'll use the following as section titles—one of them involving several major personal obstacles that constantly seemed to be in my way, while the other focused on some of the good things I did experience at this time; and more importantly, the signs that would eventually point to much better days that I saw waiting for me after graduation from here.

(1.) OBSTACLES IN MY WAY

Most of the time throughout my junior high and high school years, what would have been maximum enjoyment of this entire school experience in the Lockney ISD was severely diminished by my inability to avoid taking any sort of teasing or kidding seriously and/or personally and also by a few bullies and giants that kept getting in my way. [FYI--Specific names have been changed due to privacy and legal reasons...]

(A.) **"Pete"**—Although "Pete" seemed to be my major threat during the majority of my schooling here in Lockney, once I started here at Lockney High, "Pete" actually became less and less of a problem to me as my tenure at LHS went on. Part of it was due to some sort of time that he was entirely absent altogether during both our sophomore and junior years. (Rumor has it that he might have wound up in reform school—but I can't necessarily confirm that fact.) By the time he came back for his senior year, you can tell that he did mature a little bit. We didn't necessarily become the best of friends after that—but we at least towards the end made some sort of peace and acted a little more civil towards each other at the end.

(B.) **"Bubba" and "Earl"**—As was usually the case during my time here, it wasn't too unusual for seniors to impose some unique form of mild initiation torture of some kind towards some of their unfortunate freshman classmates. Bubba and Earl both seemed to perform the role of friendly senior tormentors very well to me personally during my first LHS year.

These two guys in particular had two very unique penchants as far as their personal expectations of me were concerned. The first was what happened when either of them took their hands in the form of a pistol, acted like they were firing a handgun at me, and shouted "BANG!" When either of them did this trick, I was expected by them both to literally fall down on the ground as if I were shot and act like I was hurt or dead.

That was nothing, though, compared to what I was expected to do when either of them shouted "AIR RAID!" When one of them said this, I then had no choice but to immediately drop and fall to the ground, then take an imaginary machine gun and pretend I was trying to shoot down airplanes.

There was absolutely no rhyme or reason to Bubba's and Earl's methods. Sometimes they'd just shout one of these while they'd do both as it suited them to. But always it was at some of the most inconvienent times—and usually caused me immense embarrassment amongst my classmates for the duration of my freshman year as a result. And they always seemed to get a laugh out of it—unfortunately at my expense.

(C.) **"Jerome"**—Bubba and Earle, though, didn't hold a candle in the area of their personal harassment methods in comparison to our next featured person. Meet "Jerome"—six foot four, 250 lbs., and yet still thinner than a rail. (How he got that way—I'll never know.) His sister, ironically, was one of the nicest girls that you'd ever know—and she and I did manage to get along well during our mutual tenures here.

But Jerome sadly was an entirely different story. If I had to make comparisons between bullies and tormentors, the overall scale might read this way. Bubba and Earl would probably on the scale rate the equivalent of pesky friendly flies—they'd annoy you some, but usually turned out to be harmless little fuzzballs at their very worst. "Pete"? I'd probably think of him more as one of the laughing hyenas in the movie "The Lion King". He could do some damage—but overall in retrospect, his bark was usually worse than his bite.

So pray tell—where might Jerome wind up on this destruction scale? To me here at LHS, Jerome was the master bully and worst opposition of them all. Think of him as a cross between an F-5 tornado and a Hiroshima nuclear bomb wrapped up in one tall package. He made no bones about the fact that he absolutely hated my guts for no good reason at all. THAT alone even now I still can't figure out.

Jerome did his dead-level best to make my first two years at LHS a living H-E-hockey sticks. Anytime he saw me in class, he always maintained a consistent diatribe of verbal abuse and profanity in front of my fellow classmates that was the absolute hardest for me to endure. I dreaded being anywhere near this guy—for he was an absolute expert at getting my dander up and making me totally upset. Tattletales to teachers and other personnel never seemed to do any good against Jerome—for he seemed to have a vendetta against me that would never quit for reasons totally unknown and unexplainable to anyone except himself. Talk about a guy I was truly scared of—Jerome was it—numero uno.

Jerome's abuse and constant verbal tirades against me pushed me so much to the breaking point that I finally got fed up with it all and challenged him to a fight to defend my honor. He probably didn't think I'd follow through on my threat, but one Sunday night I wound up sneaking out of church to meet him in an alley behind the store buildings on Main Street and attempt to settle this dispute with fisticuffs once and for all.

What followed next wasn't necessarily a version of a film about Rocky Balboa, but more a TV comedy of errors on a level more along the lines of Rocky and Bullwinkle. The start of the fight between myself and Jason probably looked more like the start of Michael Jackson's video of "Beat It", but then quickly deteriorated to the point where my feeble attempts to try to punch Jerome in the face looked comically more like that of the movements of a dancing bear. It wasn't funny to me then, but even I laugh now when Jason finally lost patience with me and when both he and the rest of the small crowd of classmates gathered for this horrible excuse of a fight urged me to mercifully just give up and leave before he started really trying to hurt me.

There was one instance during the fight that was quite memorable for all of us assembled. Among those in attendance were none other than Heather herself and also her younger brother, Kip. Apparently Kip was talking and acting up so much and giving her so much trouble that Heather actually shouted out loud in everyone's hearing right in the middle of the fight, "Kip—SHUT UP!" At the sound of this, even Jerome and I along with everyone else cracked up and started laughing. It was definitely a light spot of humor in an otherwise tense and stressful situation myself. Despite the outcome of the fight, Jerome still continued his senseless tirades against me up until he finally graduated. It seemed that the only cure to this Jerome problem was to outlast him like Survivor. When he FINALLY left and I started my junior year, it was like a breath of much-needed fresh air. For once in my life, I had absolutely no physical bullies to try to fight or contend with—and I was finally able to try to enjoy what was left of my high school years.

(D.)   **MY UNSEEN OBSTACLES**—(1.) Even during this time as my interest in things WCG continued to grow, I still wasn't free as I really wanted to be on the religion front. And as I said in the previous chapter, the only realistic things I could do there was wait until I finally turned 18 and was on my own.

(2.) Around school, most of the time I tended to feel like Norm Peterson on "Cheers"—everyone definitely knew my name and I did have some semblance of popularity, but yet I was never allowed to be a leader most of the time or received many of the big titles added by my classmates (except for being elected Class Clown when I was a sophomore).

(3.) But what seemed to be the biggest obstacle of all that always stood in my way was Mother and I's financial situation. Since Mother was now primarily dependent on various types of government assistance and since I basically wasn't able to work at all during this time (not only due to my allergies, but also probably due to restrictions on Mother that might have possibly prohibited Mother from letting me work at all anyway as a condition of her receiving that government assistance), money was especially hard to come by most of the time for us (even despite the fact that we both now lived next door to my grandparents).

The combination of poverty and also not being to drive until my senior year definitely put a damper on me even being able to go out on any date with girls—much less having any girlfriends at all. I even actually went to both my Junior and Senior Proms as well as most dances by myself (with Mother usually driving me and picking me back up and taking me home afterwards). While most of those I knew had cars and/or dates with parents that had decent incomes or being rich, I actually always seemed to be on the outside looking in.

One thing that really kept driving this home for me personally was all the times I kept hearing some of my Hispanic classmates always talking about what they did or what they heard someone else say at some place or something they called "The Dance". Regardless, it just added more fuel to the fire to deep-seated feelings within me that despite everyone in this relatively small school knowing my name that I was also at the same time a social outsider and outcast in my own high school for reasons entirely out of my control.

(II.) THE GOOD TIMES AROUND ME—AND BETTER DAYS AHEAD OF ME

There is an old saying that would very much hold true here: "…What doesn't kill you actually makes you stronger." Despite the initial obstacles that got in my way when I first came to this particular campus, please don't think by any means that my time here at LHS was a complete waste. Not in the least…in fact, there were a lot of other good things I also got to personally learn about and experience in four short years:

(1.) This was a time for me when I first started being interested in current issues facing our society. For instance, this was a time here in Texas when prominent political figures such as Governor Mark White and H. Ross Perot were trying to push "no pass, no play" down the throats of students like myself who were concerned about the effects that such legislation at the time would have on extracurricular activities such as band and athletics—

especially for small schools like Lockney where Friday night football in the fall is not only the ONLY viable form of entertainment amongst our townspeople, but is also almost the equivalent of religion and church.

A sure way to insure a very small to absolutely no turnout to ANY meeting (church or otherwise) in most small Texas towns even to this day is to simply schedule it during football game nights. Doing so might even be the best indicator to who might be truly dedicated to your particular cause— because most everyone else of sane mind will NOT be there due to the fact that they're either at the football game or for something that's at least distantly related to it.

Anyway, I first learned about involvement in social issues having to help lobby people to keep Ross Perot from getting in the way of high school band.

(2.) Speaking of band, this was also when my deepening interest in music began to grow and mature more—especially in finding out careerwise things I did NOT want to end up doing for the rest of my life.

I found out among other things that I wasn't necessarily cut out for the Marine Corps Band. I actually tried out for it one time—and found out for myself just how little I really knew about music. The sum total of the results of this tryout—my concert band tryout was bad—and my sightreading was even worse. (Good thing in retrospect that I never joined the military—for totally different reasons I would find out later…)

I also realized that an earlier desire that I might have once had to actually become a band director and work in the field of music education was not what I really wanted out of life after all either. I found this out during the first two years in high school having to work very closely with my band director, James Whitis, and spending plenty of time after school practicing on my sax. Being able to see him on a more personal daily basis than most helped me to get a firsthand look at just how hard Mr. Whitis had to work at being our band director—and how little he seemed to get back in return in the way of monetary compensation. The more I began to see for myself the numerous frustrations he faced, the more attractive the music industry became to me in contrast. This was especially evident how at the time I truly got interested in such things as writing song lyrics and making up melodies to them—and making up melodies to them—and also in keeping up with such Top 40 countdown radio shows such as Casey Kasem and Shadoe

Stevens on the radio and how I really wanted to be more involved in BOTH music and radio.

During this time as I was examining colleges, universities, and career options, a group out of South Plains College called Country Caravan stopped on their summer tour one time in Floydada. The wide variety of musical styles the group displayed during their performance as well as the diversity and dexterity of the performers was a major siren song that caused me to eventually choose them as my next stop on the education trail after my graduation from here at LHS. But here in Longhorn Country, the basic cradle of my eventual musical aspirations was formed—and my dream of being in the music business began to take shape.

(3.) There was one more instance with Heather during my junior year that was priceless for me personally. When we were both in one of our honors math classes with Mrs. LaDora Aufill, before one session, Heather and I had a small discussion in which I was finally forced to acknowledge that she had no personal desire to be anything more than friends with me and officially had to once and for again give up any deeper formal intentions for her.

Soon after that discussion, in the middle of class one day, I accidentally (shall we say) exhibited a physical manifestation of very loud flatulence. At hearing the sound of it, not only did my fellow classmates tease me about it, but one of the other girls in my class even went so far as to claim that Heather was "...turned on" by it to me about it. With our previous private discussion still fresh in our minds, I winked at her as a sort of code message to here saying, "I don't believe what they're saying about both of us right now is true in any way." She winked back at me to acknowledge her agreement with this and in essence tell me in return, "I don't believe so neither." Whether or not our fellow classmates saw through our personal code or actually thought instead that our winks to each other meant something else entirely—I still don't know to this day.

(4.) I was also privileged to go to a few places I had never been—and my love of travel started to blossom as well.

During my Sophomore year, our band went on our bi-annual band trip to Durango, CO where we also had our annual band banquet and dance. I seem to recall that the DJ up there from that dance didn't give us the greatest in tunes and had absolutely no idea about how to properly conduct a "Cotton-

Eyed Joe" or a "Schottische" for a bunch of young Texans where such things were expected to be done at dances as an unwritten rule.

I also very much remember going into the glorified excuse for a shopping center that the folks in Durango at the time called a "mall". To me, it seemed to be no more than a huge TG&Y store and a few other small shops at best.

We did have some fun, though, going to Silverton and inner tubing down Molas Pass. Even though a couple of our cheerleaders/band members wound up breaking their legs down the Pass, nevertheless it was fun to some degree for all of us to romp in the snow.

During my senior year, our band trip that time was to Kansas City. While we were there, we got to tour a number of buildings downtown including what was at that time the world headquarters of Hallmark Cards. Getting to see from myself the process required from start to finish in the creation of a greeting card was definitely an eye-opening experience for me.

We also during that trip got to go to the Worlds of Fun Amusement Park not only for our band festival, but also to ride the rides as well. I even seem to recall losing one of my baseball caps as I was riding one of the roller coasters in that park.

Later during that year, our Senior English class also went to Odessa, TX to go see a Shakespeare play at the Globe Theatre on the Odessa College campus. It was interesting to see something we had only heard and learned aobut in class demonstrated in person—especially in regards to the dimensions of Odessa College's Globe Theatre replica in comparison to the actual one use in London during Shakespeare's time.

(5.) OK—I promised you earlier the brief "tale-of-the-tape" style versions of the activities I was personally involved in here at Lockney High. Here's the way in a nutshell that my 1986 annual summed up my accomplishments (with appropriate edits, as necessary, of course):

COY REECE HOLLEY—Football Manager—1; Basketball—JV 1, Manager—3 & 4; JV Tennis—2; All-Region Band—1 & 3; Stage Band-1; Band Crew-3; Fellowship of Christian Athletes-1, 3, & 4; Future Homemakers of America-2; National Honor Society-3 & 4, Annual Staff-4; Journalism UIL-4; Class Clown-2; Number Sense UIL-1&3; Elaine Hardy Memorial Scholarship-4

But looking at my official record of my overall accomplishments here at this alma mater doesn't tell the whole story. What really does speak to me most of all are the pictures of the faces of not only my own senior class of 1986— but all of the faces in these other yearbooks as well and what all happened to them after graduation.

And what did happen to some of them? Here's what little I know from these very steps I sit on right now: A good number of these people I haven't even seen personally since graduation. Most of the folks I know from my senior class have already been either married or previously divorced and even now have families of their own. There's at least one of my fellow graduates who I just heard the other day is currently recovering from major brain surgery.

At least 2 or 3 others in my class are sadly no longer with us—one of them that I know of personally that died due to some unfortunate circumstances which breaks my heart even now to think about. For this particular individual, if I had only known then what I know now about them, I would have very much regretted the way I treated them and would have done a little better in the way I acted around them. Unfortunately, shouldas and couldas can't bring the time back—and it's late to do anything about it now.

But maybe I shouldn't paint such a pessimistic picture of those I knew during my high school days. Most of us didn't turn out that bad after all. A good number of my former classmates are now on the other side of the classroom performing as teachers of their own students in their own right. Others are upstanding farmers and businessmen and businesswomen serving as solid pillars of the communities they now reside in.

I even now in my own mind think of one couple that's still married after all these years who were even probably childhood sweethearts. But I can at least tell you for sure they both were high school sweethearts because I just remembered from looking at their senior annual how they were elected by their peers as Most Popular and Prom King and Queen. Obviously as most married couples probably do, they've over the years have had more than their share of heartaches, problems, and rough rodeos. But what is even more surprising about these two is who they are now in comparison to what they were then.

Back here at LHS, these two definitely fit the titles to which they were elected and were very much what you might consider your quintessential high school cute couple. He was the big, strapping football star lad and typical West Texas aspiring farmer type. She was a cheerleader and probably got all the type of awards that any attractive high school girl could possibly get.

Now 30 years later, these two kids are not only still together, but also have a married daughter and a grandkid. And he of all things after years of being a farmer is now a pastor of two different Methodist churches while she owns her own beauty shop and dutifully serves as an able pastor's wife of those churches her husband now undershepherds.

CHAPTER CONCLUSION—MESSAGES SENT INTO THE WIND
Even now, the ghost of past students walk to and fro past us up and down these same steps we're now sitting on. My mind now flashes back to the many times I heard the Notre Dame Victory March (which also so happens to be LHS's fight song) and the School Song that echoes on the wind to me today:

WE LOVE YOU, LOCKNEY HIGH
We spend our days within your walls
Of school so dear
And may we ever heed your call
So keep us near
Senior, Junior, Soph, and Fish
Best of all for you we wish
Our trust and loyalty you'll ever hear
We love you—we'll ever sing your praise
High above you—our voices true we'll raise
We love you—and for you we'll live and die
Dear old Lockney High...

Into that very same wind that echoes those two songs throughout the years that I'd like to use to now send several very important messages that I strongly now after all this time I need to send while I still have the opportunity to do so as you as the reader and I prepare to get up from this place and move on to other things. The first is to a very unique audience that a lot of people here would like to say something personally to, but can't for one reason or the other. So maybe on their behalf, I'll take a stab at doing so.

Sadly many years after I graduated from here, I was shocked as well as many here throughout the state of Texas when this place became the object of state and national attention in January 2009 after two more recent students decided to commit arson for what I later heard throughout the grapevine was a so-called attempt to try to get better facilities and materials for this place. These students' misplaced zeal caused a lot of unnecessary heartbreak and inconvienence for a bunch of people here. While I was still working at KKYN, I happened to see the news stories on the Net and had the sad responsibility to do a news story for KKYN. Here's the initial text of the news story I filed with our Morning Show hosts at the time in regards to it to get an idea of the story:

Lockney HS Blaze Story:

Suggested Intro: The fire at Lockney High School Sunday night affected numerous artifacts of not only the history of the school, but also of the city of Lockney itself. KKYN's Coy Holley (who himself is a former alumnus of Lockney High School) fills us in on some of the history of Lockney High:

Actual News Story: [Projected Running Time—1:41]   ]

CART#: 57770 !!!

Sunday night's Lockney High School fire didn't just affect a building, but also the memories of an entire community whose current school campus has been a landmark of Lockney's existence for around 80 years. Originally built in 1929, Lockney High is a UIL 1A classification school that currently has 18 teachers instructing nearly 200 students in grades 9 to 12. Right now, there are slightly more male students than female studying at Lockney High with a significant majority of them being Hispanic (58%) while White and African-American students making up the rest of the student populations. Lockney shares a special distinction and connection with Texas Tech due to former national championship Lady Raider coach Marsha Sharp's prior tenure as the Lady Horn's former girls' head basketball coach before the time Sharp's name became famous at Tech. Besides being known for its athletic exploits, Lockney at one time was even known much more for its band due in part to the success at UIL contests of former band director Raymond Lusk who himself would eventually become the Lockney ISD superintendent. Current superintendent Phil Cotham also served in another previous role at Lockney High—that of an assistant coach under former head football coach and athletic director Bob Purser. And of course, we cannot forget the very intense annual rivalry between Lockney and its neighboring larger town to the southeast, Floydada, in which each year the annual Floyd County Championship is decided on the gridiron. These were some of the momentos that Floyd County Sheriff's Deputies were able to retrieve from the charred remains of this Lockney institution before the collapse of the roof early Monday morning. This is Coy Holley for KKYN News.

What follows below was the actual text of an email sent by one LHS alum of what was sent to LHS alums like myself immediately following the fire that sums up the general reactions to the 2009 LHS fire (part of this used with permission by the original sender, Breck Record, in which he personally responded to an email sent to Lockney High School alumni by now former LISD technology director Charles Keaton):

Charles Keaton wrote:
Good news ... I'm back in my office, the email/web server is back home and email is flowing both ways!!! Dart Carthel and Xcel Energy did a fantastic job getting power back to my part of the building and Blackmon-Mooring has also done a tremendous job in getting the JH part of the building inhabitable again. If all goes as planned the JH kids should be back on Monday. I hope many of you have had a chance to visit some of the websites I mentioned in my quick note last week and saw the pictures of the fire and it's aftermath. I hope to find some time in the next few days to put some pictures on the the LISD website. Thank you to everyone that has kept LHS in their thoughts and prayers.

Charles Keaton

Director of Technology
Lockney (TX) Independent School District

...

Charles,

Below is what I originally tried to post to you a couple of days ago.

As follows:

This is, indeed, very horrible. We all have memories, good and bad, of our dear school. Maybe we could start a memoirs of Lockney High School and sell the memoirs in a book to raise money for something to help rebuild the school.

I'm sure that everyone has a story to tell and with the school being around as long as it has, I know that there would be a wealth of history to be told and shared with others.

Also, is there going to be, perhaps, a bank account set up for those that might want to contribute to some kind of fund to help support the school to get it back on its feet??

Thanks again for the update.

Thankfully, the high school campus (as you can see by sitting here) has long since been rebuilt. And we that are from Lockney were definitely blessed to experience the gracious generousity of a number of friends and other entities who stepped in to help us in various ways to deal with the unfortunate aftermath of that tragic incident and assist us in the necessary painful transition to not just get any school up and running—but my very own alma mater at that. Please allow me to send my first message into the wind on behalf of my fellow LHS alumni, townspeople, students, and staff of the Lockney ISD—and even maybe on behalf of the City of Lockney and the Lockney Chamber of Commerce.

That message would be—thanks very much for standing with us in our time of need and reminding us that even the worst of times we face also paradoxically brings out the best in all of us. For those that gave through either personal service and/or monetary contributions no matter the sum (small or great)—please rest assured that my old alma mater that I'm sitting in front of right now is not only back up and running, but walking stronger and better than ever thanks in part to your help. And I hope that my Lockney friends and brethren would join me in extending an open invitation for those donors who graciously helped us to come right here on these steps (whether it's during our quadrennial Homecoming activities or maybe even any time you might happen to stop by our way) to come on in over here and see the final results for yourself.

The next one to send into the wind I must address to all of those in my class of 1986 that are still alive as they read this. The message is simple, but yet profound—it's long past time to come back home to here where we all started at least one more time. Some of you I ain't seen since we all graduated. Others for sure I haven't even seen face-to-face since I haven't even seen face-to-face since I moved to Plainview.

It's sad to know that we may have lost touch as the years have gone by with each other's lives. I hope that it won't require another few years for all of us to finally decide to renew and rekindle the old acquaintances we've had. Let's come back home at least one more time before it's too late. If any of my old classmates happen to read this, the welcome mat's laid out on my part for you to contact me again and get back in touch while we're still alive to enjoy it.

The final message is a more specific one to a very special woman whose annual picture I happen to be looking at right now still brings out some of the fondest memories of my school years in my mind. I feel she'll know who I'm talking about when I write what I'm about to write. (As for the rest of you--please bear with me for a little bit as I do this. We'll get back to regular operations in a few minutes.)

In order for me to do that, though, I must needfully talk to her current husband first. I hope that if he finds himself reading these words I'm about to write to his wife that he won't get jealous at me, attempt any violent action or manhunts in revenge against me, or interpret anything said here as trying to woo her away from him. In fact, I hope that after a cooler and more reasoned head prevails that he will actually see what is written here as a tip of my cap to him and a friendly reminder that in spite of what he and this woman have probably went through together that in my eyes he made one of the wisest choices of his life when he decided to take this particular woman as his wedded wife. And that's it's NOT I that should be envied—but him. If I had half the chance that he did, I would have done all that I knew to do to try to win her heart. But instead, she decided to choose you—and probably for good reason.

This man has my direct permission to not only use this as his own personal swift kick in his rear to be more conscious of his marriage vows to her, but also on those days where this woman keeps doubting herself and her true beauty and worth that he'll also use this as a sort of fully biased, personal opinion that can help him confirm his assertions to her about this woman's true value, beauty, and worth—not only to him, but more importantly to the Master of the Universe who created her.

Now finally and lastly comes my personal direct broadcast to this special woman herself that still goes on down the line through the years. As I write this, I'm looking at one of your pictures in our class's annual at one of the many well-deserved titles you garnered as one of the leaders of our class. For a number of years, you personally served as my first personal picture of true womanly beauty.

But I was basically forced to do this sort of deep admiration and desire for you from distance. I don't honestly know how truly aware you were of all the attempts I made during our school years to win your heart. But you had a different opinion than I did—and like it or not, I was forced to deal with those facts. But, madame—you probably had no clue what all I truly would have given up at the time just for you to simply have opened your heart long enough to give me the slightest entrance for your affections. I don't care what you might look now—but looking at this picture of you, I've still never truly forgotten not only how extremely physically attractive you were to me then—but more importantly how much I truly ached during those times to be intimate with your deepest heart.

Many years later, both of our lives have taken totally different directions. You went on with the man I just talked to a few minutes ago to start a family of our own and are now doing your part to help shape the minds of today's youth. But as you'll notice the more you might continue reading this book, I had to go as a result of the direction of my Lord down a trail of immense tears and suffering. You couldn't even begin to imagine the pains and heartaches that have shaped my life to this point in time. Perhaps my God in His foreknowledge was sparing you from what I now know was my own trying "walk of faith" that you might have had problems walking. Now in retrospect, I'm glad for your sake and concern that He had much better plans for you anyway.

My years would more aptly fit Jacob's description of his own life to Pharaoh when Jacob said to him that his "…years on the earth have been few to that of my fathers and full of trouble." After I finished here at Lockney High, madame—part of the paths and overall "walk of faith" that has been my life to this point has been trying to find the woman that I struggled to attempt to meet, date, and eventually marry as my own life partner. You to me were—and still are—part of the initial ideal of the lady of true beauty, class, and character that has highly influenced what I hope my God would provide in my own future wife. So far, I haven't found her yet—but that doesn't mean that I've stopped looking for her, neither.

Maybe I'd like for you to take away two things for yourself out of this long distance heart-to-heart intimate discussion with you. The first stems from one of the things you personally signed in one of my own memory books—where you wrote: "…There has never been a dull minute with you around." Madame—I might say the same about you in retrospect and add that you're a pretty hard woman to forget about yourself even after all these years.

And with that also comes a special note of thanks for showing me not as much through words, but primarily by example what a true woman of beauty, high caliber, and high standards should be like, I'm still trusting Him as I speak that whoever he may finally allow me to have as my future wife will be at least half as good or even better than you. That's because you set a pretty high bar for a lot of women to strive for and reach in order to be able to win MY own heart.

But the biggest message above all that I'd like for you to receive is that no matter how you may see yourself now, the picture of you that's forever etched in my mind as far as I'm concerned is of that young lady that I got to know in my younger years. She's the woman who I would have longed the most to be my date to the Junior and Senior Proms that I wound up having to go by myself instead. She would have been the woman above all else I would have longed desperately to have developed a more intimate relationship with. And she might have even, if I had been given the chance, the one that could have proposed marriage to you instead of the man who's now your husband.

So on those days when the washing machine goes out unexpectedly on you or your kids and grandkids make you tear your hair out…when the kids in your classroom make you question your sanity or when you may think of yourself literally looking and feeling like death warmed over—I hope you'll remember something. I've been across many parts of this country in my lifetime and have been privileged to meet various beautiful women (although unfortunately not on anymore usually than a casual acquaintance level). At least three of those I've been personally acquainted with have held important sounding beauty pageant titles. There's several other women that I even attempted to pursue for a romantic relationship that didn't quite materialize like I had hoped.

But I still haven't quit that search for my life partner—in which you were the primary initial spark that started me down that trail as well as others that I now go for Him. Without your initial involvement in my life, I wouldn't know what a beautiful woman might look like in the first place. Before your husband even first met you or had a clue that you even existed, I admired you and had the greatest crush on you that no one else could have topped.

I hope that the next time you do not feel like a beautiful woman that you'll do me a big favor. First, look into the nearest mirror you can find at yourself and reread these words I've just written you about how beautiful I truly thought you were in the past. Then afterwards, get your husband to hold you close to him and have him tell you himself about he truly feels about you now. Then after doing all of that, spend some time in prayer to the Master of the Universe who created you and read His Word to get His picture of how He might see you in YOUR future.

After that, I hope from there you'll begin to change your self-image to conform to the one of the extremely attractive and beautiful young woman that I knew and saw when we were both in school. I walk by faith and not by sight that the same woman whose picture I'm looking at now is similar to the woman I'm confident you are now. And more importantly, that your husband feels like the most blessed man on this planet for not only having met you, but to have also married you as well. How do I know this? Because I knew you—probably much earlier than he did. Shalom alechem b'shem Y'shua Ha' Meshiach to both of you as you continue your remaining adventures of life that lie ahead of you both.

Well, my good reader friend…looks like the winds of remembrance of my time here have died down…ready to get up and travel on? Got a lot of miles still left to go before we're through…

[Chapter 4:] [Levelland, TX—When My REAL Teenage Years Began]

As our winds of remembrance die down here at Lockney High, we'll also end this first Lockney-based version of our tour (you'll see why later on) as we head straight south on Fourth Street and head back towards US 70 to leave Lockney for a little while on our first out-of-town foray. We'll stay on 70 and not only completely leave Floyd County for now—but we'll even go all the way through Plainview via 70 (which in Plainview first becomes Fifth Street, then eventually turns into Olton Road).

Only after we pass I-27 and leave...

...do we truly realize why 70 is called Olton Road when the mile marker makes clear where our next possible destinations could be—

As we continue west on US 70, we'll pass by the Quarterway Gin and eventually find the wide spot in the road called Halfway where the Texas A&M Research Station is located. Just before we get into Olton proper, we also cross the Lamb County line and proceed all the way through a good bit of Olton's main business district that continues up until Olton's western city limits. We'll stay on 70 until we get to the very small town of Springlake—where we'll see a four-way stop light where US 70 intersects with US 385.

We'll then turn left onto 385 and part ways with US 70 for now because we have a more important destination to go to right now. Our journey on 385 starts around the Sandhills and also takes us through an area in which a few feedlots stand (and also smell very prominently). Before too long, we'll eventually find ourselves on the north side of Littlefield where we'll first turn left onto a business loop, then soon do an immediate right onto Hall Avenue which serves as one of Littlefield's main streets.

Heading south on Hall/US 385, the next major stop is at its intersection with FM 54 [also known as Waylon Jennings Boulevard…FYI—I almost forgot to tell you that Littlefield just so happens to be Waylon's (as in the famous country singer/outlaw) hometown…)] Continuing south on Hall, we'll eventually meet up with the US 84 bypass (i.e.—Marshall Howard Boulevard) before we finally leave Littlefield's southern city limits. We continue past Whitharral and pass one more county line into Hockley County. Straight as an arrow staying on 385, it won't be too long before we finally see the initial indicators of what our next actual tour stop will be.

385 will then pass College Avenue Baptist and a Best Western motel before we see a Stripes convienence store on our left and State Highway 114 right in front of us at the first light. The signs not only on the billboards, but also even on the public trash cans scream out—"Welcome to Levelland!"

We'll stay on 385 (now College Avenue) throughout most of town past United Supermarkets, McDonald's and a number of other prominent Levelland businesses until we come to the light at 13th Street right by the Dairy Queen on our left and the approaching KFC and Subway restaurants on our right. We'll then turn left onto 13th Street as the South Plains College campus comes into full view. Further east on 13th Street past the Baptist Student Union and Wesley Foundation buildings, we'll turn right onto E.M. Barnes Drive and pass Stroud and Frazier Halls on our left and the Creative Arts Building and the Country/Bluegrass Building on our right.

Right before the next four-way stop sign where E.M. Barnes Drive intersects with L.C. Kearney Drive, we at long last turn left onto the parking lot of Lamar Hall— the very dorm I stayed for all three years (except for summers when both men and women had to stay over in the Smallwood Apartments) of my time as a South Plains College student. Here at the front entrance of Lamar, we'll sit down for a little while and have a chat about the time of my life that I tend to now refer as my "delayed adolescence" and my REAL teenage years.

Hey, look over here—there's a few of my old momentos of my time here waiting for us to peruse through. Let's check them out, shall we? There's my degree from here that I got when I graduated in the spring of 1989. Here's my old annuals from my first two years here—and an old button with Country Caravan as well as an old bulletin from one of their summer performances. There's even my old Sophomore Recital tape…I'd even let you see it…but drat—I forgot it's in VHS format….wouldn't do us any good with the technology of today that's now available…and hey, there's even my old Lamar Studmuffin shirt! (NO—I'm NOT going to tell you what "Studmuffins" meant—and I'm most certainly NOT going to tell you where I got the nickname "Psycho"! I refuse to do it—I just won't do it! It's too embarrassing anyway!)

As you're running your grubby hands across my old momentos, I will tell you the main themes that might best sum up my time here in Leveldirt (excuse me— Levelland…pardon me in advance if I slip into old patterns as to how some locals jokingly refer to this town…): (1.) that it was truly my personal days of discovery where I began to finally establish my own personal identity independent of what my mother and grandparents thought and wanted me to do; and (2.) I began to find out for myself the hard way the importance of making right choices that will impact the rest of your life—and the negative consequences that result from making the wrong choices that result from making the wrong choices that cause lots of needless pain, heartache, and suffering not only for yourself, but especially to those you love and admire most.

MY PERSONAL DAYS OF DISCOVERY

So you're wondering why most of the time in these SPC annuals whenever a picture of me was taken that it was usually when I was playing my sax? Uh…didn't we talk about that during the last chapter? Did it occur to you that my majors at SPC were *Music Performance AND Country/Bluegrass Music*? If not, then you wouldn't understand how much in place truly playing that sax might be here. I'll have plenty to say about that in a little bit!

But first, you'll need to understand how dramatic my move here to Levelland was to me personally. Back in Lockney, most of the time I felt frankly like a semi-social outcast. Out here, though, I was semi-independent. I was still VERY tied to the financial apron strings of my mother and grandparents for things such as food, toilet paper, and the like that I couldn't otherwise get on my own. But otherwise when I was here, I was pretty much free to do as I wished—and I almost did.

For the first time in my life, I really for once got to finally do some of the things I wanted to do. Even though most of the time here I didn't have a car to drive, this place was my first real personal frontier that lent itself for numerous opportunities to not only do what I wanted to do, but also BE who I wanted to be. No real limits, restrictions, and boundaries—and I sure tested them often and a lot. I as a result found out about who I really was and began working towards who I really wanted to be and to do and to get what I wanted out of this life.

A WALKING TOUR THROUGH MY SPC LIFE

As we saw in the last chapter, annual yearbooks like these you just thumbed through may tell you some scattered facts of the story—but they don't give you the entire picture by any means. Maybe this time, it might be better if I took and showed you around some of the buildings on campus via a little walking tour. That way, you won't just be hearing me talk so much, but you'll also get to see a little bit of my former SPC life for yourself—OK?

We'll start our walking tour going across the street to the Texan Dome and through several other buildings pretty fast before saving two or three others that I spent the most time in towards the last that's closest to our home base Lamar Hall location. First, the Texan Dome is where SPC's physical education department is located. I not only had to take racquetball for a couple of semesters to fulfill my P.E. requirements here, but also where I as a member of the Pep-Jazz Band had to perform for all Texans basketball games and other special functions.

Before we go any further, I'd better explain the very generous financial aid package that I was blessed to receive as an SPC student. The first year here as a result of my graduation from Lockney High, I applied for and was awarded the Elaine Hardy Memorial Scholarship that was given to those planning to pursue college studies in either music or medicine. (Thankfully, Country/Bluegrass Music qualified!) That small amount given at least pitched in to get me started in my new life here.

Then, I found out for myself just how truly advantageous being the son of a single mother and also economically disadvantaged could be in obtaining the necessary financial aid needed to pay for my education here. I never had to take out a single student loan all the time I was here—for by the time my Pell Grants, Workstudy, and music scholarships were received, I was able to have all things I needed as far as tuition, books, room, board, etc.—they were already paid for as far as basic expenses were concerned.

All that Mother and my grandparents usually had to help me cover were the other incidental expense such as laundry, toiletries, etc. At the time, we didn't even have cable in the rooms (remember that this was in the late 1980s before the Internet was in existence and cable wasn't as advanced as it is now)—so I had to make do with all of the channels that were available on the shared TV in the lounge.

And if you didn't have money, forget about having a phone of your own. Most EVERYONE shared the common payphone that was out in the hall closest to where my room was. When someone got a phone call, someone else had to go to your room and tell you PERSONALLY that you got a phone call—then you had to go to the pay phone booth to take the call. And if you wanted to call home (or anywhere else for that matter at the time), you either had to have the correct change for a local call (usually between a dime and a quarter for a local call) OR call the other party collect and hope to bleep they'd accept the charges. (Boy, how times have changed dramatically since then as far as technology's concerned. And thankfully, it makes me appreciate my cell phone that costs me NOTHING that I have now more than ever.)

Anyway, also across the street from Lamar are the Agriculture and Telecommunications buildings (which I rarely set foot in). From there, we start to see some of the vocational technology buildings next to the Law Enforcement building. (I remember the Law Enforcement building for one reason—one of the summers I was here I actually had a Workstudy job cleaning up the pistol range. I never got to shoot a gun, but of course, I did have to clean up a lot of dirt, used magazines, old shotgun pellets, and other trash.)

We continue on towards the Technical Arts building, then hang a left to go to the Library. (Yes, I had to check out books here like everyone else—as well as a lot of research for various papers for classes I took here.) Then on the next street, we'll find the Math and Science building where I had to take several of my necessary general education requirement courses that were needed in order to transfer to Eastern New Mexico University including a couple each of math (in which I basically reprised the Algebra and Trigonometry courses I took in high school) and science courses which I barely passed with Ds in Biology and Zoology. The most memorable thing here was when I tried to take General Physics my first semester out of the chute here. Big mistake for me, though—because I could never quite get past Newton's 2nd Law of Motion and as a result found myself withdrawing from that course just in time to be able to keep my perfect first semester 4.0 GPA intact. It was interesting to note, though, that the instructor I had for my first-year Music Theory courses was also one of my fellow students for the Physics class.

Apparently one of his personal hobbies (strangely enough) WAS taking math and science courses.

Then we move onward towards the four most central buildings here on campus that I probably spent the most time in. Across the street is the Student Union Building where SPC's cafeteria (yes—like most, they had their good stuff and bad), police station, bookstore, lunch grill, and game room. Except for that one summer at the pistol range, my Workstudy job here on campus was working under the direction of Student Activities Director Jennifer McCasland and her secretary/game room supervisor, Betty Hendrickson. Both of these ladies were absolute sweethearts to work under throughout my tenure here. Who knows just how much change for our game room users I had to give out and the number of problems with pool cues, video games, and the like I had to help resolve. I also had to help Jennifer out at times with some of the special activities that her department was responsible to provide for our on-campus housed student population (including movie nights, dances, special events, etc.).

From there, we head to the Administration Building where all of the required courses for my degree here in English, History, and Government were taken. Here's where I need to let you in on a dirty little secret about being a music major. One of the prices I had to pay to be a SPC music student was that every semester I had no choice but to take course loads of no less than 20 and sometimes up to 23 hours a semester.

Before you rush to judgment about my seeming to have an almost impossible course load and feel sorry for me in having such, consider the following first. Remember earlier when I said that part of what paid my way through SPC were scholarships? Now let me fill you in on just how I was usually able to maintain enough of a decent GPA that put me on the President's List the first semester and the Dean's List during the rest of my time here. The key? If you're a music major, it's not as hard as you think as long as you don't do anything royally stupid.

First, consider that one of my obligations of each of the music scholarships I was on was that I had to play in the appropriate band for each scholarship. In my case, each semester I was involved in a Country Ensemble, Pep/Jazz Band, and Symphonic Band. Each of those have no tests—just performances. (That's 6 credit hours right there.) I also had to take private lessons on sax and piano (and even did voice and percussion to boot). Our final exams for those were usually what we called "juries" at the end of the semester. (Take off another 2 to 4 hours right there.)

Also, I usually took things like English, History, and Government during the summer months when there was more time to focus on specific courses in a concentrated fashion. That as well as taking the required academic course load was usually no more than 12 hours for the fall and spring semesters and 3 to 6 hours for each of the two summer sessions (that includes required Music core courses such as Music Theory, Music History, etc. that were usually so super easy to study and prepare for). By the time you finish your calculations, the only thing that having 21 to 23-hour course loads usually meant was that I had to spend a lot of time doing rehearsals for band, performing in concerts, or practicing for private lessons. And that's how music majors manage to keep up such high grade point averages.

I can say the following about the English, History, and Government teachers here. They were interesting personalities to be around in general—but they were usually pretty tough and rarely cut you much slack. One of my Sophomore English professors in particular was especially memorable in several ways—one, his lisp and unique facial appearance; and two, his immense sarcasm that also by virtue made the class discussion quite hilarious at times.

One of my history professors was even more memorable in several ways. First, he absolutely loved to give ALL essay exams for his midterms and finals. But it wasn't just that fact alone that should concern you. It was the WAY you gave the answers to what were usually a total of no more than six open-ended essay questions. No "open book" was allowed—and ALL of your historical facts had to be memorized and ready to go BEFORE you got there. On top of it, everything had to not only be historically accurate, but also grammatically correct WITH proper spelling and could be NO MORE than the entirety of the available blank space allotted on the exam. Talk about an exercise in brevity while at the same time playing "beat the clock"—you had it with his exams. And if you didn't study and as a result could not complete a question, it was automatically counted as wrong. A lot of us when taking his course thought that we were taking ENGLISH instead of history the way he tended to run things there.

Another thing I remember most about this particular history professor was a statement he made to us one time in class as he talked about the history of the Progressive movement. I've by now probably forgot about most everything else he taught in that course except for one thing: "…Perception colors viewpoint." He interpreted this to mean—"…what you see and how you perceive things will eventually influence your overall viewpoint on any situation." That's a quote that still speaks to me down through the years—for there's more truth in that one statement than most realize.

Now we come to the two buildings here on campus that due to my major I obviously spent a lot of time in. Let's first go into the Creative Arts Building for a little bit, shall we? This way, you can see for yourself what I learned from the more traditional end of the music spectrum.

How about heading into this classroom for a minute or two as I talk about two of my music professors who I personally considered at SPC my "musical mom and dad" (FYI—they are both married…but NOT to each other)—Symphonic Band Director Lynda Leister Reid and Pep/Jazz Band Director and now Department Head Dr. Bruce Keeling. I sure didn't know as much about music as I thought when I came here. (In fact, in terms of music theory, I was practically musically illiterate—for I didn't even have the foggiest concept of what a chord was 'til I started here.) But during my SPC years, these were the two people above all else who taught me more about music and life in general than anyone else here.

What set these two teachers apart for me more than anything else was not only their zeal and enthusiasm for life, but how they both used that energy to make studying music really FUN! Yes—with any endeavor, there's naturally work. But anytime you saw either Bruce or Lynda in rehearsal (whether they were conducting or playing themselves), it was never stuffy by any means. In high school, band always meant an overly excessive focus on the show with the three songs we had to play for UIL marching band contest and the three for concert band contest with occasional exercises in sightreading. It was at times drudgery to go through rehearsal most of the time.

But NOT Bruce's rehearsals—NO WAY!! The atmosphere was so zany and hilarious most of the time that it was a wonder that we ever got any work done. Bruce is very much a guy that's pretty bold, upfront, and brash in his style. I mean—he could be telling a story about someone in a bar; then in the middle of telling that story count you down, "…1…2…3…4…" to prompt you to start playing, then give the punchline to the joke, then say "…1…2…ready…go!", and we all went nowhere with what we were trying to play because we were laughing so hard at the joke.

Also, if someone got a little too carried away, you wouldn't be too surprised to eventually hear Bruce say something like, "Coy—TAKE A VALIUM! Please…take two, in fact, will you?"—as his personal prompt for you to basically calm down and shut up. His unique sense of humor and bubbly personality made even the most tedious and boring rehearsals FUN—and made our band and music family a very tight and close one (albeit at times bordering on the dysfunctional, of course).

It wasn't just band rehearsals either where Bruce's unique personality showed. You should have seen us music majors when we had to take music history classes from him. THAT'S when Bruce was even more of a hoot to be around. Only Bruce could talk about things in his lectures about Bach getting drunk in church or Mozart's very pompous and arrogant attitude in a way that was different from the average bear. And ONLY Bruce could talk about how folks like Beethoven and the Romantic composers that followed him bordered between depression and suicide or how a certain musical piece in German with the word "Kindentotenlider" actually could be interpreted in English to mean "Songs of the Death of Children" (how bizarre…)—and STILL make us all laugh uproariously about it. (Amazing how much music history illustrates the many tortured souls who have made contributions to the advancement of music…no wonder why some of the best musicians I know sing and play in prison choirs…)

Where Bruce tended not to be bashful, Lynda proved at times to be the perfect laid-back, relaxed, and calm counteropposite. Don't get me wrong—she could cut up and have fun, too. But she for me was the ideal private lesson teacher I needed who helped keep me focused on the things I needed to do the most in further developing my abilities on sax—but who also at the same time gave me plenty of room to explore and try some new things musically that I'd never done. Musically, she was the one who did more of the burping, feeding, and diapering of my personal musical abilities and the mother figure (although she at the time I became one of her students she wasn't actually all that old herself) that helped keep me within the musical fences I needed to grow and do things right as a musician.

Bruce and Lynda along with the other professors and teachers in the Music Department each as a musical family made their own contributions that encouraged me to learn more and be the best I could be as a musician. The biggest things they all encouraged me the most was to remember that—(1.) Music isn't just work—but by its very nature is REALLY and TRULY at its essence—FUN!; and (2.) that no matter what I'd been through or where I came from, I could always dream again and take some risks. I learned to discover a joy of music that I had not even previously found during that line or have been able to recapture since.

One example was when our Symphonic Band was to do a Halloween concert—and Lynda encouraged those who wanted to write a piece for that concert to let her know about doing so. Out of the entire band, I was the only one who stepped forward to compose a brand-new piece. I wound up writing a composition called "The Headless Horseman" which featured myself on baritone sax, our Percussion Ensemble, and two dramatic narrators that got its world premiere first (and still ONLY up to this time) performance at that concert. As a part of my private lessons, I got to have first-hand practical experience in how to compose with a large group—and especially who is REALLY in charge where musical compositions are concerned. (It's like the family farmer—the director may hold and wave the baton. But the composer trumps and feeds them all.)

Now let's go over next door to the Country/Bluegrass Building and see some things about the some of the other reasons I decided to study here at SPC instead of another college or university. One of the things I absolutely loved about being here at SPC was seeing the very close relationships that those on the traditional side of the music department had with the Country/Bluegrass Music and other related departments. There was absolutely no exclusivity or stuffy "better-than-you" attitudes here. In fact, as opportunities availed themselves, professors like Bruce could be just as easily found playing as a part of Country Caravan (SPC's old touring country group) as a Country/Bluegrass student could also be playing in either Pep/Jazz Band or Symphonic Band.

Some great examples of this included the Country Ensembles I was in. "Country Ensembles" could be a loose term—for I wound up playing in a wide variety of styles ranging from more traditional country all the way out to Christian rock. As a sax player, I was a sort of unique oddity in this Department since I couldn't play a stringed instrument. But thankfully, that didn't stop me from doing it.

In fact, I got to learn some interesting things from experiences like these ensembles as well as an additional class I had to take in Country/Bluegrass Arranging. It was almost no different than taking the Music Theory courses I was already taking anyway—just that the only difference was for the particular style of music I was doing it for, that's all. Among other things, I found out that the best way to arrange for a sax in a country band was to think of its closest musical equivalent—a fiddle/violin.

One of the Country Music professors and ensemble leaders, Tim McCasland (FYI—remember Jennifer in Student Activities that I told you about earlier? At the time I was here, Tim and Jennifer were married with one son, Austin.) was to me one of the real fun ones to be around. If you saw Tim on the surface, you'd think that he was only just a guitar picker. That was—until you got to know him a little better and constantly heard how he talked in rehearsal. Only then would you realize how very proficient in the English language he could be. (In fact, towards the last of my tenure here, he actually started teaching an English course or two here on campus. And he wasn't the only English teacher in the family. His father-in-law was actually one of my Sophomore English teachers—believe it or not.) Rarely did an ensemble rehearsal pass without Tim giving a sort of vocabulary word for the day (like "plethora" or something else like that). That was the ONLY country band that I know of in which the ensemble teacher was also definitely an intellectual type. (Who says members of country bands are necessarily hicks?)

But the one course at SPC I really loved the most and that pushed my buttons a lot could be found over in the main Production Studio. Let's pop in over there real quick and check it out…

First, the official background on what is now called the Tom T. Hall Production Studio. During my first semester here, they were actually still building this place and some of my music classes had to be conducted in other parts of this building. But during that same semester, I actually got to be a personal witness to history in the making the day this studio was officially dedicated and named for the later country singer Tom T. Hall. Mr. Hall and 184 other musicians on that day formed the world's largest bluegrass band that helped this college enter into the Guinness Book of World Records. I didn't get to play in the band—but I can at least say I was there to see it all.

During my remaining tenure here, this was one of the places our Country Ensembles might meet. But I really benefited most from this my very last semester here when I took a beginning course in what was called at the time Performing Arts Production Technology (PAPT). That one course alone would be what would change my personal desires and career direction in ways I never dreamed.

Basically, PAPT was essentially a course in how to do TV production in the context of music video production. I never thought working in TV and relating it to the music biz—until I saw a video of a production of a show that was done in the studio in which showed a keyboard player playing an instrumental during that concert. As I watched it, I was truly mesmerized by the images of the song put video form—and from there on out was forever hooked.

I wish in retrospect I'd been able to take more courses like that here at SPC—but this one course was at least the perfect preparation that would get me ready for all the mass communication minor courses that I would soon take at Eastern. I got to through this course do hands-on based training that helped me learn such things as lighting, cameras, and editing for TV that I would have never gotten anyplace else. Put that together with my love of music—and to me, it was a totally undeniable and indelible connection that I'd never forget.

The combination of all of these reminds me of one night in my life here at SPC that was also one of my busiest ones. Imagine this scenario—

6 PM (app.)—Perform in Tom T. Hall in my Country Ensemble as a part of our Music Marathon (in which I sang two songs and also did my amateurish version of keyboards)

7:30 PM—Go next door to the Theatre over in Creative Arts and perform as a part of a Sax Ensemble (classical, that is) for the Small Ensembles concert.

THEN AFTER THAT performance was through—Go BACK next door to Tom T. Hall and do the directing/technical directing of the Bon Vivants segment of same Music Marathon (you wouldn't believe how many times I said the words "fast trans mode" to my cameramen while in the studio—meaning one camera on front of the stage, another on the singers, and the third on the horn section…)

THEN after directing and TDing—I had to then help run camera for one Marathon segment and lighting for another….

(Oh, I forgot to mention—ALL of the Music Marathon was being broadcast LIVE on local cable for EVERYONE to see…It was definitely a busy and pressure-packed night for myself and the ages for sure…)

But the project that was the most fun for me to do was the tape you had in your hands a little while ago of my Sophomore Recital. It turned one of my Music Performance degree requirements into a multimedia project that brought all of my personal talents together—performing, composing, photography, and video editing all in one place. I actually had a joint recital with a piano major in which I actually wrote a new piece specifically for this recital and at the end.

One of the things I remember most was the part of that video I did of one of the songs my Sophomore Recital partner played—Beethoven's "Moonlight Sonata". The video when edited as the final portion of the piece was being played by my colleague features a night scene filmed at a playa lake near the campus in which I did at the beginning some great shots of some stuff on the lake going in—and by the end of the piece turned into a very slow zoom out away from one of the buildings on the lake. It was a lot of work towards the end—but I had a time doing the video for that Recital…and on the tape, it truly showed.

Here at SPC, I had the freedom creatively to discover the multitude of different talents and learn how to exploit and explore how those could be best used. I discovered for myself in not only music, but other realms that the only limits I had here on that front were those I wound up putting on myself. Those were liberating feelings that later built the foundations of boldness and personal character that I know now.

MY DAYS OF DISCOVERY AS A PERSON

This time of personal discovery wasn't necessarily limited to my academic and musical pursuits here on campus, either. In fact, I was privileged to at the time meet a wide variety of people from not only all throughout the South Plains area, but even from different places all throughout the nation and even the rest of the world. Talk about opening up my world that was once easily contained within the confines of the Lockney city limits—it didn't just open new doors, but SPC even went so far for me as to completely blast them off the hinges.

For instance, I actually had a roommate for one summer session who was from Japan named Hirohito. One night, he actually fixed beef curry over rice— something that I as a native West Texan had never experienced in the culinary realm before that time (or for that matter since then). It was pretty spicy—but man, I loved it! For about a day or two afterwards, I thought it was the greatest thing since sliced bread. It was a unique taste I'd never had before.

Also through my involvement with Student Government and especially through Phi Theta Kappa (PTK) (a junior college national honors society), I especially got to go a place or two I had never been before. With PTK, I actually got to go to national conventions in Dallas and Washington, D.C. For the Dallas trip, we actually had a special barbeque and dance at the actual Southfork Ranch facility where the TV series "Dallas" was shot. As part of that occasion, our Country Caravan group did a special performance for those attending the convention. I also remember going through Dealey Plaza and touring the area where JFK was assassinated and took some pictures there.

But the Washington, D.C. trip was even more memorable for several reasons. One of them was, as I seemed to recall, that it was the year where Reagan cabinet official Jeane Kirkpatrick gave a keynote address to our convention. Another was an instance during a party/dance during the convention when I would up asking a very gorgeous blond girl in a blue dress to dance. Little did I know what I was truly in for. (I don't remember where exactly she was from—probably someplace east…I don't know.) For one thing, this girl as we were dancing started doing moves that would have made Patrick Swayze or Tom Cruise blush. (Yes—it was THAT close.)

But there was an interesting drawback to the deal—she was also drunk as a skunk. That fact was obvious whenever I might try to spin her around—for she seemed so dizzy she literally fell head first into the floor. Had I not tried to be a perfect and proper gentlemen to her at the time, the temptation to take advantage of her in her inebriated state would have been too much to overcome. I considered it a true act of mercy for her when her friends that she was with decided that she probably had enough and that it was way past time for her to go back to her hotel room and head for bed.

Despite these little sidenotes, it was an interesting treat to be able to see and take pictures of some of the important landmarks of our nation's capital for myself. The big thrill of this particular trip for me personally came as a result of a special promise I made to help fulfill a request of someone back home.

I told you earlier about Betty Hendrickson in Student Activities who was Jennifer's secretary and also one of my direct supervisors. Before I left for the D.C. trip, I was telling Betty about my going on this upcoming trip and realized that my destination was going to D.C., she not only got excited over it, but she also took a picture out of her desk and showed it to me—which eventually led to a very interesting request. Betty then showed me a newspaper clipping of one of the names written on the Vietnam Veteran's Memorial and proceeded to tell me the following story…

Betty's husband served in the Air Force as a pilot during the Vietnam conflict. One time as he was making a supply run and was about to land on an airstrip, some of our own forces accidentally mistook him for a North Vietnamese plane and shot the plane and him down as a result. Her husband was subsequently killed in the crash.

But that wasn't the end of the story by any means. A news service photographer happened to take a picture of the scene—and as a result, the pictures when they hit the papers were printed and shown worldwide. All of this was within very quick succession of the military formally notifying Betty of her husband's death. She told me that the hardest part of her ordeal was the sheer trauma she had to (bless her heart) go through every time that stupid picture was printed in the papers.

Just before I left, she told me that she had seen what she thought may have been her deceased husband's name on a picture in a newspaper of the Vietnam Memorial. Then this request of me came directly from her lips—"Coy, if you see his name on the Wall while you're these, is there any way you could bring back a picture of his name for me when you come back? Please???" I responded that I couldn't make any guarantees because of the convention schedule—but if I did, I'd see what I could do.

When I finally got to D.C. and began touring the monuments that most people associate with the Capitol, I didn't necessary feel a connection with some of the other places such as Congress, the Lincoln Memorial, and the Jefferson Memorial. Frankly, they seemed rather staid, touristy, and run of the mill for me.

But when I set foot on the Vietnam Memorial, the scene and atmosphere was totally different. For instance, as you first come into the Memorial, you find a statue of soldiers out on patrol. The main monument itself is nothing but a long wall of names who died in the entire Vietnam conflict right by their years chiseled in black granite. But yet the atmosphere at the Wall struck me differently than all of the other places in D.C. I toured combined. Pictures and other momentos literally left behind by people at the Wall, all the people either taking pictures of names or trying to stencil a copy of a name onto paper—it's hard to describe the emotions of standing in a place like this unless you've been there yourself.

Finally, I came to Betty's husband's name and was able to take a picture of it. After I came back home, when I had the film developed, I arranged to get double prints of each picture that I took while I was on the trip. When I came back to work and I got back the pictures and gave her one of the prints of the picture of her husband's name. When she saw it for herself, she broke into tears, hugged me, and thanked me for accomplishing that mission. It was definitely the highlight of that particular trip for me in having a small part to personally play in helping a widow begin to at long last close a chapter of her past that was full of pain and grief.

I didn't just get to know only the folks on campus, neither. I also took part for a little while in both a local writers' group and even a chess club to boot. My love of chess (and especially really learning how to play the game properly) sprang up big time here at one of the City Hall meeting rooms downtown.

I especially had plenty of fun being a part of the Levelland Chess Club. Most people sadly have the image of chess being a pretty stuffy sport. But during the time I was a part of this Chess Club, I saw nothing of the sort with this crowd. The pretty motley crew of folks like oilfield roughnecks, farmers, city employees, and even a restaurant manager would easily tear down that elitest image in less than two seconds.

Learning chess as a novice and its varied intrecacies was especially fun when I got to hang around some very interesting characters. I especially like the very jocular environment created whenever someone acknowledged a good move was made against them in a back-handed way. [(Ex.) "…Ouch—that hurt!"; "…That's not very nice…"; "Hmmh…..very interesting…very interesting indeed."] You knew that you were playing pretty good when you were creating problems and causing havoc for your opponent.

I even got to play in a local tournament or two as a part of this Chess Club. I remember in particular how it was when I played against a guy from Midland— and lost VERY quickly in just five moves. What happened was that I forgot to develop my pieces and castle as quick as I could. I paid the price for it when his bishops and other pieces kept me from going anywhere and as a result put me in checkmate. From that game on, I found out the hard way about the necessity of castling and prompt piece development before I did anything else in this stupid game.

Regardless of the activity, I was free here in Levelland to try new things, find my own wings, and discover who I really was as a person. I also had the immeasurable privilege of establishing some very special relationships that would last a lifetime.

AN UNEXPECTED SURPRIZE

A couple of those special relationships came as a result of an unexpected encounter that I had with a long-lost classmate just a few days after I came to Levelland to start my SPC studies. One night after I moved into my room in Lamar Hall, I decided to take a walk around campus and see what was shaking. As I was walking, I just happened to meet a guy who was one of my old classmates during most of my elementary and junior high school years in Lockney named Gary Prisk. I remember times like when we were in Physical Education classes where he would also lag behind everyone else kind of like plumper individuals like myself (even though he was actually thinner than a rail). There'd also be times like when we'd have to walk the few blocks between the junior high school and the elementary (where the main cafeteria was for those that had free and reduced lunches and couldn't otherwise afford to get lunch at the Longhorn Inn).

Gary and I would definitely have some interesting conversations on the way back from the lunchroom. But what was even more interesting for Gary was that in the fall for some reason he'd always be gone for at least a week or two for some church camp that I at the time had no clue about (nor did ANYONE else in school—because no one else I knew did what Gary did). For some strange reason, I actually thought he was a Seventh-Day Adventist or something like that. Most everyone I knew at the time usually went either to the Baptist or Methodist church except for those holdouts, of course, in the Church of Christ and those Hispanics who usually went to the Catholic church on the east side of town.. Then he and his parents started attending school in Floydada and I lost touch with him after that…

UNTIL I came here to Levelland! It turns out that Gary was also going to SPC himself to study diesel mechanics or something like that. From there, I also got to know his roommate, Bobby Armstrong, and started popping in on them from time to time on them in their apartment that was right across the street from campus as I began to renew one old acquaintance and meet another friend.

During that time, my interest in WCG was still burgeoning as I was reading and devouring the Plain Truth, the Correspondence Course, and other Church literature voraciously. One night as I was over at Gary & Bobby's apartment and we were talking, I happened to spot what I saw were some very strangely familiar books on the shelf that were very similar to the ones I had from HWA—books such as "The Wonderful World Tomorrow" and "The Incredible Human Potential". And then suddenly, it all clicked for me…"…He's in the Church! He's in the Church!"

So I began to let Gary know that I'd also been in contact with the Church and receiving their literature and eventually asked him if there was any way I could go start going to services with him. Gary said, "I don't know—I'll have to ask permission from my pastor first." At first, I thought this statement strange—but then eventually let it go. Then finally closer to November, Gary got the go-ahead and I started joining them on Saturdays to Church services in Lubbock. I remember going back and forth between Levelland and Lubbock on 114 as we'd talk about various things even as we saw Reese Air Force Base that was at the time brimming with lots of activity.

Outside of semester break when I had to go back home and sometimes when Gary and Bobby weren't able to let me ride with them to church, I continued going with them to church in Lubbock throughout most of that first spring. During this time, I received my first real taste of what WCG was like and got to know Mr. Dobson and some of the Church members a little better. I got to know what being around brethren in "God's True Church" was like at the time. And I loved it and didn't want to leave.

One of those first WCG brethren I got to know besides Gary and Bobby was Burt Brown, one of the local church deacons in the Lubbock congregation. Burt and his wife happened to also live in Levelland themselves way out on Cactus Drive in a very spacious home. It was there where I took part in my very first "Night To Be Much Observed" commemorating the night Moses and the Israelites departed from Egypt. And talk about good food—for struggling college students like Gary, Bobby, and myself, it was a definite treat to have home cooking again away from the campus cafeteria (and UNLEAVENED on top of it). Yep—this was really God's Church to me—and I wanted to be a part of it.

SOWING AND REAPING THE WHIRLWINDS OF MY CHOICES—AND THE CONSEQUENCES OF DOING SO

But lest you think that my time here in Levelland was all peaches and cream and perfection, remember that these were also years where I was finally able to do things in the way I wanted to away from the constraints of the family and church that I felt restricted me back home and instead begin to live life based on the terms I wanted to truly live out for so long. It was truly a time of making some important choices about how I was going to live the rest of my life. Some of those choices were good ones—but there were also at least several that were bad.

As I stand here looking on these grounds, Hosea's words ring out to me loud and clear about the bad choices I made here that to this day I still grieve over and regret so much over choices and years and opportunities I now can't take back: "…They sow wind, and they shall reap whirlwind—standing stalks devoid of ears and yielding no flour. If they do yield any, strangers shall devour it. Israel is bewildered; they have become among the nations like an unwanted vessel, like a lonely wild ass, for they have gone up to Assyria, Ephraim has courted friendships. And while they are courting among the nations, there I will hold them fast; and they shall begin to diminish in number form the burden of kings [and] officers." (Hosea 8:7-10; JPS Hebrew/English Tanach)

Then suddenly, these very grounds turn into a courtroom—and just now, HaSatan, the chief prosecutor and accuser of myself and the brethren, on one side and myself on the other find ourselves looking towards the bench of the Creator of the Universe. HaSatan even now reads the charges against me as I reflect on the words of Psalm 101:1-8:

Psalm 101

Of David. A psalm.

[1] I will sing of your love and justice;
    to you, LORD, I will sing praise.
[2] I will be careful to lead a blameless life—
    when will you come to me?

I will conduct the affairs of my house
    with a blameless heart.
[3] I will not look with approval
    on anything that is vile.

I hate what faithless people do;
    I will have no part in it.
[4] The perverse of heart shall be far from me;
    I will have nothing to do with what is evil.

[5] Whoever slanders their neighbor in secret,
    I will put to silence;
whoever has haughty eyes and a proud heart,
    I will not tolerate.

⁶ My eyes will be on the faithful in the land,
   that they may dwell with me;
the one whose walk is blameless
   will minister to me.

⁷ No one who practices deceit
   will dwell in my house;
no one who speaks falsely
   will stand in my presence.

⁸ Every morning I will put to silence
   all the wicked in the land;
I will cut off every evildoer
   from the city of the LORD.

"…Your Honor—Mr. Holley while he was here in Levelland and attending South Plains College claimed that he was trying to live according to the doctrines of WCG and act righteous. But the State wishes to show this Court that while Mr. Holley professed You with his lips, his heart and actions were far from You."

"State may come forward to present its case…"

"Thank you, Your Honor…I now present to you State's Exhibit #1 for the records of the Court. This exhibit is a note that shows just how much I was able to get the Defendant in fear—fear about what his family would think about joining WCG, fear of losing what at the time were important things he deemed essential for his livelihood, such as food, toilet paper, and laundry money. Because of this, the Defendant was seen and witnessed by a number of my demons committing an act of spiritual cowardice against You by saying in THIS VERY NOTE to Gary Prisk that he couldn't go to services with Gary and Bobby anymore due to basic fear of his family."

"Objection, Your Honor. State doesn't show the relevance."

"Overruled…State may proceed…"

"Thank you, Your Honor…We ask that State Exhibit #1 be noted in the Court's records and submitted into evidence."

I cringe as the Judge says, "So done…"

"Thank you, Your Honor…We also stand ready to present a list of witnesses that will show the Court how far Mr. Holley was willing to go to please friends and succumb to peer pressure."

"Objection—State is engaging over mere speculation and incorrect assumptions about my activities here."

"Overruled!" (Judge gestures for Ha'Satan to continue…)

"But, Your Honor, we feel that list of witnesses isn't necessary—when we instead can call the Defendant himself to answer our questions for himself!"

"OBJECTION, Your Honor—on the grounds of my Fifth Amendment rights to self-incrimination!"

Ha'Satan chides me, "Is the Defendant afraid to answer my questions—or is he just afraid to show the skeletons in his closet?"

"I still object to this treatment on the grounds of what I've just stated!"

"OVERRULED!!! The Court will remind the Defendant that these are the courts of MY Heavens—not of the United States of America! State has the right to call all the witnesses he chooses—and you aren't allowed to avoid testifying or answering State's questions." The Judge then turns to Ha'Satan—and already I'm feeling a sense of dread and doom over this scenario. "So do I sense that State wishes to call its first witness?"

"We do, Your Honor! We call the Defendant himself as a hostile witness."

"So ordered…the Defendant is now called to the witness stand." At this, I very reluctantly do as I'm told.

"Thank you, Your Honor. (Ha'Satan now turns to me on the witness stand.)…Mr. Holley, it seems to me that you had a fairly impressive record during your time here in Levelland. President's List your first semester, Dean's List and Phi Theta Kappa the rest of the time and a very busy schedule…"

"That's correct…" (I say with clinched teeth.)

"Impressive, yes, Mr. Holley. Perfect in every way—absolutely not…"

"I never claimed by all means like I was Mr. Goody Two-Shoes…"

"BUT YOU ACTED LIKE IT!!! We've already shown that you're guilty of spiritual cowardice. But that's not the only heinous act that you committed against the Almighty!"

(Ha'Satan then pushes something towards me…) "Do you recognize this? Some of my demons personally witnessed you going to a nearby convenience store purchasing PORNOGRAPHIC materials!"

"OBJECTION—Your Honor!"

"OVERRULED!"

"ANSWER THE QUESTION, Mr. Holley!! DID YOU or DID YOU NOT purchase this explicit magazine as well as others like them for the purposes of personal sexual self-gratification on several occasions during your studies here?"

(I refuse to answer the question…but Ha'Satan keeps badgering me…) "…State submits this magazine as State's Exhibit #2." (A mumbled "…So ordered…" comes from the Judge.) "…And Mr. Holley—did you or did you not engage on several occasions in various risqué group sexual activities that were suspect and shaky at best?"

"Objection, Your Honor! State is not only badgering me, but trying to invade my privacy to boot!"

"OVERRULED—Defendant WILL answer the State's question!"

"Mr. Holley, did you or did you not do this? A simple yes or no will suffice…"

(I only respond nonverbally by starting to shed tears as the strain of this intense questioning is wearing me down.)

"I take that as a yes…But let the records show that Mr. Holley here at SPC was not only a spiritual coward and a pervert, but a backstabber, too!"

"OBJECTION, Your Honor! This whole line of questioning is totally insensitive, irrational, and inappropriate!"

"OVERRULED again! State, is there a point you wish to make?"

"We do, Your Honor—that which is also contained in State's Exhibit #3 that we now submit for the Court's record." (Ha'Satan gives a picture to the bailiff.) Let Exhibit #3 show Mr. Holley's complicity in an act called "The SAL Incident" in which Mr. Holley took part along with several other disgruntled individuals in an act of vandalism against his own Symphonic Band Director and private lesson teacher in which the letters "SAL" standing for, by the way, Your Honor, "Students Against Leister"—were shoe-polished onto her driveway!"

"NO FAIR, Ha'Satan—you're not playing fair! Objection, Your Honor!"

"I'm not playing fair, Mr. Holley? I'm just submitting actual evidence of these crimes against the Eternal for the pleasure of this Court—that's all! Perhaps it's YOU who's not playing fair! Perhaps it's YOU who needs to admit the truth and come clean and face the consequences of your actions!"

"…ORDER IN THIS COURT RIGHT NOW! Counsel, what's your point of all this questioning?"

"…Your Honor, The Defendant has already made my points for me without saying a word. He avoided responsibility and made bad choices while he was here in Levelland. He sowed his wild oats—now it's time he's forced to reap them and eat their bitter fruit. Your Honor, we, the State, contend that the Defendant is truly guilty beyond the shadow of a doubt of the charges of spiritual cowardice, the purchase of inappropriate reading materials, participation in immoral sexual activities not otherwise pleasing to You, and participation in what could have been a borderline criminal act. He's worthy of poverty, denial of Your blessings, and even DEATH for breaking some of the same commandments that You gave to man and in which he himself claimed himself he'd obey. He made his bed—now it's time for him to sleep in it. The State rests its case."

(The Judge now chimes in.) "Mr. Holley, you have quite a list of charges against you. How do you wish to plead?"

With tears rolling down my face, I start—"…Your Honor, thank you first for allowing me to make my defense before You. The charges that the State has just accused me of are the antithesis on the surface seem pretty baseless on the surface. What the prosecution has described is similar to what King David said and even sang about in Psalm 101:1-8 (NLT):

Psalm 101

A psalm of David.

¹ I will sing of your love and justice, LORD.
    I will praise you with songs.
² I will be careful to live a blameless life—
    when will you come to help me?
I will lead a life of integrity
    in my own home.
³ I will refuse to look at
    anything vile and vulgar.
I hate all who deal crookedly;
    I will have nothing to do with them.
⁴ I will reject perverse ideas
    and stay away from every evil.
⁵ I will not tolerate people who slander their neighbors.
    I will not endure conceit and pride.

⁶ I will search for faithful people
    to be my companions.
Only those who are above reproach
    will be allowed to serve me.
⁷ I will not allow deceivers to serve in my house,
    and liars will not stay in my presence.
⁸ My daily task will be to ferret out the wicked
    and free the city of the LORD from their grip.

Then with a pained expression, I finally come clean before the Judge of the Universe and admit the following: "…But yet, with sadness and a heavy heart, I must reluctantly face the facts that the allegations that the State has made are totally and entirely the truth and therefore formally plead guilty as charged to all counts."

Upon hearing this, Ha'Satan and his demons start a round of high-fives, backslaps, and celebratory motions and is even heard to shout out loud. "I KNEW HE WAS GUILTY BEYOND ANY REASONABLE DOUBT!! I KNEW IT!! I KNEW IT!!" Then I continue, "BUT, Ha'Satan, before you start breaking out your champagne, in my defense, I also cite Lamentations 3:13-33 (NLT):

¹³ He shot his arrows
    deep into my heart.

¹⁴ My own people laugh at me.
   All day long they sing their mocking songs.
¹⁵ He has filled me with bitterness
   and given me a bitter cup of sorrow to drink.

¹⁶ He has made me chew on gravel.
   He has rolled me in the dust.
¹⁷ Peace has been stripped away,
   and I have forgotten what prosperity is.
¹⁸ I cry out, "My splendor is gone!
   Everything I had hoped for from the LORD is lost!"

¹⁹ The thought of my suffering and homelessness
   is bitter beyond words.[a]
²⁰ I will never forget this awful time,
   as I grieve over my loss.
²¹ Yet I still dare to hope
   when I remember this:

²² The faithful love of the LORD never ends![b]
   His mercies never cease.
²³ Great is his faithfulness;
   his mercies begin afresh each morning.
²⁴ I say to myself, "The LORD is my inheritance;
   therefore, I will hope in him!"

²⁵ The LORD is good to those who depend on him,
   to those who search for him.
²⁶ So it is good to wait quietly
   for salvation from the LORD.
²⁷ And it is good for people to submit at an early age
   to the yoke of his discipline:

²⁸ Let them sit alone in silence
   beneath the LORD's demands.
²⁹ Let them lie face down in the dust,
   for there may be hope at last.
³⁰ Let them turn the other cheek to those who strike them
   and accept the insults of their enemies.

³¹ For no one is abandoned
   by the Lord forever.
³² Though he brings grief, he also shows compassion
   because of the greatness of his unfailing love.
³³ For he does not enjoy hurting people
   or causing them sorrow.

"…I put myself on the mercy of this court and plead the blood of Your precious Son over all of my sins and past wrongdoings."

At hearing this, Satan and his demons rise and shout in shock and disbelief, "…OBJECTION, Your Honor! The Defendant does NOT deserve the mercy of this Court nor does he have the discretion, latitude, permission, or ability to ask for such unconditional migitation of any possible punishment that may be rendered by this Court!"

"OVERRULED!!! I'M the Judge and Master of this Court—and ONLY I get to say IF OR WHEN OR HOW the Defendant receives ANY punishment from MY hand in the first place—NOT YOU!! Defense will proceed…"

"…Thank you, Your Honor." I struggle to say in the midst of my tears. "…I know I haven't always been faithful to You. For nearly three years after I wrote that note to Gary Prisk saying that I couldn't keep going to church anymore, I afterwards vowed that if I ever even started thinking about WCG again that the next time my commitment to it (and at that particular time, by extension, YOU) would be for keeps. Well, it was after that never too far from my mind. I still even during those years kept the Sabbath as best as I knew to do at that time and stayed in some sort of touch with the Church as best as I could under the circumstances…

"…As to my involvement in what I now consider shameful acts in the area of sexual perversion and immoral behavior, I won't deny it to You—but confess it as sin against You. I still pay for the consequences of those past actions in ways most people can never think or imagine…"

"…And as to what I did with the "SAL Incident" that the State brought up, please let the State note that I did my part only after coercion by other individuals and was so naïve about the whole thing and didn't understand the true nature of what was done until it was too late and all of us involved were caught. I didn't even know what the letters "SAL" meant until I was confronted by the school administration about it—and I did cooperate as fully as possible with the investigation afterwards.

"…Please let the Court accept Defense Exhibits #1 and #2 that showed the penalty I officially had to pay—which, I might add, was much more merciful than what I truly deserved. I am fully aware that I could have literally been expelled from here or even worse faced possible criminal charges as a result (not to mention having to explain my actions to my family). I not only was administratively withdrawn from Symphonic Band for the rest of that particular semester, but the relationship I had with Lynda Leister-Reid as my teacher, etc. was never quite the same after that.

"…On my SPC transcript, the scars are still there for all to see. And I came so close to throwing away my entire college education and future away over this stupid incident. It was only Your hand and mercy even at that time that protected me and kept me from an even worse fate.

"…But most of all, I stand guilty as a Pharisacal hypocrite Christian who once condemned ANYONE who wasn't WCG as a "harlot daughter of Babylon" and a "Christian falsely so-called". I was a stupid fool who at that time didn't see you for who you truly were. I'm not worthy of Your grace and mercy in my own strength—but instead rely solely on the very blood of your Son who made me righteous in spite of anything I ever did against You!"

"…Objection, Your Honor! Again, Defendant has no right to petition the Court for mercy or clemency!"

"…He does IF I SAY SO! Objection OVERRULED!"

(Just then, a commotion starts from the back of the room as Jesus/Y'shua walks through the doors and stands beside me by the defense bench.) "…Your Honor—OBJECTION! Unauthorized personnel are not allowed to take part in these proceedings…I request that the Court…"

"…State will note that this is MY SON in whom I'm STILL well-pleased—NOT unauthorized personnel as you claim! Objection overruled!"

"…Thank you, Your Honor…Abba Father…may I address the Court in support of the Defense…"

"OBJECTION once again, Your Honor! This unauthorized buffoon has absolutely no standing to…"

"…I SAID—this is MY SON in whom I'm well-pleased—NOT a buffoon! State will shut up and sit down—objection overruled! Go ahead, Son…"

"…May it please the Court to note that the Defendant has since this particular period of time in question occurred made appropriate amends to Me for all eternity and has accepted My sacrifice for his sins and has ever since he left here done what he can do to confess Me before men…"

"…OBJECTION…"

"…State, I already know what you're thinking…and I'm NOT having any of it! SHUT UP! OVERRULED!!"

"…But, Your Honor…"

"…Do you wish, State, for Me to hold you in contempt of court? Keep pushing my buttons and I WILL! Son, please go on…"

"…I also submit as Defense Exhibit #3 and #4 that further prove that as far as Your justice system is concerned, the Defendant should be considered blameless in Our sight."

"…All of this is a bunch of namby-pamby, ludicrous diatribe with no basis in fact or reason, Your Honor, OBJECTION!"

"…State, one more act of disrespect against my Son—and I will…you understand? Defense Exhibits #3 and #4 are so ordered and entered into evidence in the record."

"…Therefore, Abba Father, on the basis of the Defendant's sincere confession of his sins and his acknowledgment of Myself as his Lord and Savior, I ask that the Court formally dismiss all charges against the Defendant and forever expunge the records of these heavens of what happened during these particular years of the Defendant's life and pardon him and clear him of all charges."

"…That's it—I've had it up to here with this nonsense! OBJECTION!"

"…Well, I SAY—that's it with you as well! I've ALSO had it up to here with you! I hereby find you right now in contempt of this Court and sentence you immediately back to the Abyss where you belong! Bailiff, take him away right now! I never want to see his disgusting face again!"

"…But, Your Honor—You're making a big mistake…it's HIM (pointing at me) you should sentence—NOT ME!," Ha'Satan shouts as he's dragged out of the courtroom.

"…Will the Defendant and his attorney please rise?" (Both myself and Jesus/Y'shua do so as the tears on my face really continue to pour down like rain.)

Then the Judge—Abba Father Himself—steps down from the bench and comes to both of us at the defense table. "Mr. Holley…Coy…Son…by virtue of the blood of My Son who you've put your sole trust and confidence in, I find absolutely no fault in You. To Me, you're also My son in whom I'm well-pleased. If you've confessed my Son before men, then that's good enough for Me. All charges against you are dropped and you're now free to go. Case dismissed." The Father bangs the gavel as I hug both Him and Jesus/Y'shua and thank them both for saving my bacon in the nick of time.

As I turn to leave the courtroom, I now see you back at the front entrance of Lamar Hall where we started and realize how, in spite of the bad stuff and negative baggage I still carry from here, truly blessed I was to spend three years of my life here. More than anything else, I found out for the first time who I really was as a young man starting out on his own for the first time in his life—and that included the good, the bad, AND the ugly parts. I got to learn new skills, try different things, and meet new people I would have never know otherwise. And most of all, I started on a new road of discovery in those things of my God. The new road would take me further than I ever dreamed—and would eventually lead me back to Him.

Well, that's enough reminiscing from here for now. Time to get back on the road and journey on, shall we? How about we first stop by that KFC over there and get some chicken? I'm hungry—how about you? Then maybe we'll take a look at the map and see where we need to go next.

Chapter 5 [Western Maryland]: Havdallah—My Point Of No Return

I was still doing my Workstudy job in the game room in what we at South Plains College called the SUB (Student Union Building) during my last two semesters there. Graduation was coming closer and closer by the month and week. And I was still in the midst of finishing up the remaining part of the general education requirements that I needed in order to have them transfer to Eastern New Mexico University (where, thanks to a very generous scholarship, out-of-state tuition waiver, and much better financial aid package as well as what seemed to me at the time to be a better music business major program and mass communications program that caused me to decide not to attend West Texas State University and instead opt to pursue a Bachelor's degree at Eastern). Like most graduating college students, I naturally had to try to find a much-needed summer job. In the midst of this process, I happened to see a poster on one of the bulletin boards in the game room from some outfit called the American Camping Association that offered a book that listed all the available positions at summer camps across the USA that were looking for college kids like myself to work for the summer.

So naturally, I started putting together my resume—and once I received a book from ACA in the mail about these job listings, I started sending out resumes to jobs like these as much as what little money and/or postage stamps that I had available would allow me to do so. One of those listings was a place in Maryland called Camps Airy and Louise that offered camp counseling positions to where among the subjects I might be able to teach of all things included music (including orchestra and band) and archery (two things I knew I could teach). It was a pleasant surprise to me where, sight unseen, a letter from the Aaron & Lily Straus Foundation came to my campus mailbox that promised me a job with Campy Airy (their boys' camp). I never realized at that time how life-changing this decision would eventually be for me.

Keep in mind a few things about this: (1.) I had only just been to a Phi Theta Kappa (junior college honors society) National Convention in Washington, D.C. within the last year or so; (2.) It was probably only the second or third time in my life I had even been on an airplane ANYWHERE across the country. (FYI--When I was in high school, I did go on a couple of out-of-state band trips—one to Durango, CO and another in Kansas City—but during both of those trips, we went via charter buses.); (3.) I at the time prior to my 1st trip to D.C. had never been outside of either TX, OK, or NM at all in my life. And I had certainly never been anywhere much on the East Coast at the time; and (4.) the foundation that sponsored the camps was JEWISH. Where I lived in the Lubbock area, you could probably go almost your whole lifetime and never meet a Jew—period.

Back home at the time, if you looked at a church directory in most church newspapers in my immediate hometown area, you could find Southern Baptist churches galore—but not a synagogue or even ANY type of Sabbatarian congregation within 50 to 100 miles of where I lived that I even knew of personally (short of WCG, of course). And those that might rather go to church on Saturday were usually thought of as either Catholic, Seventh-Day Adventists, or (most usually—as groups such as the Worldwide Church of God were thought of by most at the time) members of cazy and wacko "cults". As someone of who still (despite his own personal fears of committing to be a full-fledged member of what he thought was "**the** ONLY true church") was very interested in some degree in WCG, it would definitely be a refreshing change for someone like me who really wanted to do the Sabbath in a place that was far away from the eyes of family that I was still trying to pretend to please just so that I can still get help financially (especially as far as things such as food and toilet paper were concerned).

Even the folks back home, though, were at least pleased that I at least got this summer job. So I continued working for the rest of the semester in the game room with the last few paychecks that I received after all remaining tuition, books, room, board, etc. still due SPC were paid for to get ready for this special adventure. After I go back home to Lockney from graduation and received what was left from the Workstudy jobs from SPC, I then had to go to a travel agent in Plainview to purchase the airplane tickets necessary to go to Maryland. When all the options were checked out, the travel agent said that it was actually cheaper to fly into Baltimore/Washington International than any of the other D.C. area airports—so that was chosen at a cost of what I believe was $278 roundtrip with the departure in June shortly before counselor orientation for camp started and the return back home scheduled for a couple of days right before I had to be in Portales to start my studies at Eastern.

Leaving Texas for Western Maryland was for me at the time going to the equivalent of the other side of the world. Back home in Lockney were such things as the wind and dust storms in the spring and summer and in the winter (when the cotton gins were running) the incessant smoke and dust from the Co-op gin just only a few blocks away from my house that gave me so much trouble with my allergies and asthma that my mother would have to keep the vaporizer in my room constantly going almost 24/7 in order to keep me from coughing and wheezing due to the dry air and the gin dust.

But in the Cocactin Mountains around Thurmont and just less than 30 miles from the famous Mason-Dixon Line, the atmosphere was totally different—with plenty of tree, hills, and other wildlife. (And it would later prove to be a shock to discover on top of it that Airy was on the flight path for the Presidential helicopter to go to Camp David.){FYI—I did get to hear it pass by a time or two overhead while I was at Airy.} Yep—it was surely a different world indeed for this West Texas boy…

Despite the daily work and everything else at Airy, overall it was a real joy to have the privilege to hang around and meet people of totally different backgrounds other than myself. (And I seem to recall that at least a person or two really made light of my Texas accent at times as well.) Who would have thought that I could have been able to pack a truckload of memories and experiences into that one summer? But by the grace of God, I surely did.

A lot of the counselors I met were not only from different state of the Union, but even from other countries (including a few gents from the other side of the pond in the UK). Along with some of my fellow camp counselors, I was privileged to take some quick day trips during my time off to places such as Gettysburg, D.C. (for the SECOND time—which enabled me to go to a place or two such as the Smithsonian that I didn't have time to go to during my first trip there), and even one evening in Baltimore (where myself and a few other counselors got to go see Inner Harbor at night—if you have a chance to see it while in the area, I'd highly recommend doing so…it's definitely a beautiful sight).

During the transition period between camp sessions called "turnover", a number of us even went as far as the King's Dominion amusement park in Virginia. This particular excursion was quite memorable for me for a few reasons: (1.) the night before we actually went into the park, the biggest majority (myself and a couple of others excepted) had what amounted to be a major drinking binge party. Talk about a rowdy crowd—let's say that a bunch of those who did partake in the available adult beverages offered wound up passed out either in the floor or on a bed drunk as skunks. In the motel room where we were in, there were 8 of us counselors that shared the room. I wound up trying to sleep on the floor. I say TRYING because most of the drunks were already passed out and sleeping on the bed—and the two of us remaining that were still sober (myself being one of those) weren't able to sleep a wink in the first place because we were forced to play mother hens to this room full of drunks.

But what really took the cake on this one was the particular case of one of my fellow counselors-at-large named Chuck. It turns out that Chuck was not only drunk—but as he was sleeping off the effects of the alcohol—he seemed to have a major propensity for snoring on top of it. In fact, poor Chuck snored so loudly that his snores were met continuously with calls from his fellow roommates along this line—"CHUCK—TURN OVER!! TURN OVER—CHUCK!! QUIT SNORING!!" The more Chuck persisted in snoring, the more the calls from his roommates got louder and began including increased splotches of profanity that I'll spare you from right now. Needless to say, shuteye was surely a rare and precious commodity for all of us that night. (We did, however, still enjoy—at least those who weren't too hungover—the time we spent the next day at King's Dominion.)

The campers at Airy were also an interesting lot in themselves. One of my main jobs as a counselor-at-large was to basically fill in as a substitute bunk counselor for the regular bunk counselor on their days off. It was definitely an experience for me personally to tell kids from places such as Baltimore, D.C., Silver Spring, and other places on the East Coast who'd probably never even been to Texas in their life to tell them some bedtime stories on people and places involved in Texas history such as Coronado and the Seven Cities of Cibola, Sam Houston, and other legends about my native state that would make Texas come alive in their minds and hearts while maybe hopefully slipping in a moral lesson or two that I believe my God might eventually use to help influence their lives for the better.

I also remember the time when I was in the process of recording an audio tape letter back home to Mother when I had the idea to have one of these bunk groups join me in helping me produce that tape letter. I managed to get some of these young lads to join me in my place and also used it as an opportunity to let them to get an idea what it's like to record something on tape and then later listen to it to hear themselves talk and hear what they sounded like on tape. I think I recall in a later letter how Mother told me that when she listened to each of those boys introduce themselves and tell their age and where they were from—she related to me just how much she wanted to personally give each of those boys an ice-cream cone long-distance once she heard it. (I guess from such comments are shown a true mother's heart.)

There was one boy at Airy nicknamed "C.J." that for me easily topped the list of most memorable camper. C.J. was for sure a very energetic and rambunctious kid who was very hard to keep up with. If you liked to wear caps (like I did at the time) and you valued them in any way, you dared not have it anywhere in the immediate vicinity where C.J. might be—because he could just as quickly snatch it from you without any warning and without any shame or regret. Strangely enough, when he wasn't using his almost boundless supply of physical energy to thievery (and the subsequent chases thereafter), he could just as easily manipulate and tug at your heart strings with his personal tales of woe, sad eyes, and his tales about his parents and troubled personal background.

The environment at Airy for all concerned was a unique one. Of course, the camp offered the usual assortment of outdoor and indoor-based activities such as arts and crafts, swimming, etc.—but Airy and its sister camp Louise also offered opportunities for music and drama as well. Part of my own camp responsibilities during that summer included teaching basic and advanced archery and also my primary teaching of music which included assisting with the camp band, playing in the staff band, and even teaching private lessons with campers who were sax players.

I particularly remember a few things about teaching my own specialties to these campers. One of them was the advanced archery class. This proved to be a challenge to me because of the fact that while I was trying to come up with particular games designed to primarily help refine their skills as archers by giving them shooting challenges that would help them be able to aim at anything they may need to shoot in the future--most of the time, they kind of acted like they'd rather just shoot like they did in the basic classes and resented my attempts to try to mix things up during the activity period. They probably just wanted to blow it all off and move on to the next thing on their schedules. That did eventually prove to be a situation where I probably couldn't win for losing—but that didn't stop me from implementing other games for them since I honestly didn't know how else to teach this class.

Airy's music department also proved to be an interesting place to work in. For instance, the staff band took part in the combined efforts of both the Airy & Louise drama departments of "Guys and Dolls". The '30s gangster styles, costumes, and songs such as "Rocking The Boat" [FYI—for those that have ever seen the play, remember that this is the song in which one of the main characters is singing about how God was telling one on the musical's characters—"…sit down—you're rocking the boat…"] still run through the video screens of my mind even today.

And about all those times that I was probably not all that keen on practicing for my own private lessons at SPC, Ms. Leister would have really gotten a chuckle at the way that I began to view all of the sax players that I now had to teach at camp. I figure she would have really rolled the aisles in laughter if she only knew how truly concerned I became at the lack of adequate practice time that these kids were able to have during the entire camp session. And I definitely presume that she unknowingly got her revenge on me when I realized that I had to play the role of teacher instead of student. Serves me right, I guess…

Another particular memory that might best go in the culture shock file—as earlier referenced in an earlier chapter, my passion/borderline addiction to Dr. Pepper was really put to the test in the Cocactins. Being that this was a Jewish boys' camp, most meals we usually either had only punch or water to drink. Yes, this was DEFINITELY a camp that kept kosher. And while the Coke machines that were in the camp, not a single one of them had a button that would give you the true nectar of a DP…Now there was usually Coke, Pepsi, Dr. Pibb, and other stuff like that—but the nearest machine containing Dr. Pepper was at a grocery store in Thurmont about 15 miles away. Not an easy thing to deal with when you're from the very home state where Dr. Pepper was originally created, to say the least…

[FYI for you fellow evangelicals who are looking at this like a calf out of a new gate when I say the word "kosher", let me give you a quick lesson on Jewish tradition that I learned at Airy. If you're eating in a Jewish home or group (maybe I ought to put this in Texas talk to further illustrate what I mean)—DO NOT expect to have such meats as ham, bacon, sausage, or anything with pork in it. Also, don't expect to see catfish, shrimp, lobster, or anything that violates Leviticus chapter 11 on the dinner table either. (And NO cheeseburgers and ice cream in the same meal (FYI—make that both ANY meat AND any milk products at the same time)---for they are completely out of the question, too. Now you can have either meat OR milk in a meal—but NOT both.]

But despite this and a few other minor inconvienences, this also proved to be a special time that my God was able to use in my own life away from the things of the world back home halfway across the country to finally make some decisions about my personal spiritual life and journey that would eventually become my life in the immediate future ahead. You see, I was still very much struggling at the time with the previous conflicts I had on whether or not I would finally come clean with my mother and the rest of the family come clean with my mother and the rest of the family and whether I would go back to being a Southern Baptist just to keep my family happy and off my back OR if once and for all I would finally go ahead and take the plunge and become a member of the Worldwide Church of God. Those thoughts were still very much on my mind when I came to Airy—and that summer in Maryland would play a major role in how my own personal relationship with God would be shaped (especially when I really began to learn things about Judaism up close and personal in ways I could have never dreamed back home in West Texas).

For instance, since my requested day off happened to fall at the same time as the Jewish Sabbath, it was especially a delight at the time during each Sabbath to be able to study all the literature from WCG headquarters in Pasadena, CA and began to make some personal decisions on what and how I truly began to view God and Jesus Christ. I remember a time or two that summer when on the Sabbath I was able to have some real quiet time alone with Him to express my concerns, fears, etc. to Him about all the things and challenges I faced back home. One of the places I might do that was right behind the mess hall where the camp flagpole was which you could literally on a clear day see for almost 40 miles in view to the valley below. It was especially a great place to view the sunset at the end of Shabbat.

But it wasn't just the quiet time with Him that I relished. I was able to learn things about Jewish faith and culture that probably no one back home might ever learn— in some of the most practical ways. For instance, on Shabbat (Sabbath) morning, the rest of the camp basically had what was their own form of religious worship service. And it was totally different from all of what I thought were the boring church services I knew from my own Southern Baptist church. Not only were the songs different, but so was the format. In particular, one part of the service that was quite striking for me what they called "reflections time". This was when basically there would be special music of some kind (usually a violin or something like that) where the campers were encouraged to be quiet and still and reflect on the events of the week just passed and how God should fit into the picture. (We sure didn't have THAT in the Southern Baptist church I had to go to as a kid.) I was also impressed at the unique way these people did what I called their "folk songs" and did their prayers AFTER the meal (NOT BEFORE)!!

One of those services that made a particular indelible impression on me was a special service that was done towards the end of the summer called a "Havdalah service". For those that have never been to a Havdalah service, here's the quickest explanation that I can possibly provide. Basically, think of this type of service as a sort of gradual bridge, transition, and (also simultaneously) separation between the Sabbath and the rest of the week that is their way of saying goodbye to the Sabbath and holy time and hello to the new week ahead that is conducted around twilight as the Sabbath is ending. As a part of this, more songs are sung and a braided blue and white candle is lit, then eventually extinguished in a cup of wine or grape juice.

One thing that was remarkable to me personally about this particular Havdalah service was the inclusion of one song that at first took me aback and in which I never would have expected to hear at a religious service of ANY kind—"The 57th St. Bridge Song". (You know—the one you might have heard in the 50s and 60s that goes, "…Slow down/You move too fast/You gotta make the morning last/ Just kickin' down the cobblestones/Lookin' for fun and feeling groovy…" Hearing that one song during that service spoke volumes to me…because I realized how much these people were saying—"…We've had a good Sabbath—but now it's time to go on to the new week ahead." I found out that this was an actual bridge and transition time between God-designated holy time and the rest of the week.

But most of all, I got the chance to see a quick personal glimpse into not only how exactly the Jewish people act and relate to others—but also, sadly, how other people groups may actually see and think about Jewish people. For instance, I remember when we counselors were going through orientation how we were advised by camp management to make sure we kept a low profile and checked ourselves as to how we behaved and acted outside camp when we went into town for something due to what was a very strong presence of the Ku Klux Klan in that part of western Maryland and southern Pennsylvania (let's say at the time—if you were either a Jew or associated in some way with a Jew, you were considered worse than a lowlife in their eyes because of their view that the Jewish people were "Christ killers").

By the time this special summer would come to an end for me, I wasn't completely there yet to making my final choices on what I might do with the rest of my life after I left Maryland to go back home. But I could say truly that this became a life situation for me that would be best described by a song that is sung by the Phantom to Christine Dyae at a very pivotal point of the musical "Phantom of the Opera" called "Past The Point Of No Return".

Past The Point Of No Return Lyrics
(from "Phantom Of The Opera")
PHANTOM: Past the point of no return, no backward glances
The games we played 'til now are at an end
Past all thought of 'If' or 'When', no use resisting
Abandon thought and let the dream descend
What raging fire shall flood the soul?
What rich desire unlocks its door?
What sweet seduction lies before us?
Past the point of no return, the final threshold
What warm unspoken secrets will we learn?
Beyond the point of no return
CHRISTINE: You have brought me to that moment where words run dry
To that moment where speech disappears into silence, silence
I have come here hardly knowing the reason why
In my mind I've already imagined our bodies entwining
Defenseless and silent and now I am here with you
No second thoughts, I've decided, decided
Past the point of no return, no going back now
Our passion play has now at last begun
Past all thought of right or wrong, one final question
How long should we two wait before we're one?
When will the blood begin to race
The sleeping bud burst into bloom?
When will the flames at last consume us?
Past the point of no return, the final threshold
The bridge is crossed, so stand and watch it burn
We've passed the point of no return...

[FYI—The Phantom as he is singing is trying to influence Christine to once and for all choose him over the Vicount Raoul for her affections as Christine is literally put in a position romantically (in the Phantom's twisted way) between a life of isolation united with the Phantom OR death to her true lover Raoul and basically telling her that she must make a very crucial choice—and from this point on there's no going back to what used to be.]

At that time, I might not have said it in those terms—but in retrospect, Airy proved to be a major personal turning point in which whatever I might decide to do from here, there was no going back to the old—and that I would ultimately be personally responsible (good or bad, right or wrong) for the resulting consequences entailed. In the last chapter, I described my time at South Plains College at my teenage years. That era officially came to an end here in the Cocactins as I started my own personal transition spiritually to my late-blooming adulthood.

What proved to be the biggest capstone experience of all personally of my summer at Airy was one I wouldn't have expected. Towards the end of camp and the summer, Ed Cohen (the camp director) called me into his office to come in for an exit interview. He asked me my impressions of what happened at camp during the summer from my vantage point and solicited my ideas for improvement of how he, the executive staff, and the Foundation could make Airy better the next summer. I responded basically to him that for me personally overall that it was definitely a very unique learning experience—especially for someone from West Texas who literally came halfway across the country just to work at camp that summer. My biggest concerns were primarily in regards to the development and growth of Airy's music department (which I mentioned earlier) and particularly about the lack of appropriate personal practice time by campers who were our private lesson students in order to fulfill the necessary assignments that I felt were required in order to help our sax players become more proficient on their instrument. Ed told me that he would definitely put this information in consideration in how the camp staff would plan their activities for next summer.

But what really floored me about this exit interview was what would happen next. The subject turned to details on my plans for my return trip home. Ed asked me, "What day does your flight back home leave?" I told him the date and time that I had that was scheduled on my original plane ticket. Ed then said to me, "There's a problem with that date there. That is the day AFTER everyone else will leave camp—and you'll be stuck here by yourself in camp an extra day. Do you have a ride to the airport for that day?" I told him no. Naturally, hearing this for me would cause some concern.

It was definitely the mercy of the Lord operating in my life at the time when Ed told me, "..Tell ya what—during the rest of the year, I happen to work as a travel agent. Let me see your ticket and let me see what I can do about it. There's a way I know of to where your original ticket will still be good a day earlier." From there, the exit interview ended. I then later brought him the ticket—and from there, he was able to make it possible to where I could go home on that same ticket **at no additional charge**!! Go fig—of all the things I saw at this camp, I never in my life thought that of all things the very head of the camp itself also just happened to be a JEWISH TRAVEL AGENT!!! But there it was in black and white—and it was my real joy to call back home to my mother and grandparents that I was truly going to be able to go back home a day earlier than expected.

And this blessing didn't stop there. You see, I was literally faced with what at the time would be a very close shave situation when I got back home. Starting from the time of my original return trip back home to Lubbock and then the pickup by my mother and grandparents back home in Lockney, I was left with only about a couple of days to rest, pack, and then get ready to not only go back home across the country, but then very soon afterwards cross yet another state line…all within a very few short days to start my studies at Eastern New Mexico University and get there in time for orientation and registration. Talk about a very tight time crunch I faced…

Ed had truly no absolute idea after I got back home what he had just done for me. That extra day back home was a literal Godsend and help in helping make what would be and extremely quick turnaround and transition to my new university a little easier. And as a result, not only did this particular experience forever seal my admiration and respect for the Jewish people as a whole—but I also simultaneously found myself to be forever in their debt. I personally experienced for myself during this summer at Airy the letter, spirit, and intent about what God said about His chosen people in Genesis 12:1-3 where it says—

1 THE LORD had said to Abram, "Go from your country, your people and your father's household to the land I will show you.

2 "I will make you into a great nation, and I will bless you; I will make your name great, and you will be a blessing.[a]
3 I will bless those who bless you, and whoever curses you I will curse; and all peoples on earth will be blessed through you."[b]

If there is anyone else more than me who could truly express the words, "Whenever I stand, I stand with Israel!"—I'd sure like to know who they are right now. And if you wonder what above all else is the foundation for what are now my "pro-Israel" beliefs, the answer is simple…Camp Airy. These folks did not JUST help me in some form financially in helping me get a good start at Eastern—but they more important (I feel) were used by my God to give me a much more precious and lasting gift—that of TRUE eternal salvation.

Now I hear the voices of my Evangelical friends asking me, "But how did working at a Jewish camp lead you to salvation? They don't even believe in Jesus Christ!" When they ask me this, they also might as well tell me that they don't even have a clue about what salvation even is OR how it takes place. They usually deal from the point that salvation is something that HAS to be an emotional experience and that you even need to be able at a drop of a hat to even be able to give the exact date, time, place, etc.—or surely that "salvation experience" really in their eyes isn't truly valid. To me, that notion isn't always true. You can have all the emotion you want—but if real LASTING choices aren't made to make a once-and-for-all commitment to Him, then any emotions (good or bad) one may personally experience ain't worth diddly-squat as far as I'm concerned. At Airy first and foremost, I was able to begin to decide for MYSELF what I felt I eventually needed to be (especially as far as my relationship with God The Father and Jesus Christ was concerned)…WITHOUT ANYONE ELSE TELLING OR PRESSURING ME ON HOW I SHOULD CONDUCT MYSELF FROM HERE!!!

When I came back from Airy and then just a few days later moved to Portales, I not only couldn't believe that I had just experienced the summer of a lifetime—but that I actually got PAID FOR DOING IT!! (And the final paycheck I would get from Airy sure looked good in my new bank account, too, when it was time to start paying for my books, tuition, etc. during my first semester at Eastern.] But more importantly at Airy, spiritually I passed the "point of no return"—and from this Rubicon, I couldn't go back again to an old life I used to know that on the inside I now detested. And the vows I made to my God would eventually lead to the personal storm clouds in Portales that were on the horizon that would finally cause me to go all in and say to Him that I would from here on out be in this for keeps.

[Chapter 6:] [Portales, NM (Part I)] When My Own "Berlin Wall" Fell

OK—let's see…in about the last two chapters alone in our journey so far through my present life, we haven't been on many trains (unless you count a few subways, of course)—but we've so far had our share of buses, planes, and automobiles for sure. Now together from our homebase area of Lockney and Plainview going west on US 70 all the way to...

Muleshoe (by car at least an hour; but by our own current mode of traveling much longer than that). Just as you're leaving Muleshoe, there's a Farm-To-Market (FM) Road that intersects with 70. If you stay on 70, you'll eventually head straight to Farwell and toward the Texas/New Mexico state line. You'll not only change time zones (from Central to Mountain), but also see the border town of Texico right across the railroad tracks from Farwell as well as find the city lights of Clovis a few more miles down the road.

However, if back in Muleshoe you decide to turn onto the FM Road and go west on that road, you see the following things happen: (1.) You won't hardly see a town (or anything else on that road for that matter) for miles;

(2.) This FM Road also not only crosses the state line (and eventually becomes a New Mexico state highway), but also changes time zones eventually as well;

(3.) I can guarantee you that going down this particular road will NOT get you directly to Clovis like US 70 can (in fact, it completely bypasses it);

(4.) This road's final destination is (how ironic) a DEAD-END BACK onto US 70!

And then even after you finally get back onto US 70 from that FM Road/NM State Highway, you're still required to travel a few more miles to reach what will now be the next stop on my life tour. Welcome, folks, officially to the Land of Enchantment and also to Portales. [FYI—for those of you not otherwise from New Mexico—Portales is pronounced PORT-AL-ES (Spanish translation—porches—or as you might wish to call it—"Porchtown"!] Here in Portales during the fall of 1989 is where I would start to make some personal choices that would have a MAJOR impact on my life in many ways—especially in the spiritual realm.

Since I will be devoting the next chapter primarily on my experiences with my times at Eastern and with life in the pre-split Worldwide Church of God, I plan to instead focus this chapter and the first part of our literary stay in Portales on one major theme: connecting the final dots between the previous summer in Western Maryland and what eventually led me to once and for all make what would be my final decision to join WCG (and to where later the Lord would show me that no matter what others might say about my "salvation" because I had joined a church that most thought of as a "cult"—that in HIS eyes, as far as He was concerned, this was the time where I finally stop running from God and all the promises I made to Him and finally start the process of in a sense "putting the ring on my finger" and commit to His ways and His laws for keeps—no matter what may happen to me next).

I ended the last chapter by noting how little time I had from the time I got back home from Maryland until the time I came to Eastern to register and start my Bachelor's studies in Music Business with a minor in telecommunications. One of the things I promised God is that I would soon get much more serious about Sabbath observance, correctly doing the dietary laws (at least in the way that WCG understood them at the time)—and most of all, get back in touch with the nearest

WCG pastor and start trying to go back to Sabbath and Holy Day services as soon as I could.

But there were still several obstacles in my way. One—it's a whole lot harder to be independent when you don't have a car of your own or a lot of your own money to speak of. And I still had not come clean with my family about what I now truly believed about God because of what I personally feared my family would do financially if I let the cat out of the bag.

The biggest immediate thing in my way, though, wasn't as much my family—but of all things, marching band. The reason for it was that one of my requirements of me as an incoming ENMU transfer student in the School of Music was that I was obligated to play as a part of the ENMU Marching/Symphonic Band through all of football season as one of the conditions of a Marching/Symphonic Band scholarship. Let's say having to go through another season of football games and parades brought back the eventual distaste for being in marching band back in high school. And now came with all of this one additional reason—the fact that most of the time the ballgames and parades I had to march in were all on Saturday. Talk about making me a really grumpy and reluctant camper…but due to financial reasons, I was forced to basically endure and hang on as best as I could until football season was done and my marching band obligations were fulfilled. I still tried to do the Sabbath and everything else that WCG believed in as best as I could —with another of my promises to God: "Okay, Lord—maybe after football season's over with…I'll go back to [WCG) services."

Now let's fast-forward the tape to what was FINALLY the end of football season. To set the stage a little better, keep in mind that this was all happening to me during the fall of 1989 when "perestroika" and the fall of communism in Eastern Europe and even in Russia itself were major items on the evening TV news at the time. From those world events came one memorable event for me that would eventually become the center pivot point of what some might call my "personal testimony of coming to Christ". (At the time, I would have definitely NOT referred to it in that way—but there you go….that's the sands of time shifting indeed.)

It was a Friday night after I had ate supper at the cafeteria in the Campus Union Building. Afterwards, I went back to my dorm to get ready for the Sabbath. After putting up some stuff in my third-floor private room in Lincoln Hall, I went back downstairs to watch the news in the TV lounge before the Sabbath started. As I was watching the national news (including what were two of my favorite public

TV shows—"Wall Street Week With Louis Rukeyser" and "Washington Week In Review"), they were showing the news stories of the conflicts between the quickly-collapsing Communist governments and the common people of those nations struggling to overthrow them. But what really caught my attention were the pieces of the news footage coming from the people of what was then East Germany literally using their sledgehammers to tear down the Berlin Wall.

A funny thing happened to me while I was watching those Berlin Wall stories. While everyone in those pictures were breaking out the champagne and celebrating and others were proclaiming the disintegration of the East German government to be a historical event, I was totally the opposite. I was actually crying and grieving over this turn of events and even shouting at the TV, "Mr. Gorbachev, stop this madness NOW! You don't know what you're doing! If you only knew what is really happening here…"

Why would I think such a crazy thought? Because at the time (at least according to my personal understanding of WCG doctrine at the time), we in WCG believed what Mr. Armstrong had previously said not only during "The World Tomorrow" broadcasts, but also in various church Church publications that one day the Antichrist would rise up in a sort of modern-day reincarnation of the revived Holy Roman Empire through the emergence and dominance of the European Union— and that Germany would once again take a leading role in hastening what we believed would be the initial impetus for "the Great Tribulation". [Author's Personal Note: This is no longer a doctrine that I personally support or espouse— and I have now long since disassociated myself from this viewpoint because of currently existing Biblical evidence (especially about the role of Israel in the end times) that completely discredits this former WCG doctrine.]

As the news footage continued, these other thoughts were coming to my mind: first—"GERMANY! It's coming true!" Then, someone else entirely different compelled and urged me to do something—and it was a feeling that I just couldn't completely shake off until I did something about it—"I'VE GOTTA GO BACK!!! I'VE GOTTA GO BACK!!!" By the time the news programs ended, Sabbath had already started. So I turned off the TV, left the lounge, got into the elevator, and went back to my dorm room. I tried to look in my stuff to find my old letter that I had at one time gotten from David Dobson (the same WCG minister I once knew who at the time was still in charge of both its Lubbock, TX and Roswell, NM congregations) that had his phone number. For the first time in nearly 2 or 3 years since I first attended South Plains College, I called Mr. Dobson and asked him if there was any way I might be allowed to come back and attend services again and get a ride to be able to go. Mr. Dobson then gave me the name of one of the deacons in the Roswell church who just happened to live in Portales named Tony Aguilar. Right after I got off the phone with Mr. Dobson, I immediately called Mr. Aguilar about the ride. The very next morning, I was able to finally go to my first WCG Sabbath service in several years—and at the time, I felt like I was finally where I needed to be all this time.

It's amazing just how many things in our lives can keep us from making the necessary choices required to undergo a passionate pursuit of the God who made us. For some, addictions and bondages can keep them bound. Others find that the idols of money and the things of this world seem to take away the time and attention that should be spent passionately pursuing a relationship with their God. For myself, what kept me from running TO Him instead of FROM Him was basically fear of several things: (1.) Fear of commitment to a religious system that to me basically required me to choose WCG as the ONE True Church and forsake my family forever;

(2.) The fear of what my family would think of me essentially choosing WCG over them (and the possible economic repercussions that doing so would immediately have on myself);

(3.) The fear of how I was going to make it financially on my own completely without ANY help from my family whatsoever;

and (4.) How making this decision would affect my career goals and my earnest desire to work in the music industry.

But nonetheless, I remembered another promise I made to the Lord when I stopped attending WCG services and functions the first time while I was at SPC—"If I ever even start thinking about WCG again, I will go back—and I will do so for keeps." This was the time I finally decided (come bleep or high water) to take the plunge and fulfill that old promise to Him. From there, I resolved that no matter what price I had to pay to do this that I would gladly pay it no matter what the cost. Little did I even know or dream then the eventual prices and consequences making this pivotal decision would cause for myself and others. Nor did I even fathom to understand just how much I would have to go through (at least not in the way I felt at the time) and suffer in various ways for the next few years for the cause of Christ as a result.

Chapter 7: [Roswell, NM AND Portales, NM (Part II)—Growing Up In The Pre-Split WCG

For this part of our tour, we'll need to tell my version of Charles Dickens' "A Tale of Two Cities" by breaking this down into two parts. To do it, we'll only need to go down one familiar road—US 70. (How's that for simplicity?) In fact, our current starting point of Eastern's Administration Building is just about as close to the highway as you can get. (You can tell by the sounds of all the trucks passing by, of course.) There's a pedestrian walk bridge that spans close to the Student Academic Services building which will lead you to Greyhound Arena where the ENMU Greyhounds and Zias play basketball.

But instead, we'll head straight as an arrow southwest towards Roswell. One thing about southeastern New Mexico—there's no lack of ranches, deserts, and nothingness throughout the duration of our 90-mile trek to the slightly larger town of Roswell. And my advice if you go down this way on 70? If you have to get gas or food along the way, Elida's your best and ONLY hope—because of the Allsup's store that's there. Stock up on your burritos, cokes, and everything else while you're there—because it will be your absolute last chance for about 60 to 70 miles until you get into Roswell proper. (If you get stuck on the side of the very constricted two-lane road that is the state of New Mexico's glorified excuse for a major paved highway without these necessary items and with a bunch of coyotes, don't blame me…you were fully warned.)

After miles and miles and even more miles of torturous wastelands and endless dirt roads branching off 70, we finally meet and merge with US 285 just north of town that serves as Roswell's Main Street. We'll know for sure we're inside Roswell itself when we pass by the New Mexico Military Institute. But we'll continue on south on Main until we find Union Street at the elementary school where the Roswell congregation of the Worldwide Church of God once met. This Roswell congregation held a very special place in my heart—for it was my spiritual incubator and family that helped me grown from a newborn baby in Christ and taught me the ropes of what it truly took to be a WCG member.

PART I: MY DAYS IN THE WCG INCUBATOR

(A.)   After my initial phone call to Mr. Dobson and my new found
commitment to WCG—for the rest of the time I spent studying at
Eastern, I would find myself going down this road or others like it most
Sabbaths (that was, when I didn't have to go back home for holiday

weekends/resupply missions or when one of the Aguilars weren't otherwise able to pick me up). There were times when for a little while I wound up with Tony's daughter Jeanie and another girl from Tularosa who was also attending Eastern.

Other times, it was Tony and Judy themselves with their two younger daughters, Karla and Adela, in tow in an old beat-up yellow and brown station wagon that smelled like Fritos and looked like it had seen its better days. But through the grace of God and Tony's adept auto maintenance skills (partly due to the fact that he had previously been a truck driver before becoming a WCG member), "Ol' Yellow" would usually never fail to take us down the many miles to church.

The usual group including myself that would pile into the Aguilar's station wagon was a pretty fun group of personalities that was a perfect place to call a sort of second spiritual family during my time at Eastern. Tony at times tended to be a bit softspoken, but could also be a little bit of jokester at times. He was always, though, the man that best represented the best qualities of a church deacon—a definite humble servant of the Lord willing to do above and beyond what was necessary to help you be the best.

Tony's wife, Judy, was his perfect opposite—so I'll try not to overstate the obvious here too much. Judy could be emotional at times, forceful in her opinions, and it was never too hard to hear her voice above the road noise of the winds going through the windows rolled down at all times. But she definitely managed to fix us up with good food and was overall a very jovial lady to be around.

Karla and Adela tended to keep to themselves and stayed busy during these long car rides with either coloring books or other activities. At various times, another one of our church prospects, Ivy Smith and her daughter who lived in Clovis, would usually when they rode be first picked up by Tony before coming to my dorm. Ivy especially was a pretty fun gracious lady who at times definitely displayed an extremely wicked sense of humor. (This trait probably came in handy for her, too, since she had to deal with a husband that was not only hostile to her beliefs, but according to her didn't always act like the decent husband that he needed to be overall to his family.)

This, for better or worse, was a major part of my spiritual family that helped raise me in my newfound, reborn faith of WCG. This motley group gathered in "Ol' Yellow" most Sabbaths shared their good times as well as bad on our weekly trips to Sabbath services and other trips for the Holy Days to not only Roswell, but also Lubbock and other places as needed. We not only shared bread and various items (whether they were burritos that Judy had made or when we would need to make our usual obligatory stop at that Elida Allsups' store for bathroom breaks or food purchases), but also our tears and fears and questions that faced all of us inside WCG. And all of this as we passed through the vast ranchlands of Roosevelt and Chaves counties—those are miles that are hard to take back even if I wanted to. For a true youngster in the faith, it was the perfect safe place to learn and grow in His thoughts and His ways.

The rest of the small, but still faithful congregation in Roswell eventually proved to be just as welcoming and comfortable to a struggling college student who was just starting his own walk of faith. Several members and leaders stood out to me as pillars and examples of "God's true church". Among them were one of the local church elders, Lawrence Lovato, and his wife, Rosie. Lawrence (or as some of us in the congregation—myself included—nicknamed "Lorenzo") was a big bear of a man—over 6 foot tall and at least 240 or more pounds who at one time worked for the railroad before he retired.

"Lorenzo" was definitely a big teddy bear and gentle giant of a man that could give the biggest possible bear hug and toothy grin to prove it. If you wanted someone that was a concerned shepherd and servant of the people here in Roswell, you needed look no further than Lorenzo. Rosie was also the perfect match for Lorenzo—especially in the area of hospitality. It was always a welcome sight to see one or both of them any time at WCG services.

Mr. and Mrs. Tom Batho were also very memorable in a number of ways. One was their house that had a very spacious den that a number of the

Roswell church's smaller meetings such as "Spokemen's Club" were usually held. No telling how many times I personally went into that house for special meetings like these...The other was the optimistic attitude that the Bathos displayed not only about life, but also about the things of God. Even in their older, twilight years, I was privileged to hear at various time his wisdom and insight helpful to this young cub in the faith.

Some of the other Roswell members at the time included Clarence and Linda Cummins and their daughter, Carrie (Clarence being another one of the deacons while Linda served as church pianist); Mr. and Mrs. Rudy Luker from Ruidoso; Kari Fitzpatrick, her son, Travis, and her nephew, Earl Robinson, Kenneth and Mary Bratcher and their infant son, and an elderly man we called "Ol' Jack" who had to use oxygen which he had to carry alongside him in tow just to get around. These people were among the group who would hear Mr. Dobson and/or the elders and deacons give sermons and sermonettes each Sabbath and Holy Day (that is— when we didn't otherwise have combined services with the Lubbock congregation on Holy Days).

(B.) INTERESTING HIGHLIGHTS OF MY ROSWELL TENURE
When I say I learned a number of lessons from my time in the Roswell incubator, I'm not just being figurative. From not only words, but primarily example, I literally learned some basic virtues that would later shape the way I still view life today:

(1.) *Patience*—The value of waiting on rides with Tony and Judy wasn't completely lost on me at the time. Consider, for instance, the age of the Aguilar's station wagon and the almost sacrificial demands they had to place on it just to go to church on the Sabbath. Church in Roswell usually started about 10 AM Mountain time unless certain special events on Mr. Dobson's schedule had to rearrange it otherwise. Depending on whether or not Tony had to be there early to set up for church, we'd have to have an early start. If Ivy and her daughter also planned to come, then you had to tack on at least another hour to the trip required for Tony and Judy to go all the way to Clovis to pick Ivy and her daughter up. Then from there, back to Portales where I had to be out front of my dorm waiting for them to show before our long combined trek to Roswell. After church was over (depending on if we had a monthly potluck or special activity such as Spokeman's Club), it would sometimes be dark and very late at night before we finally got back to Porchtown.

One of these times proved to be especially interesting. One Sabbath due to mechanical breakdowns and other frustrations, I wound up waiting outside my dorm for the Aguilars for up to three hours for a ride. If there was even a time I'm glad I got over my childhood temper tantrums and was forced to learn proper anger management back in junior high, it was then. I found out that my capacity for patience was easily challenged and strengthened simply by waiting on the rides of others.

(2.) *Intricacies of WCG Doctrines*—Several particular instances in Roswell stuck out that illustrated the pre-split WCG environment I was raised in as a spiritual baby:

    (A.) *Meticulousness in dietary laws*—At the time I took the plunge towards WCG, keep in mind first that this was still in the years immediately following Mr. Armstrong's death and Mr. Tkach, Jr. assuming the reins as Pastor General. Inside WCG, we were expected to among other things keep the Biblical dietary laws of Leviticus chapter 11. We didn't just avoid pork or other unclean meats—NO! This point was driven home to me one time when I went with Tony to a Roswell grocery store. When we went to shop in the bread aisle, Tony didn't just price labels—but even went to see if there was—bleep forbid—LARD—listed in the ingredients label contents. The same was usually true when it came to things such as refried beans. Catfish was also just as verboten. And don't even think about shrimp or lobster, either—those were entirely out of the question.

    (B.) *Dealing with governments and employers*—When I first formally came into WCG, we really took the Sixth Commandment to an extreme. (Remember—it's the one involving killing and murder?) That even meant for us that

we couldn't even THINK of being a part of the military and still be a WCG member in good standing—regardless of not you were drafted or not. I know this because I remember a time or two how I was advised to file for conscientious objector status.

We also took Matthew 7:1&2 to an just as interesting extreme. When the Scripture said, "...do not judge.."—we thought that it actually actually meant what it said and said what it meant. Combine that with the above-mentioned Sixth Commandment and for us it at times meant one thing—DO NOT do jury duty...and if you're stuck with a jury summons, do what you can to get out of it.

But those things didn't compare to one of the biggest ones of all—working OR going to school on the Sabbath or on a Holy Day. To us at the time in WCG—we believed that we had to do the Sabbath and Holy Days to the point that we had to be prepared to face the consequences if push came to shove on the matter. Many a Church member had their own horror stories of either facing termination from their jobs or troubles dealing with school officials for taking their kids out of school for Holy Days. And sadly, participation in most extracurricular activities for Church kids past junior high was out of the question because of Sabbath and Holy Day issues. (I was sure glad at the time that I had NOT joined the military in retrospect—and that I was in college—NOT high school. At least I had control of most of my time.)

(3.)   *Baptismal counseling*—You found out the hard way as a newbie in WCG how far you were willing to go in your commitment to Christ by how patient you were with your minister in your request to him to be allowed to go through counseling for baptism. This one needs a little more detailed illustration.

When I first started coming to services in Roswell and after a while asked Mr. Dobson to be a candidate for baptism, it wasn't usually done the way most churches do it. For one, we NEVER EVER had altar calls or invitations during church services—period. You did NOT go up and just shake the preacher's hand, "make a decision for Christ", and consider yourself "converted". That was simply not done inside WCG at that time.

INSTEAD—you first had to ask your minister and request that you be allowed to go through baptismal counseling. Note that at the time, EVERYTHING was done IN PRIVATE between you and the minister. From there, the two of you scheduled special times where the minister would visit with you and talk to you about the basics of the faith such as salvation, repentance, and other necessary doctrines so that he could make sure for himself that you had a decent idea of what would face you as a WCG member.

After each visit, you were then given a list of appropriate booklets and materials to study and familiarize yourself with more WCG doctrine to prepare for your next counseling visit with your minister. ONLY after the minister was sufficiently satisfied that you understood what it meant to be baptized and be a member of "God's True Church" would he then start making arrangements for your baptismal service. Keep in mind, this entire process could take a period of months to complete. I know this for a fact because it probably took at least six months from start to finish for my baptism to become a reality.

(C.) WHEN I FINALLY CAME CLEAN TO MY FAMILY ABOUT WCG—

One of the first problems that I had resolve as a result of my formal commitment to WCG was the absolute hardest for me to do—to come clean once and for all to my family about certain things that I now believed about God. And I knew that doing this would not only take prayer, but also the grace of God to go through—for I was personally prepared for a reaction from my family of no less than H-E-double hockey sticks (especially from my granddad).

The time eventually came on a Christmas holiday break when I had to come face the music and formally inform my family of my decision. At the time in WCG, it was practically forbidden among other things to observe Christmas or Easter due to their pagan origins. The hardest time of all for folks like myself at the time to go through, therefore, was Christmas because of family pressure and their fears that you no longer wanted to be a part of the family any more. I found out about this myself the hard way just what this decision might cost me. Despite my best attempts to be as sensitive as possible to their feelings, the idea of my not observing Christmas anymore was received by the rest of the family like a lead balloon. I told them not only did I not wish to celebrate Christmas anymore, but that I didn't wish to give any gifts or accept any from anyone. And the fight after that was on.

Right even up until Christmas Eve as they were about to leave for Uncle Randy's house, the appeals still came from my mother, Aunt Arlene, and my grandparents to change my mind and come with them—but I held firm in my decision to stay at the house while they were gone. I kept my mouth shut as they made their last-ditch appeals. In my mind, I sarcastically thought of those appeals as a sort of talking and singing as a quartet—with one crying and pleading me to go and another tongue lashing and attempting to put me to shame for this latest decision.

But what was really the loudest voice angrily shouting at me was when Papa said something along the lines of, "…Son, you are about to regret doing what you're about to do. There's going to be a time when you're going to need some help sometime—and you're going to wish that you hadn't done what you've done." After that, they finally left me alone to my own devices and went on to Uncle Randy's house. But the battle lines were now drawn with my family officially— and there was no turning back from here.

Maybe this is a good point to stop this particular story and, in accordance to the instruction of the Holy Spirit, minister to some of you today facing hard choices today about how to either admit to your loved ones about mistakes you have made—or on the other side of the equation, inform them of a significant decision that you have made concerning certain changes in your belief in God that will be extremely hard pills for your loved ones to swallow.

Let me illustrate through a situation that many years later I had the privilege of helping someone else through a similar situation. One time as I was staying with a certain friend in Lubbock, we were eating at a Taco Bueno and catching up on the various things happening in our lives. In the course of the conversation, this friend told me about his decision to start adopting similar Sabbatarian/Messianic beliefs to mine and begin more active involvement with a local Messianic Jewish congregation.

I had been alongside of this guy (who used to be one of my coworkers at the time at the radio station I worked at) a number of times in the past as he began struggling with his religious identity (especially since his family is primarily Church of Christ). So it was a sort of pleasant surprise to me in a way that he had decided to make a clean break and be upfront with his family on his true religious convictions. As he related these things to me, though, he also told me of the current dilemmas and conflicts he was having at the time with his family and asked me for my advice on what to do in the situation.

I told him the following in response, "Congratulations, sir—join the club. You're now going to have to work at least twice as hard to earn the respect and trust of your family that you once had." I then gave him the following advice that I hope those going through similar situations will take heed and remember if you're facing a possible family conflict over your beliefs and relationship with God:

(1.)   Realize that their statements may not necessarily be about what you might believe, but are usually more primarily based on their fears of losing the personal relationship that they have with YOU. Your job is to convince them that even though your beliefs and might change—THAT DOES NOT necessarily mean that your relationship with them must change. Let them know you still love them no matter what and that you still care.

(2.)   May I especially urge you today to especially heed the admonition of Psalm 126:5&6 where it says: "..Those who sow in tears shall reap in joy, bringing their sheaves with them..." In essence, I told my friend to simply sow love to his family in whatever ways he could. For instance, as long as it didn't compromise his religious beliefs, go the extra mile as needed. If say you are one that prefers to observe the Sabbath on Saturday, but your mom or dad just has to have the lawn mowed THIS Saturday morning for some reason and they might be extremely mad at you if you don't—might I first suggest that if you have the ability to do so to see if you can work with them to find a better time to perform the same task. THEN once you have promised to do such-and-such a thing, honor your word and commitment to do so as promptly and as close to time as possible to the original time agreed to AND in as high quality a fashion as is possible.

(3.)   Don't compromise what you believe, but don't be too insensitive or inattentive to the needs of your loved ones either. Have you ever heard the saying, "They won't know how much you love them until you show them how much you care."? Well—it's true, I tell you—for you truly reap what you sow. I see that new believers in Jesus/Y'shua especially have a tendency to jump into the ditch on one side or the other.

Some will compromise even their most basic beliefs in order to retain the affection and love of those they care about. Or conversely, they are so legalistic (like I once personally was) and inflexible about what they believe that they unnecessarily steamroll over loved ones for the sake of faithfulness to their most strongly held beliefs to the point where they lack even the most basic consideration for the feelings and viewpoints of others. Both of these viewpoints in my opinion in retrospect are absolutely stupid and shameful.

The reasons are these: (1.) What good of an example of the Savior are you if you're easy prey for people who don't like what you believe –BUT YET who will not eventually respect you if you let down your guard too much? And what good is one who in the name of the very God they claim to serve are so abrasive and hostile in their approach that others are actually turned off by what you claim to believe?

Not only is your Master and Savior watching, BUT THEY ARE, TOO! When you're able to exhibit an appropriate balance between the two, you'll not only be amazed at what consistency and compassion will do for you on your behalf, but you'll also be additionally surprised just how much of an impact on others your example and actions will have in preaching the gospel in a way that St. Francis of Assisi would be proud of: "...Preach the Gospel at all times—and if necessary, use words."

(4.)   God will in due time and season find a way to eventually turn your present situation into something that's at least half-tolerable for you if you'll only first be patient and then completely obedient to whatever He may directly tell you to do. The human tendency in these situations is usually to try to eliminate your personal pain by trying to fix everything right then and now. But maybe in YOUR particular situation, it may not necessarily be the wisest course at the present time.

Remember my Messianic friend? When I next visited him, he told me that he had taken these ideas and put them to work. I was pleasantly amazed when he told me of how implementing these simple ideas truly impacted his family relationships. This man eventually was blessed to find a decent young woman of similar beliefs who lived in Pennsylvania.

The two have not only since married, but the last time I heard from them were even proud parents of a newborn son.

I may not have myself personally experienced such dramatic results—but I also can attest that time, patience, and commitment did help my own family relationships as well. I won't guarantee rose gardens on this. But I will tell you once again that you definitely will reap what you sow. The final outcome will very much depend on how much and what you specifically invest in it.

While I'm on this subject, I must also needfully address the concerns of families, friends, and others who find themselves in a relationship with someone they know that they feel or claim is in a "cult", sect, or derivative/fringe movement outside the normal bounds of what they might consider orthodox evangelical Christianity. I don't claim to know it all on the subject, but having been on both sides of the fence, maybe I can give you a few words of advice as well to help you make the best of the situation:

(1.)   **BE INFORMED!** Part of the problem I see is that most people's perception (right or wrong) of what they might think a "cult"/sect/etc. might be is usually influenced way too much by what they see in the media. If I say the word "cult", chances are that the most common mental pictures will pop up in most folks' minds might be of such things as the Marshall Applewhite/"Heaven's Gate" group, Jim Jones in Guyana with the Kool-Aid, or David Koresh and the Branch Davidians near Waco. And as a result, they unnecessarily prejudge others before making a honest effort to first find out for themselves what some of these folks really believe and making decisions out of unnecessary religious prejudice and overly emotional reactions. If appropriate discernment, wisdom, and cooler heads prevailed before putting disparaging labels on those not in complete agreement doctrinally with the Nicene Creed, we'd all be a lot better off (especially relationshipwise). (FYI--I ain't just preaching to you, either, about this--I need this friendly reminder from our state department of highways as well.

Not all folks in these suspect groups are on the surface quite as wacko as you might think. For instance, I keep seeing nicely-dressed Jehovah's Witnesses volunteers occasionally when I have to do retraining to maintain my eligibility as a TDCJ prison ministry volunteer. It's also quite rare to go into my local library and not see at least two or three Latter-Day Saints missionaries doing something on its Internet computer terminals. Both types (even if most are suspicious of their doctrines and methods of evangelism) at least make some sort of effort to reach others outside of their faith and build some sort of bridges and relationships with them much more than a lot of folks I know in most of orthodox evangelical Christianity.

The name of the game is simple—do NOT go by surface appearances or perceptions. RESEARCH and get the facts for yourself! There's plenty of good, reasonable apologetics and cult-watching material on the Net and other media these days. (For example, I would personally commend to you the work of such entities as Hank Hannegraf's Christian Research Institute and also Living Hope Video Ministries as good starting points in this journey.) Get the facts—and turn off the TV as you do it.

(2.) **Study the Word for yourself and make bleeping sure that YOU know what you personally believe.** If you can't even articulate well what you believe to others, then how in the world are you going to be able to help turn someone away from error and lead them into HIS real truth?

(3.) **Reread the four points I gave earlier to your affected loved ones.** What's good for those gooses is just as good for the rest of you ganders, too. Your approach to your loved one will be a good indicator to them of what is required to maintain a personal relationship with you. Again—you WILL reap what you sow on these things.

(4.) **[THE BIG ONE:] ALWAYS, ALWAYS** leave at least one door open and available to them to come back to you! The reason is that the ONLY time you may finally get a chance to speak to their heart WILL BE during their biggest storms of personal trouble.

A prime example of this was what Mother said to me and how she acted after I told the family that I wasn't keeping Christmas anymore. She told me basically, "I don't care what you do. You'll always get a Christmas present from me no matter what." She also never failed to help me out many times in the years afterward when I was in my deepest times of personal distress and do what little she personally could when I needed it most.

The rest of my family may have been against her for doing this—but to this day, I'm still grateful for her courage and willingness to see past the differences and still see me first and foremost as the little baby boy she gave birth to many years before. Several years later when not only my personal financial foundation would go south, but when even the entire WCG would dramatically change at the same time—that above other things was what helped melt my heart the most and start the journey away from legalism and towards the deeper relationship with Him that I have now.

For both sides of these religious type conflicts, there are ways in the end to find common ground in these situations that all sides can live under. The main key is to keep in mind first and foremost the original ties that bind you all together in the first place. The biggest one above all is the very One who created all of you to start with.

(D.) MY FIRST FEAST IN BIG SANDY

After the start of my second school year back in Portales, I had my very first opportunity to go to a WCG Feast of Tabernacles. They say there's nothing like the first time that you do something. It was certainly the case here for this West Texas boy who didn't really know what to expect. All I knew about it was what I heard from the brethren—and I just wanted to be a part of it.

So after arranging everything at school to where I could go without too much inconvenience on my studies, I took the one-way bus to Roswell to meet up with Kari and Travis Fitzpatrick to stay the night at their place before Earl Robinson and Kenneth and Mary Bratcher joined us to start our eastward journey to Ambassador College in Big Sandy, TX. (The first night at Kari's place, FYI, was a long one as far as sleeping was concerned since the Fitzpatricks had a cat—and I was obviously sneezing all night long as a result.)

Just getting to Big Sandy with our little caravan was an adventure and a half in itself—especially as we literally had to go across miles and miles of Texas. The first memorable snippet occurred when we got to Post. Earl and I were riding in his car while Kari and Travis rode in Kari's beat-up LTD with the Bratchers dragging up the rear of our caravan in their camper pickup. We all stopped in Post at a store—when after a little while, Earl and I got back in his car. As we were leaving town, we didn't see the other two cars of our caravan. So we proceeded further down US 84 to Synder. When Earl and I got close to Snyder and tried to locate the rest of the crew, they were nowhere to be found.

So Earl decided to turn back around to Post in an attempt to try to find them. Nothing doing—because we actually wound up going back and forth between Post and Snyder like chickens with their heads cut off frantically trying to find everyone else at least two more times with no success.

Finally, Earl decided that we might as well prepare to go along the rest of the way to Big Sandy by ourselves if necessary—so off we went again back to Snyder. Wouldn't you know it—at a roadside park near Snyder, we FINALLY found them. When we got to the park, the questions immediately flew amongst our caravan. "Where were you?" "Well, we were looking for you—but couldn't find you. WHERE WERE YOU?" "Well, we hadn't pulled out of Post—and we were here waiting on you!" Needless to say, Kari gave her nephew a pretty good chewing out before we resumed our journey.

That was nothing compared to what we experienced much later in that same trip when we approached the town of Grand Saline late at night on US 80. Apparently, a local cop saw Kari's car swerving back and forth in her lane of traffic and thought she might be driving drunk. So off went the flashing lights with all of us in the caravan pulled over on the side of the road reaching for our drivers' licenses.

It turned out, though, that Kari hadn't obviously had a drop of alcohol at all—she was just really tired and sleepy after a good number of hours behind the wheel. The officer thankfully let her go with only a warning. But Earl did manage to get a slight bit of revenge on Kari as the rest of us would razz Kari for driving drunk and saying things in jest to her like, "Now don't go driving drunk, Kari..."; "Don't swerve on the road, Kari!" After all of these unique travel adventures JUST to get there, we finally arrived very late at night on the Ambassador College campgrounds to all of our relief.

Once I arrived, I was in for a major treat fit for a poor college student like myself. To someone who had never been to a Feast in my life, I thought that I was in paradise (or at least in the "place of safety" in Petra), I thought to myself, "THIS IS truly God's TRUE Government at work right here at this campground!" Captains of 100s, 50s, and 10s just like in the Old Testament—all functioning just like it would in the "World Tomorrow" that I'd only heard about for many years watching Mr. Armstrong on TV or by reading Church literature.

The environment on the campground was electric. Staying in a tent there did have its drawbacks—including having to go to the building where the showers and restrooms were where the showers were sometimes cold or lukewarm at best and contained spiders and other crawling insects. And of course, no true Big Sandy campground experience would be complete unless it rained right in the middle of the Feast on your tent and got everything inside it (including your stuff and the tent bottom) soaking wet.

But the slight drawbacks and inconvienences couldn't compare to all the fun you could have on the campground. No matter where you were from or how far you came to get to Big Sandy, you could always find something going on here. Cookouts of great food to eat, lots of brethren to meet and see—this to a newborn WCG guy like me was truly the life.

Here was also the first place I'd ever seen things like students actually dress up in tuxedos and evening gowns just to go to church on the High Days of the Feast in an attempt to look their best before God. And seeing the special live closed-circuit Festival broadcast from WCG main headquarters in Pasadena was a memory in itself as we would see the Ambassador College Chorale and Orchestra perform Handel's "Hallelujah Chorus" from the "Messiah" oratorio. At last, I was truly free here to worship God in the way I felt he wanted to me to do. Away from my family and the pagan influences that bound me at home— yep, this was where I felt I belonged—and I never wanted to leave.

But church wasn't the only attraction for a red-blooded male like me. No, sir— not where there's (FINALLY) some very decent looking young ladies in the Church around mine and Earl's age to meet, greet, and get to know at the singles' activities that were available at the Feast.

One of those activities was when we went to a miniature golf course in the Gladewater/Longview area. Earl, Travis, and I happened to play our respective rounds of miniature golf behind several young ladies who were from Missouri and Iowa. Talk about cute—a man could be easily smitten by attractive ladies such as these.

One of these young ladies who was particularly unforgettable for me was a girl named Judy who was originally from Illinois, but who was then attending college at a university in northwest Missouri. This pretty brunette proved to be an interesting young woman to get to know and that seemed to be a woman that I might actually really want to be my girlfriend. We even seemed to share similar interests and backgrounds ranging from our majors (she was an English major in college who also loved being involved somewhat in choir and music while my major was in music business) to the fact that we were both children of divorced parents (her dad was in WCG while her mom wasn't).

After the Feast, the two of us maintained a relatively close pen pal long-distance relationship that lasted for several years (even through what would be WCG's most tumultuous years) until she eventually got married to someone in her hometown and we finally lost touch with each other. Judy along with a couple of other very special young ladies that I personally got to meet during the Feast added further motivation and resolution that this would not truly be my last Feast.

But the biggest memory of all came from someone in our Roswell congregation who wasn't able to go to the Feast anywhere at all that year—Ol' Jack. Before I left for Big Sandy, this elderly man who could hardly walk or even breathe without oxygen one time at Church gave me some money and said to me, "Have a good Feast for me." The original amount that Ol' Jack had given me back home lasted me until about halfway into the Feast. When I ran out of money and didn't know what to do, Kari gave me some more money on behalf of an anonymous donor that wanted me to also have a good Feast. I found out later this money was also a gift from Ol' Jack.

Here I was—a struggling college student who was literally the ONLY one in "God's True Church" in my entire family. And yet one of the least of the brethren who might never in his lifetime get to go to a Feast ever again literally sacrificially gave of himself to make sure that a young man like myself who had never previously been to a Feast at all would have the best one possible that he could have ever had. This story is all the more poignant when you realize that not too much later, Ol' Jack was found dead due to problems with alcohol and other various medical ailments—and apparently felt isolated from others…even from other brethren.

Jack's sacrificial example to me in a perfect illustration of what I would later see demonstrated in many ways in the "walk of faith" that has been my life to this point. The facts are these—

(1.)   That it's sometimes next to impossible to take even the smallest baby steps of faith unless some more mature saints first take you under their wings and show you how;

115

(2.) And our God sometimes uses those whom we think are the absolute least among us to give us the most help when we may need it most. That was Ol' Jack in a nutshell. When I came back from the Feast, I tried to bring back a souvenir from AC in appreciation for his most generous and sacrificial gift. I hope that when I get to see him again in the Kingdom that I'll be able to do more than that to truly thank him for his help in helping this spiritual baby get off to a good start with his spiritual life. And most of all—for helping make a memory of my time in WCG a truly unforgettable one at that.

PART II—LEARNING TO WORK IN THE CROSSFIRE

Lest you think that my entire life at Eastern was wrapped up around WCG, that is not even hardly the case—especially when you had to consider that I was doing BOTH a Music Business major AND a Telecommunications (Eastern's operative term at the time for Mass Comm) minor.

The good part of the deal about being at Eastern was that the biggest majority of my course credits from South Plains easily transferred as credit towards my Eastern Bachelor's degree. That even included about ALL of my core required Music courses, general education course requirements, and even credit for some of the Country/Bluegrass Music program courses I took that were included as electives. (FYI—that was a sum total of about 144 credit hours from the three years I was in Levelland.)

All I had to concern myself with taking as far as general education requirements was Speech (in which I didn't necessarily do as well as I thought—but still managed to pass). Otherwise, all I basically had to concern myself with was my required core of business-related courses (such as marketing, merchandising, business law, business writing, etc.), all mass comm minor courses, and the two Music Business courses I needed to complete my degree.

I did take a few other Music courses just to stay active on the music side of things including private lessons on sax and piano and even still participated in Jazz Ensemble. But after my first year going through what I did just to finally get back to WCG services again, I did drop out of Marching/Symphonic Band after my original scholarship requirements were met.

There were several specific classes and experiences that I was also able to derive some benefit from to enhance my career potential and also my personal interests as well. Among them included a marketing class for non-profit organizations that was taught by the director of development for Eastern's public TV station. Not only did I learn plenty from this course public relationswise—but when I first heard this course was going to be offered and asked my degree advisor if it would be an elective course that I could use to get credit on my degree plan, my Music Business advisor after checking on this not only allowed me to take it, but seemed to also manage to strongarm my other two fellow Music Biz majors to also take the same course along with me.

During one of the summer sessions (in which I mainly enrolled in to where I could have a legit excuse to stay in my dorm and get student loans and other funds), I even got to take an advanced English course called "The Bible As Literature" which even Mr. Dobson looked favorably on my taking it to enhance my personal study of the Bible.

It was not only the very first time I laid my eyes on the Apocrypha, but also my first and ONLY time that I read the Pseudepigrapha. (I say ONLY on the Pseudepigrapha because when as a part of this class I had to read "The Infancy Gospel of Jesus"—I personally though that the mere portrayal of my Lord and Savior as a juvenile delinquent was so blasphemous in my eyes that I almost wanted to throw up into the toilet after having to read such horrible dribble. The idea of my Savior as a kid carelessly throwing thunderbolts from heaven or disrespecting his mother was NOT an appealing thing for me to contemplate at all. But the rest of that particular summer course was useful in providing further needed intellectual grounding for my faith in Christ.)

I also benefited from taking some private lessons in composition and in instrumental arranging as a way to further develop my interest in composing that I had started at SPC. And even the two required Music Business courses that I had to take had some practical class assignments that I was able to use to further complement my Workstudy jobs and/or other studies in other ENMU departments.

Towards the end of my last semester in Portales, one of the things myself, my other two fellow Music Biz majors, and our professor did as a capstone to our second and final music biz course (in which I had a feeling that part of the reason for the timing of it all was how close I personally was to graduation in comparison to my fellow Music Biz majors) was to take a three-day trip to both Albuquerque and Santa Fe to visit several music business-related establishments to tour their facilities and get an idea of what those in the industry were doing at the time in preparation for going into that career field.

One thing about that particular trip I remember most was when we were trying to get around the city of Santa Fe. Most cities here in the U.S. are usually built on what is called a "grid system". But NOT Santa Fe—no, sir—because EVERYTHING in that blessed city is primarily based on the Spanish way of laying out streets—revolving around the location of the place you are at in relation to the Plaza downtown.

You think your town has strange streets? Try going down the Paseo del Peralta and you would be as convinced as I am that the one who originally designed Santa Fe's streets in the 1700s should have either had their head examined OR shot AND/OR hanged and quartered on the spot for even dreaming up such a horrible street scheme. WHY—you ask? Because you might find the Paseo del Peralta to be one of the longest streets you've even been on due to the fact that it meanders all over the place and you sure as bleep haven't got the foggiest clue where in tarnations it stops or ends. Talk about a street of confusion—that one definitely tops my list.

For the most part, though, my Eastern coursework was primarily dedicated to doing those things that might prepare me for a possible backup Mass Comm career in case I couldn't find anything in the music industry. This included a lot of work as a part of Radio and TV Practicum courses for KENW-FM and TV (the PBS TV and NPR radio stations for southeastern New Mexico). It was a definite privilege and learning experience to be a part of a mass communications program that was at the time one of the best in the country.

The mass comm program at Eastern was unique in comparison to most other comparable universities in the fact that it was such a hands-on based program that there was basically no way you could even hope to graduate without at least having been able to really get your hands dirty to some degree and learn in some way how to use at least some of the available equipment there.

From the public radio station in which I had to work an unpaid six-hour Sunday night shift a week to the TV side where I had to run camera and/or learn other functions for an actual functioning public TV station complete with daily newscasts and locally-based programming—I found out for myself how much of a pressure cooker, high-adrenaline world TV could really be. And overall despite its quirks, I loved it and appreciated it.

The mass comm class core curriculum was just as practical in nature in its training methods. Opportunities were definitely made available to learn not just how to shoot and edit video tape coverage, but even how to do things like audio and even technical directing. I even got a taste of how to work in the area of master control as well. And of course being a public TV station, we did have to help with such things as election coverage and even pledge breaks for telethons.

One of my most memorable mass comm class assignments came when I had to take a "Directing for TV" course. The professor who taught that course (as well as a number of others in the Mass Comm department) was probably one of our most favorite professors in the whole university to take courses under. He didn't cut much slack in grading you, of course—but was fair to all. If you wanted to see someone who might be the perfect look-a-like for Santa Claus, he was definitely your man—right down to even having the appropriately jovial personality to boot.

One of the assignments this particular professor gave our class was to take some footage from a classic video or film and re-edit it into a short trailer or documentary project that would synopsize the basic intent of the original film. Which film was I given? Charlie Chaplin's "The Great Dictator".

To those who've never seen "The Great Dictator", Chaplin made the film during the WWII years to be a spoof and parody of Adolf Hitler. The majority of the film honestly didn't seem to be much to write home about—until you get to Chaplin's monologue of around eight minutes towards the end of the film. Critics during Chaplin's time lambasted him for doing such a thing. But when I saw the last eight minutes of the film, it profoundly impacted me because it hit home right where I lived being a sort of religious minority at the time myself. Chaplin's very stirring and almost prophetic remarks to an imaginary crowd led me to base my whole project as a video montage centered around that very monologue.

When the finished project was completed and we discussed and reviewed the class projects during class, the professor was thankfully appreciative of my efforts to turn something that Chaplin did that the critics originally hated into something that had a positive intent and purpose. Out of the projects I did for that class, the Chaplin short got me the highest grade of all because it involved a subject that I was truly passionate about.

Even the various College of Fine Arts Workstudy jobs I had helped me to grow and take responsibility (in a safe place and without too much risk, of course) for projects in which a lot of money and other things were on the line. Among them included a semester or two where I actually directed a promotional video project for the School of Music. (I wound up bombing that one, but was able to get some practical experience for myself and even helped the School make decision of what it eventually wanted in a similar future project.) I also toward the last of my tenure got to work in the School of Music's Recording Studio helping record concerts, recitals, and other special music department functions. (Plus it didn't hurt neither in helping me at least get a basic recording ready of songs I had previously written.)

I even had the privilege of working in the CFA's Promotions Office under Sandi Bergman where I learned a little bit of the practical side of how to do public relations-related work for a fine arts entity. Sandi was an absolute dear of a boss who helped expose me to the finer points of how to write a press release and other media-related stuff that further enhanced my practical experience and complimented my coursework in both of my own declared majors.

And just like SPC, Eastern had its own rich mixture of people, culture, traditions, and personal experiences. Among those experiences included involvement in the ENMU Student Senate, Epsilon Mu Beta (one of the honors societies on campus), and the Lincoln Hall Council. I even had an opportunity or two to once again experience my love of chess through the Portales Chess Club that actually met on one of the buildings on campus and in which the director of our school orchestra was a part of.

I probably didn't get to know quite as many people as I did at SPC (partly due to my increasing interest in WCG), but there were a few interesting campus experiences that were still memorable nonetheless.

The first was the fact (and I AIN'T joking when I say this either) that I actually got to be personally acquainted with not one, but TWO different Miss New Mexicos that had been involved with the Miss America pageant system. There were a couple of provisos to this, of course. One of them was that I didn't even get to meet either one of them until AFTER they BOTH lost in the main Miss America pageant. The other part, sadly, was that despite how very physically attractive both of them were that I didn't get to date either one of them. (It was just as well—they probably already had serious boyfriends by the time I met them anyway—plus my WCG religious beliefs at the time absolutely forbade me from even going out with any women who was not otherwise a part of WCG.)

BUT I CAN say that I was at least acquainted with them! (FYI—one of them was a fellow Mass Comm major who was in at least one of my mass comm classes and who was also one of the news anchors and reporters on our TV station's daily 5 PM newscast while the other was a vocal music education major.)

Another time involved a party I was invited to go to by some of my fellow music majors at a house off-campus. Let's say this Saturday night party was a pretty raucous one involving a lot of drinking games and such. I as always opted not to partake of the available adult beverages offered there.

In the middle of the festivities, people in their various drunken stages of stupor kept wondering and asking me why I did not want to partake of such beverages. Then one of my fellow sax players in the School of Music named Ben (who was a Seventh-Day Adventist vegetarian type with black-rimmed glasses, a goatee, and a face that resembled one of the lead singers of Van Halen—and who was MUCH easier, ironically, to get along with drunk than when he was uptight stone cold sober) piped up with this most perfect hilarious response in my defense—"He don't need that! He's on a natural high!"

PART III—TWO OF THE PROUDEST MOMENTS OF MY LIFE

In the final days before I completely finished all of the courses that I had to take on the ENMU-Portales campus, I was able to experience what I felt at the time were two of the greatest moments I had ever experienced in my life—one of them that finally came after several long months of waiting and the other which would come as a complete shock and surprise to me.

(A.) **THE DAY I OFFICIALLY BECAME A WCG BAPTIZED MEMBER**
After having undergone several months of waiting, intense study, and several hard-to-schedule baptismal counseling appointments with Mr. Dobson, the day finally came just a week or so after the Feast of Unleavened Bread on April 13, 1991 (the day that I still even to this day consider my official spiritual birthday) when myself, Ivy Smith, and one

other lady all took the plunge (literally) in a horsetank in the patio of the Bathos' house in Roswell.

That day, Mr. Dobson after asking me the necessary questions to assure the validity of my conversion in Christ and before dunking me in the watery grave of my past said these words to me that I'll never forget—"I baptize you not into any sect or denomination, but in the name of Jesus Christ." After years of wandering and indecision, I finally counted the cost and decided to finally keep my end of the bargain to God that I was now going to be in WCG for keeps—for better or for worse. To me, it was the spiritual equivalent of putting the ring on my finder and once and for all marrying the Lord.

For about two years, this Roswell congregation served as my immediate spiritual family who raised and disciple me in the ways of "The Truth", who answered my questions, fed and supported me through my college studies, and burped and changed my spiritual diapers from Sabbath to Sabbath and Holy Day to Holy Day. I saw some of the best things that the pre-split WCG had to offer through the eyes of brethren who loved and cared for me and showed me that the ways of Christ were far better than the way of the world I was attempting to come out of.

These brethren showed me such love and acceptance in ways that could not be forgotten. As my time in the Roswell incubator drew to a close, it would be the joy and memory of these truly fun times of initial spiritual growth that would propel me through the upcoming storms of life that I would soon face.

Years later, I faced a situation that made me almost doubt and take a good hard look at my "salvation" and whether in the eyes of some I had truly "accepted Christ as my personal Savior". I for a fact am very much aware of the suspicions that some might have when I tell them that the time I might best consider "my day of salvation" was in a church that was still at the time considered a "cult".

As I went through that trying situation, the Lord said two things to my heart. The first was, "Don't worry about them—I'LL take care of them!"—inferring to me that I was to forgive such people and not attempt to do anything in an attempt to curry favor or get back in their good graces.

The second thing He said to me, though, was what really spoke to me the most—"When you did what you did six years ago (meaning the day I was baptized as a WCG member), that was good enough for Me." From there, I felt the peace of God that truly goes beyond understanding and have hardly doubted the true state of my relationship with Him since.

Why can I still say this now without reservations? Because I knew the road it took for me to get to that place. I remembered the many promises I made to Him in my youth that I couldn't either fully fulfill either because I wasn't completely free to make my own decisions or my fears of what my family would think or what I would lose financially should I make such a radical decision.

Here in Roswell, I found the spiritual security and support I needed to finally take the leap and plunge right into the waters of His grace. I decided that if I lost everything I had—even at the risk of being disowned by my own family—I was never turning back from this Rubicon. If I perished financially, I perished. I took the leap once and for all blind and scared and not knowing what would happen next.

This leads into something I must say to people in regards to how some might view the process of how someone should make their decisions for Jesus/Y'shua. It seems to me that a lot of my evangelical Christian brethren might have at least one if not some flawed views about this subject called "salvation"— including:

(1.) *The "Chicken Little" Syndrome*—I'm HIGHLY concerned that a good number of these brethren sadly use inappropriate evangelistic methods these days unnecessarily based in fear and a lack of trust that our God and the Holy Spirit can't adequately do a good job in Themselves in saving a loved one's soul. They seem convinced that if they can't pin that individual down and make their decision for Christ right that minute just so they can put another evangelistic scalp on their wall, that loved one is absolutely surely doomed with no hope for eternity.

(2.) *The "Magical Millennialist" Syndrome*—This is the exact opposite of "Chicken Little" in which such individuals are so complacent in their belief that there's no need to try to evangelize the world right now because Christ will come back, straighten everything out in the

123

Millennium, and give everyone that hasn't believed their shot at salvation then.

(3.) *Overemphasis on emotionalism and pinpointing dates*—I'm concerned that this is unnecessarily based on a flawed "sawdust trail" approach that legalistically requires you at a moment's notice to be able to recite the exact date, time, etc. for a salvation to be considered legitimately valid as far as a personal testimony is directly concerned.

(4.) *Underemphasis on developing TRUE disciples instead of simply making converts*—Even if the process I personally went through during my pre-split WCG baptismal counseling might have been flawed in some ways in retrospect, I still regard going through that process as a good thing overall because of the things it helped me develop spiritually—

   (a.) Patience with others (especially with the desires and needs of authority)

   (b.) Encouragement to be more diligent with the study of the Scriptures and in learning how to properly handle Biblical doctrine

   (c.) Persistence to stay the course and let my desires be known to the ministry about my true intentions as far as my decision for Christ was concerned

   (d.) Advice not to take lightly this very important decision and the commitment, responsibility, and hard work it truly takes to turn those decisions into appropriate actions

Through this process, I didn't just become a convert—but more importantly learned how to mature (even if some of the ways were proved wrong later) more and more into a disciple of Christ. It honestly saddens me that more evangelical groups will not adopt similar policies that would make BOTH their evangelistic and discipleship training methods much more effective.

The sum total of what I just said here is this—When it comes to the subject of salvation, you can't always judge the book by its cover or by predisposed fears or criteria that might actually run contrary to what the Spirit would prefer for you to do. It involves FIRST AND FOREMOST a quality choice to make an INFORMED decision for one to truly count the cost of being one of Christ's disciples and not just make such a choice based out of fear or unabounded emotion. A REAL disciple should do things for our Lord based on a commitment to do them EVEN when such an action is very much inconvenient for them to do.

That to me should be the soundest criteria to truly determine the state of one's commitment and faith to the cause of Christ. And in my eyes, you cannot have traveled half the roads I've gone or walked the trail of tears I've had to experience over the years without knowing for a fact that Jesus/Y'shua is truly my Lord, Master, and Savior to the glory of God the Father.

And to further illustrate my personal commitment to Him, consider this—(I hope, FYI, no identity thieves are reading this!) Would I in my right or wrong mind prefer to use my spiritual birthdate INSTEAD of my physical birthday for such mundane things as ATM, debit, and credit card PIN codes if I STILL didn't believe what I mean or mean what I believe? With that, I'll rest my case on that point.

(B.) **EXPERIENCES IN THE ENMU STUDENT SENATE**

But to me above all else, the proudest time of my Portales tenure was my involvement in Eastern's student government (otherwise called at the time ASENMU and/or ENMU Student Senate). Please allow me to put the nuts and bolts background on all of this first to explain what I mean.

During my second semester at Eastern, I heard of an opening in the Senate that was an appointment to be a Student Senator for Lincoln Hall. I was afterwards appointed to that post for the remainder of that first year. Serving as a Lincoln Hall Student Senator was good in itself, but didn't seem to me to have quite the legitimacy as being an ELECTED senator was.

So when the next school year came around and it was time for student government elections, I decided instead to file as a candidate to serve as the Student Senator for the College of Fine Arts. I did this for several reasons:

(1.) Noting that most of the folks in the College of Fine Arts were usually way too busy with various artistic projects and were usually disinterested in anything having to do with student government, I figured I had a better chance getting elected by this constituency rather than by Lincoln Hall (which proved to be even more true since I eventually ran unopposed for the CFA slot);

(2.) The Senate, as I found out from my previous semester's experience, had control of one major thing on campus—the purse strings of the amounts collected in student fees during registration that were available for student groups to use as money to pay for special projects for different campus departments;

AND (3.) If I DID NOT run, the College of Fine Arts might have absolutely NO say or voice as to how such fund were spent.

Even though my senatorial campaign was unopposed, I still ran it as if I was running it against an opponent. The strategy worked well enough to garner over 40 votes from the entire college—enough to secure my election to the post.

But the tougher challenge for me lay ahead as a Senator. The CFA during my term as its Senator in comparison to the other colleges and departments at Eastern was actually the SMALLEST in representation. This meant that in the ENTIRE Student Senate, CFA had a grand total of ONE Senator este todo—and I was it. That meant that if I didn't do this job well, the WHOLE CFA would get extremely short shrift on student funds.

My solution to this dilemma? I decided that if I were the ONLY voice that CFA had available in the entire Senate—then I would attempt to be the loudest one. The others could ignore or disregard me if they wished—but they could not say that they never heard a word I said.

How was this strategy implemented? I did it in several ways. First, I spent outside time on college computers and such creating and posting in all the affected buildings within my CFA jurisdiction to keep my constituents informed as I could about the goings on in the Senate—especially in regards to upcoming resolutions that were pending in the Senate. If there was a student group within my CFA jurisdiction that had a funding request before the Senate, immediately upon finding out of their filing, I attempted to seek out the group and/or its leaders to talk to them about the resolution and give them some advice about how to best insure their chances of Senate approval of their funding request.

My usual stock advice to them? Cut down the size of your request and do more fundraising on your own. Then when the resolution of a particular CFA group went before the Senate, I usually beforehand arranged for the Senate office to leave a copy of a letter of endorsement of the group's request in each Senator's box as an attempt to sway the votes of my fellow Senators towards approval of the request as well as verbal personal endorsement on the Senate floor.

I also noticed something interesting that was a part of our Senate meetings. Towards the end of each session, there was a time specifically devoted to allowing Senators to make other Senators (and by virtue, their constituencies) aware of important events going on in their constituencies. From that, I noticed an interesting problem unique to the School of Music. Most of the students of the School (whether it was a student recital, ensemble concert, or special event) were always in need of one thing above all else—people to make an audience. And they couldn't get out the word about their special events to the rest of my fellow Senators and student body like I could.

So the idea came to me—why not use that time to inform my fellow Senators and ask them to pass on the word to their constituents about these special events? Most of them were free of charge for them to attend anyway—why not urge them to come to whatever events they could be a part of?

It was the little things like those that I did during my term in that office to make my voice as CFA Senator an influential one in the entire Student Senate. It wasn't through power grabs or political backstabbing where my God allowed me to make my mark as a student government official—but instead simply by doing the necessary grunt work as best as I could and to as much of the benefit of my constituents as was possible.

I didn't get paid anything for this seemingly thankless job (which even most of my own constituents either usually didn't know about or would have cared less)—but I found out later in the year just how much this hard labor and effort would pay off in the end.

One night shortly before Passover, I happened to be watching TV outside the cafeteria in the Campus Union Building. The Student Body President asked me to come to her office to talk to me about something on her mind. Prior to this, I was spiritually preparing myself in various ways for the upcoming Passover and Feast of Unleavened Bread—especially in studying a recent sermonette by one of the deacons of our Lubbock church as well as another sermon by Mr. Dobson about questions we should consider asking ourselves to get an idea of what He might feel our true state as Church members of our spiritual progress might be in His eyes. I was truly contemplating at the time how I was doing spiritually. But when I came into the President's office for her talk, I needn't have worried—for before she was through, she would definitely make it obvious to me where I probably stood.

Her real intention at the time, I found out, was to try to garner enough votes and support for a pending Senate resolution that basically would change the way New Mexico university student government entities would lobby the New Mexico Legislature for increased funding for higher education. What the President was saying to me at times caused me to wonder whether she really meant what she was saying to me or if she was trying to do this simply to get my support for the resolution. Whatever her true intentions may have been in saying what she did, the way she was saying it sounded almost as if she were reading my mail and giving me her honest evaluation of what I would later consider the final results of my Passover exam:

"...Coy, I have been around people that don't care about me and that stab me in the back. But Coy—there's something different about you. I can't place exactly what it is—but you're not like them—you're not like everyone else. There's something different about you—but I don't know what it is." I later saw that it was probably the Holy Spirit speaking to me right through her—even if she wasn't necessarily aware of doing such a thing.

Anyway, I told her that I would need to discuss the affected resolution with my constituents before making a decision. From these, we ended the discussion and I left the office. To make a long story short, when that resolution came up for a vote in the Senate, I not only advocated for its passage, but even immediately "...called the question" to end all debate on the resolution and bring it to an immediate vote. Little did I know the consequences such decisions would provide for me personally.

Prior to the very last Senate session of the school year, I informed the Senate Vice-President that due to the before mentioned Music Business class trip, I would not be present for the upcoming Student Senate banquet. So when I came as always to the last formal Senate meeting of the school year, I really didn't anticipate what would come next.

One of the awards presented each year by the Student Body President to Student Senators was the "Most Outstanding Senator" award that was voted on by all the Senators. I had my own ideas on who might get this particular award—and believe me, I was the absolute LAST one that I would have expected to get that award. Surely there were better senators than I in the mix.

That was UNTIL the Student Body President called one name out of all other names she could have called out—MINE!! To say I was completely shocked and flabbergasted at such a development didn't even begin to describe what I truly felt. And it was given to me at all possible times towards the end of my very last meeting in which I had to leave early for a special assignment at the TV station that night. After making my last announcements on record (including my thanks for the granting of the award), I ceremonially resigned formally from the Senate. After getting my things and taking my placard, I walked out of the Senate chamber for the last time to a standing ovation by my fellow Senators and others present. Talk about a way to leave a place with class and honor—I couldn't have asked my God to arrange a final scene like that any better than He did for me that evening.

There were several major lessons above all else that my God impressed on me during my time in both Portales and Roswell:

(1.) I learned for myself not only how much my God really loves me for myself and who I am, but also what happens when your brethren who also love the same Lord you do don't just tell you how much they love you—but more importantly step up to the plate and show you themselves.

(2.) I found out the best way to practically apply such Scriptures at Matt. 10:29-42, Luke 9:57-62, and Luke 14:25-33 is to simply keep one thing in mind—that there's a price tag, commitment, and high cost required to become a true and real disciple of Jesus/Y'shua. Before you even dare undertake such a risky endeavor, you'd better ask yourself some very crucial questions: "Have I TRULY counted the cost of being His follower?", "Do I have what it really takes to seriously commit with all my heart, mind, and soul to do EVERYTHING He wants me to do—no matter what may come my way?"

(3.) I found out for myself that a REAL leader doesn't always have to have a big fancy title. In fact, it's truly amazing to see for yourself how even those you might otherwise perceive as outsiders and unbelievers may actually view YOU as a true leader THEY might admire! And it is an almost certain fact that people WILL take notice of your leadership capabilities IF first and foremost your primary focus is on simply being a servant to all.

(4.) I also saw demonstrated with my own eyes that it only takes ONE person to make a true impact and difference in the lives of others. Even if you see yourself small in your own eyes and as the very least in a particular group, He will enable you through His inspiration and guidance to serve just as much as I did in the Student Senate as the loudest and most influential voice in the bunch. They can run or hide from you as they wish—but if you do things right according to His power, they in the end WILL NOT have the option to say that they didn't hear a single word you said in the first place. THAT to me in my personal experience is a great indicator of how much your Christian example can truly shine the light of His glorious Gospel in the lives of others.

(5.)   Above all else, I was shown by God Almighty Himself the many marvelous things He very much longs to do for those who put their trust in Him.

All of these proved to be valuable lessons that I learned in my spiritual and physical incubators that were Roswell and Portales. I would later find that I would need these important foundational pillars to get through the massive storms that I would soon face in my life on the remainder of my personal journey that still awaited me.

[Chapter 8] [Albuquerque, NM: Learning From "Ifcomes"]

After I finished all the courses that I could at Eastern by the time my final semester in residence in Portales at the end of the 1991 spring semester was completed, I only had just two more final requirements left in order to finish my Music Business Bachelor's degree (and that included ALL of the Mass Comm courses I had to take for my Mass Comm minor)—the Corporate Finance course I could never seem to pass and the required necessary Music Business Internship job that I could never seem to find.

Dr. David Willoughby (my main Music Biz advisor) and I were literally working right up until the time I had to move out of my dorm and my mother and grandparents needed to pick me up to help me move back to Lockney. Three of Dr. Willoughby's particular favorite Santa Fe and Albuquerque contacts were worked to the bone in a last-ditch attempt to find a suitable job that would fill the bill for my internship. But it was to no avail—and I went back home to Texas empty-handed and with just two courses left that I had to have to graduate.

After I returned home, from there it was off to the job hunting trail I went. Trips were made to Lubbock to make contact with all possibly musically-related businesses (including stores, recording studios, and even radio and TV stations) to take care of the internship requirement. Similar contacts were made closer to home in Plainview and Floydada and even up as far as Amarillo towards the same end—but I came up with nothing but zeros. As the summer went on, I then had to start finding ANY job that would at least provide some cash so that I can finally finish the degree I started back in Portales. It got to the point where I even had to do a telemarketing job doing carpet cleaning sales in Plainview. (At least the boss on that one somewhat understood that I couldn't work on the Sabbath…)

But the pressure mounted to find a job—and my granddad in particular DID NOT like the fact that I told employers that I no longer could work on Saturday or on the Biblical Holy Days. It had only been within the past year or so that I had finally come out of the closet to my family about my WCG beliefs—and they certainly didn't hesitate to make their dissatisfaction known to me about it. My granddad was of the persuasion that the ONLY legitimate response that you should provide an employer who wants you to work ANY and EVERY day of the blessed week he/she wanted you to do was to respond, "HOW HIGH?" when someone asked you to jump. And any attempts to convince my granddad otherwise were essentially futile—despite the fact that I always offered to prospective employers my willingness to work on Sundays and other major national holidays as needed in exchange,

With this in mind, I took the notion to pay for a want ad in the Albuquerque Journal to entertain offers to find an apartment there. I also tried to reapply for more student financial aid to try to not only cover the costs of this, but also retake one more time the necessary Corporate Finance course I needed at the University of New Mexico (UNM) as well as enroll for the Internship course through a special cooperation agreement that ENMU and UNM had with each other.

I found that no grants were available back at Eastern—but instead that I had to take out student loans in order to do what I needed to complete degree requirements. In the meantime, I did get a few responses to the Journal want-ad—in which I eventually decided to commit to a furnished apartment several blocks south of the UNM campus. And it was just as well that I did—because I was itching to get out of Lockney as fast as I could again.

When August finally came and a new UNM fall semester was about to start, I packed up about several suitcases of my belongings, was then taken by my folks to the Plainview bus station where I said my goodbyes to them (for good, I hoped at the time, I admit), and left Lockney far behind again.

Oh—the directions from Plainview to Albuquerque, you ask? Of course—I'd better not forget that…The bus route directions went like this—I first had to go early in the morning from Plainview to Lubbock, then wait nearly 12 hours at the Lubbock bus station for the one and only daily connecting bus to Albuquerque. Then after loading most of my luggage that I was moving as carry-on stuff on board (in which I had to use two seats in order to hold those things—including my sax and keyboard), the bus went all the way up US 84 to Muleshoe, then crossed the state line in Farwell/Texico and then stopped in Clovis for about 15 or 20 minutes.

From Clovis, we continued west on US 60/84 to Fort Sumner, then in Fort Sumner turned right and went northwest to Santa Rosa. (FYI--It was already dark when we got to Santa Rosa.) We then met up with I-40 and continued west through Clines Corners and eventually went into Albuquerque itself—continuing on I-40 until we got downtown to the bus station (which was at the time just a few blocks from the Amtrak train station, I might add…) I then took a cab that went west onto University, then onto either Lead or Coal Streets (I forgot now which one specifically …but it was definitely one of the two because both of these are one-way streets going in totally opposite directions from each other...) until the cab finally dropped me off at the offices of Campus Property Management across the road near to a Smith's grocery store in the middle of the night.

When I finally got to the office, I was confused at first where my apartment specifically was—but at least the property management company left the key to my new apartment in the office box outside with a note where I could get to it and the apartment. I had to then first leave my luggage behind at the office, then walk down a couple of blocks or so to the new place at 2428 Garfield SE so that I can find where the apartment was. After finding that I had to go up a flight or two of stairs, I started the process (STILL in the middle of the night) of transporting all my luggage between the property office and my new apartment. And that was how my new life in the Duke City unceremoniously began.

If I thought life in Portales was interesting, then I really thought I'd hit paydirt once I got to Albuquerque. Besides my apartment's convient location to the grocery store and to UNM, it was also great that the Garfield Street Laundry was a couple of blocks away. I even appreciated the convient location of the Sun Trans city bus routes which I was able to use fairly often as well.

Once I got settled in to my new surroundings and also took care of enrolling in the UNM Corporate Finance course as well as my concurrent Internship registration, I then had to also wait a little bit on my financial aid to come in. Thankfully (even after the first of what would be many eviction notices from them), my new landlord understood the situation I was in as a college student and was willing to wait until my student loan check came in where I could catch up on my balance that would quickly go into arrears. I even during this time was able to go a few times into the nearby Frontier Restaurant on Central Ave. (I tell you—that restaurant was HUGE and stretched for an entire block or so BY ITSELF!) for a chess club that was held there to get back in touch with my love of the "sport of kings.

But one of the things that thrilled me most at the time was my new local WCG congregation that met at an Elks Club ballroom near University and I-25. This congregation was definitely a happening bunch artistically—AND I LIKED IT!! Felix Heimburg was the head pastor and Sam Butler (who was originally from Australia) served as the assistant pastor over a WCG church circuit of Albuquerque, Santa Fe, and Farmington. This place even had BOTH a choir AND orchestra (a rarity amongst most WCG congregations in those days). Ed Ronish (who also served as one of our local church elders) and his wife, Dr. Marty Ronish, led our church's orchestra in which a good number of them had been to some degree professionally trained or previously employed in either classical and/or jazz music—a perfect environment for a musician like myself to keep up his sax chops and yet still be able to play for God and His True Church.

We all had some seriously fun times in the ABQ congregation. For instance, on the Day of Atonement during what would normally be a lunch break between services, a group of us singles went to a park, spread blankets on the ground, and had what was called a "picnicless" picnic. We all just sat, talked, and had a grand ol' time…even on a day where lunch was not allowed to be served as part of the menu.

I also on one Sabbath I was in ABQ see some hot-air balloons flying in the air as a part of the Albuquerque Balloon Fiesta as a part of their big "balloon rodeo" right from the Elks Club parking lot. It's sure a sight to see when you get a chance—especially when you see hot air balloons like one I might have seen that was in the shape of Garfield The Cat.

Thanks again to Festival assistance, I got to go back to Big Sandy once again for the Feast that year. I was by that time beginning to get under some financial pressure from the landlord and other bills—but I still went to the Feast regardless. There were some interesting memories about that particular Feast trip when I went with Evelyn Timmons and her son and a couple of other brethren who were from California (one of them who was actually a freelance radio announcer).

The first occurred when I was told by Evelyn to be ready to go at a certain time when she would pick me up from my apartment. So I packed and was ready to go and waited by my phone and also checked outside to see if I could find her car driving up.

One hour went by—and she didn't show. Then two, three, four—still no sign. I was beginning to wonder if something might have happened to Evelyn and her son. Most of the day went by without any sign or phone call from her—and my bags were STILL packed and waiting.

Then FIVE-and-a-half hours later (on what should have taken no more than about a 30 minute to 1 hour one-way trip even with traffic from Rio Rancho to Albuquerque), they FINALLY showed up. Evelyn explained to me that they had a ton of trouble getting their stuff in their car and tying it down as well as getting that same car across the city limits. And so, later than originally planned, we started on our way to AC in Big Sandy, TX and the Feast for another year.

Our trip going to Big Sandy took even longer than expected because our California brethren insisted on stopping every two blessed hours—no matter where they were. Both of them apparently also had significant eye problems—with one of them wearing a prescription so thick you would have thought he actually had Coke bottles for his glasses frames. These two liked to stretch, move around a little bit, mosey on down, and take their time. Evelyn was the exact opposite, though—she wanted to get moving and keep going as fast as we could get there to the AC campus. She was the type that didn't mind driving for up to 12 hours straight with minimal stops for the bathroom, eats, and gas until we got to where we were going. Let's say that these two diametrically opposite travel approaches between Evelyn and these California guys mixed like oil and water.

Once we finally got to the big AC campus campground, the majority of this particular Feast for myself was basically a blissful repeat of the debut edition I had the previous year—but with a couple of exceptions once I checked in with my voicemail back home in ABQ.

The first involved troublesome phone calls from my creditors (my landlord being among them) for past due bills. The other involved calls from my mother and grandparents wondering where I was, why I hadn't called them, and if I had found work yet. When I finally called them back on a AC campus payphone, I reluctantly decided not to tell them the whole story and make them think that I was still back in the Duke City finding work INSTEAD of really being on a campground in the East Texas Piney Woods as I attempted to call them. Talk about putting a damper on my Feast fun—the pressures I faced back home seemed to catch up with me even here on the AC campus.

Then I happened to see Fred Acker, one of the brethren who was in the Lubbock congregation that I had met last year at this same place. I wound up confiding in him what was happening in my life right then back in ABQ. He graciously gave me in turn what was great advice and counsel at the time—"…Don't sweat it—it'll all work out." Fred's encouraging words helped lift up my spirit and kept me from not going into a complete state of panic even at the Feast over such things as eviction notices and credit card bills that I couldn't pay. From there, I was able to somewhat enjoy the remainder of this Feast without too much more incident.

When my Feast was over and we were all on the way back home to ABQ, Evelyn's car broke down somewhere around Eastland. We first spent the night at a local hotel. Then when the tow truck came, it was a good thing that I did have my credit card with me—because Evelyn sure needed it to pay for the tow truck and repairs. It was also a good thing that Evelyn was a AAA member herself—because she said that she would reimburse me for all of this when we got back home (thereby covering my own back).

There was two problems, though, with the tow truck—one, the nearest place that Evelyn could get her particular car fixed was back in Fort Worth; and two—there was room for only two of our party to fit into the tow truck. So it would up that I had to wait on the next eastbound bus from Eastland back to Fort Worth while Evelyn and her son got in the tow truck. I was stuck outside at the Eastland bus station for quite a while until that bus finally came.

Once upon my arrival back in Fort Worth, Evelyn, her son, and a couple of WCG brethren she had found all brought me to this couple's house. I by that time didn't even have much on me except the clothes on my back and the stuff in my pockets I originally had on my person at the Eastland bus station. The lady of the house was so sweet to even wash said clothes after I had to first take them off and then get underneath the covers on a pallet since until those clothes were washed, I was literally jaybird naked. (When I remember myself in this scene, it still amuses me to no end after the fact…LOL…)

After I was finally reunited with my newly-washed clothes and able to put them back on, Evelyn, her son, and myself were privileged to spend the night with this sweet couple who really helped us in a desperate time of need. After the car was finally fixed, our original party was then able the next day to resume our journey back to ABQ.

(FYI—Evelyn DID hold up her end of the deal on the reimbursement after we returned home and she got her check back from AAA. We then met up at my bank at the time—where she signed over her check to me and I was then able to deposit it in my account. (I don't think, though, that I was actually able to use if to repay the credit card—for I had a much more urgent need at the time.)

I also enjoyed the Spokesman's Club group that our ABQ congregation had in which Mr. Butler directly supervised. I really got to develop more in the area of speaking skills there that I had started in the Roswell club. There was one time during a Club meeting in which one of our Club leaders asked us this interesting question: "What ministerial rank are both Mr. Butler and Mr. Heimberg?" We had answers from all over the ballpark. I amazed myself when I turned toward Mr. Butler at that meeting and gave this answer: "You and Mr. Heimberg are both of the same rank—preaching elder. The only difference between you two is your function—with Mr. Heimberg being the head and you being the assistant." Even Mr. Butler seemed impressed at my answer to a question that stumped the rest.

We in the orchestra even did something radical for us (especially since we didn't observe Christmas—but in which most of us who were alone appreciated anyway)—we actually had a NON-Christmas Eve party. Marty Ronish wasn't just a good church orchestra leader—but she could really cook to boot. That party was a penultimate example with a spread of Mexican food that would rival any Mexican (or any other) restaurant. The sight and taste of the chili rellenos she made in particular is still a treasured memory to this day.

The coming onset of winter in the Duke City brought about some lean times financially for myself. But I did finally come across an outfit called the New Mexico Music Industry Coalition that I was able to do an unpaid internship with to help with my degree. It did allow me to meet a few people in the music industry in the ABQ/Santa Fe area that gave me a taste of the practical side of the business that I only learned in theory about in Portales.

Folks like Jonathan Knight (who was an active musician and songwriter from Grants as well as the leader of the Coalition) and Jose Ponce (who while I was there managed to get a job for an independent R&B record label as a publicity and promotions representative) were gracious in allowing me to see the day-to-day challenges in working in a very demanding and fickle music industry environment. My internship for the time I worked with Jonathan and the Coalition consisted a lot of not only office duties, but also writing a few articles for the Coalition newsletter. (At least it helped me later on when I needed writing credits in creating my personal bio sheet..)

Jose in particular also told me about his past experiences starting with only a high school education at a radio station and having to muscle in to an industry that can be very clannish at times. It sometimes was hard to watch—but those were much-needed doses of reality meant to help me realistically reevaluate my career goals in the midst of a changing corporate environment.

I also had the privilege to briefly try to do some side work as a booking agent for Angelito Productions who managed a musical stable of primarily Tejano and

Spanish acts. I say TRY because I wasn't even able to do a single booking or anything for them. But I did at least get to meet yet another Miss New Mexico. This one had been in the Miss USA system (different from the Miss America system that the other two Miss New Mexicos I personally knew had went through). She happened to be the secretarial person for several other small businesses that were in the same office area that Angelito was in. She also did dance classes for kids on the side.

But since I didn't have a paid job, I was forced to really start looking for ANY paying job FAST to not only keep one step ahead of the landlord, but to try to pay for all of my continually mounting expenses (of which there were many). And on top of it, I flunked the necessary Corporate Finance course AGAIN. And if that weren't enough, I started having problems with my vision on top of that. Things in my right eye started looking like I was seeing through a frosted glass outside. I couldn't practically do anything with my vision (or anything else in my life, it seemed...), but I still had to maintain a decent front for the folks outside.

And the job search trail was a pretty hard one to hoe at times in ABQ—especially without a car. I eventually wound up having to take up the offer of one of my fellow Spokeman's Club members to work in his janitorial company that he was a district manager over. For about a couple of months, I had to work overnights at a Kmart basically cleaning the bathrooms and the lounge area while the rest of the crew buffed and waxed the floors.

It seemed like a humiliation to me at the time having to clean toilets as the TV in the lounge was set to an all-night news channel when I should be working instead for a record label—but it was a way to help keep the rent paid and food on the table for a little while. But when the district manager had to resign, after a while I had to also quit because I couldn't keep up with the crew who wanted to constantly hurry up and get things done as quick as possible. I was more concerned with the quality. But the pressure to keep up the pace was a bit too much for me.

So back on the job-hunting trail I went...I eventually wound up for a few weeks helping some sort of political consulting firm do phone surveys of political candidates for the 1992 Democratic primary. But the work went down and I wound up losing the job as well.

After New Year's Eve, the beginning of the end started for me when I had to have cataract surgery on my eyes (without any medical insurance, I might add). I later realized too late that the ones who did that surgery may have botched it—because I still see a small hair that looks like a sliver that floats around in my eye even today.

Through various circumstances, I wound up in Albuquerque, NM having MAJOR problems trying to support myself financially and just couldn't seem to get things right. I was a little bit too proud to take ANY job that didn't fit into my little plans that I had made. I also took on medical expenses on a surgery on my eyes that there was NO way I could even think of paying off anywhere in my lifetime on my own because I had no insurance. And there were a number of times where I had to ask the church for help in keeping my landlord paid so that I could stay in my apartment.

But what was even more of a mistake than anything else I had done was to try to buy a car from someone at work whose title had not changed hands in at least four previous owners at the time I got it (...who knows if it was possibly stolen...) with money I couldn't realistically part with because I should have used it to take care of my rent (which I was SEVERELY behind in at the time). (By the way, I also had no insurance on the car as well.) Guess how much that car cost me? The grand total of $375 got me the following:

(1.) A car that was a VERY expensive ride for me because I only got to drive it twice since I couldn't afford the insurance, license plate, or other stuff that I needed in order to use it legally

(2.) Two traffic tickets that eventually required me to spend about three days of community service to pay it off by picking up trash on the side of the road near Rio Rancho and also the northwest side of Albuquerque

But it also caused a couple of other people in my church some problems, too, because:

(3.) It wrecked a relationship of trust between one of my friends in my church and an auto mechanic he dealt with (which, incidentally, he took that car I bought on a mechanic's lien because I couldn't afford to pay for the repairs on it)

Other events escalated to a time that I remember well and which served to be one of the major turning points of my life. One day, when I was in my apartment, the associate pastor and one of my fellow members of our Spokemen's Club knocked on my door and asked to talk to me for a little bit. What followed next was the equivalent of a confrontation that someone in Alcoholics Anonymous might give to a drunk.

They sat down and expressed their concern for the financial condition that I was in. I tried to deny it and put a good spin on it, but they saw right through my disguise. It was to them the last straw when I pulled that stunt with the auto mechanic. Then, the friend said something that has haunted me since throughout the years-- "'Ifcomes' don't work in Satan's world." What this man meant by an "ifcome" is "'...if it comes, I will pay.'"

Mr. Butler during this conversation revealed to me that before he became a minister that he had once worked in finance and had plenty of experience in dealing with situations with mine. As a result, Mr. Butler asked me to hand over my checkbook and basically allow him to handle my financial affairs on my behalf. By that time since I didn't have too many job and financial options, I didn't have much choice.

And just as things couldn't seemed to have gotten worse, I had to go to my eye doctor with a big black spot in my right eye. The diagnosis—a detached retina…the worst eye ailment according to the doctors that I could have because if it wasn't fixed IMMEDIATELY that I would soon go blind. But I didn't have the money now to even pay the doctor bills or the surgery. So I was referred to the University of New Mexico Hospital where I had to be in the hospital recouperating from this brand-new surgery on my right eye.

Strangely enough, this time in the hospital painful as it was—especially after finding out from the doctors after the surgery that I couldn't read, drive, walk very far, or do any heavy lifting for several weeks until the retina healed—was also a sort of peaceful break from the financial turmoil that awaited me back at my apartment.

The only ones from my church that even came to visit me in the hospital or that even knew of my situation were Mr. Butler and the Spokeman's Club friend that were literally guiding my hand there during the remaining time I was in Albuquerque. I had asked my pastor to call my family to let them know that I was having the surgery--and he did so. My mother and grandparents came all the way to Albuquerque to see me in the hospital (which now I am very thankful that they did in spite of my horrific attitude towards them at the time). They urged me to come back home--but I was very unwilling to at that time because my personal desire was to try to fight the situation as best as I could.

Sad to say, I regretfully treated them in a disrespectful manner. They gave me what I now realize was probably an easier way out of that situation--but I was so stubborn and set in my ways at the time that I absolutely refused to take that road. Little did I know then that the very road that I did not want to go (even if I was dragged kicking and screaming) was the ONLY road that I was allowed to take at all.

The minute I came back to my apartment from the hospital, it was if whatever bottom that was still under me at the time completely collapsed from under me. The eviction notices were more and more taped on the door; any attempts by my associate pastor to find me an alternate place to live in the area were soon met with failure; and any possible hopes for finding ANY job were for now completely out of the question. Plus I didn't have a phone to boot—so no employer could contact me at all even if there was a job for me to go to.

It was when I went to services at church that next Saturday when I got what seemed to be the worst news of all. The associate pastor talked to me and told me that the ONLY option that I had left was to do the ONE thing that I DID NOT want to do under ANY circumstances--go back home to Lockney. That was to me the most devastating blow to me and my pride at the time--it meant running away from a problem that I thought I could solve.

But I also saw later on that staying and fighting that problem would be an even worse disaster. When it came down to the nitty-gritty, the most unpleasant decision I was forced to make was this: to either swallow my pride and go back home to a situation that I thought was absolutely unbearable (or at least uncomfortable) OR face the music of eviction and complete homelessness on the streets of Albuquerque, NM and going through who knows what. Basically, I had no choice at all--so it was time to surrender and give up the fight and go back home.

In the final day before Mr. Butler, the Spokeman's Club friend, and I made my arrangements to go back home, I stayed overnight with another of my fellow church members in his apartment. I saw the things that he had in comparison to what I didn't and only then began to realize how far down I had went. And the worst part of all was this--this same young man was the last one who said goodbye to me at the same bus station that I had arrived in Albuquerque about eight months earlier (which seemed to be a lifetime ago).

The bus ride from Albuquerque back home to Plainview, TX was the LONGEST bus ride of my life. 6, 8, even 12 hours seemed to be eternity--for I was still holding on to the faintest hope of going back to the place of my personal defeat while at the same time feeling like I WAS in my spirit dragged kicking and screaming back home to Lockney. When I arrived later that night in Plainview, I was welcomed home by my family, but I didn't feel that welcome back home. From that point on, my own combination Great Tribulation/Siberian Exile period began—with plenty of time for me to learn some valuable lessons through the school of hard knocks that I only started listening to much too late.

[Chapter 9:] [Lockney (Part III-W. Locust St.) Going Back To Siberia--My Siberian Exile/Great Tribulation Period]

The longest bus ride of my life from Albuquerque back home to Lockney would start a period of time for me that I even to this day still call my combination Siberian Exile/Great Tribulation. Even as I very reluctantly was forced to come back home, my pride and ego felt like it was being dragged to the gulag after the debacle I had just been through in Albuquerque.

First, it's once again directions time. Starting from the Duke City that I did not want to leave at any cost, I went regardless on the Greyhound bus back down east on I-40 with stops in Santa Rosa and Tucumcari before crossing the Texas/New Mexico state line around San Jon. Continuing from there, we go all the way into the TNM&O bus station in Amarillo to change buses for the southbound back to Plainview (where from there the bus continues on towards Lubbock, Big Spring, San Angelo, and eventually San Antonio).

Along the way, this particular southbound bus going down US 87 makes very quick stops in Canyon, whizzes by "the town without a frown" (otherwise called Happy), stops again briefly in Tulia, and then passes by Kress. As we start coming towards Plainview we first notice the wide spot in the road called Finney Switch at 87's intersection with FM 788, then the Excel meatpacking plant at FM 3183 (which was eventually renamed Cargill Meat Solutions--but which was closed just about a year or so before this book was written) on the left hand side of the road. [Author's Note: Please keep in mind that I'm writing this as is was at the time-- before I-27 was eventually expanded to the north to extend into downtown Amarillo.]

The massive Producer's Grain Association grain elevators remind you that you're certainly now approaching the northern city limits of Plainview. From there, you'll immediately take the Business 27/87 exit (also known as Columbia Street) and continue south on Business 87 until you get to the light on 11th Street. Hang a left at that light, proceed east for three more blocks, and you'll find yourself very late at night at the Plainview bus station across the street from the Texas Employment Commission. (Neither of these are now the case at the time of this writing.) My mother and grandparents then met me at the bus station where I was then taken from there south on Broadway to...

We then continued on 70 back to Lockney on the exact same trial that I had originally traveled just months before to get away from this place. Coming back to Lockney, we then turned left on FM 97 (which, FYI, the mile marker sign says "Flomot--32 miles"). FM 97 then curves around east and passes the Lockney Co-op Gin before crossing the railroad tracks.

A couple of blocks further to the east, my mother's and grandparents' houses can be seen on the right side of the intersection of Sixth and West Locust Streets--the place of my incarceration in what I now call "Siberia". I went through what I first thought was my party time in ABQ (where I desperately wanted to go back to--but now that route, as I would later find, was closed). But from here, I would be required to endure what I would eventually consider to be the roughest three-and-one-half years of my life.

Now in the one place I DID NOT want to be--back home again in Lockney--the chickens came home to roost on all the seeds I sowed back in ABQ. My old unpaid debts were piling up faster than I could even pay (which was virtually nothing at all). The two major right eye surgeries I had back in the Duke City (one for a cataract and another for a detached retina) not only provided me with the privilege of more debts to pay since I didn't have money at the time to even get insurance...much less pay for it, but also required me to avoid even finding a job (much less working at anything) for several weeks until I finally was able to recouperate from the detached retina surgery I had at UNM.

The doctors told me before I left ABQ that I was not allowed to do several things for 4 to 6 weeks--no reading, driving, bending, or heavy lifting. Strangely enough on top of my prescribed "do-not" list, the doctors told me that watching TV was definitely okay and was actually quite helpful to my recovery because of the minimal effort and strain it caused my eyes.

Pretty soon after arriving back home, one of the first items of business I had to take care of (thanks in part to a convoluted, complicated bureaucratic process required in order to get indigent medical assistance with the Texas Tech University Medical Center (TTUMC)) was the need for more eye surgery--this time an infection in the buckle of the right eye. With this surgery came yet another brief hospital stay at TTUMC in Lubbock and even more doctor and hospital bills that I couldn't pay. I wound up having to go through even more paperwork--first at the local level, then eventually to the Texas Tech Health Sciences Center itself since Lubbock was about the closest place to Lockney to have the comparable services of an opthamologist. I even had to on top of that actually apply to Social Security for disability for the sole expressed purpose of getting a DENIAL so that I could qualify for this other assistance. (That's your tax dollars at work for you for sure...)

Even after the immediate medical rodeos were finally dealt with, I still had several simultaneously several situations staring me back at the ranch. No job, no car, and no money all combined meant massive problems in even being able to simply go to church on the Sabbath as much as I would have liked. Add to that a family that was quite anxious for me to find a job--ANY job--even if it meant violating my conscience and religious beliefs. And I was still looking for that elusive radio, TV, or music biz job that would be my ultimate ticket out of this morass. But most of the time, I came up short.

I did manage with the help of my family to make an appointment later that summer to meet with the Dean of the College of Business at Eastern (who also happened to be one of its finance professors) to take a challenge exam to get rid of that one pesky remaining Corporate Finance course that still separated me from finally receiving my Bachelor's. After I was finally cleared by the eye doctors to read again, I started rereading and studying the Corporate Finance textbooks and notes from the now THREE times I previously tried to take the course (twice at Eastern and once at UNM). This stuff STILL made as little sense to me then as the previous times before.

The day came when I went back to Portales to take the exam. I met with the Dean--and then promptly wound up flunking THAT exam as well. After grading the exam, the Dean asked me--"Would retaking this course again be of any help to you whatsoever?" Considering the long distance I had to come back there with my mother and grandparents in tow, I promptly replied, "No--absolutely not." The Dean said, "Ok...let me talk then to the Dean of the College of Fine Arts and see what we can do." Later that summer by the skin of my chinny-chin-chin, I FINALLY at long last got my hard-earned degree from Eastern in the mail back home. I didn't get to have a graduation ceremony this time to receive my degree like I had at SPC. But by that time, I didn't particularly care. The main thing was that I was finally through with college for now and was officially an ENMU alum.

But the fact that I now possessed two college degrees didn't necessarily guarantee smooth sailing for me from that moment on. In fact, it was only the start of many troubles to come. For instance, graduation from Eastern left me with two different student loans to pay for a combined total of around $6,000. Add that to my mounting debts from my recent time in Albuquerque--and you might as well thought the judge had thrown the book at me financially with a prison sentence that would take years for me to serve.

Before I go any further with this discussion, I need to formally define for you what I mean when I seem to talk about the hometown of my birth as "Siberia" or a "Siberian prison camp". In case the Lockney City Council and/or the Lockney Chamber of Commerce are reading this--please DO NOT infer or misunderstand what I'm saying about Lockney. I'm NOT necessarily talking about the TOWN of Lockney being "Siberia". Understand that the use of the term "Siberia" whenever I may use it for the rest of this book is only referring to a particular period of time in my life when I was struggling with the loss of personal independence (financial and otherwise) combined with tensions with my family over my overt WCG doctrinal beliefs and also frustration at not being able to find ANY decent employment (whether in my desired career path or not).

And how about adding a few more spices to the mix? For one, my continued permanent stay with my mother very much put all of her government benefits at immense risk--especially Section 8. I remember times when I would have to act like I lived with my grandparents next door when my mother had inspections from the housing authority so that they wouldn't get wise to the fact that I was actually living instead with Mother.

My grandfather especially would be one of the most challenging people I ever dealt with during my harsh Siberian prison sentence. The best way I can delicately put it without too much disrespect or dishonor to my family is probably this--that he was an extremely interesting and difficult character to put up with. His behavior and attitude towards me showed in what I perceived as some extremely troublesome and peculiar actions.

One of them was his penchant of requiring you to do something to help him around the house [whether it involved painting, doing something in the garden, or helping him in his shop doing something mechanically or construction-related (neither of which was ever my personal forte by any means)] at the most inopportune times. It didn't matter if you were watching TV or doing something YOU wanted or needed to do. The unwritten code in his presence was that YOU HAD to stop and drop EVERYTHING you were doing RIGHT THEN no matter what--OR he'd get madder than an old wet hen at you...and you were automatically in trouble with absolutely no appeals allowed. He ruled the whole roost over everyone--and made it clear and obvious that he did so.

Also, another thing he tended to do would have been really comical to think about--had it not also been madly infuriating and frustrating at the same time. In the winter when there was any sort of amount of ice and snow on the ground and you needed to go out of the house and do something in the car, he'd absolutely put his foot down and say something like this to you, "...It's slicker than an owl's butt out there!" Immediately after he said that, you knew better than to risk his wrath and set foot even one inch outside of the property.

But what was even more infuriating about this entire scenario was that the same ice, sleet, and snow that he seemed to keep you bound and shackled with never seemed to stop him from going into his pickup and making what he thought were his mandatory twice-daily visits to the Dairy Queen to meet up with his precious coffee klatch. You would not believe the many times both Mother and I would scratch our heads and incredulously roll our eyes over the senselessness of his words and actions towards us.

I'll spare you all of the detailed stories about "Papa" (partly because I want to be cautious of spreading what the Jewish people would call "lashon hara") except for two memorable instances that are forever etched in my head. One was on a day where he required me to help dig up tree stumps that were in the grassy area between our two houses. I remember him and I having to really get in there with the shovels, dig real deeply around each stump, and once each stump was loose, rock the stump back and forth until the root system, stump, and all were out of their former place. We especially had a real hard time getting one of these stubborn stumps dug up (despite my best efforts to dig around it) which led him to provide this infinite piece of wisdom: "…Son, if you're going to get it, you've got to get it by the roots."

But my all-time favorite recollection of Papa that was severely annoying and irritating to the rest of the family (but now still strangely amuses me when I think of it) was the peculiar ways he tended to act in severe weather situations. The procedure around our house since my grandparents had the basement in their house that also acted as our storm cellar was usually for Mother and myself to go next door if the weather outside was getting too bad. I am convinced to this day that if my granddad had known about the existence of the Weather Channel at the time, he would have been an absolute addict to it 24/7. (And it wouldn't have been due to the extremely gorgeous and attractive lady meterologists broadcasting on that channel these days neither.)

But what really took the cake about Papa's strange behavior were the path of his movements around the house and property during a severe storm. Imagine him CONSTANTLY pacing through the house in this manner: front porch, back porch, back porch, front porch—stand outside for a few minutes and look stupidly at the clouds and lightning….THEN back porch, front porch, front porch, back porch—watch the severe weather update on TV! (and you'd better hush while he was watching it or he'd really get mad at you…)…front porch, back porch, back porch, front porch--sit in chair and snore!—and on and on this peculiar pattern with him seemed to go until HE finally determined that it was safe for us in his opinion for Mother and myself to go back to our house. When these things happened, the rest of us really wanted to first pull our hair out…and then promptly choke him with it—anything to stop this insanity—PLEASE!!!

And on the church front, relations between myself and the rest of the family at the time were still the equivalent of a game of constantly butting heads. Christmas Eve in particular usually proved to be one of the hardest times of all for me personally—with immense family pressure seeming to indicate that my attendance at this and other family functions was essentially obligatory and mandatory on my part while I in the meantime resented the idea of being involved in a holiday that was in my eyes (and also in the eyes of WCG HQ at the time as well) immensely "pagan".

I was very grateful for what we in our WCG area congregations called at the time "Amarillo Weekend" where several congregations in our region would all meet at West Texas State University in Canyon to meet to conduct a lot of our regional youth group sports activities [which in WCG at the time was called YOU (Youth Opportunities Unlimited)] and Sabbath services that were usually held in fairly close proximity to the Christmas Day weekend since (even though we WCG members at the time didn't formally observe the holiday) a lot of the brethren were off during that particular time anyway.

The rare and few times that I was somehow able to get to go to regular Sabbath and Holy Day services (especially when we did have the privilege of eating out afterwards and fellowshipping with brethren) was a pretty good treat indeed. And even finally being able to go to the Feast of Tabernacles in Tucson in 1993 (thanks again primarily due to Festival Assistance) was even better for several reasons other than the obvious fact that I was able to in a sense got to go on a sort of much-needed vacation leave from my Siberian jail cell.

That year for the Feast, I was able to join Lucy and Bower Wood (two of our Lubbock congregation's elderly and disabled members—for the record, they were mother and son), Dorothy Holbrooks (otherwise nicknamed "Dot"), Dorothy's daughter Jana Devlin, and Jana's daughter on our trek to the Grand Canyon State. I stayed overnight at Lucy and Bower's house in Cotton Center where we awaited Jana and her daughter's arrival. The five of us then loaded ourselves in Lucy and Bower's handicapped van where we then went to Dot's house between Seminole and Hobbs to pick Dot up.

The journey going to and coming back from Tucson was remarkable in a couple of ways—one of them the enduring hours upon hours of Bower's endless supply of puns and bad jokes; and the other coming as we approached the military checkpoint nearest the White Sands Missile Range east of Alamogordo, NM.

If you think you've seen traffic jams, you've never seen one that quite like the one at White Sands. Imagine this scene: You're in the middle of the desert with nothing around you for miles and miles. Suddenly you see a road sign that says that EVERYONE MUST STOP because you're now approaching a missile range. Oh, by the way—you also just happen to be going down a major four-lane highway which is basically the combination of US Highways 70 and 82 converged into one road. Military police (MPs) are stationed at these checkpoints with a major stoppage of traffic BOTH in front of you and also behind you. It's hotter than the blazes in this widespot in the desert—and absolutely NO ONE can move until the MPs say so.

You also eventually find that leaving your engine running for a long period of time is totally useless. So you eventually find yourself turning off the ignition and rolling down the windows to save both gas and the water in your car's radiator. The average MINIMUM wait time for this entire process (for BOTH ways, I might add)? At least 45 minutes to an hour each way. And did we ever see a single missile fired? NO—just a bunch of cars parked on the side of the road—that's all. (Your country's tax dollars once again at work indeed…)

When we did finally get to Tucson, this particular Feast had some decent memories for myself. One of them was the Park Inn Santa Rita. My reservation to this place was arranged for me as a part of my Feast assistance—and the Church definitely did it right in putting me up there. The Park Inn not only offered a decent continental breakfast, but even free drinks and hors'de'ouerves in the evening. I also while at the Tucson Feast got to go to a place called Old Tucson where I not only got to see some actual Western movie sets, but even wound up getting wet in the middle of a gullywasher.

I was also able to hook back up with some of my old ABQ church friends at one of our Festival activities and reassure them that I was still somewhat alive and well back at the homestead in Lockney (despite my continuing present financial difficulties). It was a real boost to me personally to get to see them again one more time.

This Feast was also remarkable in the fact that it was the year where Dr. Ross Jutsum of the Ambassador College music department formally debuted WCG's new church hymnal. The hymnal was a combination of the former WCG hymnal that primarily consisted of hymns originally composed by HWA's brother, Dwight plus a number of new hymns that Dr. Jutsum wrote just for this hymnal as well as other popular hymns. All of us who attended the Feast that year who were baptized members were privileged to receive a personal special edition copy as our Feast gift from the Church that year. (FYI—that original hymnal copy still sits on one of my bookshelfs at my apartment to this very day.)

Other than these occasional breaks and respites away from the house, a good bit of my time during my Siberian exile outside of the many hassles and burdens placed upon me by my family was spent in a continuous unavoidable merry-go-round of employment instability in which it was very rare (if not next to impossible) to find any decent job that could generate any sort of decent living for myself that would last any longer than two months at a time.

Fairly soon after I came back to Siberia (hmmmph…--I should say Lockney) and was cleared by the doctors to work again, I did finally manage to work at one radio job…doing ad sales for the local radio stations in Floydada. I found out the hard way for myself the truth of what one of my mass comm professors at Eastern said in class one time about radio ad sales—that it was "…the easiest job to get in radio—and simultaneously the hardest one to keep." I even tried to get this job to include production work to some degree so that I could at least make minimum wage for part of my work there—but wasn't successful in the attempt.

The stations (which had a traditional country format on the FM and a southern gospel format for the AM) was bought by a guy out of the Coleman, TX area on a loan and desperately needed sales and revenues PDQ. The trouble was (I found out later) that in comparison to the other sales reps, I had the worst territory of them all. Floydada was obviously the most coveted area for us as a station—but someone else had that territory. I wound up going to OTHER area towns outside of Floydada trying to do cold calls on businesses (and even at times trying to compete with the Plainview stations)—and ended up striking out a lot.

The pay basis for that particular job was a "draw on commission" (defined as basically a salary on loan that would be paid on future commissions). I only made during my very brief tenure with those stations ONE entire sale—which was to a close family friend who was the manager of a grain business. I soon found out how ill-fitted I was for the sales profession when I was fired after just a month. Not only did I wind up OWING the station owner for the loan off commission I was forced to take (which he did forgive), but the constant trips I had to take in my mother's car caused a lot of wear and tear on it plus the costly additional burden on my grandparents (financial and otherwise) via long-distance phone calls on the phone that both my mother and grandparents mutually shared that I had to make for station purposes didn't exactly make my mother and grandparents happy campers neither.

The Siberian employment merry-go-round continued when I was able to get another job—this time as a cook at Sonic. Needless to say, I didn't last long there neither. One of the assistant managers proved to be particularly annoying to all of us employees. We were expected as a team to literally get an entire fast-food order from start to finish in three minutes or less—or the you-know-what would hit the fan by management.

This particular assistant manager took the cake, though, in constantly harassing us with this tirade—"HURRY UP! HURRY UP! HURRY UP!" If we even fell behind on the burger grill or messed something up…ohhh, the tongue lashings by this man were sure soon to follow. When I told my mother (who herself has over 20 years of experience as a short order cook and waitress) about this situation, she incredulously told me, "…You can't do that and expect to have a decent burger that is done like that." Nevertheless—the expectations were high—so unrealistically high that I was eventually fired from that job after only a month.

The Siberian employment carousel continued into another position as a house supervisor for a men's substance abuse halfway house facility called Serenity Center. I had absolutely no clue about what someone going through substance abuse problems actually deals with until I started working at that place. And the clients themselves even wound up (like it or not) being my teachers—since I didn't have that type of experience as a part of my personal background. One of them in particular was a real Mountain Dew soda addict. (I know that because when I had to borrow a few bucks from him one time I had to wind up paying him back in 2-liter Mountain Dew bottles.)

They even let me know in no uncertain terms that I wasn't as great of a breakfast cook as I thought I was. And while I was there, two of the other guys who had been alcohol and drug addicts who eventually became house supervisors wound up flipping out and skipping on their duties leaving me holding the bag. I was (guess what?) let go from that gig after just two months.

My employment situation at one point actually got to the point where even my own church pastor began to think that I might have something seriously wrong with me mentally and psychologically and even recommended (despite my reluctance otherwise) that I pursue treatment with Mental Health and Mental Retardation in Plainview to see if I could further refine my social skills. Even THAT didn't help the situation one bit.

Eventually, though, I was able to find a couple of small jobs that would at least provide some small amount of desperately needed income that would enable me to make whatever small payments I could to my creditors (especially towards my student loans which I had to continually put in forebearance status due to my continually troublesome financial condition). These I was able to use as I continued what seemed to be my never-ending mandatory job search.

One of them was writing feature articles as an area correspondent for the Lubbock Avalanche-Journal (A-J). An "area correspondent", FYI, in the eyes of the A-J was basically their high-falluting term for a freelancer. At times when I'd see an interesting story in the Plainview Daily Herald, I might myself try to contact those same individuals to do a similar interview and story for the A-J. I'd also at times stop by the Hale County Courthouse to see what was shaking as far as court cases were concerned that might be of interest to the broader regional audience that the A-J reached.

Among some of the most fascinating interview subjects I had a chance to work with included a Plainview lady lawyer who was an ex-Marine and who also participated in long-distance horse racing competitions and a Catholic priest whose rectory was actually located inside an old bank vault. It was a lot of work having to transcribe all the cassette tape interviews via handwriting first unto regular paper and then arrange everything to type up a suitable article via an old manual typewriter my grandparents used to use many years ago. But from my Siberian vantage point, ANY sort of money that I can get (no matter how small the check might be) was truly better than nothing at all.

I also benefited for a while from being a substitute teacher for the Plainview Independent School District (PISD). Even if it was the sort of position where I was basically on-call, at least this was one place where my two college degrees (even if they weren't in education) did work to my advantage a little bit due to the pay scale for each job assignment I performed on their behalf.

For the PISD, I worked at a real garden variety of assignments ranging from kindergarten to special ed to all the way up to high school. And I didn't even go to college to be a teacher in the first place (although my mother and ESPECIALLY my grandparents really made a federal case over me on this...mainly for monetary reasons, of course). And despite my best efforts to convince my folks otherwise about how current conditions in our current educational climate and environment truly were, those efforts to convince them were of no avail.

A few of these sub teaching experiences stand out most in my mind. One of them was when I had to sub for an elementary special ed teacher's aide that helped students who had major problems in reading. During one of these periods, one of the Hispanic students definitely had a hard time with one of his reading assignments that I was helping him with. Each time this little fella tried to sound out words and/or letters (bless his heart), he grew more and more frustrated at his failure to read and understand the assigned story as he should.

During the course of my interaction with this student, I kept noticing that he was squinting his eyes so much that I actually wondered in my mind if he actually could see the words on the pages he was reading. Remembering my own recent medical rodeos involving eye problems that were still relatively fresh on my mind, it didn't take a rocket scientist to figure out that this little one might be having similar vision problems, too. Further inquiry and investigation (and his response to my questions) only served to firmly confirm these initial personal hunches.

Later on before I left for the day, I brought this to the attention of the main teacher and suggested that she might consider approaching this student's parents about seeing an eye doctor to find out if the lad might need glasses or corrective lenses of some kind—and that there were appropriate social services available to them if they didn't have the money to do so. The main teacher was very appreciative of my suggestion and said that she had been dealing with this boy's problem for months—but was at a loss as to what to do in that situation. She assured me before I left that she would bring this up with the parents at the first available opportunity she had to do so.

The most humorous sub experience that I had, though, by far was the day that I had to fill in for half a day for a fourth-grade teacher. One of the assignments the regular teacher had me to give to the class was to have them draw a picture of what they wanted in their idea of their perfect room. Little did I know what I was in for next…

After giving the class the assignment and giving them a few minutes to draw their pictures, I then had everyone show and share their pictures to the rest of the class. The sum total of the overall content of these pictures was absolutely amazing to contemplate.

Most of the pictures—believe it or not—involved the use of water to some degree. One wanted various objects involving the sea and water. Another wanted a sailboat in water—while yet another student even went so far as to want to flood and drench their entire room with water. This very peculiar trend amongst these students' pictures developed so much to the point where I eventually had to ask the class the following question: "…Okay, now—is there anyone here that had a picture of their room that wanted something else BESIDES water?"

One of the boys raised his hand up in response—and I called on him. I asked him, "Okay—so, what would you want in your room?" His response was classic as I exasperatingly rolled my eyes, "WATER!!" Everyone else in the room cracked up at that comment.

When the regular teacher came in during lunch and I was filling her in on what happened before I left for the day, I told her personally about this little incident. She responded, "It figures—the whole class is a bunch of comedians." (And you don't think an entire group can have a collective personality? I stand confirmed with these hunches.)

There was also one sub incident at another elementary school within the PISD that would not only affect my future ability to do further assignments for the PISD, but would also months and years later cause me to be fired from another job for bizarre reasons that were truly beyond my direct control.

As I did a sub assignment on this one particular campus, I had to go down the hallway at one point in the day to use the restroom. For some reason, I must have had something either spilled…or something must have slipped from my grasp…Whatever the situation was, I reacted to it by saying the word "shoot". I didn't think anything much about it at the time.

That was UNTIL I got a call from the main office saying that they were doing an investigation on me in which the principal and her staff alleged that they actually heard me say an inappropriate four-letter word of profanity on school premises while performing an official capacity for the District. I responded to the investigator that the charge was totally baseless because I not only knew what I actually said (and the difference between the two words), but because my religious beliefs with WCG would strongly prohibit from even wanting to think such a ridiculous thing—much less say the word the principal claimed that I had said.

The charges to me were so baseless that I was even pleasantly surprised that even when I had to tell Papa about the situation that he actually came the closest he ever did during his lifetime in offering any form of moral support to me at all. He told me, "…Well, if you didn't do anything, then you don't have anything to worry about." That statement of support from Papa was between very rare and never in my eyes—for RARELY IF EVER did he ever try to say anything positive to me within my immediate presence and hearing.

I later found out from another source that the principal and staff of this particular elementary school had a pretty unflattering reputation within the District for being a pretty highstrung and snooty lot for anyone that was outside of their particular social circle. I don't know why (despite my best attempt to express to the District administration my willingness to meet personally with this particular principal and attempt to resolve and straighten the conflict out), but this principal for reasons unknown seemed to have it out for me. I don't know if it was some sort of personality conflict or something else entirely…but I kept getting the sense that she for the weirdest reasons just didn't like me.

Later, I saw this very bizarre and seemingly meaningless incident come back to bite me once again in a couple of ways. The first was when the PISD's final results of their investigation against me determined that I should still be allowed to remain on the substitute teaching list, but under the proviso that I would not be allowed to sub anymore for this particular school campus.

The second time, though, was when it really hurt after I became a school crossing guard for the city of Plainview. One day, I wound up having to fill in for the guard who regularly served this very same school campus. The same principal happened to see me and apparently went ballistic at the sight of me (even though she didn't let it show to me when she saw me)—because I wound up losing that job as well thanks in part to her.

Job situations such as these caused what seemed to be my continual two-month max tenure job carousel to spin out of my control here in my Siberian prison camp. But even these didn't hold a candle to yet another unanticipated medical problem that would further eject me off the merry-go-round.

Around the fall of 1994 fairly close to the Feast, I happened to go on one of my periodic nightly walks around town designed to not only get me exercise, but also some semblance of personal privacy outside the house. One evening, I was in the middle of one of these walks and was even just a few blocks away from home. Then, I tripped on a curb—and my right ankle really started hurting. At first, I thought it was just a sprain and that it was simply pain that I could easily walk off.

But when I got closer to home, the pain in my ankle started getting worse and worse. By the time I got home, my foot was hurting so bad that I decided to try soaking my feet in salt and hot water. At first, I felt some sense of relief from the pain. But in the overnight hours, I found out the hard way that soaking my feet in hot water probably wasn't the wisest move I could have made. In fact, the pain in my ankle got so bad that my mother and I had to ask my grandparents to drive me to the Methodist Hospital emergency room in Plainview.

The doctors' diagnosis? A fractured right ankle in two places—and surgery was required to do it right away. (Just when I thought things here in Siberia couldn't get any worse—they did.) The cure? Surgery, then a one-week hospital stay. Then bedrest and pain medication for the pain for 4 to 6 weeks and sleeping in a bed with my injured right foot in a cast sky high with LOTS of pillows underneath said foot. The ONLY place that would fit the bill was one of Mama and Papa's spare bedrooms in their house.

So my right foot was elevated sky high and with the pain in my foot so bad that I couldn't even walk on it, But what was even more challenging about the situation was that since I was way too heavy to walk on crutches, I actually had to use the walker to even go to the bathroom on top of it. And for a while, I was temporarily forced to move from general population on the Siberian prison camp to a sort of solitary confinement cell waiting on the day I could finally take off the ankle cast.

If my ankle was any indication of something, it was this: that I should not expect my personal Siberian Exile/Great Tribulation to end any time soon. I was in a sense imprisoned here in Lockney not only by past seeds I had sown, but also by the weirdest and most bizarre current medical and financial circumstances that no one in their right OR wrong mind could have dreamed up. (But I assure you…I didn't…I truly didn't. It just happened to me that way…that's all.)

Even after my recovery from my ankle surgery was complete, the chains of Siberia still shackled me and kept me from escaping its cruel clutches. My creditors were my jailers—and my medical problems served as judge, jury, and executioner over me and my case. And the unanimous verdict was in—that not only would my release be much longer in coming than I first thought, but that the worse of everything was still yet to come. And I found out later that I surely wouldn't like the final results of it all neither.

[Chapter 10:] (Lubbock, TX) Going Into The War Zone After "The Changes"

While my life was still in personal turmoil in what were my immediate surroundings in my Lockney/Siberia emotional prison camp, of all times, this was when what seemed to be the one place where for even the briefest of time I was somewhat free began to itself change into something that I totally did not expect. And what seemed to be for all practical purposes my "god" (though I didn't think so at the time) that was the WCG organization began to crumble right before my eyes.

To show more what I mean, we'll now have to go to the place where it originally happened. To do so, we'll need to leave Lockney from my mother's house in order to get there. First, we'll have to go east on Locust for two blocks until we get to Fourth Street. Then on Fourth, we'll continue south until we dead-end with US 70, take a left, and then an immediate right in order to continue south on FM 378 out of town with the Lockney Meat Company in front of us on the left.

We'll then stay on FM 378 for a good 25 to 30 miles (Yes, I know—there's a TON of curves on that particular FM road…) until we get into the city limits of Lorenzo. We'll continue through Lorenzo's downtown district until we get to the combined roads of US Highways 62 and 82 and Texas Highway 114. We'll turn right at the stop sign and then merge onto 62/82/114. We'll stay on this road all the way until we get to the eastern outskirts of Lubbock. When we get to the intersection of Loop 289, 62/82/114 diverge into two separate roadways—with US 82 forming Parkway Drive/4th Street and 62/114 becoming 19th Street. [FYI for those of you in the Lubbock area—keep in mind that I'm for the purposes of this chapter still pretending that neither I-27 or the Marsha Sharp Freeway has been built yet…which was the situation at the time this all took place.]

We will go onto 62/114 as it eventually becomes what is 19th Street. We'll stay on 19th all the way past the South Plains Fairgrounds and downtown Lubbock until we get to University Avenue. At University, we'll turn left and continue south until we get to South Loop 289. We'll turn onto the Loop 289 westbound frontage road, then get into the left lane and look for the Quaker Avenue exit. At Quaker, we'll turn left, then do another left to get onto the Loop eastbound frontage road. As we get into the right-hand lane, we'll pass Indiana again and then right by Pyramid Plaza see our next location—the Holiday Inn Park Plaza. At this place, I'll tell you what it's like to see a church completely change and a "cult" begin to die.

First, though, let me put the historical bones in place on this skeleton. In WCG congregations worldwide towards the end of 1994 and the beginning of 1995, we were eventually required in our local congregations during our regular services to watch what we now in WCG/GCI history call Mr. Tkach, Sr.'s famous "Christmas Eve" sermon which was originally taped in Atlanta. (For us hearing these things, this was definitely ironic timing, to say the least.)

I seem to remember that the day we played the sermon video in Lubbock that due to the length of Mr. Tkach, Sr.'s sermon (FYI—it was about THREE hours long just by itself!), that we had to adjust the format of that day's service significantly as a result. Also, just as personally memorable to me was Mr. Tkach, Sr.'s opening statement on that video: "Brethren, I can tell you that this is going to be a very long afternoon." Then, he started talking about the differences between the Old Covenant and the New Covenant in a way that we as WCG members had NOT previously heard up to that time.

Soon after that, due to my ever-continuing problems on a consistent basis about getting a ride to services (i.e.—usually meaning for me that there was absolutely no way for one of those members to pick me up at my house in Lockney and/or no way for me to come to Plainview myself to where I could meet either one of my consistent rides at their house because I wasn't allowed to drive my mother's car or one of my grandparents' vehicles), there was about a couple of months where I literally had no choice but to stay home despite my best efforts otherwise. Of course, there had been other times in the past where this had happened to me—but not to the extent I faced then. My main contact with the Church was through local church sermon tapes and Church HQ publications from Pasadena—so I had absolutely no clue what was truly going on in my own church surroundings….UNTIL..

Passover and Unleavened Bread of 1995 came—and I finally was able to ride with one of my fellow Plainview members again to go to Spring Holy Day Services. As she and I were traveling the earlier aforementioned route to Lubbock and I was trying to catch up with her about what was going on in the Church, it was only then where I began to realize what was truly going on behind the scenes locally. The way she talked about recent events was so distressing and disconcerting to me that I wound up asking her this point-blank question—"…Do you mean to tell me that we're about to step into a war zone?" She didn't answer the question directly—but her subsequent words, actions, and reactions basically told me yes. And what happened next would be a Holy Day that for me will live in infamy.

Here at the Holiday Inn Park Plaza, our combined Roswell and Lubbock congregations gathered together for combined services that Holy Day. The services that day seemed at first to be very much like they used to be when I first started in WCG with one remarkable exception—our recently resigned pastor was still in attendance, but had basically stepped out of the formal limelight and didn't speak at all for anything that day for the strangest of reasons that I didn't know about at first. Instead, it seemed like all the local church elders and deacons did all the sermons and sermonettes that day. All the sermons in the first service were constantly emphasizing the old familiar stuff about the Old Covenant that most of us members already knew instead of the new things about "the changes" that Pasadena was giving us these days.

Then, a group of our brethren went to eat lunch at a nearby Furr's restaurant—and it was only then when the full impact of "the changes" Pasadena was proposing finally hit me. During lunch, I heard a conversation between that same recently resigned pastor and one of our fellow members who I had really gotten close to for several years (even to the point of staying one weekend at his house) started talking about some upcoming conference in Indianapolis that was coming up that I wasn't previously aware of. These two seemed to be talking about it as if they were talking amongst themselves in some special secret code. Hearing all this strange talk only further increased my suspicions and added to my own personal distress.

But what really broke my heart was when this same friend started talking to me in ways in which (unbeknownst to me) he sounded like he was actually saying goodbye to me. When I asked both of them questions about their views of whether or not they supported the current things that Pasadena was espousing, their individual and joint actions were extremely disheartening to me to say the least.

The afternoon service followed in similar fashion to the morning service. We all said our usual greetings and other stuff to our fellow brethren not realizing that it would possibly be the FINAL time I would ever see a good number of those same folks again. And I also realized too late that for some it was going to be their last hurrah in WCG for all of those speakers the way they preached that Holy Day.

Why was that the case? Only after that Holy Day did we find out that a spiritual tornado had hit our local congregations—and hit it HARD! Many of the same brethren that I saw during that Holy Day of Unleavened Bread were by Pentecost no longer attending WCG at all and had instead joined a brand-new splinter group called the United Church of God…and neither of our groups would ever be the same again.

The damage to Lubbock? Guess who led the charge for most of those brethren to quit? That same former WCG pastor I ate with during that last Holy Day! Talk about having to live out the words of Psalm 41:9…."…Even my close friend, someone I trusted, one who shared my bread, has turned against me."…all of us who still stayed and didn't jump ship in Lubbock really felt this firsthand. This pastor took with him to the newly-formed UCG one of our local church elders, several of our deacons, and at least half of our congregation—and did it not only literally behind the backs of Pasadena, but also unsuspecting members like myself. The other remaining local church elder decided to stay put in WCG, but he and his wife opted to instead move and join their daughter and son-in-law in Arizona. And the Roswell congregation from what I heard didn't fare much better either—with only one local church elder still left that was loyal to Pasadena. Talk about breaking hearts and stabbing us in the back…And Pasadena was sadly forced to now send another replacement pastor to help clean up the mess that former pastor made of our Lubbock congregation.

How did that former pastor do it? It was only later after the dust settled that those of us still left in WCG found out. First, he and others that would eventually become dissident pastors basically tried to stall and hold off preaching and teaching on the changes as long as possible. Then the pastor all of a sudden decided that he needed to preach a sermon and/or Bible study series on a safe, noncontroversial topic like marriage and family. Then, he suddenly resigned as pastor—but said that he would stay active in the congregation. After that, the local church elders started running the show. Then, UCG forms—and they start leaving WCG completely. We found out later that our Lubbock congregation wasn't the first or last to see this happen—but that all of those things were a pretty common pattern amongst congregations who experienced similar problems to what we faced.

After David Carley, our new pastor, came and took over the reins of our Lubbock congregation, Pasadena wound up giving him the direct supervision and responsibility of FIVE—yes, I said it—FIVE different churches in TWO different states. Imagine a pastor being forced to shoulder the responsibility of THIS local church circuit: Hobbs, NM; Lubbock; Midland; Abilene; AND San Angelo, TX.

Even with local church elders in each congregation—no one surely in their right (or even wrong) mind envied him for shouldering this enormous task. Talk about wear and tear on your car—not to mention the emotional and physical strain on Mr. Carley and his wife, too....After about a couple of years of this routine, he understandably burned out and wound up resigning.

Mr. Carley wasn't the only one facing this gruesome local church reconstruction task in the middle part of 1995. There were a number of other post-split WCG pastors who faced similar dilemmas. Add to that massive budget cuts due to decreased church revenues, a constant stream of people leaving for UCG and other splinter groups, and gaping wounds among everyone else that was left that were still fresh and raw—and you can easily see why during that time most of our WCG membership that I personally knew seemed to resemble a bunch of emotional basketcases.

I might be jumping a little bit ahead of the full story on the surface—but it is also necessary to mention Mr. Carley's successor while we're here talking about local pastoral leadership in Lubbock. In the book "Transformed By Truth", Dr. Tkach, Jr. mentions the role that Tom Lapacka had as WCG's Church Relations Director during the time when Pasdaena was first in the process of implementing the new doctrinal changes. Well, I can tell you that Mr. Lapacka himself also left a little legacy with our Lubbock congregation. Mr. Lapacka was allowed by Pasadena to transition into part-time WCG employment and start a business to support himself and his family here in Lubbock.

Mr. Lapacka was of great help to me personally while I was in the process of being approved as a Prison Fellowship volunteer and trying to get involved in prison ministry. But as a pastor, he really started doing things that for us as WCG members were probably a little too much on the deep end for most of us.

For instance, he kept wanting us to do communion like we were a LUTHERAN church. Mr. Lapacka started talking about stuff such as "transubstantiation" and other gobblydegook that were foreign terms for a church body that was used to doing The Lord's Supper (which we celebrated on the evening of Nisan 14 and called Passover). More sermons such as Luther's view of grace kept popping up within our congregation's midst.

Before too long, you'll never guess what happened next. Mr. Lapacka did what seemed unthinkable to most in our eyes—he actually resigned his part-time WCG pastorate here in Lubbock to become the new pastor of a LUTHERAN church!

And once again, our little remaining remnant of what was still our Lubbock congregation was thrust right back on square one aimless and adrift.

And because my immediate family was still very hostile to me being involved with WCG, I couldn't even feel like I could count on them for any emotional comfort and support whatsoever because I had to keep a front for them about the Church that they were still not happy in me being a part of. With all the other personal turmoil in Siberia still surrounding me, this new pressure of adapting to the post-split WCG environment added additional concern and uncertainty that made it possible for my faith in God to fail and grow weak due to circumstances that seemed to be totally out of my control.

For folks like me still trying to pick up the pieces and make sense of what was now the new WCG, it was sure a long, hot summer ahead. And the Fall Holy Days were still approaching fast around the corner. This time around, they sure didn't seem to be the Festivals that they used to be…and it was apparently clear that we were about to attend our own funeral.

[Chapter 11:] [(Fort Worth (Part I)—The Feast of Funerals That Changed Everything]

Have you ever known someone who you loved and cared for deeply die right before your eyes? How about some dreams that you made sacrifices to prepare for—were you disappointed when your previous hopes and dreams were dashed? I do. And it's not a pretty picture, either. Our next tour stop all the way to Fort Worth demonstrates the trauma and aftermath of what happens during a church split—and, more importantly, what happens when you're forced to face that something you once loved and worked for has died.

In order to do this, we'll start from our current location in Lubbock going east on South Loop 289 until we find the 62/82/114 exit. We'll take that exit and prepare for a VERY long drive straight as an arrow east towards Fort Worth (which, FYI, will take us at least 6 to 8 hours by car—not counting pit stops and meal breaks, of course). We'll be able to stay with State 114 all the way until we get close to Bridgeport and the D/FW Metroplex. After that point, I'll have to ask you to rely on your GPS system to get us from there to downtown Fort Worth until we get to the Fort Worth Convention Center. (Besides—I'm not that great when it comes to following directions in the D/FW area anyway.)

It was here at this very convention center where I experienced in 1995 a Feast of Tabernacles that I'll always remember. First, let me back up about a few weeks before (especially during the period between the Feast of Trumpets and the Day of Atonement) to better set the stage here. More WCG members in a number of congregations were leaving as fast as they could for UCG. Then, if that weren't enough, we heard word that Mr. Tkach, Sr. had died of colon cancer. I definitely remember on the morning of Trumpets when I was staying in a Lubbock hotel room while spending the night in town for that particular Holy Day. One of the local church leaders who picked me up that morning for Trumpets services told me of Mr. Tkach, Sr.'s death—and it was the first time I had heard about it from any source.

That fall was an especially sad time for those of us who were WCG members. And Mr. Tkach's seemingly quicker-than-expected death and subsequent funeral was the perfect metaphor for what we all had faced through most of 1995. The more info we kept receiving from Pasadena and other sources, the more that some of us really began feeling that we all in WCG were losing our way.

During that year's Feast, I actually had the privilege of going with Charles and Ellen Spoon and riding with them back and forth between my home in Lockney and Fort Worth. I was only able to go that year because of what we in WCG called "Festival Assistance" (this was a special WCG fund that usually came out of member contributions that we called "third tithe" at the time that was set aside to help brethren like myself at the time who were economically disadvantaged as well as the elderly, disabled, etc. attend the Feast). I was able to stay that Feast at a place called the Care-A-Lot Inn about a mile's walk from the Convention Center.

There were sure some memorable things about this Feast in Fort Worth. For instance, most of the talk and conversations amongst the WCG members who did attend that year centered on questions like these: ""…How many members did you lose after the split?'; "What about (such-and-such congregation)?'; or 'What about (such-and-such pastor)?'"

The average consensus amongst those I had a chance to ask these same questions to was usually this—most (including my own Lubbock congregation) lost a MINIMUM of between a third and up to a half of their congregation's membership due to "the changes"…and a good amount of the time in a number of instances, at least one local church elder on average (and even in some cases the pastor himself) left WCG for either UCG or another splinter group. And believe it or not, there was even one TX congregation that I heard about that not only lost their pastor, BUT ALSO up to NINETY percent of the entire congregation.

Just as there was turmoil in the Convention Center, there was also a little controversy brewing outside, too. There was this wacko group of folks that had parked a bus on the Convention Center parking lot in which some elderly gentleman (in this instance, I regretfully will have to use that word VERY loosely…) was blaring things on the loudspeakers and bullhorns attached to his bus that called Mr. Armstrong such nasty things as a "maggot-infested-you-know-what" (I'll spare you the detailed graphic terms here…) and declared that Mr. Armstrong and anyone else who followed him would burn in hell. I and other brethren who found themselves subject to this verbal tirade kept our mouths shut and/or had a good laugh over it…but I know what I literally would have liked to shout out through my tears to that guy and those working with him, "…If you only knew what we are going through right now—you wouldn't be saying things like that!" Talk about inner pain—it was as if Satan himself was using these folks to really kick us when we were already down low enough as it was.

And to add insult to injury in a literal sense, in the middle of the Feast as I was on my way to services one morning at the Convention Center, I happened to trip on a curb and fell on the same right ankle that I had hurt the previous year. I was wearing my dress clothes including my cowboy boots –and it got harder to walk in them the closer I got to the Convention Center.

It felt like a dull pain in my ankle at first—but the more I stood in my boots (especially during services), the more I hurt. It even got to the point where I had to go in to the Anointing and Counseling Booth to receive prayer for healing. It just so happened that Mr. Carley was one of the ministers that were on duty at the Booth that day.

During my private session with Mr. Carley, the ankle got so painful that he decided that I needed to go to the emergency room. Unfortunately due to my dire personal financial situation, I once again didn't have any medical insurance. Mr. Carley then told me that in this situation the Church had funds available to take care of this. So he took me to John Peter Smith Hospital—where after several hours of waiting and examination, they determined that (to my relief) all I had was a severe sprain on my ankle and that I needed to keep the ankle elevated until the swelling went down…but that it should be ok by the time I got home and saw my primary physician (which I didn't have).

From there, I spent most of the last part of the Feast basically lying in my motel room with Mr. Carley and others graciously paying for room service to bring meals to me either to my room and/or when I would go down the elevator on my crutches to the ground floor restaurant. It was a good feeling for me personally when I was finally able (with some assistance, of course) to attend services on the Last Great Day.

But this Feast in Fort Worth wasn't all just a big list of problems. Before I tripped and fell on my ankle, I was at least able to go to a very interesting Family Day at Medieval Times that was full of jousting and eating an entire medieval-style meal (including a whole chicken—WITHOUT UTENSILS, I might add). I also got to go on an afternoon bus excursion to the Ambassador College campus in Big Sandy again (where I had gone to my very first two Feasts) and even leave a message for Judy (the same young lady I mentioned in an earlier chapter whom I was a close pen pal with who at the time was herself attending classes at Ambassador ; but who was gone attending the Feast some place else). (This, of course, was right before Ambassador was finally closed and sold to someone else.)

During what I call this Feast of Funerals came an occasion that not only grabbed me musically, but also spiritually, too. One Festival service I attended had things that we in WCG had surely not seen or experienced—and was also the very things I saw my God use to speak some much-needed words of comfort and encouragement.

The service was primarily music-oriented featuring an audio-visual presentation with slides containing pictures and/or the lyrics that accompanied the actual songs sung by the original artists. To really understand the major whammy impact this particular presentation had on me, I need to first give you a quick idea of the way those of us who were in pre-split WCG viewed the use of music during worship services.

During any service before the split, we seldom if ever played ANYTHING but either hymns that were in the official WCG hymnbook or selections of classical music. And no self-respecting WCG member at that time would even dare think of playing ANY sort of music even in their private times EXCEPT either classical or country. (FYI—an unconfirmed rumor had it at one time while Garner Ted was still in WCG that one of the main reasons why country was somehow still considered kosher in WCG circles was because Garner Ted liked it and wanted to keep it. But again—I can't confirm this or verify this claim's accuracy...so you didn't hear it from me...)

During the presentation, two particular songs really grabbed my attention—"The Anchor Holds" by Ray Boltz and "Still Listening" by Steven Curtis Chapman. Before this time, what was called "contemporary Christian" music and/or "Christian rock" were definitely verboten in our sight. But God used of all things Messrs. Boltz and Chapman to set me straight. It woke me up finally to the fact that there ARE other Christians outside WCG—and there's a bigger world in His eyes.

Especially, though, when I saw the way that Mr. Chapman's song "Still Listening" was displayed as a part of this presentation, it was a light bulb that went off in my head. And then this fact hit me—when everything you know is collapsing around you (and to me at the time, it seemed like it was)—there's only one place you're allowed to look—and that's up (to Him, that is). THAT was when I finally started on my road out of exclusivity and isolation—and came into His glorious light of acceptance. You see—for once in my lifetime, I didn't have to jump through hoops any longer to get to my Abba Daddy—for He was already running towards me in ways I didn't know then.

Back home, my WCG church home was collapsing. I couldn't find a steady job that would allow me to be off on Sabbath to save my life that would last any longer than a couple of months at a time. And I also had to constantly butt heads with my family because of what I believed. But now I was forced to confront the fact that my God had some bigger purposes to all of this than my own personal comfort and fulfillment of my personal dreams and desires.

And it was this—had I not been going through what I was back home in Lockney, I might well have been one of those that would have instead went to UCG. I started beginning to realize how insensitive I was in judging other Christians (especially my own family) as "Christians so falsely called" just because they didn't hold to the same WCG beliefs that I did. Even those in my own family…boy howdy—how roughly did I treat or disrespect them sometimes (even though that's the way I thought I was supposed to do it as a loyal WCG member).

Only when I was forced to face those facts were my Siberian emotional prison gates beginning to open up for me just a little bit even as I had to mourn the loss of the original dance partner that had brought me to this dance in the first place. Myself and other WCG folks in a sense had the funeral service of our previous pasts right here in Fort Worth. It was now out with the old WCG—and in with the new—and things for myself and others would never be the same again.

And at this Feast of Funerals, I had to necessarily bury some judgmental attitudes that were hindering my relationship with not only the very God I served and worshiped, but also the family and friends I loved. But it was also simultaneously at this series of group funerals where I truly began to live the life that I had so longed to live for years.

[Chapter 12:] [(Plainview—Part I—FM 2286/"Spann Road") Finally Leaving Siberia FOR GOOD!!

Throughout the final part of 1995 and the first part of 1996 after I got back from the Feast in Fort Worth, not too much changed in my financial and employment situation. Still the same ol' same old—I was STILL stuck in my without walls Siberian prison camp, never seeming to get a job that lasted any more than two months at a each for each (most of the time due to bizarre reasons beyond my immediate personal control). Other than occasional substitute teaching assignments and Avalanche-Journal area correspondent article submission opportunities (which even eventually got phased out as well due to the A-J's decision to open a new Plainview office that housed a full-time reporter), I hardly had much income at all to speak of come income tax refund time because I hardly made enough to even qualify for it.

But a chain of major events starting in the springtime of 1996 would finally start the ball rolling towards my final release from Siberia. The first one was when I got the call from some lady from Anderson Merchandisers asking me to come in to Plainview for a job interview at Wal-Mart (then located at the time near Stonegate Shopping Center). I was then hired after that to become a part-time merchandiser for Anderson—first starting for a couple of weeks working with baseball trading cards, then being eventually moved over to work with magazines in that same Wal-Mart store. It was nowhere near full-time hours—but it least was FINALLY a steady source of income that I could rely upon (even as I continued doing occasional substitute teaching assignments for the Plainview ISD). The first anchor was down.

Then after school started that following fall when I finally saw that this Anderson gig might actually be able to get me somewhere, I was informed that it might also be a good idea to consider applying for Section 8 government housing assistance with the Hale County Housing Authority. So my long-awaited search for apartments in Plainview finally began.

Before I go further, it's time for the directions again in order to see where that apartment search took me. We finally get to leave and go west on Locust Street in Lockney all the way out of the Lockney city limits (YAY!!!) until it dead ends on US 70. We'll stay on 70 for a few miles until we get to Aiken at the intersection of US 70 and FM 2381. We'll then proceed north for a few more miles until it intersects with FM 2286 (or as many of the area locals prefer to call it—"Spann

Road". Don't ask me why…because I don't know either.). We then turn left on Spann Road and continue west for 11 miles until we find the Plainview city limits…

where FM 2286 then passes Plainview's "barrio district" and finally dead ends at FM 400 (North Date Street) right next to what used to be a Jolly Roger, then afterwards a Friends' convienence store. (At the time of this writing, it was the location of a liquor store that has now long since closed.)

As I awaited the final results of my apartment search and status of my Section 8 application, I wasn't able to attend that year's Feast of Tabernacles primarily for two reasons: the first being once again financially-based in nature due to my most recent change in employment; and the second being that due to what happened the previous year in WCG with "the changes", I wasn't able to get Feast assistance like I had in the past. I did get to, though, go to some of the Holy Day services that were held in Big Spring (the most central point possible for what was still Mr. Carley's incredible two-state, five-church circuit at the time).

During one September weekend that year, Lockney High School held its quadrennial Homecoming weekend—and it just so happened that my 1986 graduating class was also going to have its 10th-year class reunion as well. The Lord instructed me to go ahead and stay home to go to it and even added the following instructions with it: "…This may be your last chance you may ever see some of these people ever again. Say your goodbyes—because after this, you'll be leaving Lockney FOR GOOD!" I struggled to understand the impact of these words from Him—but nevertheless did appreciate and enjoy gathering with some

171

of my old classmates once again and catching up with what had gone on in their lives.

My Plainview apartment search continued with one major criteria—I wanted a place to rent which I would not have to be responsible for paying utility bills, but instead be able to have one central rate in which everything (utilities included) would be encapsulated in one full price. There was also another factor looming with this major decision. My mother and grandparents basically told me that the minute I moved to Plainview, I would no longer have access to a car. That meant that I would from there on out start having to get used to walk EVERYWHERE I went. So a close location to places like the grocery store became a must.

I finally found such a place at a complex on East Givens Street owned at the time by Warrick Properties. With help securing one of these apartments from Section 8, I was able to obtain an efficiency for a grand total of less than $225 a month with all bills paid INCLUDING water, gas, lights, AND even some basic cable. My folks weren't necessarily too thrilled at first with the looks and specific location— but for the Plainview market, it was the ABSOLUTE cheapest I could find (especially considering that most of the other HUD-eligible places usually had either a much higher price tag on rent AND/OR didn't meet my exact criteria of the concept of "all bills paid").

I then had to wait for Section 8 approval as well as get the money together that I needed in order to pay Warrick the necessary amount for initial deposits, fees, first and last month's rent, etc. But my wait FINALLY ended just before Thanksgiving. November 16, 1996 would later become a sort of second personal Independence Day for me when for the last time I left Lockney and what had been my Siberian prison camp behind and when my mother and grandparents helped me move my stuff in my new apartment on Givens Street. I did have to come back home that following week for Thanksgiving—but except for any necessary brief visits home, I was in essence a FREE man once again. No having to constantly report to my folks….I can now go to church on the Sabbath with much less hindrance than I used to have because now both of my usual rides to church didn't have to go to Lockney if necessary to pick me up.

During what I would afterwards call my Siberian Exile/Great Tribulation period, I kept praying to Him to help me find a decent job in my career field at least in Lubbock or Amarillo to where I would be closer to church. But instead, He decided to shift my personal residence axis just 15 to 20 miles down the road to

Plainview—which by virtue also automatically put me almost equidistant to BOTH Lubbock AND Amarillo. And if I needed to take a Greyhound bus to either place, all I had to do was purchase a ticket and then wait for the bus downtown.

On a cold November day in my apartment, I was never so grateful to God for anything in my life. A brave new world of possibilities now awaited me outside my new door. Back in Albuquerque three-and-one-half years ago, I nearly lost everything I had and left the city in disgrace and disgust and feeling like I was being dragged kicking and screaming back home to Lockney. Now in Plainview, I finally got the Divine second chance to have something I lost back in New Mexico—FREEDOM!

There's a saying I once heard that says it so well—"Political freedom without economic freedom is merely an academic exercise." I saw the truth of that statement when I moved to Plainview. My Siberian Exile and Great Tribulation had finally and mercifully come to an end in my new place and hometown. With this second chance, I resolved to do one thing above all else—to NEVER EVER go back to the Siberian torture chamber I had just left behind again. After all, it was my long-awaited and delayed personal July 4th. There weren't any fireworks displays by any means—but once again I was FREE AT LAST! And in the end, THAT'S what mattered to me the most anyway.

Chapter 13 [Plainview—Part II—Sam Hearn and Givens Streets] Eviction Notices—How I Had To Learn About God Being My Provider

We actually won't have to go very far from where we stopped at the end of the last chapter to get to where we need to go next now that we're finally in Plainview. (And, FYI—for the rest of this tour, Plainview will now serve as our primary home base location as well.) All this short trip will require is a quick right onto North Date Street from our present FM 2286/"Spann Road" location. As we go right onto Date...

...the road will immediately curve around Date Street Housing (DSH) (or as some of my fellow Hispanic locals might still call them—"the campasitas" or what once was Plainview's version of the labor camps that a number of agriculatural migrant workers used to live in).

At the very next street north of us (Givens Street), we'll turn left and proceed west until the end of the block where...

....Givens intersects with Sam Hearn Street. To the south of us, we'll still see the north side of the DSH apartments in view. Across the street, there's a vacant lot on one side and the main sanctuary of Happy Union Baptist Church on the other. Right here at the Country Village Apartments (now unfortunately deserted and abandoned) will be our next tour stop where we'll spend time focusing in on what I faced in the initial months and years finally getting readjusted to my long-awaited personal freedom in Plainview. We'll also talk some about the numerous economic, employment, and transportation obstacles I was forced to face after I moved here to my new home.

A little bit of the history of this particular place first—this actually used to be some of the former buildings that used to be a part of the old Amarillo Air Force Base before they were moved here sometime in the 1950s or 1960s. For many years, this used to be referred to as the "Givens Apartments" way before I moved here.

As for me, the sad memories of my months in Albuquerque and the still-fresh scars of my recent Siberian experiences wound up being part of the baggage that I had to take with me to my new apartment here at Country Village. For about the first eleven years, Apartment #308 on the east side of this complex was home. But then in 2007 because of the physical deterioration of the entire building that #308 was in, I had to move to the next building across the parking lot to #209 for the rest of my time here.

The same division of time also reflects the number of landlords the place went through while this was my home. Warrick Properties first owned this place from the time I first moved here until not long after I had to move to #209. There used to be a saying here in Plainview that held true—"…J.B. Roberts owns one-half of Plainview while John Warrick owns the other half." I just so happened to live in the half that the Warricks owned.

I will publicly say this about the Warrick family (especially about the senior Warrick). In my personal dealings with them over the years, I will at least highly commend them for being solid, locally concerned Christian businesspeople that have attempted to be as fair and cooperative in their business dealings with me as I have been able to do so with them. I've not always at times seemed like one of their greatest clients—but I have appreciated their willingness to cut me as much slack as possible until I was finally able to appropriately catch up with any balances that I had been in arrears with them at various times in the past.

The entire family overall in Plainview has been very active in a number of civic and religious endeavors—with the senior Warrick having himself been active in the local Gideons' camp and even preaching himself at our local prison units for years until his death a number of years ago. John's son, Randy, continues their family tradition of local involvement in his own way with his own involvement in one local church as well as our Emmaus Community here.

After my move to #209, Country Village began to go in a state of flux for my last three years here—first having been bought by someone in San Antonio for a short time until the new owner unexpectedly died of a sudden heart attack, then for the last two years by the pastor of a nearby local church (which I will not identify here for personal reasons) until the physical condition of this place eventually forced me to move across the street to DSH in June of 2010.

But back again to the new world I faced during my arrival here…one of the big scars I carried of my Albuquerque experiences was a carefully developed fear of eviction notices (either left on the door--or worse brought in person by Mr. Warrick himself). I even for a while put on my front door one of the eviction notices I received while I lived in Albuquerque to remind me of my former Waterloo there and how I did NOT want to move back to Lockney AT ANY PRICE!

But eviction notices weren't the only thing that stared me straight in the face in my new Plainview frontier. The chains of my old debts and financial bondage weren't too far behind me—so much so that I eventually had to find a lawyer to file for Chapter 7 bankruptcy.

After some research, I finally found a lawyer that was willing to take my unique case. It took YEARS, though, for this case to be formally filed due to the time it took (which to me seemed like FOREVER) for me to pay the required fees necessary to file the case in federal court. There were even times where the absolute MOST I could send was five to ten bucks at a time per paycheck.

FINALLY in 2005, due to upcoming changes in the bankruptcy laws, my attorney decided graciously that I had paid more than enough in fees and waived the balance of what I still owed due to time constraints and the urgent need to get the case to court before the laws changed—and I was finally able to make the necessary office visits to my attorney to get my case filed in federal court. One Saturday that year was particularly memorable because I had to go into the attorney's office in Lubbock and look through all the legal papers my attorney was to file on my behalf. It was only on that day where the full weight and magnitude of what I was about to do hit me.

As I went through these bankruptcy papers and had to start signing them, I thought to myself in absolute shock and dismay, "…I am about to ask the federal government to literally forgive me of $30,000 worth of debt? What am I thinking?" I sat dumbfounded at the startling realization that I owed THAT MUCH money to that many people all at once since I left Albuquerque. It was definitely one of the hardest pills I ever had to swallow. Paradoxically for me, bankruptcy in comparison to all of the roller coasters I had went through in recent years was actually somewhat of a joyous personal event—but still bittersweet at best.

Then just as if I didn't have enough balls to juggle, let's add all the required financial rectal exams I continuously had to undergo in order to maintain my eligibility for Food Stamps and HUD Section 8 Housing Assistance. And let's not forget either the other additional bureaucracies that are required should you bleep forbid need other forms of food or emergency rental assistance (especially in cases where the eviction notice is on the door RIGHT NOW and you're out on the street in three days or less if you don't get completely caught up on rent).

You're wondering what I mean by "financial rectal exams"? For some of you, about the next closest example that might illustrate what I mean by that phrase is to ask you the process you have to through each year when you have to file your taxes. Some would quip that preparing for a tax audit is about as much fun as preparing for a root canal. Well, I'd say that you should be so fortunate to only have to do it once a year. Imagine if you have to do the exact same stuff every three MONTHS for food stamps (by itself) PLUS an additional separate time for Section 8 AND add a detailed "white glove" inspection of your apartment on top of it. Oh—and each time you have to get special help on food or rent in emergency situations, you're ALWAYS asked for proof of income (i.e.—meaning paycheck stubs or bank statements) and other detailed information that makes filing your tax return seem like a walk in the park.

Now let's add a few well-intentioned bureaucratic limitations to the mix. Now don't get me wrong—I need to work with my hands as much as anyone. But what if despite your best efforts, you can't find a job AT ALL? Or worse, you fall under a technicality like I have in the past where if you do not work enough VERIFIABLE hours to qualify under "welfare-to-work"? Not all of us are COMPLETE deadbeats or substance abuse addicts that are forced to receive government assistance, you know. Verify this type of income....send proof of that...sometimes I wonder if having to file for help from bureaucracies is just as much work as trying to find work.

And don't get me started on the business of "...if you'd just try and apply yourself—there's tons of jobs out there."—that is, if you'd like for me to remain in a half-decent social mood. Not that such self-help advice doesn't help at times— but sometimes there's only so much of a bootstrap you can pull up before it tears. And in case you're wondering, I HAVE worked at various places at the bottom. The problems usually occur the most when you try to reach for the top at the same time you're also forced to work from that very bottom.

Maybe at this point, I'll illustrate through a few more employment experiences that I went through during my first few years here in Plainview. In the last chapter, I mentioned that I finally got a part-time with Anderson News to merchandise magazines for our local Wal-Mart just a few months before I moved to Plainview. There were some disadvantages to that job—(1.) the 3½ miles I'd have to walk between my apartment and Wal-Mart when I didn't have the money for the fixed-route bus (25 cents one-way);

(2.) the limited amount of hours per week that I could do this job (usually 10 to 12 depending on work load) since this was the ONLY store our company served here in town;

AND (3.) the amount of time I'd have to spend sometimes just twiddling my thumbs and waiting on a shipment to come in and process...

So at various times, I'd always have to work at least one or even two additional jobs in order to even keep my head above water financially even as I did my stuff for Anderson. They included such outfits such as:

(a.) Allsups'—I actually had to work for these as a convienence store clerk for several months primarily doing the night shift. Let's say the expectations at the time virtually required for me to almost be Superman because I had to try to do the work of two or three people all by myself. Note this did not just mean cashiering—but also keeping the cooked foods fresh and cooked as much as possible, doing cleanup duties both inside and out, and (IF time permitted) merchandising. This was a place where you really took a risk just going to the bathroom in the middle of the shift—especially if you wanted to avoid being the victim of a theft. (FYI—I even wound up being stolen from two or three times—one or two of those times involving cigarettes and another involving a gang of youths who actually stole $20 worth of cooked foods. I had to testify one time in municipal court in one of those cases—but had problems identifying the defendant...therefore, the case eventually got dismissed.)

We also had to help get the truck deliveries inside twice a week—with the major one coming in Friday morning. This just made a long shift even longer—especially if you had just worked a long shift on your feet. And let's say the definition of an "easy shift" for me was when I had to help train someone else...that way, I could make THEM do some of the hard work. That was probably what I would at the time considered the closest thing to a semi-night off.

What was most remarkable about this was the way I was actually terminated from this job. Let's say the area supervisor found himself on the hot seat—so he apparently figured in order to save his own skin that he could at least get himself demoted back down to store manager. Sadly, it was at the expense at BOTH myself and the store manager I was under. The area supervisor was even upfront about it—but still went through the pretense of letting me go due to baseless claims about my job performance. At least at that time I did receive partial unemployment for a little while for my trouble.

(b.) I also wound up working several times through the years for the local Salvation Army corps as a bellringer (fundraiser for their annual Christmas kettle drive). Even though it was primarily temporary work, it did help keep me somewhat financially afloat at times. The hours were long—and I wasn't always one to be content with simply ringing a bell. OH NO! I somehow developed a reputation for being pretty tough on bells—and even when I stood in front of stores, I used those as occasions to hone my singing skills. I even a time or two played my sax some—but was eventually told to cut it out by store management due to the noise. And the year-end money did help boost things financially when I needed it most.

(c.)   I was also privileged for a few years to write for Suite 101.com—primarily as the Contributing Editor for Texas Culture and Politics and then later on took on the additional title of Managing Editor of Asia, Africa, South America, and Other Regions. It sounds like a high-fallutin' title—but it really didn't pay much (at most—usually between $25 to 50 month to compensate for internet access charges…which since I didn't have a computer hooked up to the Net and had to use public terminals to get my work done, it practically didn't cost me too much to do most of the time except when I had to send something to the company headquarters in Canada.). But I did find it to be a pretty good outlet to continue my side writing career and use it as an excuse to go on a few trips throughout the state of Texas.

And I did get to interview some very interesting people during my tenure there (both in person as well as via e-mail) that provided excellent material for my weekly articles there. Among those I was glad to interview included the executive producer of "Austin City Limits' and several prominent political figures and important people in the area of "restorative justice ministry". I was able to use a conference at a church in Amarillo to interview some prominent Christian people including a brief interview with Darrell Scott (father of Columbine shooting victim Rachel Scott). And I even got to do an interview with a West Texas-based country group that were some of my biggest heroes growing up in Lubbock. This along with other opportunities made my literary journey that I took with the Suite for several years a useful and profitable one in many ways. (And I didn't even have to leave Plainview most of the time to do it, neither.)

(d.)   Also—I bet there's not too many guys out there that can actually claim work as a church secretary to be a part of my resume. But I can—because of the several years I worked part-time for an Episcopal church. I saw this one time in the paper—and wasn't sure how much a chance I had in getting it. But let's say my computer skills were a big help in landing that job for me. And the place when I came in really seemed to need it—especially for a parish priest that didn't know too much about how to exactly use one.

This church secretary job (even though it was only a very few hours a week) did help further my own personal computer skills—especially in stretching and developing my abilities in website design, newsletter publishing, and even at times spreadsheets. And it was even a privilege to join them at various times for some of their functions and develop some relationships with the parishioners there.

You can say that coming to Plainview didn't necessarily end all of the rodeos I had in regards to my continuing financial problems. But I did at least begin the process of putting down some new roots in brand-new territory that would help preserve me for the many things my God would start having me to do further down the trail ahead.

[Chapter 14:] [Plainview (Part III)—Wheeler & Formby TDCJ Units—WHY Restorative Justice Ministry?

I once had a friend in my church who I met one time at the Feast in Fort Worth who I had the privilege of corresponding with via mail. We would play chess by mail (which we never did finish that particular game) and send certain information about ourselves back and forth. I would usually write longer letters while he would tend to respond back by postcards. In the course of our letters, I had mentioned to him my increasing interest in the area of prison ministry. He wrote back to me one time something that was very short and sweet--but has proved to be a very profound thought that has never escaped me since: "We all live in prisons of our own making--and we don't even know that we have the Key (this presumably meaning our Savior Jesus Christ)."

Considering all of that...hmmh...what does it take for someone to work with the needs of prisoners? Let's see...driver's license or state-issues picture ID? Check! No prior felonies, outstanding warrants, etc. that would keep you from being allowed into a TDCJ unit? Check! Reliable transportation? (Buzzer sounds...) No? Sorry about that, but you lost the game...but thank you so much for playing...(At this point, most people would give up and stop completely.) Hold on, though— we're walking by faith and not by sight—RIGHT??? So wouldn't this (that is, if the prison you're going to is close to town) qualify as "reliable transportation"? And hey—wait another cotton-pickin' minute! If we managed to take a Greyhound bus to get into town, couldn't we also do similar things out-of-town while we're at it?

Let's find out...we can do so by going the exact same way that we went to Lockney when we first started this journey. But this time, we're not going to even get close to Lockney. Instead, just as we're getting out of the eastern city limits of Plainview, we'll see a huge water tower on our right.

Then just another half-mile or so down US 70 across the road from the Plainview Co-op Compress, there it is—plain as day. A road sign will lead you to turn right into County Road AA right into the first parking lot. Right here are the Texas Department of Criminal Justice's J.B. Wheeler and Marshall Formby Units as well as the prison farm and even the Regional Correctional Officers' Training Academy (FYI--Wheeler's in the front and Formby's in the back.)

It's especially interesting to see the lights around these two units at night. These days, you know for certain that you're almost in Plainview because the lights are so bright on these two units you can see them for at least several miles away. You also could be fooled into thinking if you didn't know better that the place was one of two things—either an airport (which isn't the case for Plainview because the airport's on the SOUTH side of town) or a football stadium (for the record, Plainview's is actually on the NORTH side of town). Right here is where we'll have a little chat about how I wound up going to assist in such a ministry as this.

All the time I was growing up, US 70 was always usually the way we got from Lockney to Plainview and back. But I remember a time when there was absolutely no razor wire to be seen on this property. In fact until the 1990s, all this place had been was a bunch of old farm land that grew crops and even had a playa lake on its property.

Then TDCJ due to an ever expanding prison population decided to do a massive prison building expansion project throughout a good bit of the state. West Texas in particular really got a desperately needed boom in the area of economic diversification (the Plainview area included) starting from just one unit in Snyder to over 30 different units across the Panhandle and South Plains like there are right now. Small and large communities alike out this way fought long and hard to entice the state to pick THEIR city for a new prison unit—especially the promise of tons of jobs that came with them. And if THAT weren't enough, even my current hometown was even chosen as the site of TDCJ's Region 5 (Panhandle/West Texas) headquarters on top of it.

So where do I specifically fit cogwise into this vast machine called the Texas prison system? I definitely did NOT seek out to actively do prison ministry at all (especially during the WCG pre-split years). During that time, frankly, prison was definitely the farthest thing from all of our minds anyway. Then one day I happened to see an announcement on one of our local information channels on our cable system promoting a special training class that was going to be taught by Prison Fellowship on how to minister to needs of those in prison. So I called in to the number and came to the training to see what it was all about.

First, understand that when this happened, the aftermath of "the changes" was still pretty fresh on the minds still in WCG while we were in the process of shedding our long-held tradition of exclusivity of other churches and denominations of ANYONE that wasn't us. I was still popping in occasionally on services or various other local churches and working to expand my personal sphere of relationships within the general Body of Christ. Also, let's say that my Siberian Exile/Great Tribulation period experiences (even though I have never been truly incarcerated—or plan to be any time soon) made me sensitive and aware enough of just how it feels NOT to be truly free to do as one wishes and pleases. And since I couldn't always be at church in Lubbock and serve actively in church in some consistent fashion there, I was looking for some sort of ministry outlet to where I could be of some definite assistance to the Universal Body of Christ.

Only the Lord for sure could have set me up to do this (especially given my WCG background up to that time) when I first met Dr. Patricia Herman. Patricia, who was a professor of education at Wayland and who later at one time became our Prison Fellowship Area Director, had a passion for ministry to offenders and their families that was self-evident (due in part to her being at one time a spouse of an offender). Patricia's teaching style was fun and quite lively—especially given her propensity for using tons of charts, graphs, and visual aids during her presentations.

Another thing that was quite remarkable about Patricia was that we actually had a mutual acquaintance—the daughter of one of the ladies I'd ride to church in Lubbock with was a fifth-grade teacher who actually took some of Patricia's education classes as part of her own collegiate studies at Wayland.

When it came time to fill out the application to be a Prison Fellowship volunteer, that was really when I was truly wondering if my past AND current WCG membership would be a liability in doing this type of ministry in the first place. My answers, I later found out from Patricia, actually made her question my relationship with the Lord due to her own lack of knowledge of WCG and, in particular, our most recent doctrinal changes.

To get an idea by what I mean by that—keep in mind that before the split, we in WCG didn't believe in the Nicene Creed—in part due to what Mr. Armstrong had taught us about the Trinity as well as the overall way we as a church fellowship tended to view what and/or who the Holy Spirit was in the first place. AFTER the split, though, it was a totally different and opposite story. So one couldn't naturally fault Patricia and her supervisor for being extra careful for reviewing my volunteer application. I was QUITE glad at that time that the same Tom Lapacka who was right there in Pasadena when "the changes" started coming down the pike and had to help Joe Tkach, Jr. communicate these things to the rest of the world was now MY pastor in Lubbock.

Talk about a real setup by my God on this thing—if it hadn't been for Patricia spending a couple of hours or so on the phone with Mr. Lapacka, I'm sure that I wouldn't be making ANY trips to ANY prison whatsoever—period. After Patricia's phone call with Mr. Lapacka, I was finally approved as a Prison Fellowship volunteer. Afterwards, I was also able to get in my required four-hour TDCJ security training (which required me to make a special trip to go to the Montford Unit in Lubbock to get that done)…and from there, my journey in the area of "restorative justice" ministry began.

At first, I was graciously allowed to go in with a group of Gideons who held church services on Thursday nights at both Plainview units as well as the Tulia Unit for about 3 years. I was, though, eventually asked to step aside from being what seemed a perpetual guest to their programs because I failed to meet the main requirements for Gideon membership (the primary one being that I either had to own my own business or at least be in some sort of management position over several employees).

During this time, I had also gotten involved with a weekly Promise Keepers small group Bible study. Eventually I also attempted to start the process rolling to help them get some things going for them in our local Plainview units—but things fizzled out due to other unexpected factors—and I was then left in the cold without any way to continue this type of ministry. Thankfully when there seemingly was no other ministry outlet left, I was blessed to be able to start actively going as my personal financial situation could afford (and I sure took a ton of risks financially at times to do it-even at times at risk of eviction from my apartment) with Don and Donna Castleberry and Freedom In Jesus Ministries to assist them in conducting prison crusades in many units across the state of Texas.

It has been a privilege personally throughout the years to consider Don and Donna some of my closest personal friends. Don in particular has been a true example to me about what a real man of faith is truly like and just how once changed life by God can have an enormous impact on many lives. Don also has served as one of my foremost primary spiritual mentors who has taught me many things over the years not just through words, but especially though his actions and deeds over the years how a relationship between a man and Christ his Savior should truly be lived and walked out.

The many hours we've spent together up and down the roads of Texas sharing things about life and the lessons each of us has individually learned from our Maker—my, oh, my. This from a guy who used to be a bank executive, but wound up leading guilty to federal charges of bank embezzlement…only through the mercy of the Lord was he only required to serve a very small portion of that sentence in the Lubbock County Jail followed by 3 years federal probation.

Through the times he has had with several ex-wives before meeting the love of his life in Donna (next to his Savior, of course) nearly 30 years ago, various family and financial situations, and even staring down prostate cancer in the face and winning, I've been privileged to see a man who has had to endure many things plus lead a vast and varied international ministry—and who still has an unshakeable fiath in His Creator and Abba Daddy who loves him…Don to me has not only been one of my biggest cheerleaders and personal supporters from the start, but has even been gracious and kind enough to even let me speak a word or two occasionally to some of the prison crusade audiences that FIJM holds. It's folks like Don in which without their direct contact and participation I could not have survived—much less thrive and keep up the "walk of faith" that has been my own personal path most of the time over the years.

Let's say through the years I've had an interesting nickname for Don that I still use to this day whenever I call him on the phone or address him otherwise in person. We were once at a prison crusade in Pampa, TX where three of our lady volunteers who came with their husbands began addressing one of our most senior of volunteers on our team, Dr. Noel Williams, for the strangest of reasons "Charlie" (as in the voice you hear on "Charlie's Angels"). I finally just had to ask why they started doing this—so I asked one of the ladies about it—and the conversation went like this:

"…Well, then, if you're now calling yourselves "Charlie's Angels", who's Charlie?

"Noel…"

"…Well—who's Bosley?

"Don…

"Well, then, who am I?

"…You're the Director!"

[We all got a good chuckle from that one. And ever since, I've even started calling Noel "Charlie" and Don "Bosley". To give you an idea of what I mean about Dr. Williams, you have to understand that Noel gets around in a motorized wheelchair whenever he goes most anywhere. You wouldn't believe the number of times I've had to constantly shout at Noel—"Hey, Charlie! SLOW DOWN!! Quit trying to do races around us! Give the rest of us a chance to catch up, will ya?" Usually, he never listens to me when I say that…but that's neither here nor there…]

For the rest of this chapter, I'm not going to throw every prison-related story at you because I already have others scattered throughout various parts of this book. But I will at least try to let you in on some of my own most interesting war stories about working in this type of ministry.

For instance, during a period of time when I was regularly going to assist a certain group in the area of prison ministry at a couple of state penal facilities near where I live, I initially depended on rides from one of the men involved with that group in order to even have the privilege of participating (i.e.--if I didn't have a ride, I usually didn't go).

But after a while of this, it got to where this method was unreliable on my end--especially when I personally realized that I was virtually walking the exact same distance on a frequent basis to where I work in the other direction to where I live as where the units close to the city where I live were in relation to where my apartment was. So finally one night, I decided to do something to test God out and to see how far my faith really was and see how God might probably see my relationship with Him from His perspective. I literally decided to walk to the place where I was going-- exactly 3 to 4 miles away. (I figured--hey, even if I was late, at least I'd be getting my exercise and enjoy what I considered my personal weight loss plan--"poverty and walking". Unfortunately, my immense amount of exercise never exactly kept up with my propensity for eating--but, ah well...that's neither here nor there.)

So I experimented with this for a while and took the leap of faith necessary to get to the unit and back--not sticking out my thumb or doing anything that others might interpret as hitchhiking, but just simply relying on Him to virtually take care of my transportation needs to continue my involvement with this group. The results of this experiment were, to say the least, quite fascinating. Not all of the time, but the biggest majority of the time sometime right in the middle of these walks, ten would get you one that somebody would eventually ask if I needed a ride somewhere. Sometimes they were members of the group itself while at other times they were either friends that I knew personally in the past or were total absolute strangers to me. But nevertheless, my God was always faithful and somehow managed to get me there. But the more amazing part of this was that I rarely if ever had to walk back home. This continued for the rest of this period of time that I have opportunity to participate with this group. [Talk about literally walking in faith--I'm a complete walking, talking example of it...]

Over the years, I've had the privilege of learning a lot about how our prison system here in Texas works—not only through conferences and various trainings, but even through practical experience. At one of those "restorative justice ministry" conferences in Austin, I began the process of undergoing training for a very unique program started here in Texas by a Lutheran minister named David Doerfler called Victim/Offender Mediation/Dialogue (VOM/D) that is still conducted by TDCJ Victim Services in which a victim of a violent crime now has an appropriately structured opportunity to meet face-to-face with the person who actually committed the crime as a way to assist them in their own personal healing process and answer the hidden questions of the heart that only the offender can help provide answers to. When I first heard about this, it was like a light clicked on inside me as a possible unique future area of personal ministry that I might be able to do.

So I underwent the application process necessary for me to take part in this training. There was an interesting quirk or two about this—one, the training was only held once a year; and two—I had to go all the way to Huntsville to do it. And of all the people that probably in the natural SHOULDN'T be doing this, I probably would be the LEAST likely candidate to do this. But my God did at least work it out that the particular training for this program one year was going to take place fairly close to the Feast of Trumpets. That year in lieu of what would have been my normal trip to Huntsville for Tabernacles, I had to go ahead and move up my trip in order to be a part of that training. Doing this very thing would prove to be one of the biggest personal trips I ever took—not only for the specific training itself, but for further practical spiritual applications in my own life during that particular overall trip as well.

After traveling on the bus all night again, I arrived in Huntsville on the previous Sunday before the training was to start. I didn't exactly have a very auspicious start to the trip upon my arrival into town—because I found that the Motel 6 I was staying at didn't accept the money order I had sent them in the mail because they only accepted cash and/or credit or debit cards. Having no other monies available until I got my next paycheck into my account that Tuesday, I was basically stuck out on my own for the first night or two without a room. So I went south from the motel with my luggage in tow (yet again…LOL) and first wound up at an Assembly of God for their Sun. night service. During the service, I went up to the altar and once again prayed to Him for the needs that I had for the remainder of the trip.

After the service concluded and with no other apparent solution immediately at hand, I decided to just start making my way anyway towards the place where the training was going to be several miles away and taking my time in getting there. It was definitely a very long sleepless night in the rain as I was walking south along the northbound I-45 frontage road. And I was VERY glad that I brought my poncho—because it definitely proved to be handy this time.

I wound up first for a little while near one church with a park bench or two to be near. But I decided that I didn't want to stay too long in one place because I needed to avoid being arrested for trespassing or vagrancy because of suspicious police. From there, I wound up (with rain literally pouring down on me and my stuff, I might add) at another place on that frontage road that used to be a mobile home sales lot which had a pretty good tree and stuff to hide in. (That was definitely an experience—especially having to, shall we say, utilize the bathroom facilities out in the elements in the middle of a rainstorm and a bunch of mud.) Eventually as time got closer for the training to start that Mon. morning, I just decided to head towards the Sam Houston statue and find another place as close as possible to there and also the place where the training was going to be.

I wound up at a Pentecostal church where thankfully there was a correctional officer that was also a church member who at least allowed me to use their bathroom quickly and stay outside on their porch until time to finally head to the training facility. So out there, I waited for several hours until time to go in. At the time I left, I just decided to trust the Lord and left the remainder of the luggage that I didn't need to carry with me to the training itself.

After that first day's training was done, I went back to the church to check on the luggage, etc. Apparently, the sight of my luggage spooked someone because the local cops were called. But it also happened that a federal agent was on the scene and noticed my plight when he asked me about what I was doing. He gave the local cops kind of a good verbal dressing down (unbeknownst to me at first, of course) and then took me to the local homeless shelter facility. Believe me, I was never so glad to even have ANY bed to sleep in and a decent meal for the night as I did at that place. I was so tired by the time I got there that I did something I rarely did— went to bed REAL early and slept so soundly that I was dead to the world until I got up the next morning.

From there, I was graciously allowed to leave my luggage there until I could get back in the afternoon from the training. Then on top of it as I was heading back to the training facility for the next day's session, I stopped in at a convienence store and saw that my paycheck had come in—thereby insuring that I could finally go get that room at the Motel 6 for the rest of the trip. I had stayed at that place before on previous trips to Huntsville, but was never too thrilled with it. But THAT trip, even just being at this motel (which for Huntsville was at the time the cheapest place realistically available) proved to be a good thing in itself. And I was able to stay there even through the Feast of Trumpets itself and until that Sun. when I had to catch the bus back home.

My own outside personal turmoil only further served to illustrate to me the Divine timing of this particular VOM/D training. One of them that really stood out in my mind was a victim impact panel that was held about the second or third day of the training in which a group of three women shared their stories about what they had went through as a victim of crime. One of the younger women had a story that really tore my heart out. She shared how when she was a child she had to endure incest and a number of unspeakable things as she was growing up. But what really got my dander up was when she told us how as a young adult when she was still struggling with these horrible childhood issues she asked the pastor of a church she had started attending for counsel in dealing with these things. She told our class that the pastor gave her such bad advice that it literally caused her to stop attending ANY church all together. When I heard this, I wanted to find this pastor and SLAP him for this stupidity and for attempting to lead such a precious child of God totally off-course.

Instead, after she was finished and it was time for Q&A, I said this to her: "…I want to say this to you. Now you are NOT required to accept this or take this—you may do what you want. But for what it's worth, I wish to formally apologize to you on behalf of our churches and the Body of Christ for that bad counsel and advice that pastor gave you. I and those that I know would never had condoned such conduct and are ashamed that you had to go through and endure such things."

While I was saying this, I also actually had another question that I really wanted to ask these women on the panel about what things our churches could do for folks like them. After I had said this to this younger woman, the older woman on the panel sitting beside me shot back: "Now you know what to say to your churches!" After she said that, it was like that older lady read my mind and knew exactly what I was thinking—and there was after that no need for me to ask that question…for it was already answered.

From that experience, I believe that they would have me to say things like the following:

The first is to share with you a FIRSTHAND experience of what it's like to be a victim of a "misdemeanor" crime. One night about 4 or 5 AM, I was awakened by a knock on the door of my apartment. When I opened the door, there on my front steps stood two Black ladies, one of them who I had seen on two previous occasions and that had asked me for various things, and the other who was pretty overweight. When I opened the door, one of them asked me if I could give them money for a bus ticket to a nearby town. When I told them I didn't have it, then the lady asked if I could fix them a glass of water. After I let them in, I fixed the glasses of water and them gave them to the ladies--in which they left pretty quickly afterwards and I turned off the light and went back to sleep.

The next morning, I tried to find my cell phone and tore the house up and down looking for it--but couldn't find it. Then I had the idea that I might have left it at a church I had went to the previous night for a singles group. So I took some time to go to that church to find the phone that I thought I might have misplaced there--and came up with zero. After going down the exact trail I had walked the night before, only then did I realize that those same ladies that I had let in during the night may have also stolen my phone. All of which caused me to go to the agent for the cell phone company I was using at the time to get a replacement phone...which then required me to file a police report...which then afterwards required me to go back to the cell phone company to pick up the replacement phone. A whole day wasted on my part due to the actions of someone else...

But what really got my goat was this: I was virtually dependent on that phone in order to keep my job and maintain all appropriate contact with the outside world. But what was that phone worth to those ladies? I soon found out after one of the city police officers told me what happened to the phone. The police had found that phone just blocks away from my apartment in a nearby park. What did the ladies get for the trouble of stealing my phone? To them, it was a quick high of an illegal drug and quick cash to do something stupid. To me, it cost a whole lot more in terms of time spent trying to rectify this situation and inconvienence and hassle in having to replace a phone and then having to return the replacement phone and get the original phone that I had back in operation again.

To add some clarity to this situation, let's take an example or two from my past experiences in assisting various prison ministries to get a clearer picture of what I mean. I had an opportunity to assist an older man with a certain men's group with a 10-week men's Bible study within one of the state prison units near where I live. There was a time or two where it seemed that I had an occasion or two during this period of time where I was able to hopefully contribute a lesson of some substance given to me by my God that might make a difference in their lives.

During one of these times with this group, I started teaching a lesson on how all of us should view the various roles and functions within the greater Church. I focused the discussion on passages in 1 Timothy as well as in Titus and even found a way to incorporate my love of chess as a way to give the men (whom most of them may have problems understanding through reading) a practical way to visually see how different people playing different roles contribute to the overall operation of the Body of Christ. (FYI—it was a miracle in itself that I was even able to clear my chess set through security that night...)

In the course of this discussion, I asked the men of what they saw and thought the role of women should be both in society and in the Church. The answers each of them gave in general disappointed and shocked me--and almost broke my heart. Here I am a typical man--and yet I was discussing the role of women...and no woman was able to be present to tell them what SHE truly felt her proper place should be in comparison to a man.

The responses of the men present? The majority basically gave her almost no role at all EXCEPT for her to be barefoot and pregnant and to be no more than the equivalent of a glorified housekeeper. This sadly revealed to me what major problems of perception face those who are offenders both behind bars as well as those just released. They just could not see that a woman has just as much value to our God (if not more so to a man) as they do. It definitely opened my eyes in seeing how much they so desperately needed to learn about these subjects and how our Adversary has done a very good job of deception in the area of how our women should be treated by a man.

Anyway, as I begun the chess portion of the lesson, I had the small group of men two at a time that knew how to play chess (which happened to be most of them-- which thrilled me a lot having played seriously in a few tournaments myself in the past). I allowed the first two to start the game, then after a few minutes I stopped them in the middle of their play and had the next two men continue the game right where it was--and so on and so forth down the line.

In the process of this "controlled chaos", I also simultaneously had one of the inmates read some Scriptures dealing with roles and functions while the chess game was going on. After a little bit of time was taken with the chess activity, I then was led to bring the lesson to a close by challenging the men to also consider the roles that women and children can play in His work. To say the least, I was privileged to learn a little bit about what was in their hearts and minds and encourage the men to try to see things from other perspectives outside of themselves and get a better grasp of how God might view our unique roles and functions in His Son's Body.

But the lights began to come on about the problems in our prisons once I found something else out--especially in regards to the scourge of domestic violence. Another night, I was able to get a ride back with one of my fellow volunteers back to my apartment. This man and wife also happened to serve as one of the "volunteer chaplains" and also headed an anger management class at one of our local units. On the way back home, I asked them both two questions just out of curiosity (because at the time I was myself thinking a lot about the issues of domestic violence and sexual assault through various other training that I was undergoing at the time). I asked them, "I want to know two things. In your anger management group, I'd like to know: first--how many of those men in that group have been involved in some way with domestic violence, whether they were a batterer themselves and/or were abused as a child? And second--how many of those men in that same group have been involved in any way with sexual assault?" [Before I give you that answer, I do need to let you know that the particular unit this is referring to is what is considered in my state a prison facility specifically designated for the treatment of probationers dealing with substance-abuse problems.]

The answers of that couple to my questions nearly threw me back for a loop. The man said that at least 65% of the men in that group have been batterers themselves. But that was nothing compared to the statistic that he gave for sexual assault. He further said that 90%--folks, that is NINETY percent, NINE-ZERO--that were at minimum at least sexually molested or abused as a child.

From this, it became quite obvious to me why our criminal justice system in our nation has been a total failure in the area of recidivism. Through this, I realized that we cannot expect to solve the problems of our system UNLESS we first in the Body of Christ wake up to the knowledge that we must help those that have suffered with these devastating problems resolve these unfinished issues of their childhood before we can even expect them to begin the long journey that they must take to become productive citizens.

But what might all of this connect with the subjects of domestic violence and sexual assault from a Biblical perspective? AH--THIS is where the discussion gets even more in-depth and interesting from here. If my God has not dissuaded you from these activities through my own personal experience, then maybe these statistics and other statements out on a limb might shock you to reality:

(1.) One study that I have heard about in regards to domestic violence and sexual assault in my own local area says that 95% OF ALL cases that ONE CENTER has dealt with were usually the result of the MAN being the offender!

(2.) A currently growing cause of the breakdown in the communication and the health of marriages (EVEN among, BLEEP FORBID--CHRISTIAN ONES) is the habitual use of pornography by the male partner in that marriage.

(3.) Several notorious serial killers and rapists have personally attributed the use of pornography of some form as playing a major role for their incentive to commit various heinous acts.

(4.) Numerous celebrities (EVEN those in the Christian world) have been caught in adulterous acts and other inappropriate behaviors that have cost them respect, trust, and even the existence of their careers. We have even in our nation had a President who was nearly removed from office as a result of various inappropriate sexually-related behaviors.

But what has seemed to be the biggest reason of all why I still take part in this type of ministry whenever possible? One more related experience might help sum it up for this chapter--

During a period of time when I was regularly going to assist a certain group in the area of prison ministry at a couple of state penal facilities near where I live, I initially depended on rides from one of the men involved with that group in order to even have the privilege of participating (i.e.--if I didn't have a ride, I usually didn't go).

But after a while of this, it got to where this method was unreliable on my end--especially when I personally realized that I was virtually walking the exact same distance on a frequent basis to where I work in the other direction to where I live as where the units close to the city where I live were in relation to where my apartment was. So finally one night, I decided to do something to test God out and to see how far my faith really was and see how God might probably see my relationship with Him from His perspective. I literally decided to walk to the place where I was going--exactly 3 to 4 miles away. (I figured--hey, even if I was late, at least I'd be getting my exercise and enjoy what I considered my personal weight loss plan--"poverty and walking". Unfortunately, my immense amount of exercise never exactly kept up with my propensity for eating--but, ah well...that's neither here nor there.)

So I experimented with this for a while and took the leap of faith necessary to get to the unit and back--not sticking out my thumb or doing anything that others might interpret as hitchhiking, but just simply relying on Him to virtually take care of my transportation needs to continue my involvement with this group. The results of this experiment were, to say the least, quite fascinating. Not all of the time, but the biggest majority of the time sometime right in the middle of these walks, ten would get you one that somebody would eventually ask if I needed a ride somewhere. Sometimes they were members of the group itself while at other times they were either friends that I knew personally in the past or were total absolute strangers to me. But nevertheless, my God was always faithful and somehow managed to get me there. But the more amazing part of this was that I rarely if ever had to walk back home. This continued for the rest of this period of time that I have opportunity to participate with this group. [Talk about literally walking in faith--I'm a complete walking, talking example of it...]

One night during this period of time, as I was going in to the Central Control part of one of the units with this group, I saw (as we would normally do) a couple of men from various Churches of Christ in our city that would usually hold a Bible study at the same time the group I was with would hold our church service. All of us in our group knew them well and as we waited to present our drivers' licenses to the front window for the correctional officers to check their records, one of the men who was the minister of the only Black Church of Christ in our city told me that he saw me as I was walking to the unit as he was passing by in his car. He said to me that he was talking to the other man who was assisting him with their Bible study and telling him, "That young man is dedicated! I think I'll give him a ride..." Unfortunately, by the time he thought this, someone else with a similar notion who was a part of the group that I was with had already beat him to the punch--so he lost his chance. But I was, to say the least, highly flattered by his comment.

Over the years of doing this, I have found above all else the importance of having what I like to call "...the faith of inconvienence". It's not an easy path of faith to travel. It requires a lot of stretching of yourself to do some things that are out of the ordinary customary stuff in our lives. But it has been one of the tools that makes a vital truth from Galatians chapter 6 flash like a neon sign—"...what you sow, you shall also reap." I've been privileged to sow a lot of seeds over the years and also in turn reap abundant harvests into my life that I never would have seen otherwise had I not done so.

It is the exercise of this unique type of faith that makes every mile traveled for any prison crusades and other related endeavors worth every mile of the trip. And it lets me see the many miracles our God can do in a changed life. So is there any reason I see that I need to stop doing so? Not that I can see in the near future at least…Besides, there have been brethren behind razor wire fences that I have taught me a lot over the years. The only difference is that I don't have to stay here. But I also look forward to days like when I might have to go on another bus and I happen to ride with some guy who just got released to go home from one of these units. I might not have much—but if He directs me to do so, I at least try to do something to celebrate with them. They probably hadn't had a good Coke in quite a while…And it's always good to help them start their own new journeys of faith in Him off right.

[Chapter 15:] [Plainview (Part IV—W. 21st St.) How I Found Out About "Pigs In The Parlor" And Came Home From Vietnam]

Ewww—wwee!! Do you smell that gross smell? I'm talking that one—that one downwind of us…No, silly—I didn't cut the cheese. I mean it smells like a SERIOUS pig farm out here. Oh, I forgot…there DID used to be a pig feeding operation out even further east of these prison units about a couple of miles down the road, but it shut down many years ago. Soo-ey!! Boy, that's stinking to high heaven! Let's get out of here and go west back towards town before we both go crazy, shall we?

I just remembered something—now that we're on the subject of pigs, we might as well stop off someplace else here in town that also at one time dealt with porkers. (Now you're really thinking I've gone off my kosher rocker—going from one pigpen to the other…) I'm not talking about physical livestock, of course. Besides, I think having significant amounts of livestock is still prohibited inside of city limits if memory serves me right…

To find this place of swine, we'll only need to continue on further here on Fifth Street until we get to Quincy. A quick right will put us on Quincy/State Highway 194 in which we'll proceed north on Quincy until we get close to the bowling alley. At 20th Street, we'll then take a left and then on Smythe do an immediate right. Smythe will then curve around to reveal a three-way intersection with West 21st Street and Castro Street.

At that three-way intersection, we'll turn left onto West 21st and keep going until we dead-end on Utica and the First Presbyterian Church parking lot with the east grandstands of Bulldog Stadium facing us.

What in the bleep do these porkers have to do with bulldogs? Absolutely nothing except for one major spiritual reason—West 21st Street just so also happened at one time to be the home of a very internationally-known minister named Frank Hammond—the same man who originally wrote a book that is still regarded in the Pentecostal/Charismatic movement as a watershed book in the areas of deliverance and spiritual warfare named "Pigs In The Parlor".

I didn't start at first knowing about Bro. Frank. In fact, given my past WCG background, I didn't even have a clue who Bro. Frank was or what he even did in the first place. And I sure didn't know until some time later that we both shared at least one common thread—he just so happened to live across the street from where one of my usual rides to church in Lubbock, etc. had her house.

That would change, though, not too long after I moved here to Plainview. During the first few years here, I started popping in at various local churches not only just to learn more about Him, but also in light of my past experiences, attempt to get to know other Christians within the Body of Christ in my area.

One of those times led me to the doorstep of a monthly "Cowboy Church" service led by New Covenant Church pastors Ron and Marianne Brunson that was usually held in a barn right near their residence that was at the time within the boundaries of Seth Ward (an unincorporated community that straddles the northeast Plainview city limits).

As I started attending these Cowboy Church services more and more, I eventually found out that New Covenant also did something each month called a Deliverance Weekend which featured various speakers who talked about things such as how demon spirits manifest, spiritual gifts, and practical applications of the concept of deliverance.

This was brand-new different stuff for this Baptist-raised boy who rebelled TOWARDS the traditions of WCG. Now, the Church DID at least teach some about healing—but we in WCG were taught that if you needed to be anointed and prayed for re: physical healing, you asked the pastor or one of the local church-level elders to pray for you—IN PRIVATE. Under NO means was there to be any public display of any kind whatsoever.

And plus—keep in mind that in pre-split WCG, members did not even dare do public prayer in services outside of the way the pastor and/or elders did. The basic rule was that everything was to be done decently and in order. You prayed to God PRIVATELY in your prayer closet—period. Such things as small group studies, etc. NOT organized directly by the pastor and local leadership was simply NOT done. So if we didn't quite have a full grasp of the doctrines of Divine healing or spiritual gifts, most of the WCG folks that I knew personally probably had even less of a clue about what this thing called "deliverance" was.

And to be honest, at first I only started going to some of New Covenant's Deliverance Weekends for only two primary reasons—(1.) free food (at breakfast, that is); and (2.) it was someplace else I could go to church on the Sabbath at times if there was no other way I could otherwise go with one of my usual rides to Lubbock for church.

But I found out the more I went to these things about how very little I knew about not only the Word, but more importantly the things of the Spirit. Even if WCG wasn't teaching anything like this at the time, at least realizing that I had a unique privilege of sitting under the teachings of Bro. Frank and others like him that had been doing this for a while that there were truly more to the things of the Spirit that I originally realized.

Some people in certain theological circles may have severe criticism and intense questioning to those who deal with concepts such as spiritual warfare, demonic possession, and things of that nature. I know for certain that there was once a time where I surely either didn't know much about it at all or, worse, considered those who practiced such theological concepts to be full of the devil himself. But, after what happened to me one Memorial Day weekend, it will be very much harder to raise those same criticisms ever again. After what happened that weekend, I will only say one thing for sure--without a few people that I know who work in this particular area, I certainly feel that I would have never come back home from the Vietnam-like struggles of the past I once faced.

One of these particular Deliverance Weekends proved to be a major personal milestone in my life that showed me how much this deliverance thing could get me through the trail of tears that I went through after the WCG "changes". I remember quite well the day I came back home from my Vietnam. No, I was way too young to have even been able to go through the Vietnam War, much less fight in it. I wasn't hardly in kindergarten when the War ended. But I know a little bit of how it is to go through a war in your emotions that never seems to end.

It was interesting how it all happened. I forget whether or not I had decided deliberately to stay home from my home church that weekend or if I had trouble getting a ride there. It just happened to be that one of the non-denominational churches in the city where I live was having a "deliverance weekend". I originally didn't take much stock in this concept...UNTIL this particular Memorial Day weekend came. This time proved to be so radically different for me than other times. It was as if a compulsion came over me to come to this weekend and behave in extremely unorthodox ways in my manner of worship to Him than I was personally accustomed to--just compelling me that I just had to be there, no matter what effort it took for me to get there.

It wasn't the fact that I had to walk over a mile one way to where the meeting was held--that to me didn't seem unusual. NO--it was the fact that during this weekend, I constantly felt compelled to do two things. One--that I had to make a COMPLETE list of ALL of the prayer concerns and needs that I wanted to pray over for myself and others. The second? (And this was REAL strange to me...) It was as if I wanted to pray (especially during the ministry time), I could ONLY pray in one position--prostrate face down on the ground lying as if I were shooting a target with a rifle.

But why this thing about praying ONLY in a prostrate position? Part of it was the compulsion of what I felt I needed to do within the spirit of that particular moment I was in. But the other reason was even more Scriptural in nature. I found this out during a previous one-day fast that I went through in which I found myself not being able to pray to the Lord effectively in any other way EXCEPT to completely lie prostrate. A picture that was burned in my mind that I saw on a made-for-TV movie was very prevalent in my thinking at that time--a picture of King David himself going into total abandon in his worship and praying entirely in a prostrate position. But what got me really in this mood to pray prostrate was when I looked up the word "prostrate" in the concordance in my Bible. There are only two times that I could reasonably find that very word in Scripture--and both of those are located in Deut. 9 in the New International Version when Moses was making his final address to the Israelites. [Can you guess what BOTH of those instances within that chapter (verses 18 and 25, that is) refer to? The answer might surprise you. Look it up real quick as an exercise--and you'll see what I mean.]

Now back to the weekend. This went on through both of the services of that deliverance meeting that Sat. Then I had to get back to reality. I did some other things that night and went to bed, noting that I had to do laundry first thing in the morning. The next morning, I was again compelled by the Spirit to go back to that church--THIS TIME to schedule a personal appointment for ministry. One slight little problem with this, though...THE LAUNDRY!! And a BIGGER problem in doing the laundry? The laundry room in the apartment complex where I lived operates on a time lock that closes the place between 8 PM until 8 AM. Believe me, when I got up at around 7 to 7:30 AM the next morning, it was a VERY long wait for the laundry room to open back up to get the laundry done.

By the time I was finally able to get into the place and get the laundry started, it was 8:30--and the church service at that place starts at 10:00. By the time I was finally able to get to that church, the folks were already most of the way into the music service. But nevertheless, I managed to slip a note to the pastor of that church requesting an appointment for that afternoon. After the service, I spoke with that pastor--and he said to speak to his wife and that she would set up a time for me. I did--and arrangements were made for later in the afternoon (which, by the time I left there for the lunch break so that I could finish folding the clothes that I wasn't able to do during my rush to get to the church service--it would prove to be an hour-and-a-half later).

When I came back for that appointment, needless to say--I came prepared. I had to first wait on the folks on the ministry team to handle those that were from out-of-town as a courtesy to them so that they could have time to get back to their homes at a decent hour. Then, my time came and both of the wives of the pastor and one of the assistant pastors would later prove to be the ones performing ministry on me.

When I came in the room, the very first thing I did was to spread out a number of things that I had put in a duffle bag as points of contact to pray over. Then guess what happened AGAIN? You got it--I wound up face down on the floor again. (For an EXTREMELY fat man like me, it's, to say the least, a VERY uncomfortable position to be in--ESPECIALLY in terms of being able to breathe properly!!] When they did their initial assessment of my situation, I told them all that I had been felt compelled to do throughout most of that weekend up to that point and the things that I had needs that I desired prayer for quite a number of issues.

I was quite amazed to hear the response of one of the ladies after relating my concerns to them: "I think that we can take care of this by simply dealing with the spirit of rejection." "All these needs could be taken care of by working with this?" I sarcastically thought to myself. "This surely can't be." Nevertheless, I went along with the flow of the Spirit.

The first thing after that remark the ladies asked me to do was to sit up to where I could breathe. (That in itself was a relief--ESPECIALLY when I just couldn't do ANYTHING BUT pray in a prostrate position.) THEN--things got even more interesting from there. NO--in case you're wondering, I did not experience anything along the lines of "The Exorcist". (Besides, some things of a spiritual nature don't always necessarily require sound, fury, and thunder anyway. Some of our God's best little victories and most effective solutions are sometimes the most quiet ones of the spirit.] INSTEAD--the ladies started speaking over me some of the most life-changing and affirming words I had ever heard. These were not as much "I rebuke you, Satan!" or things like you might commonly associate with flashy teleevangelists in today's media. They were for me more along the lines of "God loves Coy. God cares for Coy..." and so on and so forth.

But what eventually proved to the pinnacle of it all and the ultimate testimony of God's infinite insight, timing, and grace was when one of the men that was there who was trying not to intrude on what was happening actually would serve the most valuable role of all. I did not realize it until then--but it seemed that, above all else, there were some issues of father abandonment, rejection, and neglect that I had not worked through up until that point. The very man who was trying not to intrude would actually be the very thing that gave what took place a whole lot more credibility. I will always remember what he said to me as I hugged this man for dear life as I for the first time in my life dealt with deeper issues that the previous problems I had went through so far in my life up to that point were at best mere symptoms of. This time, that root--the trunk of that tree, so to speak--was finally being destroyed for good as he said to me, "As a representative of Jesus Christ, I accept you as a man and affirm you for who you are." I may not have the exact words right and in their entirely--but the essence of the message that God gave to me through this man was this: "You've talked a lot about Vietnam and Siberia. Well, son, you are rejected no more. You can finally come back home from Vietnam."

I was literally crying a river of tears in the midst of this scene. Some people might call this foolish, unwise, and undignified. But if that is the only way that my God felt that I could realistically come back from Vietnam, come back home from the rejection, the misery, the pain, the shackles of my emotional past, the devastation, and the loss of things I once held dear...then who am I to call the process that He may desire to liberate me from those things that hold me back as useless and stupid? How could I even think or dare to call the King of the Universe on the carpet for a method that isn't necessarily easy to fit in a certain box that I might otherwise imagine for Him?

After the ministry time was completed, I had occasion to ask one of the ladies (ESPECIALLY since I was still a little new to the concept of spiritual warfare) how she was able to tell and discern that the root problem of it all was that of rejection. She told me that it was by "observation and discernment of the Spirit" and that she could tell by the look on my face and in the way I acted when I was in the room and had literally surrounded myself with objects on the floor.

After I came back home from the church, I reflected a little bit on what had happened and then turned on the radio to a prominent Christian radio network. The song that I heard not too long after I turned on the radio gave even more of a bit of closure and the turning of all the events to a completed full circle. It was a special honoring veterans for Memorial Day that I happened to come upon that had a song by Ray Boltz called "It's An Honor To Serve" that I will also remember for a long time to come. As I sang the chorus of that song, I could hardly keep from thinking one thing: The wars that I have faced are finally over now--and I have as of now OFFICIALLY in my mind and heart FINALLY come back home from my Vietnam. Back home from the chains that had bound me--and back from the pain and grief that I had suffered through. And I couldn't help but especially sing this line with gusto: "It's an honor, an honor to serve." I was now officially dismissed by Him to move on to other things that life had to offer and dismissed from the duties and responsibilities of the past.

Some time later, I had occasion to assist another prison ministry at a prison unit in another town. As a part of this, all of the members that went to one of the units on the part of the crusade team that I was on prayed over the Chaplain of that unit as we felt was in harmony with the moving of the Holy Spirit. Somehow in this process during the second time we prayed over him after that service, I felt led to pray for this Chaplain that he be delivered from the spirit of rejection and did so appropriately. It turned out that I had previously heard a little bit about this man through the prison ministry grapevine about him in regards to possible problems that he may possibly be having in regards to time management and organizational skills. During the course of this, this Chaplain had mentioned that he was a veteran of the Vietnam War. Somehow that came up in my prayer over him, too.

After we finished the crusade, the head of this ministry remarked that he thought that I might have the spiritual gift of discernment because he had previously discussed these issues with this Chaplain before--AND that I had seemed to pick up on this WITHOUT ANY prior knowledge whatsoever of that particular situation. This also amazed me in itself. But what was more remarkable on my end was my response to his remark: "...I don't call it discernment. I consider it only hard-earned experience at best since I have been myself previously delivered from that same spirit."

To those of you that have your doubts about the concept of deliverance, let me fill you in on something—I personally found that in order to even begin to do effective ministry to offenders, utilizing this spiritual tool is essential and almost mandatory in order to help them break the chains of bondages and addictions that still haunt them. And having a little more spiritual insight on the root causes of deeply-seeded and embedded problems surely helps the recipient know that there's something our Lord has given them to do that can be positive—not negative.

I came very late to the party in regards to the things of the Spirit—but Bro. Frank and others under his tutelage started me on the path to be not only hungrier for the things of God, but especially of the Spirit. Sadly due to my recent WCG past, I didn't get a chance to really see Bro. Frank in his prime or even get to meet his wife Ida Mae when she was alive. But I can say that I'm still grateful to Him at least for the privilege of having some sort of relationship with him in the last few years before he died.

In my recollections of Bro. Frank, I still recall him to be a man that was very zealous for the ministry given to him by the Lord. Those of you who knew Bro. Frank long before I did can rest assured (at least from my vantage point) that he stayed as active as long as he possibly could…constantly answering letters and emails and phone calls from throughout the world and continually writing new books for those precious last few years before he passed on and even as the time came for him to where he could no longer travel internationally and as extensively as he once did.

He truly was an example to me about finishing his race before the Lord stronger than when he started. I can even personally tell you that Bro. Frank kept a keen and sharp mind as well as an active ministry of writing on subjects such as "The Perils of Passivity" that he was able to finish before his passing. It was even a privilege of mine to stop by his place occasionally, say hi to him, and give him an update on some of the things I had recently been involved with at various times in the area of prison ministry—and maybe even leave a few prayer requests for him from time to time from the chaplains of prison units I had just been to for various prison crusades so that he could maybe at least still feel like he was a part of the game spiritually. And I was even present at his funeral when all of those who were with New Covenant and others affected by his ministry gave Bro. Frank his "homegoing".

But what impressed me most about Bro. Frank wasn't necessarily what he may have taught me personally. Oral Roberts once said, "…Success without a successor is failure." From the scores of pastors and others that would be some of his most outstanding students, I don't think Bro. Frank will ever need to worry about his ministry for the Lord being a failure. There have been plenty more that are even now taking the torch he left them and are running with it as hard and as fast as they can.

The experiences I had at these "deliverance weekends" makes me wonder about the following: Could it be that a possible ROOT CAUSE of your turmoil in various areas of your life be attributed to possible spiritual effects of rejection, abandonment, etc. from one or both of your parents? Could the valid reason for your current troubles be partially be due to the fact that certain issues in your own life have NOT been completely, fully, and honestly dealt with in the way that they should be properly dealt with? Is your search for love, fulfillment, and favor in the eyes of man instead of God a possible cause for your current pain and heartache-- and are these things also partially due to these issues? May I give you at least one thing that I learned from Bro. Frank and others like him—if you'll let HIM have those things and stop striving for His love and let Him handle it and give it to Him, He'll be more than glad to help you make something out of even those things that once caused you pain.

All of this I would have never thought of or dreamed of learning on my own in the WCG pre-split years—but I did…and it was from a man whose teachings helped me come home from my own Siberia and Vietnam…and who also was a neighbor of one of my own closest best friends in WCG itself. SOO-EY!! Thanks for the memories, Bro. Frank—and see you in the Kingdom. Shabbat shalom—and rest well.

[Chapter 16:] [Plainview--Part V--Interstate 27: How to Walk By Faith And Not By Sight--WITHOUT MONEY! (PART 1)]

Well, we finally came home from Vietnam--but I regret to inform you that we'll already need to leave those filthy pigs in the parlor and get back on the road again. (Besides, they truly stink A LOT--don't you think?) And make sure you got your walking shoes laced up tight and that you're nice and comfortable in them--because we've really got some walking to do from here--ok?

So let's leave West 21st Street behind and go up Utica for a couple of blocks until we get to the convienence store right by State Highway 194/Dimmitt Highway. Why don't we stop there and make sure we're loaded up on drinks and snacks before we hit the trail? Oh, you say--you didn't bring any money with you? That's all right--I'll cover you this time. The Master during the chapter break managed to slip me something. Come on--let's go in...

(We go inside the store and start looking around.) Go ahead and get what you want...honest...it's on me...Serious!...Ok, let's see--there's my Dr. Pepper on special...but hey, wait a minute--Red Diamond Tea's also on special, too! Drat...it's only for a gallon. I need something much more portable than that. Hmhh....there's Arizona Tea for 99 cents each...I oughta get a couple of those...Or HEY--why not get both? I am fancying a Cherry Dr. Pepper right now....How about this...maybe I'll get a couple of cans of tea for later and I'll get a Cherry Coke fountain drink (44 ounces, of course). Yeah--sounds good...Oh--Hershey's Cookies and Cream King Size's also on special. Is this my blessing day or what? Maybe some peanuts might also be good...ok, I'll get a couple of packages of that, a little non-perishable beef jerky...yeah--okay, I should be good with that...

WHAT??? You didn't get anything? You can't afford it--and you're not worthy of receiving it? Come on--you're gonna get thirsty before too long where we're going--and I said I got you covered. Get ya something--NOW! While you're deciding, I've got to go to the restroom for a minute. Just put what you want here on the counter beside what I've got and I'll pay for it after I'm through. Besides, the more you get, the more I get blessed, and the more He'll provide both of us in turn, right? Be back in a minute...

(After coming back from the restroom...) Ok...got what you wanted? Cool...hmm...bottles of water, sunflower seeds, Poweraide fountain drink, and pickles? Real health nut, aren't ya?

(I address the clerk and get ready to pay the tab.) Aaahh...don't worry about it. I've been in your shoes--LITERALLY! (Clerk rings up items on the register and gives me the total.) Boy, that's shaving it close! Let's see--what was that total again? 20 dollars and 56 cents....ok...there's 10, 15, 16, 17, 18, 19, 20...let's see...and 25, 35, 50, and 60....man, that's about everything I got right now...just barely...Nah, keep the change...we won't need it where we're going...Appreciate it...thanks!

Ok, let's put all this stuff here in my traveling bag so that if we need it, we'll have it. I'm glad it's got a handle with wheels that roll. I hate to have to carry suitcases with handles. Besides, those other bags aren't too sturdy anyway....Let's get back on the road again and stay on the Dimmitt Highway for a few blocks, ok?

Let's see--go past Covenant Hospital, then...ah--here it is...Interstate 27's just up ahead. Let's go under the overpass and take a left on the southbound frontage road, ok?

Good--you got your Poweraide with you. Let me know when you're ready for one of those waters you got. That's also why I brought this large rolling traveling bag for both of us to put our stuff in so that we don't have to carry this in our hands or around our necks when we're not using it.

Oh, wait a minute! You didn't know that I didn't get a ride for both of us--and we don't have any more money after what we bought at the store? Oh, sorry...I forgot to tell you...**that's the theme of this chapter!** Welcome to the Coy Reece Holley Boot Camp Short Course on Walking By Faith And Not By Sight! I hear you groaning again--"MORE WALKING?" Trust me--it'll be fun--ok?

Let's stay on this southbound frontage road for a little while until we get out of town, ok? That'll give me plenty of time as the traffic wizzes by us to take you through some of the major points of this short course. Let me give you the rules of the road first...

(1.) **NO HITCHHIKING OR STICKING OUT YOUR THUMB to get a ride, all right?** Our God is our source and HE will provide what we need--just like He gave us enough to cover the stuff we got at the store.

(2.) **Here's the BIG one--NO COMPLAINING OR BELLYACHING as we go along the way, ok?** I don't give a flip how your feet hurt or how many blisters you got on them--keep your mouth shut if you can't say something praiseworthy or if it ain't otherwise a decent prayer to Him, ok? Not only does He not like it--but I also get a little annoyed with it myself when it happens.

(3.) **If the Lord does happen to provide a ride for both of us along the way, let's be gracious to whoever may help us out and try to be a blessing to them as much as possible in return, ok?**

Now with the road rules established and as we cross...

  US 70/Olton Road and continue out of town, I'll let you in on some of my own past travel experiences (both the highlights and the lowlights, that is) that God has personally used in my life to demonstrate His grace and mercy to me in some of the most practical ways.

Maybe I ought to start with some of the lowlights first. On one of my past Feast trip attempts, I decided to first help out at a prison crusade in Colorado City, then go on from there to Davenport, Iowa for the remaining part of the Feast ahead. I went down this very same highway on the bus to Big Spring, then waited for a bit on the connecting eastbound bus (which once I got to Big Spring I found out that it might be up to 12 hours before the next one to Colorado City would show up).

But thanks to the mercy of the Lord, I didn't have to wait for too long for the next eastbound bus. The catch, though, was that this middle-of-the-night bus didn't technically stop in Colorado City. But the driver did say that once we got there, he would drop me off on the side of the road. So when we got into town, I had the driver drop me off right at the exit where the motel our crusade team was staying at across the road. I got there somewhere around 2 AM and checked in and went to my room where the next morning I finally called the head of the ministry to let him know I was there. (FYI--I only had enough money to take care of about 3 nights at this motel--as you'll see later.)

We did the crusade--and then after we were through and as everyone else was heading home that Sunday, for some reason the ministry head asked me if I also wanted to go back home with them as well. (I had told them during the time they were there about my Feast plans.) I told him no and refused his offer--saying that I had one more night here at the motel and then from there that if I had to go by faith in order to get to Davenport, I'd do it. So they left and went home while I stayed the extra night at the hotel.

As I pointed out earlier, there was one little problem with this arrangement--I definitely didn't have the money to go to Davenport on my own. But now my course was set and I'm now stuck in Colorado City. The next morning, I stayed as long as I could at the motel before I finally went to the bus station. If I recall right, one of the motel employees even graciously gave me a ride out there. (It was a good thing, by the way, that when I first got into town that I DIDN'T go directly to the bus station because I later saw that it was way out on the other side of town from the motel.)

There was yet another problem when I got to the convienence store/bus station--the ATM showed that my checking account had a negative balance. Now I really started to regret not taking up that offer to go back home the previous day. Thankfully, the convienence store/bus station was also a RV park that had a picnic bench--OUTSIDE! So I and my luggage (including my alto sax) found ourselves roughing it that night outside by the park bench. Throughout that night for appearances, I would go back inside the store to use the restroom and also check the ATM machine again (same result each time with my debit card--still a negative balance).

This process went on through the night until daylight came. (It was a real cold night--and I definitely didn't get much sleep either.) Finally, the store clerk noticed my predicament and asked me what the problem was. I told her that I was trying to get Davenport, IA, but I didn't have the money to buy a ticket to get there. She had noticed that I'd been out in the cold all night and asked me when I informed her of this where I came from. I told her Plainview. She said they couldn't necessarily help with getting to Davenport, but that they did have some sort of charity/emergency fund in which they could at least give me a one-way back home.

Reluctantly knowing my current predicament (especially since I had attempted to call that head of the ministry for help—but those efforts were to no avail), I had to swallow my pride and accept this way out of Colorado City. It hurt me to do so— but I was forced to abandon my original plans for Davenport and head back home.

But it was a much-needed lesson learned about presuming too much about what in future situations like these could and couldn't be done—and that I definitely needed in the future use a bit more wisdom in all that I might do for Him.

(Horn honks suddenly from a car pulled off to the shoulder on the side of the main road as we get near Azteca Milling on the southern edge of the Plainview city limits. The driver asks me what's going on and where we're going…) Uhhh…we're heading first to Lubbock, and then from there wherever our God decides He wants us to go…(Driver asks me how…) We're walking by faith and not by sight…(Driver invites us in…)

You sure?...Ok—sure appreciate it. Give us a minute and let us get across the road first to you. (I turn back towards you, the reader.) See-what I'd tell ya earlier? Let's hop in, shall we? The Lord provided once again for us, didn't he? (You nod your head…)

(We put the bag with our belongings in the trunk and then get into the cars back seat—myself on the left and you on the right. I speak to the driver…) How ya'll doing today? Yeah—I'm blessed and highly flavored—with coconut pieces and chocolate sprinkles…But I hadn't decided what flavors of ice cream I want yet…(all of us chuckle at that remark) Oh—by the way…meet my friend, the reader, who's along for the ride…They don't say much—but they're sure a good observer and listener. (We both shake hands with the driver. The driver restarts the ignition, pulls the car out of Park, and makes his way back onto the I-27 main road traffic.)

Where we heading?...Right now, Lubbock—and then we may go east from there depending on what He (I point up…) may direct us to do. Uhhh…you're going on to Midland? Ok…tell ya what…maybe if you could drop us off somewhere around the South Ave. Q/US 84 exit…in fact, there's a Valero convienence store right where 84 hits Loop 289…could you just drop us off there and maybe we can go from there?...Great!!! You need directions from there? Yeah—I'll let you have them once we get there…

(Driver asks us what we both do for a living and tries to engage us in small talk…) Hmmm…let's say we're both pilgrims and strange travelers on the earth and leave it at that…What about you?...Hmmm, insurance salesman, eh? What types?....Did you get to sell much today?....AWHHH….rough day for you, eh? Bottom fell out? Lost your job because you didn't meet the sales quota? Such a shame…Gonna be hard to break the news to the family when you get back home, eh? Hey—I hope we're not any trouble for you. (Driver nods no—he's fine with that…but then is in tears and seems frustrated at this latest personal development.)

Hey, my good man—I've been in your shoes, too…I've done my share of sales jobs myself…Not an easy row to hoe—that's for sure…(I find a Kleenex from the back seat and hand it to him…) There you go, man…Just keep your eyes on the road and the hands on the wheel for now…Listen, I know it's hard to believe right now—but trust me on this. If you'll let GOD be your provider and do what He said for you to do, He'll be more than faithful to do for you what He promised to do.

(We all approach the city limits of Hale Center.) I was just telling my friend here some things about "…walking by faith and not by sight…" You interested in hearing about them? Driver says yes, through his tears…) Ok…Uh—where's that found? Well, I just happen to have my New Testament here…let me find it real quick and read it to you since you're driving—and maybe you can check it out for yourself when you get home, ok?

2 Corinthians 5

New International Version (NIV)

Awaiting the New Body

5 For we know that if the earthly tent we live in is destroyed, we have a building from God, an eternal house in heaven, not built by human hands. [2] Meanwhile we groan, longing to be clothed instead with our heavenly dwelling, [3] because when we are clothed, we will not be found naked. [4] For while we are in this tent, we groan and are burdened, because we do not wish to be unclothed but to be clothed instead with our heavenly dwelling, so that what is mortal may be swallowed up by life. [5] Now the one who has fashioned us for this very purpose is God, who has given us the Spirit as a deposit, guaranteeing what is to come.

[6] Therefore we are always confident and know that as long as we are at home in the body we are away from the Lord. [7] For we live by faith, not by sight. [8] We are confident, I say, and would prefer to be away from the body and at home with the Lord. [9] So we make it our goal to please him, whether we are at home in the body or away from it. [10] For we must all appear before the judgment seat of Christ, so that each of us may receive what is due us for the things done while in the body, whether good or bad.

In particular, I was just starting to tell my friend here about some times where I literally had to put this Scripture into practice. I hadn't told him this yet—so maybe this might be a good chance to tell you both what I learned about Psalm 126:5 & 6 and Psalm 20 :

Psalm 20[a]

For the director of music. A psalm of David.

[1] May the LORD answer you when you are in distress;
  may the name of the God of Jacob protect you.
[2] May he send you help from the sanctuary
  and grant you support from Zion.
[3] May he remember all your sacrifices
  and accept your burnt offerings.[b]
[4] May he give you the desire of your heart
  and make all your plans succeed.
[5] May we shout for joy over your victory
  and lift up our banners in the name of our God.

May the LORD grant all your requests.

[6] Now this I know:
  The LORD gives victory to his anointed.
He answers him from his heavenly sanctuary
  with the victorious power of his right hand.
[7] Some trust in chariots and some in horses,
  but we trust in the name of the LORD our God.
[8] They are brought to their knees and fall,
  but we rise up and stand firm.
[9] LORD, give victory to the king!
  Answer us when we call!

Psalm 126

New International Version (NIV)

[1] When the LORD restored the fortunes of[a] Zion,
  we were like those who dreamed.[b]
[2] Our mouths were filled with laughter,

our tongues with songs of joy.
Then it was said among the nations,
   "The LORD has done great things for them."
³ The LORD has done great things for us,
   and we are filled with joy.

⁴ Restore our fortunes,[c] LORD,
   like streams in the Negev.
⁵ Those who sow with tears
   will reap with songs of joy.
⁶ Those who go out weeping,
   carrying seed to sow,
will return with songs of joy,
   carrying sheaves with them.

Hey—you know what Psalm 126 says about sowing in tears? No—we're NOT asking you for ANYTHING—keep your money in your pocket right now...you'll need it to keep that mortgage and utilities paid around the homestead...But I remember Bible teacher Joyce Meyer one time on TV saying something along the lines of this: "...If you'll get out of yourself and do something for someone else, then He is released to mighty things on your behalf in return." It's not an exact quote of hers that I just quoted, granted—but it can still work in any situation you may face today.

I also want to emphasize verse 3 of Ps. 20 where it says—" ³ May he remember all your sacrifices and accept your burnt offerings. ⁴ May he give you the desire of your heart."

I could tell you of many times where all of this has held true for me personally more times than I can count—so many, in fact, that I don't have time to tell all of them to you. And I ain't joking, neither—I mean I have had my rent paid for at times even when I've gotten eviction notices...(no—I didn't see no "secret millionaires"...just people like you, I might add)...people like you have given me rides out of the blue, meals paid for, and even hotel rooms completely covered when I didn't have a dime on my debit card.

(Driver looks at me incredulously as we pass the rest stop between Hale Center and Abernathy.) I'm serious, man. Maybe I've got a little time after all to tell you one experience similar to this. In fact, since we're heading towards Lubbock, it reminds me of a time when I actually got a ride with a drunk cowboy....(Driver nearly swerves to the right side of the road upon hearing this…) I know it's hard to believe—but it actually happened…trust me!! (Driver manages to self-correct…)

I had just finished a weekend visit with my cousin who lived in Lubbock at the time. On a Sunday night, I decided to go to a Nazarene church on the South Loop to see a "Jews For Jesus" concert before heading back to the bus station to catch my midnight Greyhound bus back home. During the concert when the offering was passed, I was led to sow a few bucks to the offering plate as well.

After the concert ended, I started making my way back towards the bus station downtown. Mind you—I didn't even have a way to get from that church to the bus station—especially with the luggage that I now had to tote around with me…Now you talk about walking in faith—you try doing it with heavy luggage in tow and see where that gets you…Anyway—I continued first going east on the South Loop until I got to University. It was dark by that time—but I was definitely at least making good time after I turned left onto University and went north.

Then somewhere around 34th and University where the Plains National Bank Building used to be, as I was crossing the intersection with my luggage, a guy in a pickup truck in the middle of said intersection asked me, "Where you headed?" I responded, "To the bus station downtown." "Why?" "Because I'm heading back to Plainview." "Get in…" So I put my luggage in the back and hopped in. After I did this, the first words out of his mouth to me were, "…I've gotta go take these boys back home, " referring to a couple of other guys sitting in front of and also beside me. "…they're drunk as skunks."

It was only then that I immediately realized a few things about this scene: (1.) the driver ALSO seemed drunk as a skunk himself; (2.) there were beer cans scattered all in front of me in the floorboard in the general area where I was sitting; and (3.) they all seemed like they were just coming from a party or a nightclub or something like that. A thought or two even briefly crossed my mind in the form of a prayer, "…Lord, what have You gotten me into this time?" I was about to find out—like it or not. We finally got to this house where the other two got out of the truck and I was urged to move to the front seat. This drunk cowboy and I then drove off back onto 34th Street and into the night.

As he was driving, our conversation started taking a strange turn towards religion and why I was there during the weekend just passed—including his even asking me about the current state of my personal relationship with the Lord. Then out of the blue, he asked me, "Are you one of them Jehovah's Witnesses?" I said, "No."

He then relaxed and said, "..GOOD—because if you had been, I would have dropped you off on the spot!"

We continued towards downtown and the bus station. When we got there—as I was thanking him for the ride and preparing to get my stuff out of the back of his truck, he said to me, "Coy, I really like you—and I want to do something for you and give you something." I responded, "No—don't worry about it. The ride's more than good enough." But he insisted, "No, I really want to do this…" So he got out his checkbook—and to my incredulous surprise, he wrote me a check for some unknown amount that I couldn't see. At first, I strongly protested against him doing this and told him that he didn't need to do such a thing. But he wouldn't take no for an answer. So I reluctantly took the check (figuring that maybe it was something like 5 or 10 or no more than 20 dollars). I asked him after that if I could at least pray over him and his seed (to which he agreed). Then I said my goodbyes to him, got my stuff out of the back of the truck, and went inside the bus station.

A few minutes after he left and after I had went inside the bus station, I decided to go back into my pocket and see how much the check was actually for. Believe it or not—he had actually written the check for $100! My jaw literally dropped to the floor when I saw that. Then I had another thought or two cross my mind. First, I remembered during the ride when he told me that he was actually the president of a bank in Kress. Then I immediately thought, "Oh, great—what if this check doesn't cash?" But I put the check back in my pocket and continued waiting on my bus back home.

The next day after I got back home to the ranch, though—I found out for myself that I needn't have worried so much about the validity of the check. And how timely that check was for me—because I had a credit card bill that I needed to make a payment on.

(Driver takes a quick glance at me and mouths the word, "WOW! Really???" As we all start leaving the Abernathy city limits and cross the Hale/Lubbock county line, Driver says the following to both of us…)

Driver: "…I wish someone would help me like that."

Me: "Hey, man—the God I serve is no respecter of persons. What He did for me, He can do the same and possibly even more for you."

Driver: "…You say God did that for you…that's good. But I've done too much in my life wrong for God to even care for me." (Before I attempt to respond, Driver continues.) "…Hey, listen—I even lied to you. I ain't no insurance salesman…In fact, I just did something that I'm totally ashamed of. Now I'm gonna lose my family…and I'm only just about a month or two from being completely released from my parole…If my parole officer finds out what I did…you won't say anything, you promise????"

Me: "Don't even tell me what it is or what you did. I don't even need to know the details, ok? If you don't go telling me something about that, then I won't be able to tell anyone anything anyway. Right?"

Driver: "Ok…"

Me: "Besides, me and my friend here—I think I can speak for them also…(You nod in agreement.) We could care less about what you did."

Driver: (Shouts out loud…) "BUT I DON'T WANT TO GO BACK TO JAIL, MAN!"

(We're all shocked to hear this at first…but then I continue as we all approach the New Deal city limits.)

Me: "Well, as I said—if you don't tell us anything, we can't say anything—ok?"

Driver: "Ok…"

Me: "And as I was about to say, more importantly to God—HE doesn't care what you did either!"

Driver: "But when I got out of the penitentiary last time, I threw my Bible in the trash can the minute I got to the bus station. No one was there waiting for me but my old buddies when I got back home. NO—GOD can't help me no way out of this situation!"

Me: "YES, HE CAN, man—IF you'll let HIM do it! Genesis 18:14 says, "Is there anything too hard for the Lord?" I SAY NO!!! Now I'm not guaranteeing that everything's gonna go peaches and cream and rose gardens for you—don't get me wrong. But I DO know for sure that He's got the answer you need for your situation. Let me ask you a question or two, ok?"

Driver: "Shoot—go ahead…"

Me: "Number one is a question I heard someone say that's so perfect for this situation—"How is it between you and the Lord right now? How is your peace with Him right now?"

Driver: "And number two?"

Me: "...If you were to die this very night and then you suddenly right after that were to find yourself standing before a holy God and He were to ask you—"Why should I let you into My Kingdom?"—what would you say to Him? What would your response be?"

Driver: (hem-haws for a moment, then says...) "...I don't know...I don't know if I could even face Him. He'd strike me down dead if He knew what I just did..."

Me: "...Listen, man—God loves you just the way you are right now. Don't run from Him—run TO Him! (I say this as we find ourselves in between the Regis St. exit and Pharr RV...) You don't have to go clean up just perfectly or jump through any hoops for Him to even let you see Him or love you. In the first place—YOU CAN'T clean yourself up before Him...only He can do it anyway.

"...Do you know that my loving Abba Father sent His only Son to die on a cross for those things you did wrong? But not only—that same Son was then buried and later rose again just so that you can reconciled to Him and be able to sit with Him in heavenly places. This Jesus—FYI, in Hebrew...he's actually called Yeshua or "God is my salvation"...this Jesus wants to have a relationship with you..."

Driver: "...He does?"

(We're now approaching the 19th Street exit on the Interstate...)

Me: "...Yes, he does...And I tell you—it's not that hard to do. Would you like to do that?"

Driver: "You bet I would. How do I get to know this Jesus dude?"

Me: "...Tell you what...we're getting close to that 84 exit I was telling you about earlier...not this exit, but the next one coming up...how about we turn off there and get on 84 East and I'll show you where that Valero store is that you can drop us off at? Then when we get there, we can pull off and stop there for a few minutes...and me and my friend can tell you more about how you can do that. Deal?"

Driver: "It's a deal...you said turn off on this next exit?"

Me: "Yes…then when you get to the light, turn left and head towards Slaton and stay on 84 until I tell you otherwise."

(From here, we all safely go into the west side of the parking lot between the Carriage House Motel and the said Valero store. You and I help lead Driver through the Sinner's Prayer and also pray over him about the current situation he's facing. After the prayer's done, Driver thanks us—and I hand him a phone number of a good friend I know who has a ministry to ex-offenders in the Midland/Odessa area that he can call for further help and guidance in what he's currently facing. We then thank him in turn for the ride and start to get our stuff out of his trunk.)

Driver: (shouts) "HEY—one more thing…"

Me: "Yes?"

Driver: "…You said something while ago about sowing in tears? I need to give you something else."

Me: "No, man—the ride's good enough…Besides, you really need your money now more than we do…and I told you earlier that our God is more than able to supply all of our needs."

Driver: "I know—but I'm not going to need this where I'm going. And it sounds like to me that you two have got a long journey ahead…PLEASE take it!!! PLEASE—and pray for me again, will ya?"

(Reluctantly, I take the contents of what's inside the closed fist when I shake his hand—then when I've grasped his hand, I immediately pray over him one more time…this time over his seed into us and believing God for his harvest into whatever needs he faces in his previously described situation. Then I thank him again for everything….)

Driver:" I'll do it…By the way, what's the best way to get back home from here?"

Me: "Just get on the Loop and stay there all the way until you get to the South Plains Mall and the Loop 327 exit. Spur 327 will eventually take you to the Brownfield Highway. Then stay on 62/82 until you get into Brownfield. Go all the way through town…then just as you're leaving Brownfield, you'll find State Highway 137 that can get you to Lamesa. From Lamesa, I think there's another state road from there that'll take you straight back towards home. That help for directions?"

Driver: "Sure does…thanks…see ya later.."

Me: "No—thank you for everything…Have fun, be blessed in Him, and drive safely, ok?"

(Driver rolls up his car window, drives off, and heads for the Loop. After this, I once again turn my attention back towards you, the reader…)

Isn't our God good? (You nod in IMMENSE approval…) Here I go—just about to tell you all of my old war stories—and here HE goes—giving BOTH of us a real-life down-to-earth practical lab time illustration that just showed you what I'm talking about much better than I could. That was a story that's gonna go in the record books for both of us—that's for sure.

Say—while we're here, let's go into this Subway for a little while to take a break so I can tell you a couple more of my other stories and get a REAL meal for a change, shall we? We can save all the stuff we got back home for later anyway—it'll keep…If you'll help me get this luggage in and find us a seat, I'll be back in a second. I got to go over to the other side of the store and practice what I preach. I need to get a money order real quick before we get back on the road, ok? Be right back…

(After we get settled in to our seats at the Subway and ordered our food, we pray a blessing over the food and also especially over the driver that helped us.)

Hey—I got an idea for you…I mentioned earlier about the Carriage House Motel nearby…looks like we might have enough cash to get a room for the night. Want to see about doing that after we're through here? (You nod your head in DEFINITE agreement over that prospect.) Besides, we still got a long journey ahead on this segment—and it wouldn't hurt to get a good strong rest before we travel on, right? (You keep nodding…)

While we're eating here, maybe I'll tell you a couple more of my travel war stories…This reminds me of another Feast trip in which I started over in Plano to attend an international prison ministry conference before I planned to go from there down to Huntsville for the last part of the Feast. The Lord even blessed me in a few ways—one of them being that after I barely had enough money to take care of my first night there that the Lord used some others at that conference to pay for the remaining night I spent at the motel that I was staying at that was next door to the hotel where the conference was held. (I did have to spend a night or two sharing a room with some Nigerian bishop I never knew who loved to keep the TV blaring all night to a Dallas Christian TV station that basically played nothing put Creflo Dollar and other "word-of-faith" preachers—but hey, only a minor inconvenience at most...)

That Sunday morning after the conference in Plano, I wasn't able to get a ride to the nearest bus station in Richardson that would enable me to get a connecting bus in downtown Dallas that would in turn allow me to go south towards Huntsville—thereby causing me to miss that originally scheduled bus.

So I wound up literally having to start going south down US 75 (with luggage in tow, of course). After I realized, that I wasn't going to make it to the bus station in time, I eventually found myself near a church that was having their regular Sunday morning worship services. I popped in for one of their services and also used it to also take a load off of my feet for a little while. After the service was over, I continued on what seemed to be my long journey towards the downtown Dallas bus station. After I had just gotten back on my feet from a rest break on the side of the road, some guy in a car that had just been to church earlier that morning and then went on to some sports bar watching a Dallas Cowboys game on TV pulled over and offered me a ride.

He first stopped at a convenience store where he told me to buy whatever fountain drink I wanted. (That 64-oz Dr. Pepper sure tasted great to a thirsty camper like myself at the time.) From there, he graciously brought me all the way to the Dallas main Greyhound station.

What was remarkable to me in particular about that ride wasn't, though, what he necessarily did for me. The driver apparently attended a very large Metroplex Methodist church—but was going through some very significant marital troubles that were bordering on the edge of divorce. He personally alluded to me that I must have been to him some sort of angel sent to him unawares into his situation. I wouldn't personally agree with his assessment after the fact, but I was nevertheless glad that the Lord did allow me to speak a little personal counsel into his life that might could help him appropriately deal with the situation at hand for him (including some stuff I was aware of about Oral Roberts and the principle of "see-faith"). It was one instance among others that helped me to find by personal experience that when you're walking in faith for Him, sometimes it's not always necessarily for you—but it is most likely primarily for the benefit of the one that needs to give and sow through you to the Lord.

Hey—how's that foot-long sandwich? (You respond with food in your mouth, "Hmmm…pretty good.") Perfect for a health nut like you, eh?

Maybe one more quick story before we see about calling it a night, ok? It's getting late and dark out there anyway…I also remember a trip I took to another prison ministry conference one time in San Antonio. What was especially memorable for me personally were the last two nights of this particular trip. After the conference was over, I decided to try to go to the Saturday night service of Oak Hills Church (you know—the famous one where Max Lucado has preached a number of times in the past). It proved to be a struggle that was to no avail by the time I caught several city buses as far as I could and then eventually walked several more miles worth in an attempt to get there in time.

But I wound up getting there long after that night's service had concluded and the folks at the church were in the process of closing up for the night. But the lady who met me there at least was gracious enough to receive the offering and prayer requests envelope I had wanted to leave there and even allowed me to look around the place a bit and take a few pictures of the church for the benefit of the folks back home that might never get to see it.

After the church closed and I finally had to leave and head back towards my hotel, I then faced a very long walk of about 15 miles or so one-way (thankfully WITHOUT very much to carry at all) that literally took me all night to do. I barely got back to the hotel around 7:30 AM with only about an hour-and-a-half total time for a quick glorified nap and then an even quicker shower and change of clothes before getting up to go to another church Sunday morning.

After that church was through, the ride I had went to in order to go that particular morning graciously dropped me off at Cornerstone Church (where John Hagee preaches) to await their Sunday night service. This one service—I tell ya—was definitely a memory for the ages here.

That night's service at Cornerstone also just so happened to be the very same night where Mathew Hagee actually gave a concert that would be the official launch of his debut CD (which was also taped for later viewing worldwide…Every time I see that program rerun on the "John Hagee Today" program, I recall being there in person having the privilege to see it for myself as the program unfurled…). But what really got me was what happened AFTER the concert. Before the senior Pastor Hagee gave the benediction, he told those assembled that there would be a punch-and-cookies reception immediately following the service.

"…My staff told me that we're having a punch-and-cookies reception after the service tonight. When they said that to me, I asked them—'Well, do you know how many punch and cookies my congregation eats?'

"…They said, 'Yes.'

"…'Well, do you have enough?'

"…'Yes.'…So we're having punch and cookies after the service tonight."

A brief footnote to this story—I can personally attest to the fact that I was present at that reception—because I had several glasses of punch and three sugar cookies about as big as my hand. I can tell you that it was definitely work the 10-mile walk back to my hotel before I had to go back home to Plainview early the next morning…

Well—looks like we're finished eating…Why don't we make tracks and split for the Carriage House and see if we can check in for the night, ok? I'm tired already…and I bet you are, too.

[Chapter 17:] [Lubbock--Part II—US 84: How to Walk By Faith And Not By Sight--WITHOUT MONEY! (PART 2)]

(Fast forward to the next morning after we check out of the Carriage House and we get back with luggage still in tow onto US 84 East heading southeast towards Slaton and Post.)

You sure you got a decent night's sleep in that room last night? You sure were snoring ZZZs and sawing logs ALL NIGHT long…I mean I could hear you louder than the air conditioner….Oh, I'm sorry that the motel didn't have a decent continental breakfast. Maybe we can pop back into the Valero and get a quick burrito or two and a drink for the road…Don't worry—I've got you covered again…get what you want…

(After we make a quick stop at the Valero again, we continue on our journey southeast on US 84.) Man, that traffic getting off the Loop's rough, ain't it? (After crossing the intersection of US 84 and the Loop, we begin making our way out of the Lubbock city limits.)

But you know what to me was one of the most memorable trips of all? It was another Feast trip in which I literally went across the country over a two-week span. First, I attended the first part of the Feast in Huntsville where the brethren there as always were extremely hospitable and helpful to me during my stay. Then from there, I continued on to Houston on the Greyhound to go to a Precept/Kay Arthur training seminar and then hopefully to Lakewood Church for a Saturday night service before I was to catch a flight early that following Sunday morning at the Hobby Airport to Charlotte, NC to meet up with my cousin who lives in Asheville, NC (about an hour's drive or so from Charlotte).

The fun really started on this adventure when I was about to leave the church where the Precept seminar was at to go to the service at Lakewood. I called a cab company to see how much a cab would cost to get between the two places. I was informed that it would be around 52 bucks. I only had on my person a combination of cash and an unendorsed money order of slightly above 40 bucks. So I had to just go ahead and tell the cab company that I'd give them as much as I could and get me as close as possible to Lakewood, and if I had to, I'd try to hoof it from there the rest of the way. So when the cabbie got there, I told him of the predicament and asked to just got me as close as he could to Lakewood with what I did have available. That's when the miracles really started.

To start off with, the cabbie didn't even turn on the meter. (That was a shock and a half to start with.) He also called his wife on the two-way radio who happened to be one of the dispatchers and basically did an end-run around his bosses to do my cab ride. And gasp—of all things, he even went so far to stop at a convienence store and buy me Doritos and a Dr. Pepper on top of it. And he even for good measure drove me right up to the doorstep of Lakewood itself. (THAT was one cab ride that I was more than glad to give that cabbie all I could to bless him.)

But (as the TV commercial would say)—THAT'S NOT ALL! Once I got to the service at Lakewood, I came into a scene I will never forgot. For those not otherwise familiar with Joel Osteen and Lakewood, keep in mind that their current location of their main campus used to be the old Compac Center where the Houston Rockets used to play ball. There was absolutely no doubt how welcome they made me there when one of the first sounds I would hear upon entering the vast main sanctuary would come from a 300-voice youth choir and orchestra belting this song at the top of their lungs—

["Not Forgotten" lyrics, aongwriters: LINDSEY, AARON / HOUGHTON, ISRAEL; Warner/Chappell Music, Inc....]

I am not forgotten
I am not forgotten
I am not forgotten
God knows my name;
He knows my name.

...

Warner/Chappell Music, Inc.

[P.S.—I happened to come in during their youth night service. Joel didn't preach that night, but other Osteen family members were present and one of his brothers did.] I was, to say the least, fairly impressed with the way they did their service.

But that was nothing compared to what happened next. I was on my way out preparing for my 10-mile or so walking journey to the Hobby Airport for my flight to Charlotte. I greeted one of the ushers and thanked him and their congregation for their hospitality and the great service. I also asked him for directions on how to get from the church to the airport. The usher must have seen my luggage and (even though I didn't directly tell him) realized my true predicament because he asked me to "…wait just a minute—I'll be back…" Then presently he introduced me to another gentleman and said, "…This man will get you a ride to the airport…"

It turned out that he didn't just get me a ride to the airport—but on top of it, he first took me to a Golden Corral restaurant and sprang for my supper before taking me over there. It was even more of a treat to meet this guy for a little while and hear of some of the things that were going on at Lakewood and share with him in turn various things going on in my life at the time. And he got me to Hobby in more than plenty of time for my flight (in which I spent the rest of the night until my departure trying to get some sleep in the airport chapel).

(We now have already left the Lubbock city limits and are passing by the TDCJ Montford Unit Hospital and Trusty Camp. After we've passed by Montford (since there's a sign urging motorists NOT to pick up hitchhikers)...

...we stop somewhere along the side of the road and take a break for a few minutes to get a load off of our feet. You now are toting the suitcase with all of our valuables—including food and drink still unused from yesterday.)

Hey—would you mind handing me one of my teas and one of the packages of peanuts and the beef jerky? (You do so…) Thanks…Sure glad now that we got that stuff we did yesterday, eh? It might not be cold as it was yesterday…even if we did put it in the motel fridge overnight…but at least it's something to drink, right? (You nod…) I told you yesterday that you'd get mighty thirsty on the trail if you didn't get what you did. (I'm saying this as you open one of your water bottles and start to drink from it as the West Texas August afternoon hot sun beats down on both of us.)

Oh—I forgot to finish the remaining part of my trip story. After leaving Asheville and ending my two-day visit with my cousin (thanks in part to a one-way bus ticket between there and Springfield, MO that he and a couple of other folks in his church bought and sowed into my life when I didn't have a dime to do so on my own), I then started towards the last and most challenging leg of my trip to Branson, MO to attend a Billye Brim Prayer Conference.

I say that leg of the trip was challenging for a couple of reasons:

(1.) There was NO direct bus that even went to Branson AT ALL at the time…instead, the nearest bus station was in Springfield which was about the same distance between here and back home in Plainview (about 45 miles). Let's say I spent a good deal of that bus ride between Asheville and Springfield silently praying in tongues. I even remember when I had a layover in Nashville I stood outside in the bus station parking lot at night (at least as best as I could) basically having an all-out, no-holds-barred talk with Abba Father about the particular situation that was about to face me.

I said to Him in Nashville, "…I came all this way to do this trip…The minute I hit Springfield, I have absolutely NO WAY to even get to Branson there and no money to speak of to pay for the hotel room and everything else I need when I get there. Lord, if YOU don't do it, then I absolutely will not get done at all—because I sure can't do it on my own!" And the closer I got to the Missouri state line and also to Springfield, the more I silently prayed in tongues over His Divine provision for the rest of my trip. I finally got to Springfield—and promptly found out that even a shuttle bus between there and Branson would cost around 85 bucks. Which led to problem #2—

Not even hardly having a penny to my name (not even on my debit card), I then started to make my way with several deals of luggage towards the main highway. Just a few blocks away from the bus station, it seemed like most of my luggage somehow disappeared or got stolen. I would up at a store right next to US 65 with only one suitcase left which thankfully had about three days' worth of changes of clothes and a few other significant items that I needed right then. So figuring that it was too late to turn back now, I started going south from US 65 towards Branson.

I had gotten about a couple of miles down the road when a pickup truck going the opposite way happened to notice me and eventually turned around and picked me up. The driver took me to a place several more miles down the road called the James River Fellowship.

Have you ever heard the Pam Tillis song "Mi Vida Loca"? Well, this is where things really got crazy. I was first taken to the church office where one of the Fellowship's counselors who happened to live in Branson said that he'd be willing to take me there. I happened to also be able to stay for their Wednesday night service which was a very good one in itself.

After the service was over with, there were a couple of twists to this— (a.) Security got spooked at the suitcase I left outside the Sanctuary and wound up calling the local police (who then promptly confiscated it); and (b) The counselor that had originally promised to get me into Branson forgot about me and was just about on his way back home when the church office was finally able to call him on his cell phone (which then caused him to have to turn around and go back to the church where I still was waiting).

So after another one of the James River Fellowship folks called this counselor, it was probably a good hour or so before he finally showed up back at the church. First, we went to the local police department so that I could claim the remaining piece of luggage still in my current possession before we sped on to Branson.

This counselor guy proved to be a very interesting chap. For one, his voice sounded all the time like he had just shouted himself at a football game so much that he was hoarse. (I found out the reason was because he had permanent laryngitis.) Then I also found out during the ride that he actually written a book or two in his time—one of which was actually read by President Bush #43 (George W.—that is). [To prove it, he even showed me a letter he had received from the First Couple themselves.]

When we finally got inside the Branson city limits, he proved to also be the consummate tour guide—pointing out things to me, "…This is the Mickey Gilley theatre…" and "…This is where Barbara Fairchild lives." He even told me a story and a half on Ms. Fairchild—even going so far to tell me that he'd actually met her personally and that she had been in his church a few times.

But what really floored me was what came next. We finally got to the Chateau on the Lake Hotel where the Billye Brim conference was being held. He asked me if I had a room—and I said that I didn't have the money for it. So he checked with the hotel's front desk about the rates—and the cost was going to be somewhere over $100 per night. Thankfully, though, I remembered that I had originally reserved a room at a Days Inn that was considerably cheaper and had a good continental breakfast.

So you know what this guy did? He actually took out his credit card and paid my bill for the two nights I had on my original reservation. Before I had time to thank him and ask him if I would pray over him and his major seed of generosity into my life, he had to split fairly quickly. I was just definitely thankful and praising God that I had just been able to get into town—but having this room reservation supernaturally paid for on top of it was a definite confirmation that I was supposed to be there during this time. (And the fact that a daily continental breakfast came with it was even more helpful since I didn't have any monies available to speak of for meals.)

Being at Sister Billye's prayer conference proved to be a real faithbuilder for me in a number of ways. Included were a couple of interesting experiences during the first two days in Branson like when I had somehow had sudden doubts the second night about how long the James River counselor guy had actually paid for the room. I wound up after the next night's service wandering for several hours in the city (including a VERY cold time outdoors next to a car wash) before I finally got the gumption to go back to my hotel room sometime around 1 AM and see if I STILL had a room or if the hotel had confiscated my luggage. It was a real relief when after putting the room key in the slot I found that I could still get in. I was never more relieved to have a room for the night.

Another one was on Friday when I had originally planned from there to go back to first to Springfield, then from there attempt to go to a weekend conference of the Worldwide Church of God at a camp across the state from Branson. But it had been all I could do just to get here and there was no way by now I could get back to the Springfield bus station on my own. I therefore decided to test the Lord and see by His provision where He wanted me to go next—whether He felt I needed to be at the other conference across the state or to simply stay where I was in Branson until Sunday night.

So I checked out of the hotel and headed for the Chateau for that day's service with my luggage in tow again. After winding up getting a ride back to the Chateau by a couple of Mormons (who both seemed to have no absolute clue who Billye Brim was), I sat my luggage down in an out-of-the-way spot in the hotel that was fairly close to where the conference room was. (I'll pick this part of the story back up in a minute or two.)

The entirety of the Billye Brim conference itself had a number of great highlights for me. At one point, Bob Oakes (now deceased who was Shelli Brim Oakes' husband and Billye's son-in-law) gave a mass altar call for people who needed to be prayed for concerning healing for back pain and other arthritis-related ailments. Another service actually saw 101-year-old Mama Jenkins (now also deceased) and Sister Billye pray over all of the youth present at the conference who were 20 and younger. Among those prayed for Sister Billye and Mama Jenkins during that service (and I can truly attest to being a direct witness of this) was Richard and Lindsay Roberts' youngest daughter, Chloe. A number of the greats in the charismatic/"word-of-faith" movement were there at the conference including Kenneth and Gloria Copeland and Mac and Lynne Hammond.

But that wasn't all there was for me...no, sirree...One time during one of the Conference services, someone from out of the blue who was under the inspiration of the Holy Spirit actually gave me a $10 bill. Another time between services, someone got up out of their place in line, went to the nearby hotel ATM machine, and after withdrawing gave me another sixty bucks in cash.

...which leads me to take off the pause button on what happened that Friday once I got back to the Chateau for the Conference. In between services since I didn't know whether I was going to leave that day or what—so I sat in the floor at the place inside the hotel where I had parked my suitcase.

When it was eventually apparent that I was NOT going to leave Branson that day and that from here I was completely stuck here until my next bus in Springfield Sunday night, I then figured that if I had to sleep outside around the Chateau and wait on services there without a room, I would do so. (Besides, I had checked out of the Days' Inn not only in accordance to my original travel plans, but also not to take unfair advantage of the counselor who had helped me out so graciously in the first place.)

As I was waiting on the Lord's direction on what I was to do, one of the ushers happened to see me and my suitcase. When he asked me what the situation was and he saw the direness of my present circumstance, he graciously allowed me to stay the rest of the trip in his room at a different motel in town. It turned out that the place he was staying was even better than where I had just been at—for not only did this particular motel that this guy stayed out have a pretty decent breakfast in itself, but also had free ice cream and cobbler each night for its guests to boot.

(There was one little proviso to this—after each night, this guy did ask me to go ahead and pack up the next morning. But he thankfully wound up not only hosting me the rest of my time in Branson, but even took me back to Springfield on top of that on the following Sunday afternoon in time for me to catch my bus back home.)

This Conference usher happened to be a RHEMA Bible Training Center graduate who was working as an paramedic in Tulsa. During the remaining part of my Branson stay, it became clear one of the reasons I didn't get to leave town on Friday. This guy was really going through some marital troubles to the point of divorce due to his now-estranged wife getting up and literally leaving him…and who was not only in his eyes living a life of outright rebellion against him, but more importantly against God. It did prove to be a pleasure to share our war stories and personal struggles with a previously unknown brother-in-arms.

As you can see, I came into Branson with nothing but one suitcase with three changes of clothes. By the time I returned back to Springfield on Sunday evening to catch my bus back home, I left Branson with a high hand and my immediate needs for the return trip fully fully supplied! HALLELUJAH! Not only was I supplied and sent back home with sufficient food, snacks, and money (in which I was able to before I left Springfield get a very BIG meal at a Waffle House that had what I wanted), but I even was able to take home a book on the life of John G. Lake that I had just heard about earlier in the trip.

But we ain't done yet with this story—because there were a couple more final surprises from the Lord that still awaited me back at the Springfield bus station. One of them was that all of the other luggage that I thought had been lost before I first left Springfield for Branson was found by someone just several blocks away from the bus station immediately after I had to completely ditch them and were taken back to the bus station to await my return.

The other was that I even got credit back on my debit card on top of it for the two separate in-state Missouri bus tickets that I wasn't able to use. (Good thing I did get that credit—because I later found out that my checking account was running a negative balance anyway.) You can say that the first part of the Branson leg of that entire extended Feast trip was a real challenge—but I definitely came back home from the entire trip not only much better financially, but even more pumped spiritually as a result of having gone in the first place.

(We now find ourselves about halfway between Lubbock and Slaton and are coming close to a nearby Christian radio station.)

Hey—how about this spot for another brief rest break? Besides, you remember me telling you yesterday about the road rules? Well, this money order I still got has something to do with them. And it also reminds me that I forgot to tell you about **Road Rule #4—that whenever the Lord uses someone to provide and sow a significant financial blessing (for example—do you recall that driver that brought us into Lubbock yesterday?), I try to make it a personal custom in return in order to do my part to be a wise steward of all the resources I'm given to sow a portion of their gift to me as a sort of "twice-sown" seed on their behalf to whatever ministry the Lord may have me to give to and use that as my way to believe (especially since they have already blessed me—but in which as a result of their generosity to me I believe that they are due the bigger harvest from Him) that our God will return their seed back to them pressed down, shaken together, and running over in whatever way they need it most.**

And as I do that on their behalf, sometimes I might bump up the total given a little bit as an additional seed offering to believe for whatever other needs I may face from here. Since He supernaturally provided for us, there was a reason I got that money order back at the Valero. The Lord reminded me of a pastor friend who lives here in Lubbock who has a weekly paid church program on this station—and that I needed to drop off this money order here as a payment and a credit he might use towards paying for his airtime here. Go ahead and stop and take a load off of your feet for a moment or two. I'll be right back…

(I go inside the radio station and drop of the money order with the receptionist. After I come back out, I rejoin you where you're sitting and sit down beside you.)

Ok…done…Hey—could we while we're sitting here pray over that driver and this seed and believe that He will do what is the absolute best for all of us as we continue on this present journey?

(We join hands and bow our heads in an appropriate prayer of agreement.)

Abba Father—thank you so much first of all for the many blessings we have just received even since we left home base in Plainview. I especially thank you in particular for making this particular chapter as well as the previous one in our current journey not just a collection of my old war stories, but for taking the unique opportunity to show my friend (YOU— the reader) who may not have had as many experiences and adventures in faith as I've had a true-life based practical lab time-like illustration of just how You have personally taught me what it is to "…walk by faith and walk by sight" and how they might appropriately put those lessons into practice in whatever situations they may face in their life today.

I ask You that You not make all of this so much to the point where they will need to learn those same lessons I did through the school of hard knocks, but that instead they be able to learn from much easier instruction from myself, You, and others to where they can learn those same lessons much faster—and they won't have to go through too much inconvienence personally as they do it.

And as for that driver we saw yesterday who blessed us immensely in the way that he did—we sow officially sow a portion of his gift to us into the work of the Kingdom on his behalf as "twice-sown seed" that in which You promised in Psalm 20:3 that You would remember all of our offerings. We both don't know the particular details of the situation he was referring to—nor do we care to know. But YOU know everything about what he's facing now. We intercede on his behalf that You or man not judge him in accordance to your judgment, but instead with Your loving grace and tender mercy. Give him right now Your wisdom and discernment on what to do—then help him to listen to Your voice and do what You tell him to do. And we trust that as he does what You say to do that it will be THE right thing to do AT THE right time—and that it would be the best thing that will benefit all parties concerned and give due honor and praise to You in the process.

And for both myself and my friend here, we ask that you continued blessings and traveling mercies be present throughout the rest of our present trip. And in accordance to Mark 11:22 & 23, we thank You for it in advance and declare it done in the name of your Son—Y'shua Ha'Meshiach…Jesus Christ, our soon-coming King, Master, and Lord…AMEN!!!

(We now begin to get up from our brief rest break and start again going southeast towards Slaton.)

Ready to get going again?

(Just as we're getting up and starting again down US 84, a Texas DPS trooper car behind us slows down, pulls off towards the shoulder, and flashes his lights at us.)

I hope you got your driver's license and/or appropriate ID with you…PLEASE don't do anything stupid, ok?

(DPS trooper gets out of the patrol car, says hi, and asks us what we're doing and where we're going.)

Howdy, officer…No, we're not trying to cause trouble here. We're just mindin' our own business—that's all…NO, we're not hitchhiking or trying to panhandle or do anything like that, sir….the people can do as they wish—and we don't want to get in their way…
(Officer asks to see our licenses. We give them to him—then he asks me where we're going and how we plan to get there…)

Uhhh…We're heading towards I-20 and Abilene—then waiting to see where we need to go from there…(Officer asks me how we're going to get there….).Uhhh, sir….we're walking by faith and not by sight…(Wink…) (Officer goes back into his patrol car with our licenses, then calls in the info to Dispatch….)

[Chapter 18:] [Fort Worth (Part II): How I Finally Received The Baptism Of The Holy Spirit]

Boy, that was a close shave back near Slaton…Earlier in this book, I talked about how during the 1995 Feast in Fort Worth would prove to be a personal gamechanger for me. Well, it's amazing what happened exactly seven years later at about the very same time where another trip to Fort Worth would prove to be yet another demarcation line in my life.

So since we went back on the road again (literally!) during the last chapter, we might as well go back one more time to Cowtown so that you can see what happened to me that would have such an impact on how I have lived my life since. (P.S.—I'm going to take a break again this chapter from being the GPS directions guide on this one.)

As has seemed to be the case in my life, it was once again another development on the financial and employment fronts that would bring things to a climax. Through the first part of 2002, I was still doing the part-time job I had with Anderson News Company that involved maintaining and merchandising the magazine displays at the local Wal-Mart in Plainview. It always seemed to be a struggle trying to make ends meet financially—especially in trying to find more substantial employment in town that DIDN'T require a car.

From time to time, those ugly eviction notices and all my other bills would continue to pop up like a jack in the box. And you know the old saying about robbing Peter to pay Paul? Well, it still seemed to me that it was more like robbing Peter completely just so that I could make SMALL payments to my bankruptcy attorney to have a chance in filing Chapter 7 (which was seeming to take forever at the pace I was paying them at the time), THEN paying Paul (the landlord, that is) all I could pay him, then from there making more small payments to James and John, too…all the while hoping to bleep that Nathaniel would be patient with me and stay off my back long enough until I can finally have the chance to take care of him as best as I could.

During this time, I started looking at the one very small benefit that came with being a part-time Anderson employee—being able to save a portion of what little income I had in a company-owned 401(k) fund. Especially at times where I saw that all the money I had accumulated in the 401(k) (if I could access it, that is) could surely help me out of this or that short-term financial jam, that money started looking pretty good to me. BUT there was a BIG problem—the only ways I could even be able to access it were either if I was terminated in some fashion from my employment with the company OR if I were in what was called a hardship situation (meaning that I basically had to either be in an accident, an emergency medical situation, OR be in imminent threat and danger of eviction from my apartment that would cause me to be homeless). For a while, I didn't come close to technically satisfying any of those conditions (despite my best attempts to try to prove otherwise that I WAS truly in a CONTINUAL hardship situation)—so there in the 401(k) my money continued to sit.

This continued throughout the spring until one day when I came in to work. The delivery driver who was acting as my interim immediate supervisor at the time happened to come and see me at the store. He told me that the company due to budget cuts was going to completely let go of all part-time merchandisers in all stores and start having the delivery drivers also do the merchandising in each store from here on out. He told me that it wasn't anything against me or the work I did—but that it was strictly business.

He apologized for the lack of proper notice and gave me instructions to finish out the current week as well as the next week before I would need to officially consider myself terminated. After that, I followed those instructions to the letter, finished my final shifts, and the next Friday left my badge inside the returns, and stopped acting in the capacity of merchandiser for this particular store.

Now things were really beginning to get lean again financially for me—and what were once funds that I couldn't previously access would now be monies that I now had no choice but to either take as a lump-sum check or rollover into another separate 401(k) account. Urgent financial needs (despite the fact that I would wind up having to see 20 percent of the proceeds taken out for Federal taxes) dictated that I take the former route.

Meantime, I filed for unemployment benefits with the Texas Employment Commission (TEC) (now called Texas Workforce Commission—TWC). But in the process of filing for unemployment (which I did receive and kept receiving as I waited for the final response), Anderson suddenly decided to appeal my claim for unemployment due to their contention that I was in their view STILL employed by them (despite significant evidence I had to the contrary) and therefore not entitled to receive unemployment benefits.

I had to spend a lot of time drafting my response to Anderson's appeal (isn't that BIZARRE—actually having to prove that you're NOT an employee?) that showed that I was told by my immediate supervisor about the changes in my employment status and that I had NOT acted in any official capacity as an Anderson employee since my actual date of termination (given the just-described chain of events I mentioned above). One of the biggest pieces of evidence that I was able to use against them of all things as a part of that official response? You guessed it—the 401(k) paperwork. After all, I told them (in detailed legal gobblydegook, of course)—according to THEIR own rules and those of THEIR bank, I legally could not access that 401(k) UNLESS I had been officially terminated from employment in some way. (Thankfully after that, they finally backed down and allowed the original decision for me to receive unemployment benefits to stand.)

In the midst of all this personal turmoil, I had planned to take another extended Feast trip that year to several locations which included yet another attempt to finally get to Davenport, IA, then eventually go to Fort Worth for something that Eagle Mountain International Church was holding called "The Days Of Refreshing" that of all times that year was being held right during the Feast itself, then head on from there to head to Gatesville to take part in a prison crusade with a ministry I had never worked with called Law of Liberty Ministries before heading back home.

Let's say that to take the above trip was going to be yet ANOTHER literal walk of faith—especially as far as being able to do this and still keep the rent on my apartment paid was concerned. So I waited and waited for the 401(k) check to show up—but it was slower than molasses in coming. By the time I should have been on my way to Davenport for the Festival (FYI—that year, it was actually scheduled closer to the time between Trumpets and Atonement), still nothing in the mailbox—and I was still stuck at home.

One week of the planned trip had passed—until I finally got the check in the mail. I had been watching "The Believer's Voice of Victory" broadcast all this time—and decided that if I couldn't go to Davenport, I'd at least make the best of what was left of this Feast. So off I went anyway on an all-night bus to Fort Worth with barely enough money to cover a number of necessary expenses for the first part of the trip (including two nights at a Days Inn in White Settlement and monies for other incidental expenses along the way).

I left Plainview for the long bus to Fort Worth and didn't get into the city until very early the next morning. After arriving in Fort Worth, I then found a city transit bus that I was able to go on to get to the nearest bus stop possibly to the motel. I arrived at the motel and managed to check in and pay for my room up until Friday morning when it would be time for head on to Gatesville. A quick shower and a change of clothes—and it was time to call a cab to go all the way across the Metroplex to EMIC and the headquarters of Kenneth Copeland Ministries.

It was a very expensive cab ride to Eagle Mountain (around $43 or so ONE WAY which I barely had enough to cover)—and I managed to get to the church as Keith Moore was wrapping up not only his sermon for that morning, but also for his part of the entire meeting for the week. So after the morning service (since I was basically planning to be stuck out there for the rest of the day), I took advantage of the opportunity to take a look at the KCM headquarters building, look around in the bookstore for a little bit, and even eat in the KCM cafeteria. (That cafeteria, by the way, was almost like dining in a gourmet restaurant—not only in ambience, but also in the quality of food. That was a treat in itself.)

After going through the facilities, I then went back towards the main church building to await that evening's service. I took some of that waiting time and found a spot that overlooked Eagle Mountain Lake and then had a very candid discussion with the Lord about everything that I still faced back home.

"...Lord," I prayed in desperate frustration—"...I came all this way to go and do what You told me to do!" I then reminded Him of what I faced with my employment and financial situations as well as the deep issues and desires of my heart that still faced and haunted me. I shouted to the Lord over the lake to a point where I thought others might even possibly hear me—but I didn't care. "...Lord, I don't have enough money for my motel in Gatesville—much less to get back home! IF YOU DON'T DO SOMETHING NOW, then I can't go any further from here in ANYTHING I DO! It's either YOU do it—or it won't get done at all!"

I poured my real heart to Him, crying over all of this with my tears, and beating the air in total frustration and hopelessness at all of these financial, transportation, and employment problems that could never be solved at home—UNLESS HE STEPPED IN AND DID IT! I then went back towards the main church building to once again further await that evening's service.

What transpired that night will be indelibly engraved in my head as long as I live. The worship team started out the service with the song "King of Glory" by James Hall:

Lift up your heads
O Ye gates
Be lifted up ye everlasting doors
And the King of glory
Shall come in
King of glory shall come in

...

From that point on, I was taken to a place in the Spirit that I had never really been before—especially during praise and worship.

Then Kenneth Copeland preached a sermon that was like he was talking directly to me when he gave it. When he said the following, it made me pay attention more than any other sermon (even in WCG/GCI itself) that I ever heard in my life up until that time:

"**...FEAR TOLERATED IS FAITH CONTAMINATED!** You cannot be in fear and still be in faith. Fear and faith are opposites...Fear has torment. Perfect love casts out all fear. There is no fear in love—and there is no torment in your God."

Boy—did THAT one make my hair stand up! All these years I constantly feared another eviction notice on the door—or worse, a knock on the door from my landlord...that was the key! I was always afraid of the financial wolves at the door—and I sure as bleep DID NOT want to move back to Lockney ever again in disguise—having to move back to my mother's house because I couldn't stay in my apartment. And all my financial resources at home were dwindling by the minute.

After Brother Copeland's sermon was done, Pastor George Pearsons extended the invitation not only for those who needed to be saved, but also for those who wanted to receive "the baptism of the Holy Spirit". I didn't feel a need for salvation due to those things the Lord had told me years ago about being in WCG. But having by this time been around the folks at New Covenant and hearing them talk about deliverance and this "baptism of the Holy Spirit"—I realized just how little I really knew about the things of the Spirit. And they sure didn't teach THIS in WCG! (In fact—years before within WCG/GCI, ANY displays that were interpreted to be in any way, shape, or form "Pentecostal" or "charismatic" were not only highly discouraged, but also outright condemned.)

And yet here I was raising my hand in a service to receive this "Holy Spirit" in a church that just 10 years before I would have never darkened the door of—and of all places, this was occurring in the very same city where just 7 Feasts ago I had to deal with the painful aftermath of "…the changes". It was HERE in this town where my God finally began to close the circle on what I'd been through. I went down the aisle to the enthusiastic reaction of the congregation present to do this "receiving the Holy Spirit". I prayed with the altar counselors who counseled me about what this second baptism was really all about and gave me some literature to read later.

The service ended and everyone went out the doors towards home. As I gathered my things to go, I faced another problem…how in the world was I going to get back to my motel in White Settlement 17 MILES AWAY? Keep in mind—I basically spent just about every dime I had for the one-way cab ride to get here. I definitely had nowhere near enough for another cab for the return trip—or even anyway to call one.

Then I thought to myself, "Well, if I have to walk the 17 miles back to White Settlement, I'll do it." I started walking—and I didn't get any farther than the front entrance to the KCM campus when a young couple with a young son happened to ask where I was going out their car window. When I told them that I was heading back towards my motel in White Settlement and they realized my predicament, they graciously offered a ride.

When I got in the car, the father told me, "First I need to get my wife and kid back home…that kid's crying and they need to get back home quick." So we first stopped by his house—and after the wife and young child got out and I said my goodbyes to the wife, the husband then said to me, "…Hang on a minute—I got to go back into the house and get something."

When he came back to the car, he started bringing in a bunch of sport shirts and dress shirts hung up on hangers. As we continued our journey back to my motel, he told me that he had actually been saving these shirts upon the direction of the Lord for someone that He didn't know yet. But when he saw me, he apparently felt the leading of the Lord to give them to ME! (Talk about the Lord literally wanting to put new clothes on me both physically and spiritually…) Mind you—this wasn't simply just one or two or even a few shirts. Instead, this guy gave me so many shirts that I didn't know if I could pack all of them in the garment bag and suitcase I had brought for this trip.

But nevertheless, by the time we got back to my motel, I very much graciously thanked him and we prayed over each other before parting ways for the night. Act I of our Fort Worth drama ended with my taking those same shirts into my room and realizing that night that the Lord didn't just want to clothe me with His Spirit--but that He also wanted to clothe me physically as well. With prayer and a new way of expressing myself to Him in my mouth, mind, and heart, I called it a night.

Act II of the Fort Worth part of this trip started with myself oversleeping (in part probably due to the lack of sleep I had on the bus getting there) and missing my originally planned time to go back to EMIC for the next morning's service with Billye Brim. After weighing my options financially and otherwise, I realized that if I just went up a major cross street as far as it would go north that I could eventually dead-end with Loop 820 and from there wind my way back to Boat Club Road which eventually led back to EMIC. So I went ahead and did that for several miles (with appropriate rest stops on the way to get something to drink and rest) until I got to Loop 820, then I continued for a few more miles proceeding northeast on the Loop until I got to Boat Club Road. At a shopping center, a guy in a pickup truck managed to see me and then eventually help me to the EMIC campus.

If I thought my Act I from the previous night was something, it wouldn't hold a candle to what I'd see next. That night for the first time during praise and worship, I practiced speaking in my newly acquired prayer language. I even laid prostrate on the floor and experienced a new freedom in speaking and worshiping Him that I'd never known before.

Then Sister Billye started preaching about "The Glory Of The Lord"--and especially what it meant in the actual Hebrew and how the Jewish people viewed this interesting phenomenon. Billye related some of the same things of the Spirit that I had previously heard from other sources--but in unique ways that finally made sense to me--and in which I had truly never heard or seen before ANYWHERE. For one thing, it definitely got my attention when Sister Billye talked about things like the Sabbath and the Festivals and Holy Days--stuff that only someone from WCG like myself might have a faint clue about. Talk about someone else preaching right to me--she did not just with the specific sermon content, but also within the current context of the Feast of Tabernacles that was going on as we were at that service read my mail right where I lived.

What was even more remarkable about this service was what happened (or maybe to be technical--what DIDN'T happen) after she finished her sermon. Sister Billye then dismissed the service for anyone that needed to leave right that moment.. But NO ONE moved--and it was so quiet in the sanctuary that you could have heard a pin drop...and no one would have still moved an inch. This probably went on for at least 30 minutes, 45, maybe even an hour--in complete DEAD silence. Then out of the blue, someone attempted to start prophesying in an unknown tongue--but Sister Billye firmly stopped them from doing so and said sternly, "...Hold your peace! Hold your peace! This is a holy moment and this is holy ground. Hold your peace!"

More silence ensued, followed by someone groaning like a pregnant woman giving birth in sheer agonizing pain and travail. As this was going on, Sister Billye's daughter, Shelli Oakes (now Baggett) started singing this song:

The Glory Of The Lord (Betty Jean Robinson)

Verse: 1
I was down at the alter, talking to the father,
when the glory of the Lord came down,
I cried father please save me, he came and forgave me,
when the glory of the Lord came down.

Chorus:
The glory of the Lord came down, the holy ghost fell all around,
I was praising my Savior who lives and reigns forever,
when the glory of the Lord came down.

....

Soon Sister Billye started joining Shelli in that song--and both sang it ad infinitum--first for a while in a slow, relaxed speed. Then eventually the Spirit's move grew into an absolute tidal wave engulfing everyone in the room with it. By the end of it all, Shelli's original song speed sped up to the point where the whole scene was like Mardi Gras in New Orleans--and the mood was so celebratory and festive that there were even people "...drunk on the new wine of the Spirit" to where they could hardly even stand up or walk half-decently. And both Sister Billye and Pastor Pearsons were among them--as they both eventually ended up on the platform face-down eating carpet (honest--I'm telling you the truth here) passed out together. (And for those asking or even thinking that someone somehow snuck any adult beverages into EMIC--you can perish the thought right now. If you're still in doubt on this, I would refer you to Acts chapter 2 and recommend that you check its details for more info.)

Finally after all of these escapades were over with, Sister Billye and Pastor Pearsons finally one more time dismissed the service somewhere close to midnight. I hated having to leave this atmosphere--but I had to catch the bus the next morning to Waco to meet up with the crusade team. But talk about a great note to leave town on--there couldn't have been any more perfect way to do it. And I would certainly need THAT encouragement for where I was heading next.

The next morning, I checked out of my White Settlement motel and headed towards the Fort Worth bus station. By the time I got there, I only had enough for a ONE-WAY ticket to Waco. There was absolutely no way that I had enough to turn tail and head back home--so I had no choice but to put myself at the mercy of the Lord from there. What I dreaded most was that I didn't even have the money to cover the hotel room I had reserved in Gatesville. And I wasn't exactly forthright at first neither with Cindy Richter (one of the heads of Law of Liberty Ministries)--at least not until we actually got to that motel (and only after I went through the motions of checking in, but couldn't since all I had on my person was $2 on my debit card). Cindy was really ticked off at me when I had to admit what happened.

But it was too late to turn back--so Cindy and her husband, Randy, told me to go ahead and keep my stuff in their truck until they could figure out what to do with me next. During this time, I literally went from being as high as a kite with what I had just experienced back in Fort Worth to being down in the dumps and ashamed of myself stuck in Gatesville without even a room or the money to get a ticket back home.

Nevertheless, we went on to the first night's service at the Woodman Unit. It was, out of all my time so far volunteering in prison ministry, the first time ever I had even stepped onto a women's unit. Even with what I was facing outside the gate, I was still in for a treat being in the same service as these women. I had previously been in a number of crusade services at various men's units throughout the state of Texas--but they didn't even hold a candle to the unabashed way these ladies did it. They held NOTHING back during their praise and worship times--and weren't ashamed to do so neither for their Master.

What broke my heart, though, in seeing those women come in was the way they looked in their physical appearance. Some of them looked like they had makeup similar to what a Cover Girl model might look in a magazine. Who knows what pain and suffering these ladies had probably went through during their life--and most of it sadly due to what a bunch of jerks of my own gender had done to them. It really made me want to cry for them and over them.

That night after we got back to the motel that most of the crusade volunteers stayed at, I left my luggage in the truck, found some bushes in a place close enough to the motel to where I could be there in time to go to the unit the next morning (but yet far enough away for anyone else on the crusade team to see me), and hid in shame. The motel happened to be very near a Wal-Mart. As I looked at the Wal-Mart and the surroundings around me, I then thought of the state I was in the previous night. Last night, I was in Fort Worth in a motel room. Tonight, I'm stuck outside by a bunch of bushes next to a motel WITHOUT a room of my own. What have I gotten myself into this time?

While the others on the crusade team slept comfortably in their own rooms, I basically spent the night outside alternating between said bushes and sitting in a chair around the motel pool--trying to keep a low profile in case I might get arrested for vagrancy or trespassing. When the sun rose that next morning and I met up with the rest of the crew on the truck, I realized too late that they had been trying to find me all night to let me know that they did find a room I could have stayed in with a group of other guys. If it weren't for myself and my stubborn pride--trying to do things in such a way to attempt not being an unnecessary burden to others...and what did it get me?

The next morning we went on to a different women's unit where the group I was in did visitation with the ladies inside their pods. The remainder of the day went fairly well--with a pretty good meal fixed for us in the Officers' Dining Room by some of the offenders themselves who were great cooks. (And it was almost the equivalent of good home cooking at that, too!)

The Richters and the crusade team after we left that unit that day then generously bought my supper and even loaned me around $100 or so to where I could get a one-way bus ticket back home from Waco. They then took me back to the Waco bus station and sent me back home from there. (FYI--it did take me a while to pay the Richters back--but I'm thankfully that He allowed me to do so eventually.)

I may not have had a completely easy time of travel during that particular Feast. But I learned through practical experience what it is to not just be washed in His blood--but more importantly born of His Spirit. I learned also that faith NEVER mixes well with fear...in fact, they're like oil and water to each other--and that fear is NOT His best for me. I found out that He has a much better plan than I might think or conceive. But more than anything else, I found out an old truth that He had me to once again rediscover--this time through different conduits and channels. What is that truth? That He loves and cares for me and that He's more than able to protect and provide for me whenever and wherever I need it most.

The first time I was here in Fort Worth, I thought I was attending the funeral of things I once knew. But at that time, I realized here in Cowtown of all places that even in the darkest times He's still there for me. This time in Cowtown, He didn't just remind me of something I should have already known by now--but He even gave me a deeper understanding of that truth in ways I had never known before. This new knowledge would guide me back home as I would soon start another brand-new chapter of my life--finally being able to pursue a very long-held desire of my heart that I so desperately wanted and craved for many years.

[Chapter 20:] [Plainview (Part VI--N. Quincy St.) Learning To Be A Voice For Him--The KKYN Years (2002-2010)]

Man, that was a LONG bus ride back home from Fort Worth--but it sure beat walking back home, right? Now that we're back home at the ranch again, we might as well start heading to our next stop here at the homefort. Now don't get gripy with me again, ok--because I don't want to hear it!

From our present location at what was once the Greyhound bus station downtown (but is now a rental hall facility because Greyhound after switching their bus stop location several times in several months finally settled on stopping at one of the convienence stores on I-27), we'll this time just need to go down two streets. The first involves going straight west here on 11th Street, passing the traffic light on Columbia and also New Life/Nueva Vida Assembly of God as we go. When we see Highland Elementary on our left, the next light on Quincy Street/State Highway 194 is where we'll then take a right and head due north. We'll pass Harvest Christian Fellowship and the newly renovated Plainview High School along the way.

Then when we get to the Plainview Bowling Alley, Highway 194 will branch off from us and start heading towards Dimmitt while we still continue north on Quincy passing the Xcel Energy Service Center, Plainview Tire, and even the back side of the Wal-Mart Distribution Center. When Quincy intersects with 32nd Street, we'll see a sign that says New Covenant Church (remember the pigs in the parlor we left behind before our recent "boot camp" session?) is 4 blocks east and one block north of us.

Up a little farther than that, it will be clearly obvious what our next tour stop will be by several glaring indicators. The first is the very big vacant lot with a large antenna to the east of the main building. The satellite dishes on the north side are the second clue to our puzzle. By the time you see a sign of a metal guitar attached to a tree stump, a red vehicle that displays this place's call sign letters and other promotional logos, you'll no doubt easily recognize what place we're at now.

And I have no doubt that by the time we're through with this chapter why this place for all practical purposes will be the final cutoff place historically and chronologically of this book where we will be covering the actual history of my life. After this chapter, the remainder of what I wish to say will primarily personal general commentary and wrap-up.

Let me first give a brief technical note before we proceed. At the time of this writing, I am actually still on my SECOND different tenure with the stations here at Plainview Radio. However, to preserve and protect the privacy, self-respect, and dignity of my current colleagues, this chapter will ONLY talk about the significant events that happened during my first go-around of employment here. I needed to find a good jumping-off point of the overall part of my life story—so I figure that the best way to do it is to simply talk about how one of my dreams after many years of waiting came to pass—and the numerous things that happened within these very studios from start to finish.

When last we left my life story, I came back home from Fort Worth and Gatesville still needing to find another job after being dismissed (sort of) from Anderson

News. About two weeks after I came back from the trip, I got an e-mail from a Brandy Haines at KKYN asking me to call her back for a possible job interview. The receipt of this e-mail for me was particularly remarkable in itself because at the time (once again due to financial reasons) I didn't have a working phone at my apartment. So I not only e-mailed Brandy back, but also called her right from the library to respond back. We were able to arrange an interview for the next day—and by that following Friday, I first started working for the four stations that now currently make up Plainview Radio as a part-time football game board operator.

Late that Thursday night/Friday morning after Brandy told me I was hired, I made the celebratory phone calls to several phone calls (from various nearby payphones, of course) to close family and friends to let them know the great news. Among the back slaps and hallelujahs, I will admit that I had one question in the wind for the Lord. That was—after years and years of trying to apply and get interviews with about every blessed radio and TV station in the Amarillo/Lubbock area (KKYN definitely being one of them) seeming to shut the door in my face and not even give me the time of day--WHY NOW...and WHY THIS PLACE?.

The Lord's clear response to the question on the floor came in the middle of the night when I felt a prompting to go back and listen to a tape of an interview that one of the priests I had worked for at St. Mark's had done years before with a radio station in New Jersey. During the interview, the priest talked about what he had personally went through growing up in Pakistan as a Christian in a predominantly Muslim nation. Hearing the stories on tape reminded me of what I had heard him personally speak about at various occasions at the church I was still working at part-time.

After I finished listening to the tape, the Lord spoke to me   "I have called you to be a voice to speak for those who can't speak for themselves, who are humble in heart for those who are afraid to speak for one reason or another." Hearing this from Him humbled me very fast to say the least and blew me away at the wisdom and His timing required to bring me one of my life's major dreams to finally come to pass in my life at one of its most critical junctures.

The first few months at KKYN were interesting in themselves for a couple of reasons. One was when Jerry Larsen (the first general manager) I worked under) actually died suddenly on Thanksgiving weekend within the first year after I started working for KKYN. Most of the time, I was forced to keep my focus on keeping an eye on the station and doing what I was told. But I did have some contact with Mr. Larsen—and he at least was nice enough of a guy who died way too soon and unexpectedly of a heart attack. It definitely left a void in management in which Tom Hall, the program manager here in Plainview, and the general manager of our company's radio stations in Big Spring, had to temporarily fill.

Just prior to Mr. Larsen's death, our stations were owned by a group based in the Bryan/College Station called Equicom who were in the process of trying to sell our stations to another prospective owner. One particular group visited our stations in consideration of buying them—consisting of a limited partnership with a father, son, and one of their best friends—Jerry and Michael Rhattigan and Guy Gill.

The day I met them, I was getting ready for a ballgame later on—while this partnership group was meeting with others at the station. Finally, it came my turn to talk to them. Noting that I was the new kid on the block, I didn't have too much to contribute to the conversation—except for one thing.

At the time on the wall near where Tom and Brandy had their joint office, there was a bulletin board that contained a lot of pictures of newspaper clippings, photos, and other whatnot about the people and things going on around the station. One of those pictures that clearly stands out in my mind is that of Tom on his motorcycle that he occasionally liked to ride in good weather. Pictures like that led me as the very last person who would speak to them that particular day to point them towards that board and to look on the faces of the people on it as a way to make my own appeal on their behalf.

I then basically told these potential owners—"…Look at all the faces that you see on this bulletin board. These people have families and life stories and lives of their own. This station and community from what I know about it has a proud tradition stretching for many years. You can have an impact not just on the lives that you see here—but on an entire community.

Then in one last final desperate plea, I said to them: "Please for the sake of the people you see here—don't let this place die." I don't know whether it was a factor in their ownership group's decision—but in 2004, this same partnership trio would eventually buy from Equicom our four Plainview stations along with three others in Big Spring and several others in Uvalde and Eagle Pass.

GOOD FRIENDS IN A STORM

One of the things that is most apparent in the radio business the more you work within it is a consistent LACK of consistency in personnel, format changes, or

ANYTHING else for that matter. For example, I was one time asked by Tom whenever our Tejano DJs for one of our FM stations were suddenly fired that same afternoon to start simulcasting our sister country stations until further notice. That particular station would eventually change its format dramatically to classic rock, playing primarily '70s and '80s heavy metal type rock.

That fact about the radio biz made me appreciate more the continuing presence throughout most of my tenure with the company that would be eventually known as Rhattigan Broadcasting TX-LP—the Rhattigans, Guy Gill, Tom, and Brandy. In a period of nearly eight years of employment, our stations went through FOUR entirely different General Managers (not counting the time that Tom had to fill in as Interim Manager), who know how many different sales reps, and no telling how many different board operators.

These five through who knows how many different changes served as constant anchors at various times that I've needed them most. In this current world of corporate mergers, restructuring, and the like, it was been a great help to me at times to know that whenever needed that I at least knew the owners of our stations on a first-name basis. The Rhattigan partnership trio throughout the years I've worked with them have graciously treated me with respect as a valued employee and have been helpful in many ways in not only advancing my own career, but also in advancing the interests of our stations as a voice for Plainview and the surrounding communities they serve.

But two of the biggest reasons that kept me for a pretty good time from even wanting to work anywhere else for years were the persons of Tom and Brandy as my immediate supervisors. As the years at KKYN went on and the three of us bonded much closer together, I was not only grateful for two special bosses that didn't just tolerate my little quirks and idiosyncrasies, but have since become two of my closest best friends who were always there for me to help me as much as they could—especially when my back (financially and otherwise) was up against the wall.

Several things in particular strike me as quite remarkable about Brandy. The first was her age—and especially how I viewed it. Believe it or not—she and her husband are both younger than me. And yet (mainly because she has worked in radio longer than myself), I sort of actually viewed her most of the time as an OLDER sister to me. (Strange, I know—but I guess that's how most relationships are..]

Also something that continually exasperated me was what seemed to be her almost endless supply of indefatigable energy. Get this—this woman and her husband have several kids (two of them their own and two others they adopted as a result of their serving as foster parents). She on several occasions I know of has gotten up early in the morning just to bake chocolate brownies for all of our staff for our "sharing table"—PLUS worked a full workday starting around 5:45 AM or so [sometimes—as rumor might have it—WITHOUT makeup (which she might actually put on DURING the Morning Show)] until who knows when...THEN leaving shortly after I came in for work in the afternoon, THEN pick up her kids from school, THEN either have to come back and do some production or something like that before going home for the day—THEN on top of that, exercise her obligations as a wife and mother to her family. I STILL stand incateduously amazed at how adept this woman was at getting the most that she possibly could get done within ANY 24-hour period.

But what really strikes me as remarkable about Brandy above all else are two things that speak about her personal beauty and Christian character. One of these things is a statement that I hope her husband will not only mind me saying—but will even take as a sort of back-handed complement from a single guy still looking for his own potential life partner. What would that be? That if Brandy weren't already married to him with kids AND she weren't also my boss and she were ever single again, the temptation would be VERY strong for me to desire a more intimate romantic relationship with her. Thanks to her husband, though—this urge has been EASILY resisted...but nonetheless, I hope this man will never fail as long as he lives to continually and lovingly remind her why he originally wanted her as his wife to start with and how truly blessed and most envied by a single guy like myself.

The other involved both what I would personally later see in terms of personal generosity at various times towards myself when she didn't have to and another instance that I didn't know about until after she left that would reveal the true depth of her relationship with the Lord.

One of my remarkable remembrances about Brandy were those times when she was forced to ask me to come in to board op a Saturday ball game—the very day that I needed to be off on the Sabbath due to religious reasons (as well as the fact that it was my scheduled day off due to the fact that I worked on Sunday morning instead as a part of my own job responsibilities). I was usually reluctant to do so at these times—but there were various occasions where there was absolutely no choice but for me to come in. (And I usually wasn't a very happy camper in doing it, either, when this type of instance happened.)

Being the true sweetheart that she was, she would literally take additional money out of her own pocket and give that to me as a special personal bonus from her for me doing this special favor for her. To me, that is a real boss going above and beyond the call of duty to make something that was otherwise unpleasant and distasteful for me personally into something somewhat more bearable and tolerable in doing.

But something Brandy probably didn't realize that she left behind on the computer to me personally spoke even louder volumes about her personal relationship with her God. Brandy before she left KKYN for good started taking classes at Wayland Baptist University to finish her college studies that she abandoned years before in preparation to become a kindergarten teacher.

One day after she left, I happened to be going across her old computer files when I saw a paper she had written for an Old Testament history course in which she interviewed her pastor's wife and did a sort of comparison/contrast study between that pastor's wife and Queen Esther. I knew that Brandy and her family were active at a church in Tulia with her husband serving as one of the elders. But Brandy wasn't as a boss necessarily one who displayed her religious beliefs outwardly on her sleeve. When I read that paper she did for that particular class assignment, I saw for the first time a totally different side of Brandy that I never really knew about her during all the time I worked under her.

Just as Brandy would eventually prove to be one of my closest friends through the many storms we went through at KKYN, Tom Hall would become that and even more to me in his own way. And I would find myself thinking that if I had a chance to name a replacement dad to replace the one that I never got to have in the first place—Tom would definitely be very high on my list of candidates I would have loved to have the title of "daddy/father" in many ways.

Tom himself could be a very good disciplinarian. He could definitely give you grace—but you'd better not violate it because you could almost take him at his word that if you ever did something wrong again in his presence—you were most certainly going to be fired. As the play-by-play sportscast announcer I worked under the most, you DID NOT in either your right or wrong mind want to be on the business end of the broadcast phone line if you ever messed up anything during a ballgame or even have to tell him something that someone else did that he didn't like. If you wanted to hear real cussing, just listen to him during the commercial breaks when he was off air—because he might be prone to utter one of his most colorful phrases that could almost make you blush.

Tom, though, was also a sort of McGyver of broadcast equipment. I am still convinced to this day that if you only gave Tom a box of matches and some copper wire, he could fix just about anything in any of our stations in no time flat. Need to get a simulcast of a game onto another one of our stations? Tom could simply take a cable, hang it on the wall near the ceiling, and stretch to the other station with the greatest of ease.

But Tom also more than anything else has pleasantly surprised me with his own version of remarkable generosity—especially in my times of utmost need. For instance, when I had to work at the station on behalf of everyone else so that they could take off for Thanksgiving (Tom in particular because he had to help with the Queens Basketball Classic)—there he'd be showing up with a great big plate fully of food from his own family's table coming just for me.

Many time during my tenure at KKYN, Tom would be there doing what he was able to do—whether it would be food, money, or whatever else I needed most. One time as a Christmas present, both he and Brandy chipped in and actually bought me a brand-new TV set when the one I had went out. It didn't matter what the personal need might be—Tom proved to be a salt-of-the-earth type friend most appreciated when you were in a time of storm. Were it be that I had more folks like him—for remembering those acts of generosity made any times I might have had problems working here seem a little sweeter.

When I first started at KKYN, I found out I knew absolutely nothing about being a board operator. That was a situation that only time (and not necessarily education) could cure. I started by cutting my eyeteeth doing our live broadcasts of Hale Center football games
.

Most people usually don't have much of a clue at all as to what it sometimes required to put on any sort of live radio broadcast—especially where sports coverage is concerned. The best ways I can put what a radio board operator in does in the first place in layman's terms are twofold.

First, think of a sports play-by-play announcer as a sort of performing poodle on a unicycle on a highwire. The board op's job is basically make sure not only that the highwire is safe for the poodle to walk on, but that the poodle is able to perform on said highwire like it's easy to do for anyone (which we ALL know that is nowhere near the case). On top of this description, also think of that same board op as a radio equivalent of an air traffic controller—especially in knowing that the hardest parts of any flight are the takeoffs and the landings. If you can manage to juxtapose those two images in your mind, you'd pretty much get the nutshell board op job description.

And the only real difference between a board op and a disc jockey is usually the fact that board operators don't usually talk on the air live during a broadcast. But both in radio must attempt to exhibit at all times some reasonable amount of personal poise, tact, and diplomacy towards not only their co-workers, but especially towards the listeners and/or callers who to them are asking you life-and-death (or that's what seems to be like to them) questions such as "What's the score of the Bulldogs game?" that they probably weren't listening to or as lost as snowgooses in the first place to find. (Sometimes, I will admit, I felt like I worked more for the Bureau of Stupid Questions rather than a radio station judging by the calls we might get.) All that was required to insure your eventual climb on what I called the "board op" ladder.

For us at Plainview Radio when I started, the bottom board op rung was doing Hale Center football broadcasts on KVOP, our news/talk/sports station, where you got your basic training on how to work with play-by-play announcers (especially in regards to their own individual little quirks). I especially got my fill of dealing with announcers when during high school basketball playoffs and baseball season we had to do what we called "Sports Express" games (i.e.—these were games which our stations were paid by another Lubbock station to broadcast because of KVOP's unique signal reach).

Two specific incidents come quickly to my mind about these KVOP games. One of them was the number of times our Hale Center announcer would say on the air ad nauseum—"...And that's something you don't want to see from your senior..."—or different variations of the same.

But another one of Sports Express origin will forever live in infamy. I actually had another announcer that I had to board op who was broadcasting from Big Spring that was a real ordeal to work with. The guy talked to me as if he were sweet as sugar, but seemed like he couldn't hear my cues to go back on air to the point where I actually doubted if he could hear off the side of a barn. Most of the time through that game broadcast, I thought that each time I cued him through a break that I was literally having to jumpstart a mule every time I turned around. Needless to say, I was VERY glad when we were done with that particular game.

But despite the lowlights, there were definitely several play-by-play announcers I loved working with. Tom was obviously my first choice since I had the unique privilege to work with him for so many years. But his brother Bobby and his sidekick Phil Cotham (who ironically used to be one of my coaches I had played and/or worked under while at Lockney High) weren't too bad to cut up with during commercial breaks, either. (I just wish, though, that they didn't do as many of what I called "shirttail shoot" late broadcast starts like they did—but that's neither here nor there.)

Chris Due (former announcer for the Lubbock Cotton Kings hockey team and now Lubbock Christian University Sports Information Director) was also at times a fascinating personality to work around—primarily because he has a voice that's almost identical to Dennis Miller's. Any time I hear Chris's voice on air, I can't avoid thinking of him as if he were the President getting off Air Force One and stepping off the tarmac at the airport for some diplomatic summit—all while he was also broadcasting a particular ballgame. That image is indelibly burned into my mind—especially each time a baseball is hit out of the park for a home run— along with Chris' words—"ADIOS, BASEBALL!" being said as the ball falls into the crowd in the right field stands.

But the play-by-play announcer that would be a close second to Tom as most enjoyable announcer to work with will always be Steve Dale (son of legendary Texas Tech basketball announcer Jack Dale). Usually, I'd wind up getting Steve on Sports Express games—and sometimes on occasions where I probably if I had a choice I would have rather not have had to be there in the first place. I especially liked working with Steve a lot because I could really cut up with him during the breaks. Steve was your quintessential radio professional—turning on the charm when he was on-air and then once I told him, "You're clear...", being honest as a dickens to me that he really didn't want to be there working that day either. Those rare times when I did get to board op Steve's call of a game made even those times I was stuck working otherwise somewhat tolerable experiences that we were able to both soldier through together.

Usually during these KKYN years, if someone asked me what I did for a living, I would usually say to them—"I can sum up my job in three words—ballgames, remotes (live broadcasts from sponsors doing special events in their store or business), and churches. If I don't have my hand-in-one, I'm usually involved with another." Ergo—whenever I wasn't dealing with turning the knobs and pushing the buttons on our live broadcasts, I was responsible for making sure all of our church broadcasts on Sunday got on air. That at times proved to be the biggest challenge of all during my tenure here.

Since I preferred not to work on Saturday due to religious beliefs, I usually offered to work on Sundays in exchange as needed. Since most everyone else preferred to work on Saturday and be off on Sunday for church, they were some definite advantages to all concerned about this arrangement. This became very clear when the chief board operator that was ahead of me on the board op chain and that was at the time responsible for Sunday morning programming would up getting fired.

Tom and Brandy first approached me after this particular board op was fired about taking on the additional hours and responsibility of overseeing our Sunday programming operations. Little did I realize after I accepted the offer how much work all of this truly needed to be done here to make all of our church programs sound as smooth as silk on-air—and especially how much of a stepchild Sunday religious programming is regarded by our stations, but yet finding out just how many people really do listen to it.

When I started Sunday operations, I saw several immediate problems that truly showed me how much work caring for this new stepchild would require. The first one out of the gate was the lamentable mess my predecessor left behind. The previous board op had designed the system to be so complicated that it was doomed to fail and required HIM and his expertise to fix. After learning the ropes on this the hard way, I found that opting for much simpler methods of designing our Sunday programming might be easier for everyone to run.

Then, I truly saw with fresh eyes what short shrift our church programs had apparently gotten over the years prior to my arrival. So our church programs began seeing new intros and outros to transition in and out of programs. I began to develop more consistent methods of not only dubbing programs, but even developing a specific training manual for other board ops that had to take my place on those Sundays here I had to be gone in an attempt to make their work on my behalf as simple as possible. Both of the above (plus shouting up and down about the need for such changes) took about a year or two to achieve so that all of our Sunday programs would have a consistent sound for each station appropriate to the occasion.

Once we were able to set a pretty consistent standard on how our currently existing programs that we were aware of needed to be run, I then set our sights on how we could continually exceed those expectations and do even better. Some continually plaguing questions began to dominate my thoughts: "…Why are our churches in this area not putting on ANY paid religious programming on OUR stations? Also—we have a Baptist church and a Methodist church doing a taped program. But where are our charismatic and Pentecostal churches? Not ONE in this city is broadcasting here! And what about other churches in other area towns? What about our African-American and Hispanic churches and other congregations of color? Why aren't they doing programs HERE?"

Those questions seemed to be some of the biggest concerns I kept talking about like a broken record to our sales staff and also to upper management. You would not believe the number of times I sent proposals up and down the chain about Sunday church programming. I kept feeling at times that I was the ONLY voice this so-called "stepchild" ever had—and I honestly kept feeling like no one was really hearing me on this. Complaints about current business conditions never quite seemed to satisfy those pesky questions about Sunday that kept popping up in my mind.

But by the time I finally left KKYN, I began to see my work in this area was done and that it was time for someone else to have the baton when on the very last Sunday morning I worked we were by that time running twice the number of LOCAL church programs that our stations once had when I took over this task. We had by then added two non-denominational churches (one in Plainview and another based in Wellington, TX) and an Assembly of God church. We had also on top of that done some short stints with another Baptist church in Tulia doing a live service on KVOP and even a short failed attempt producing a one-hour taped program by a local African-American church. It wasn't a perfect picture of what I would have wanted—but to me, it seemed to be a major personal achievement of my KKYN employment I felt privileged and blessed to truly hang my hat on.

LEARNING HOW TO PLAY WITHIN THE FENCES
Tom and Brandy as my immediate supervisors tended at times to have their own ideas and limits on my specific job requirements and particular role in our Programming department—even if I might not have necessarily agreed at times on how far I was allowed to go. I would have liked, obviously, to been able to do more on-air and upfront in my job duties. But they in contrast saw my role more as a behind-the-scenes one with them taking the lead.

But in hindsight, even that in my eyes was a pretty good call for the reasons that it allowed me to have a pretty cushy and comfortable "catbird seat" to sit on (i.e.— high enough to get most of the benefits, but low enough not to have to take the responsibility and hits that's required to be a member of upper management). And two—thanks to T&B, there was rarely ever a question of the limits and boundaries placed upon me on the job. I knew how far I could go to push things and/or raise a stink about something and what point I needed to back off and say "uncle" and let it ride for another time.

This unwritten rule between T&B and myself proved to be especially handy on "the day I almost got fired". That day, I was in the midst of doing severe weather updates on our stations. Without going into too much detail, let's say the General Manager at the time decided to criticize my work and acted so much like a jerk that despite my best efforts, the GM unilaterally decided that he'd try to be "Mr. Everything" on the air and even fired me on the spot. All of this got to the point where I felt so much like a fifth wheel and decided that enough was enough. I called Tom to ask him to pick me up and DO IT NOW—because I had things to say about this GM's conduct that I couldn't say over the phone in the GM's hearing.

When Tom finally came and I got in his van and we took off for my apartment, I let him have the whole story about this GM's horrible conduct and disrespect towards me. When Tom heard my story, he about blew his top in response and told me he'd take care of it. I found out later that after he dropped me off, he went back to the station and confronted the GM about his actions and even threatened to resign if I was not immediately reinstated. The next day, I was told to come back in. When I got to the station, the GM apologized to me for his actions and basically changed his tune from the previous day. Situations like this confirmed an important fact about my employment here—that as long as Tom and Brandy were there and I didn't do anything royally stupid—that T&B would always have my back and I'd always have a pretty secure position with Plainview Radio.

Having this secure perch led me to several significant blessings that proved to be icing on the cake. Some of those did include some occasional times where I got to be in the spotlight such as after-hours severe weather coverage, news stories, and election coverage. News stories sometimes could be tedious to work on (especially when Tom told me as a general guideline to keep my stories under 40 seconds), but it was a thrill to me personally that even when I had to work at night, I was still directly contributing to the "Wake Up Kickin' Morning Show" whenever I could leave Tom a CART number with a news story or two and make his work putting together news for the Show a little easier the next morning. (Plus there was a little bit of personal gratification whenever Tom would play one of my stories on the air and I'd actually hear it for myself…)

What really got me noticed a lot not only amongst my coworkers, but especially by our listeners was when I got to do election coverage. When I first started at the station, Tom being the news director naturally wound up having to take care of our election night results. But as time wore on, Tom let me know in no uncertain terms that election coverage wasn't necessarily his favorite thing to do. When I eventually volunteered to take over these duties, he was only more than happy to do so and thrust that job on my shoulders.

Little did I realize some of the fun roller coaster rides taking over this particular job responsibility would entail for me personally. One of them was the night that I had to broadcast the results of a general election for the District 85 State Representative seat in the Texas Legislature. The Republican nominee, Jim Landtroop, was expected to win big against Democrat Joe Heflin. But based on a controversial campaign move that Landtroop made in Howard County (county seat--Big Spring...where, incidentally, one of our company' sister stations was), I thought that if Landtroop had any possibility of losing the race, the Achilles heel of the election for him might clearly start in Big Spring.

But later in the night, the results told me how totally off my original prognostication actually was. As the returns started coming in from the different counties, the race was pretty even split between Landtroop and Heflin. And eventually the race came down to three counties that had not filed their returns to the Secretary of State: Jones, Hale, and Floyd. And the questions lingered— "…What is taking so long for the returns in Hale and Floyd counties? And where in the bleep is Jones County anyway?"

In a mad dash between coverage breaks, I had to find out how to get in touch with the county clerk for Jones County—and the race was truly on. Finally after several attempts, I found out that Jones went to Landtroop. So now for the two counties much closer to home. I then finally heard from the clerk in Floyd County that Floyd went to Heflin. And it got to be a longer and longer night—just when I thought it would end…the roller coaster ride continued.

FINALLY--somewhere around 2 AM, I actually got the final returns for Hale County. Recounts and other issues delayed the counting of the vote in my home county. And the final results were even more of a shocker—by just over 200 votes,

Heflin won the seat despite coming into the race (save for a significant personal endorsement and political contribution from the outgoing occupant of that same seat who also at the time was the Speaker of the House in the Legislature, Pete Laney) with no realistic chance of prevailing against Landtroop. After I did the final update, it was probably closer to 5 AM in the morning when I was finally able to walk back home for much-needed sleep (which by that time I remember Tom happened to already be up and finding me along the way and graciously taking me back home).

Calling that election was particularly gratifying for two reasons—one of them a comment that one of our sales reps gave me that she was listening all night to the updates—and that listening to me give those returns made her proud that she worked for our stations. The other was that for me, it was one of the first of those rare times where for once I had to be in what I called a "moneymaker" position which required me to be the broadcasting spearhead and lead a whole thing from start to finish WITH paying sponsors.

Just as exciting were the times when I got to call the returns for several alcohol "local-option" elections in Plainview, Tulia, and Abernathy that would determine whether or not alcohol could be legally sold within the city limits of a certain town.

I particularly remember calling the Plainview election for several reasons. One of them was the strategies and tactics both sides utilized going into the election effort. The anti-alcohol forces went full-blast from the start by holding big rallies in prominent places in the city and conducting an all-out intensive media campaign. The pro-alcohol forces in contrast took the low-key approach to getting their message out relying primarily on print ads and emphasizing how alcohol sales would enhance economic development in Plainview.

Once again, the election night returns proved just how crucial one vote can truly be. After 100 years of Plainview being a dry city, just 200 votes made the difference to turn Plainview wet. And the remarkable thing about this election was the deciding factor WASN'T those who were wanting to vote in droves to legalize alcohol sales in Plainview—but actually those members in our city's churches themselves that bought in to the notion of "economic development". Sometimes you learn a lot indeed from those times in the spotlight.

THE BENEFITS OF WORKING IN RADIO

People tend to get the notion that those who work in radio and/or other parts of the "Fourth Estate" work in a pretty glamorous environment. I hate to burst those folks' bubbles—but those who have those flawed assumptions might need to reconsider their unrealistic fantasies. For one thing, there IS work involved in this industry—and most of it isn't as glitzy and glamorous as you might first think. (I would hardly consider sweeping the floors of our transmitter sites or being the janitor of our studio facilities to be worthy of pictures from the paparazzi.) And I can guarantee you—you WILL lift heavy equipment…and you WILL sometimes have to do things by the seat of your pants as needed.

That doesn't mean, however, that there aren't side benefits to working here. For instance, I have been able to go several times to the Cotton Barons' Ball (Plainview's big annual American Cancer Society fundraiser) and enjoy a good Texas steak now and then. I've been the beneficiary of free prizes and free tickets that have helped me at various times along the way. I even (believe it or not) actually LOST in a karaoke contest against another of our General Managers (who actually is a pretty decent singer in her own right and who has even since recorded her own album). But the GM the next day turned right around and gave ME her $100 grand prize. Talk about being a classy winner—her unexpected generosity definitely took some of the edge off of my attempts at that time to be a gracious loser to her…

And not all the special blessings and benefits came solely from my Plainview Radio employment. During my time here, I actually won a freezer as the Grand Prize (worth probably about $1000) in a contest from Schwan's which the Lord prompted me to give to a ministry in East Texas. I was even able (thanks in part to one of our stations broadcasting the Dave Ramsey radio program) to take advantage of an opportunity or two (since there was finally at least some sense of stability in my personal income at the time) to finally to get some much-needed work done on my own financial vineyard through taking Dave Ramsey's Financial Peace University to further sharpen my personal financial skills and abilities.

It also worked out for me personally that a later GM had once struggled herself with financial problems and was able to lead me to her sister who was a Consumer Credit Counseling Service counselor as well as provide some initial direct assistance to me directly in helping me meet some urgent personal needs at the same time as she was also helping me meet some personal financial goals. I wasn't always as diligent as I should have been in several financial areas and, as a result, found myself eventually falling off the financial wagon—but I can even consider those times much-needed hard lessons learned that would help me be more conscious of my financial affairs immediately after I went through Chapter 7 bankruptcy in 2005.

THE ONE DAY THAT I NEVER WANTED TO GO THROUGH AT KKYN

Within all of the good things and even the disasters we all went through, there was always one thing I eventually feared and wanted to NEVER see for a long time to come. Despite what I might have said otherwise, inside I REALLY loved this comfortable catbird seat I was in. And after all the struggle and hard times it took to get here in the first place, the LAST thing I wanted to do was to go back to the place where I was before I first came here.

But the day came in 2009 where I found myself in the same position that Job was: "…My groaning serves as my bread; my roaring pours forth as water. For what I feared has overtaken me; what I dreaded has come upon me. I had no repose, no quiet, no rest, and trouble came." (Job 3:24-26, JPS Tenach)

The basis for my nagging fear in the back of my mind and later deep concern that I expressed to upper management that we desperately needed to prepare for the one thing that would blow everything at the station we had to smithereens—the time when Tom and Brandy would eventually decide it was time to go. This realization was based in part from my own knowledge of the way T&B tended to operate as far as their decisions as heads of programming. Tom and Brandy were excellent managers and supervisors in part because you always knew for better or worse that you could always interpret the decision of one of them as being supported by the other. If there were disagreements they had with each other on certain things, they were always hashed out behind closed doors. There was never any way you could pit one of them against the other—for they always presented a united front in any decisions they made concerning what I did for them.

That's why I wasn't too surprised as to finding out that they even had an unwritten agreement with each other on how they both would leave. It was understood between them that they would never do a Morning Show with anyone else if one of them left. In fact, they went so far as to agree that the day that one of them resigned the other would also tenure their resignation from the station at the same time. The particular fear I had personally about this scenario wasn't necessarily the fact they would consider doing this—but WHEN. I felt in this situation like Linus with his security blanket. T&B WERE my security blanket here in this place—and I NEVER wanted to let them go.

But one day when I came to work, everything changed in an instant. Tom told me that he was going back to Wayland to his old job there, but with a new and different title. Then Brandy (who by this time had already resumed her previous college studies to become a teacher) told me that she was quitting, too. I was thinking as they told me all this, "…All the years we'd worked together…the fun times as well as the bad. We'd been through so much together—***now this?***"

The inner hurt and pain I experienced now could only be compared to two major events in my life—the first coming back home from Albuquerque and the second that of the aftermath of the WCG changes. Talk about another sucker punch to the gut—my mentors in the industry and two of my closest friends were going to leave here—and I once again couldn't do one bleeping thing about it. It seemed like the nightmare was about to start all over again.

After T&B told me about their impending resignations privately, they then went before the GM to formally present their resignations. The GM then basically had them go back to me and officially notify me. The second time was basically for show and ceremony for the GM—in which in response that I would be planning to stay and was willing to offer my assistance in helping navigate our stations through the transition. Here it was after all these years—Tom and Brandy were leaving and handing the baton now to me…and I almost didn't have the heart to take it from them. I wished now that I could have had the luxury to have been able to do the same thing they did and leave at the same time they did—but I couldn't afford to do so and I certainly had no other realistic place I could go.

Before this all came down the pike, I had formally submitted my request for vacation time during the upcoming Feast of Tabernacles in which I had planned to go on a trip first to Los Angeles, then to Pennsylvania to see a friend, then on to North Carolina to see my cousin, and then back to Huntsville, TX for the last part of the Feast before heading back home. (I'll have a little more to say about that trip in Chapter 25.)

Therefore, Brandy graciously stayed to first allow me to have my requested vacation time and then stay for another month or so to help train our new Morning Show hosts and help me learn the ropes of what would be my new additional programming responsibilities. Tom, though, fairly soon after his formal resignation had to start his new/old job duties as Dean of Students at Wayland.

The days and weeks after these dual resignations happened were some of the darkest days of my life that almost threw me into deep depression. Right before I had to leave for my extended Feast trip, I had the sad task of putting together the news story that on behalf of the entire company would formally announce to our listeners and the world Tom and Brandy's resignations. I was literally crying before recording it and most certainly so after. And I literally had to pray one simple prayer before doing it--"Lord, please help me to say goodbye."

It was only the mercy of the Lord that allowed me to have the poise and presence of mind to be able to record the story without completely falling apart emotionally. The piece was about six minutes in length (rare for stories like this, yes—but thankfully occasions like this even allowed me to put some personal feelings and reflections) and in which I didn't get to hear on-air because I was gone and didn't therefore get to be there on Tom's last day on the job. Tom would continue to do play-by-play for the remainder of football season—but otherwise that was it for him.

But my day of final realization that this was truly the end of it all was on the very last day that Brandy worked at our stations. As she packed up the remainder of her things, I walked with her to her car in the parking lot. As she was about to leave, I did something I rarely did with her (considering that I was single and she was married)—I hugged her long and tight. As she drove off for the final time, the tears really started coming down unashamedly down my face. The funeral service of all of this was over—and the baton was once and for all in my hands.

With Brandy, the last vestiges of an era in history I once knew drove off with her never to return. And for the first time since I started here (regardless of all the other people who had long since previously left), the fact really hit me like a ton of bricks. I was truly now alone—no security blankets, no protections or things short of my God that I could now count on. I was, like it or not, very much on my own—and no one might be there to pick me up if and when I fell.

THE LAST YEAR'S FINAL ROLLER COASTER RIDE

After Brandy left, I practically (even after all the training she gave me before she left) didn't have a honeymoon period as far as my new interim leadership responsibilities were concerned. Besides, after all this time, this was my own first chance to in a sense interview and audition through my current job performance for Brandy's old position. It was in a sense a trial by fire from the start for me—not just in learning the ropes, but on top of it seemingly to have every responsibility in the world thrust on my shoulders for the first month or two. Technically, I reported to the program director of our Big Spring stations as we worked together through the transition.

And there was definitely plenty to do. Not only did I have to run ballgames as a board op and also supervise others, but I was now responsible for producing daily newscasts, correcting the program logs sent to us by the Traffic department, recording and producing commercial spots—you name it....I just about did it all EXCEPT supervise and have control over our new Morning Show hosts (which the GM controlled—and NOT me due to reasons I never fully understood). I started having to pull 14 to 15 hour workdays at least 6 days a week (I did continue, though, to take Saturday off unless there was a major emergency) PLUS the time it took me to walk back and forth between home and work.

With football season ending and basketball season about to begin, spots had to be changed for all of our sports teams our stations broadcast. I eventually even found myself having to start training all of the other part-time board ops to do my Plainview games so that I could be freer to take care of other necessary responsibilities. To say that all of this took a real physical and emotional drain on me and my personal energy and emotions would have been a massive understatement.

What was worse about the deal was that my main personal motivation for this attempt to prove myself—the opportunity at long last for formal promotion to program director and a potential raise (to me, operations manager was out of the question since I didn't have experience in either engineering or fixing transmitters) just as suddenly got jerked away from me as quickly as the burdens were put on me. Despite my best efforts and my formal declaration and request to the GM that I would be formally considered for promotion, I wasn't even allowed a proper hearing. Someone else had already been hired to take what I had hoped was to be my eventual place unbeknownst to me—and I had no choice but to be busted back down to the level of a plain old board op.

This was also when the final roller coaster ride of the remaining part of my tenure here got really scary and weird. First, I went back down to nothing for a short time when a new supervisor came in. Then one morning just two weeks later when that new supervisor didn't know what to do when everything fell apart and the GM had to literally come to my door and wake me up and tell me to come fix everything, I was back in a semi-supervisor role. Then there were four of us with the GM micromanaging us—and then back down to nothing again. With all these up and down cycles going on here, was it any wonder I was an emotional basketcase by the time everything was said and done?

And the original depression I felt in the wake of Tom and Brandy's departure only got worse. It about got to the point where one of the board ops named Joe was about the only one in the whole place that knew how to talk to me. Joe was originally hired by Tom and Brandy before they left to assist us with ballgames and to help board op the Tejano show that got started on one of our AM stations. When Tom, Brandy, and even the new Tejano DJ left our stations, Joe and I wound up being the ones who were forced to pick up the pieces left behind.

Joe and I tended to have a very interesting and unique working relationship. Joe was ex-military, but never revealed his true experience in radio and engineering until after Tom and Brandy left. Little did I know what both of us would go through in the remaining time I was there. First, it was me being his boss. Then eventually, we were both thrust as co-leaders. But in time, it felt like Joe was practically MY boss—especially in light of the things I didn't know and the way I reacted to things in general emotionally.

Where Tom and Brandy coddled and protected me, Joe did the exact opposite and put his military management methods to good use on me and everyone else. One case in point was his very firm patience and insistence that I work on mastering my personal knowledge and skills in utilizing the recording software we used in our downstairs recording studio where we produced all of our commercials that would go out on the air.

At first, I was probably like most kids who didn't want to eat their vegetables as far as learning that program was concerned. I didn't want to do it—no way, no how. I wasn't too happy over this change—and I didn't hesitate to show my displeasure over it. If it weren't for Joe's patience and willingness to know when and how far to push my emotional buttons, I would have never learned that stupid program like I know now (and actually wish I still had).

But a bigger thing than the above that I truly appreciated about Joe (despite our sometimes challenging relationship) was his skills in one area I could never top—engineering. Regardless of what I might have thought of him at times as a person, his post-military engineering abilities could not be denied when it came to fixing a number of technical issues that were constantly plaguing our stations. He helped put in a much-needed new control console for KKYN (our flagship country station) that made our broadcasts sound better. He found lingering problems with our news/talk/sports station that had been long neglected for years. Joe may have been difficult at times for me to deal with personally—but I will admit in retrospect that I couldn't have gotten through those final months without him. Time to eat humble pie, I guess?

GETTING THE SUDDEN GOLDEN PARACHUTE OUT

Despite all the things that I went through after Tom and Brandy left, one nagging fact still remained—the initial enthusiasm and excitement I had for working here was gone. I was only there now for two reasons—(1.) I couldn't quit because I couldn't afford to do so for fear of losing my government assistance; and (2.) there weren't necessarily any other decent opportunities that I could realistically pursue without quitting this job. And if I had to leave, I didn't want to lose my vacation time in which I would get a new set in June.

Then when the winter of 2009 and spring of 2010 came along, things began dramatically changing on the personal front. January saw me finally receiving my SECOND debt-free, paid-for car in less than three years that once again enabled me to get places faster without the help of others. Then in May, the situation in my apartment on Givens Street deteriorated with my landlord to such a point where I was forced to move to another place in town just nearby from there. In the interim time, I had to stay with my mother for a few weeks and commute between Plainview and Lockney to not only work, but begin my move to my new apartment on Date Street.

As these changes started coming into the air of my life, I didn't realize that one more of those changes was also about to come my way. One Sunday as I was working my regular shift and thinking about all the church programs our stations were now doing, the Lord suddenly seemed to indicate to me that this would be the very LAST Sunday that I would be working here. I didn't think much of it at first--UNTIL….

The next day when I came to the station for work, the GM told me to meet her in her office. There was something strange about this visit (especially in the things she apparently did BEFORE I even got there or knew that I was supposed to meet with her)—because she had already cleaned out all of my stuff from my desk and all through the station and had it ready in a box waiting for me. She then told me that due to budget cuts that I was being laid off. A check of over $1,000 was already in her hand not only to pay me for the salary amount of my last paycheck, but also the two weeks' vacation time that I had just finally and BARELY accumulated a few days hence (that date being the anniversary date of my official hiring to full-time status). The GM must have known for a while that by that time I was only there anyway just to collect paychecks—for what in the past I would have regarded as an absolute disaster (that is—the loss of my primary job) was now in my eyes an act of mercy and release.

I didn't get to have all the final parties and celebrations that Tom and Brandy had when they left—but it was still a golden parachute ticket out of my present circumstance nonetheless. There was one difference this time. When I first started here in 2002, I had to walk to get here to start work my first Fri. night to do a ballgame. But when I was laid off in 2010, the future of new and endless possibilities awaited me as I drove off in MY own car towards my new apartment. At least I had enough money this time to pay my rent for most of the upcoming summer ahead and get back on the job hunt again for something else that I might REALLY want. And this time, I was even eligible for unemployment on top of it to boot. Yep, it was definitely a pretty good golden parachute indeed to those things that still lay ahead of me...

[Chapter 21] [Amarillo, TX:] Living In The "Kehillah Kedoshah"—Why I Now Attend THREE Different Churches

I just realized something about our current location on North Quincy—and doing so leads me to ask you as the reader for some extra special forbearance and patience as I suddenly remembered that in order to write this chapter correctly that we'll actually have to leave Plainview again for a little bit to answer some questions I'm sure you have of me if you've managed to read and go as far as you have in these current literary travels with me.

So to do that, we first simply will need to continue north on Quincy until it dead-ends with the northbound I-27 frontage road. Then we'll immediately merge onto the main highway and start on our way north on I-27 towards Amarillo. Oh, yeah—I forgot to tell you again that it's about 75 to 80 miles from here to get to where we'll need to go. [I know—I hear your groans, complaints, and protests! "We're actually going to WALK 80 MILES???" No, silly—not exactly. We are, though, going to have to walk in faith AGAIN….and absolutely NO HITCHHIKING or sticking out your thumb is allowed on this one whatsoever! (Besides—I don't want us to get in trouble with any law enforcement officials, you know.)]

Hey—don't you know by now anyway that if our God wants us to get to Amarillo bad enough, he'll surely provide a way to do so! [I ought to know—because I actually did it once! I started one morning having my apartment around 7 AM…and sure enough after 3 different rides, several intermittent miles of walking, and several hours total one-way trip, I finally got to where we'll wind up next some time later that same afternoon. So I know for certain this CAN be done if necessary!]

Our current route on I-27 will keep proceeding north all the way up until we almost get into downtown Amarillo where I-27 intersects with I-40. We'll then turn right onto I-40 and go east about a couple of miles until we get to the Nelson St./Quarter Horse Drive exit. On the left you'll see the American Quarter Horse Association Museum. As we exit off the Interstate, we see the Camelot Inn on our right followed by a small service station at the stop light. After the stoplight changes, we'll continue another block on the frontage road until we get to Manhattan Street and turn right once again. As we go past one church and a Jehovah Witnesses' Kingdom Hall on the left, we continue south on Manhattan immediately on our right, we'll turn into the church building of the Community of

Christ [formerly known as the Reorganized Church of Jesus Christ of Latter-Day Saints (otherwise referred to as the RLDS...keep in mind, of course, that this is TOTALLY separate and distinct from the main LDS Church based in Salt Lake City)]. It also just happens to be the main building where at the time of this writing my nearest official GCI congregation meets. And here is also where I now choose to answer what now is probably the biggest question that's flashing like a neon sign on your face—"Why on earth after all you've been through would you STILL choose to be a member of WCG/GCI?"

First, I need to clear up a slight technicality before we move further. Actually, I now don't just attend a Grace Communion International congregation—but since there's not another similar congregation back home in the Plainview, I now ALSO attend TWO other different charismatic/Pentecostal congregations as well! Ok—I can tell your head is really swimming even more so than usual over this peculiar thought. Stay with me—all of this organized chaos will make perfect sense to you later on. Just trust me on this one—will ya?

And if you're dying to know IN DETAIL WHY I now attend three different churches, you're not alone. The puzzled look I know you're having right now doesn't compare to a situation I had years ago as I was pursuing a certain young woman for a long-distance romantic relationship via e-mail. During the course of my e-mail correspondence with her, I had actually sent her an email attachment I called my "personal statement of core beliefs". I also mentioned that I actually attended THREE different churches.

After she read all of this info I sent her, she wrote back questioning why I even did this and (in my view) possibly misinterpreted from that statement that I was unstable in my religious beliefs and couldn't conceive how I could actually be a member of more than one church. I tried my best in a subsequent email to further clarify what I meant by this—but my efforts were to no avail. She sadly could not see past her personal prejudices the possibility that you COULD realistically be a member of more than ONE church. In fact, she had so much trouble wrapping her mind around that concept that what little of a relationship we had fizzled out and went south after that due in part to that unexpected conflict.

Since that incident, I have had a very hard time explaining and/or justifying my personal positions on religious matters to those who have never walked a mile in my moccasins or even know what it's like to have a unique religious background like mine. It was only recently when I read a book by New York Times best-selling

276

author Mitch Albom where I finally found what the best way to answer similar questions to what that young woman on the email asked me.

In Albom's book "Have A Little Faith", Albom recounts the story of how he was asked by his childhood rabbi in New Jersey to deliver that rabbi's eulogy at his funeral and the process Albom underwent with that rabbi to do it over an eight-year period. Alongside that story, Albom also recounts a parallel story of an African-American pastor in Detroit that he befriends and plays a role in helping meet the needs of this particular pastor's homeless ministry,

In the middle of the book, Albom recalls one particular conversation he had with the rabbi that has not only given me a good quick way of answering and rebutting any questions about the churches I now attend, but that has also very much struck a chord within me about what the Church should be in the first place…and why we should even bother being a part of it all.

"…'When I was growing up in the Bronx,' the Reb said, '…everyone knew everyone. Our apartment building was like family. We watched out for one another.

"'…I remember once, as a boy, I was so hungry, and there was a fruit and vegetable truck parked by our building. I tried to bump against it, so an apple would fall into my hands. That way it wouldn't feel like stealing.

"…Suddenly, I heard a voice from above yelling at me, in Yiddish—*'Albert—it is forbidden!!!'* I jumped, I thought it was God.

"'Who was it? I asked.

"'A lady who lived upstairs.

"'I laughed. Not quite God.

"'No. But, Mitch, we were a part of each other's lives. If someone was about to slip someone else could catch him.

"'That's the criticial idea behind a congregation. ***We call it a 'Kehillah Kedoshah"*—a sacred community.** We're losing that now. The suburbs have changed things. Everyone has a car. Everyone has a million things scheduled. How can you look out for your neighbor? You're lucky to get a family to sit down for a meal together." ["Have A Little Faith"; Albom, Mitch, pp. 62 & 63; published by

Hyperion Books; New York City; Copyright 2009 Mitch Albom, Inc.; particular emphases are solely mine...]

I think the writer of Hebrews would further put the cherry on top of the rabbi's statement by adding:

A Call to Persevere in Faith—Hebrews 10:19-25

[19] Therefore, brothers and sisters, since we have confidence to enter the Most Holy Place by the blood of Jesus, [20] by a new and living way opened for us through the curtain, that is, his body, [21] and since we have a great priest over the house of God, [22] let us draw near to God with a sincere heart and with the full assurance that faith brings, having our hearts sprinkled to cleanse us from a guilty conscience and having our bodies washed with pure water. [23] Let us hold unswervingly to the hope we profess, for he who promised is faithful. [24] *And let us consider how we may spur one another on toward love and good deeds,* [25] *not giving up meeting together, as some are in the habit of doing, but encouraging one another—and all the more as you see the Day approaching.*

I also recall the times where the Rav Shaul/Apostle Paul is found several times throughout the latter part of the book of Acts giving some of the most impassioned and eloquent defenses of his faith in the Messiah. In particular, the time Paul presented his case to Kings Agrippa and Festus is a remarkably stirring account to me personally that serves as a prime example of how Shaul/Paul as a Jewish rabbi illustrated what the Jewish sage Maimonides later would talk about in his last two principles of his "Thirteen Principles Of Jewish Faith"—

"...Principle 12—I believe by complete faith in the coming of the Messiah, and even though he tarry in waiting—in spite of that, I will still wait expectantly for him each day that he will come...

"...Principle 13—I believe by complete faith that there will be a resurrection of the dead at the time that will be pleasing before the Creator, blessed be His name, and the remembrance of Him will be exalted forever and for all eternity..."

[All further quotations of this are quoted from Brad Young, "Meet The Rabbis: Rabbinic Thought and the Teachings of Jesus"; p. 163, Hendrickson Publishers, Inc.; Peabody, MA (Copyright © 2007)]

As Paul once did his own defense in front of King Agrippa, so I will do the same right here in this particular worship hall to relate to not only the earlier aforementioned young woman, but all who my questions why I am not only still a part of the particular "kehillah kedoshah"/"sacred community" of GCI—but also all of the other "sacred communities" that I am personally involved in—which includes (but is not limited to) how I spend my time, financial resources, etc.:

(I.)   **WHY AM I STILL INVOLVED IN SOME WAY WITH GCI?** **(ANSWER:)** Although at the time of this writing I have been extremely limited due to financial and transportation problems to be as active as I once was in GCI, I still try to do what I'm able to realistically do here because of the following reasons…

     (A.)   If it were not for what I learned about the Old Testament here (especially Mosaic law, the Biblical Festivals, and other parts of what some would call the Torah and the Tenach), I could not be able as a Christian to have been able to have a reasonable working knowledge of the Old Covenant that I have now.

         Here where I live in West Texas, of all things, one of the biggest phenomenons in a number of religious circles around here in recent years has been the rapid growth of the Messianic Jewish movement and increasing interest in the Jewish roots of the Christian faith. Whenever I see someone new to the Messianic/Sabbatarian movement grapple with an issue that I personally dealt with over twenty years ago that I learned as a part of previous WCG/GCI doctrine, I keep feeling more and more like what Barbara Mandrell sang about in the song, "I Was Country When Country Wasn't Cool": "…I took a lot of kiddin'/ 'Cause I never did fit in/Now look at everybody/Trying to be what I was then…"

     (B.)   **The courageous historical legacy that Mr. Armstrong/Mr. Tkach, Sr./WCG/GCI both left behind**

In my own personal experience, most people when they might think or hear about WCG either probably have never heard or known much about us in the first place…or (strangely enough) usually focus too much on GARNER TED Armstrong (the son) INSTEAD of Herbert

W. (the father) since Garner Ted even for a number of years when WCG was in the spotlight a whole lot more than it is these days was viewed by most as the face of WCG…and then maybe later after that say something knee-jerk stupid without thinking like—"Oh, by the way—they're a CULT!"

I know, for instance, that I've heard secondhand rumors about what we supposedly actually did. GASP—Maynard…they actually do animal sacrifices on the Ambassador College campus! (FYI for those folks—we have NEVER done so…and now probably never will. PETA can calm down now. This rumor is so patently false and off-base that it's not worth spending any more space on!)

And I've even heard a story or two through the years about the ALLEGED escapades of Garner Ted himself…and they actually STILL manage to link him to us in WCG/GCI despite verified information to the contrary! [On that one—let me clear up something. Garner Ted to my personal knowledge has NOT been formally associated with WCG/GCI in ANY shape or form since the 1970s. The senior Armstrong formally "disfellowshiped" Garner Ted in about 1974 (in which is a long story in itself that I don't have time or space to go in detail here...I would once again recommend reading Dr. Tkach, Jr.'s excellent book "Transformed By Truth" that you can still find on the Grace Communion International website at www.gci.org for further details on that particular episode in WCG history...)— where Garner Ted soon afterwards formed what is now called the Church of God, International based out of Tyler, TX. Later from what I found out through other research, Garner Ted basically left that church and formed yet another sort of association called the Garner Ted Armstrong Evangelistic Association in which what is now called the Intercontinental Church of God is an offshoot of. Any more info you need on Garner Ted past that is beyond the formal direct scope of my own personal WCG/GCI knowledge.]

Let me DO say something that I might confirm based on what I now know from hard-nosed experience in WCG/GCI—Mr. Armstrong would have been, if not the very first, at least one of the first ones in my view to declare that he was nowhere near perfect—and he was usually never hesitant in the things he wrote to our members to mention his many failings and shortcomings before God and man. But one thing that saddens me the most is that not enough hay is made to mention the GOOD parts about Mr. Armstrong and the history of WCG/GCI that were easily apparent and plain as day to see. It's THOSE parts of my own church's history that I don't hear enough of these days…because each time I either hear of, read, or recall stories like these, they give me great encouragement:

> (1.)   Mr. Armstrong's seemingly tireless and indefatigueable efforts during his many world travels to talk to world leaders during his time about "a strong hand from someplace" that will someday set this world aright

{Even if some previous WCG members got frustrated over this, I think now that we as members might in hindsight owe him both an apology and also our sincerest thanks for all the frequent flyer miles he put on that Gulfstream jet—because we wouldn't now have been able to truly claim that we were legitimately any sort of "worldwide" or "international" church that we really are now (and in which I still believe we'll always be).}

> (2.)   That WCG/GCI members and pastors have always been a unique group of people whose membership and "sacred community" truly transcends racial, cultural, and national barriers

{A little secret I can tell you between you, me, and the fencepost—most people I know in other churches and denominations around me usually probably don't know too many other Christians outside of their own little churches and denominations—much less within the town they live in most of the time.

For me personally, though—it has been an absolute privilege through such things as previous Feast of

Tabernacles I have attended to meet a number of people of various walks of life and places throughout the earth and get out of my own little comfort zone every now and then—and even be able to maintain friendships that have lasted for years. Even if there is an extended break in contact that might occur, there are still times that when I next see them, we can literally pick up where we left off the last time. And if a situation warrants, that relationship can also be an opportunity for both of us to serve others not only where we each personally live—but in other places throughout the world.

(3.)   The courageous stands WCG/GCI has taken in the past against injustices in society that have faced its members

{Two main examples that I could cite would include:

    (a.) The willingness of WCG pastors and congregations to defy the wishes of the KKK and local law-enforcement officials in the Jim Crow-era segregated South and disobey unjust segregation laws because of a simple belief that white and black WCG members should ALWAYS worship as ONE congregation come what may;

    (b.) When the state of California decided to put WCG in receivership in 1976 due to allegations of financial mismanagement— Mr. Armstrong, his staff, and WCG responded to the threat by fighting one of the biggest landmark religious liberty battles the U.S. had ever seen at the time— AND WON!}

AND (4.) When Mr. Armstrong, Mr. Tkach, Sr., and their successors have continuously endeavored no matter what the cost to do two of the biggest things that Mr. Armstrong admonished us to do many years ago:

    (a.)   "Don't believe me—believe your Bible!"

282

(b.) A belief that the Word of God will never change…and that if there is ever ANY WCG/GCI doctrine that conflicts with Scripture—it is not God or Scripture that should change, but YOU and your silly doctrines that should change with it

When I have seen this personally demonstrated in front of my own eyes about WCG HQ and its leadership would be so willing to change doctrine if it is shown beyond a doubt that it is in direct contradiction to Scripture—that they would go so far if necessary to literally risk EVERYTHING they have and pay the extremely high prices necessary just so they could be in complete compliance and obedience with the will of God—and NOT just by words—but also more importantly by their actions…to me, THAT speaks volumes more to me than anything else I know.

(4.) How my God has used WCG/GCI in my life to give the messages that I am now compelled not only through the direction of the Holy Spirit, but also through my personal life experience to tell to the nations

(a.) The damaging effects of legalism of ANY kind—and the consequences it leaves behind

(b.) That we truly have a merciful, gracious, loving, and holy Abba Father who cared so much for us that He Himself allowed His most prized possession (His OWN SON!) to die just so that we could truly and finally live;

(c.) That Christ/Y'shua DID die, was buried, and rose again—AND is STILL living today ever continually making intercession for us as our High Priest FOREVER before the Father; and--

(d.) THEREFORE—we should NEVER run FROM the Father or be afraid of Him…but instead boldly come to His throne of grace in our times of need—and expect that He will be faithful to do exactly what He promised us He would do;

(e.) AND LASTLY—throughout the years, my God has used many different WCG/GCI brethren to provide various types of help to me whenever I've needed it most—some of them literally time and time again. Some of those folks are now no longer with us (either because of death or other reasons).

It is one of my biggest desires to whenever I have opportunity to do so to do what I call "returning old favors" that were extended to me many times by various brethren in the past by striving to bless someone else in need as I have the ability to do so. I consider it now one of my biggest duties and obligations to see that these brethren and their personal contributions to my life are never forgotten.

As long as WCG/GCI does what they are able to do in continuing these right and proper legacies, I officially declare now that the very figurative ring I put on my finger when I was first baptized in 1991 will never come off my finger until either my dying day or the Rapture (whichever comes first).

And WCG/GCI will never fail to at least receive whatever small amount of monies that I might be led to send to HQ nor at least know that as I'm able to have appropriate occasion and opportunity to do so that I will try to at least be present at any WCG/GCI service and/or activity that I can possibly be a part of.

(II.) WHY I AM ALSO INVOLVED WITH THESE OTHER "SACRED COMMUNITIES"

As I write this, you'll find that that GCI isn't the ONLY place where you'll find me spiritually and physically active in. I also wind up scheduling these activities and groups on a fairly frequent basis—

(1.) I also attend two other different Pentecostal/Charismatic congregations in Plainview on a regular basis. One of them believes in doctrines that focus on deliverance and healing from unclean spirits. The pastor of this particular church and his wife are true-blood redneck cowboy types who are neither ashamed of either their roots— or more importantly, who they are in Christ.

In contrast, the other congregation I frequently attend is led by a man who, according to his own personal testimonyy, who didn't even "get saved" until later in his forties and who at one time, according to his testimony, acted like an absolute heathen even though he was raised by Godly parents in a Southern Baptist church. The outreach ministry that he and his wife now run does a lot of evangelistic work amongst the biker community as well as serve as one of my own home city's major food and clothing distribution outlets to the poor and needy.

Both of these groups are about as different as night and day. But there are still good things that I personally see in these groups as well that lead me to stay active in them as well.

(2.) Also—the Walk to Emmaus-based community of many churches and members in my own area hail from different backgrounds and perspectives—but they still come together for the sole main purpose of Christian renewal and developing potential spiritual leaders in our local area congregations...

(3.) "Restorative justice"/prison ministry—This particular "sacred community" not only reminds me of the many men and women who are also fellow believers in Him in which the only marked difference between me and them is a bunch of razorwire...but also that anywhere I may go that there is always a bigger "kehillah kedoshah" of believers in my Messiah that have still not completely kissed the knee to Baal...but are doing all they know to do to make a difference for the Kingdom of God. It is always a privilege to lend whatever assistance that I can do towards these mutual efforts.

(III.) THE CONCLUSION OF THE MATTER—WHAT HAVE I LEARNED THE MOST THROUGH ALL OF THESE "SACRED COMMUNITIES"?

(A.) I have now learned (maybe even more so than most) that there's a whole lot of a bigger world to this thing called "...the universal Body of Christ".

(B.) I have learned that I (contrary to what I might otherwise perceive and think) am NOT alone in this world—and that if I limit who, what, etc. IS a true part of the "universal Church" and I attempt to be a Lone Ranger trying to conquer hell and whip Satan with a water pistol—then I will surely be trounced and taken to the cleaners. But if I allow others to join alongside me in the fight and give them a chance to add their strengths to make up for my weaknesses and be willing to do the same for them in turn—then all of us together will form an invincible team for Him against the real enemy of our souls—and that will truly do great exploits for our Savior as a result.

(C.) I have also personally found that there is a lot to be gained through appropriate relationships, partnerships, and joint participation in mutually-beneficial causes—especially in learning new things I could never know about otherwise.

For instance, from the Charismatic/Pentecostal movement, I can gain a whole new different perspective on what the "...gifts of the Spirit" are and how I can take advantage of them to live a much more victorious and overcoming life. From such groups as the Baptists (where I was originally raised) and the Church of Christ, I am reminded about the importance of maintaining the integrity and infallibility of the Word of God and just how important is is to do your part to be involved in the work of evangelism.

From churches such as the Episcopal Church (despite their unfortunate decisions in recent years to condone homosexuality within their ranks in any shape or form), I'm reminded that our

God is also a God of order and organization. Previous work with the Salvation Army puts the necessary kick in the seat of my pants to be willing to get out of my comfort zone and serve others in their time of need—no matter what their overall personal backgrounds or history may be.

And even the recent emergence and increased presence of what is now called the "Hebrew Roots"/Messianic Jewish movement in the Southwestern US as well as other Sabbatarian groups has done one big thing for someone who spent some of his formative years under the shadow of Mr. Armstrong and WCG. This above all else gives me a little personal hope and encouragement that I'm not the only one out there still trying to fully serve the Lord.

These folks might not exactly believe like I do—but I also truly believe that as they continue to properly follow the voice of their God in these efforts, they will indirectly also insure that at least a few of the good things Mr. Armstrong taught folks like me will still remain and that any and all of the previous sacrifices that many of my WCG/GCI brethren made in the past will not be entirely in vain.

And maybe who knows? Along the way, these folks might themselves decide to ask either myself or other similar brethren to share what lessons we've been privileged to be taught and specialize in so that our own gifts given to us by our God can also benefit them, too…and that EVERYONE will win as a result.

(4.) Through my direct and/or indirect involvement in these groups, I have also learned that it is absolutely futile to try to put ANY part of God in a box—because God's natural inclination will always be to GET OUT of it. It's a crying shame we don't break down our denominational and theological walls that separate us all—for we'd sure make a great team for Him TOGETHER!

Maybe the best way I could describe the ideal is to go one more time to a later instance in Albom's book:

"....Two weeks earlier, on a Saturday night, the temple had held a gathering in the Reb's honor, commemorating his six decades of service. It was like a coming home party.

'I tell you,' the Reb said, shaking his head as if in disbelief, "...there were people who hadn't seen one another in years. And when I saw them hugging and kissing like such long lost friends—I cried. *I cried.* To see what we have created together. It is something incredible.

Incredible? My old temple? That small place of Sabbath mornings and funny holidays and kids hopping out of cards and running into religious school? Incredible? The word seemed too lofty. But when the Reb pushed his hand together, almost prayer-like, and whispered, 'Mitch, don't you see? We have made a *community*," and I considered his aging face, his slumped shoulders, the sixty years he had devoted tirelessly to teaching, listening, trying to make us better people, well, given the way the world is going, maybe 'incredible' is the right description.

'The way they hugged each other,' he repeated, his eyes far away, "...for me, that is a piece of heaven.'" (Albom, pp.223 & 224)

"...Principle 12—I believe by complete faith in the coming of the Messiah, and even though he tarry in waiting—in spite of that, I will still wait expectantly for him each day that he will come...

"...Principle 13—I believe by complete faith that there will be a resurrection of the dead at the time that will be pleasing before the Creator, blessed be His name, and the remembrance of Him will be exalted forever and for all eternity..."

To that, I can only add the following prayer—May His Kingdom come speedily and swiftly even in our days...and may all of the "kehillah kedoshahs" that we are a part of not only continue to blossom and flourish—but even grow into much bigger ones than we realize. For in desperate times like these, we are so in need of every "sacred community" we can get AND keep—because it reminds us so much of Him who died for us and longs to be in relationship with us. May we never completely walk away from these communities—but stay more fully attached to them as the days grow darker and the time gets closer to His Final Glorious Appearing. Then in THAT day—we will see the greatest "kehillah kedoshah" that will have ever covered the earth…one without boundaries or limitations…but with one common thread…the one who paid a costly price for even us.

As I start this chapter, I realize that we had to make an urgent side trip across the Texas Panhandle. (Believe me—when I first started writing this, I didn't exactly plan it that way. But as they say, that's the way life goes sometimes…) But I felt that in order to finish the specific things that I needed to say about WCG/GCI, that sudden out-of-the-way trip was truly necessary.

Now we're back home again at the ranch—and after our quick Amarillo diversion, maybe here at Bulldog Stadium will be as good a place as any to talk about something most people might most people might normally dread doing. Recent events that have surrounded me in my life at the time I originally write this have spurred me to prepare something for the loved ones I might leave behind. At first, I thought about doing this separately from the book. But any opportunity I can get to be able to kill two birds with one stone is definitely hard for me to pass up. After all, I certainly didn't get to choose the humble beginnings I started out with—but maybe while I still have some life and breath left, I can maybe have at least a little say-so about how I might wish to take my final exit from this life into my final irrevocable entrance into the eternal Kingdom of His Dear Son. (Whoever the executor of this will turns out to be—are you listening and reading this closely? Please pay close attention to what will follow…)

The current impetus for incorporating these will revision efforts during this book's original writing was when I had to help my grandmother and one of my aunts begin to move stuff of my mother's former house that she had lived in next door to my grandparents since I was a freshman in high school when my mother on the advice of her doctor decided that it was time for her to become a permanent resident of a Plainview nursing home.

During this time, my eldest aunt and I had at least one conversation about what final arrangements would be conducted upon my mother's death. [FYI—this was necessary since this particular aunt holds power-of-attorney privileges over my mother.] During that conversation, I happened to mention to her [probably to her for the very first time] that I was an organ donor…and also revealed maybe an additional thing or two about my own final arrangements that she may have not been previously aware of. As we were talking, I heard my aunt rightly and wisely emphasize the need for me to get my own final wishes down on paper as well. While we were in the process of going through some of the stuff in my mother's house, I happened to find a handwritten version of a will I had drafted years ago and sneakily put in my mother's bedroom cabinets—but never told my mother or anyone else in my family about.

I then took a quick look over what I had previously wrote—and then realized that it was way past time for some major revisions on this will. (This also included the possibility that since the original version was never typed up by myself that it might not be interpreted as valid will since it couldn't be legibly read by someone else other than myself.) And on top of it, over the years at various times, I've also pondered some additional interesting thoughts about how to best take my final exit from this earth—especially in a way that would more fittingly and appropriately give glory and honor to my God and do my part (even if I did nothing else than this during my short lifetime here on earth) to see that the cause of my Savior is more effectively established and published on the earth.

But why make Bulldog Stadium my backdrop for this? It's because during a certain pre-Holy Day fast years ago, one of the things that I sensed the Lord talking to me about was that part of my own personal destiny of my life would possibly run through two particular locations here in Plainview…one of them the old Hilton Hotel…and the other right here on the very football field that the Plainview High School Bulldogs play their home games each fall. I haven't always cared to watch any games here…but I've certainly done more than my share of helping broadcast games on the radio that have originated from here.

At first, I thought I'd just go ahead and give you the entire legal document here. But then I remembered that reading all that legal gobblydegook wouldn't exactly be that sort of fascinating reading that would keep you on the edge of your seat. (And it might be better for legal purposes, too, to keep the actual will separate from the book anyway. But I might still go ahead anyway and at least attach a copy of this chapter as a part of the final will to serve as a basic outline of how I would rather see my own official final exit from this earth.)

After careful reevaluation and reexamination, I have decided to insure through my will that no matter what else might be done in my lifetime one part of this particular personal destiny is appropriately fulfilled in a way that might honor Him…one way or the other. So I now officially update and revise my last will and testament in the following manners specified here while I've still of the presence of mind to do it. Therefore, here's what I now wish to consider as of the time of this book's original writing (unless and until I give additional codicils and amendments otherwise) my final statement of my desired final wishes and requests that I would like to see take place upon my final demise in the form of a general checklist that can be used for all to judge whether or not my final wishes were appropriately carried out to my taste and standards:

[SECTION I:] (1.) I first wish to officially make known by my own hand that I have registered with the Texas Department of Public Safety and specified that I wish to be an organ donor of any usable organs, tissue, etc. necessary upon my demise to those appropriately in need of them;

(2.) That AFTER all necessary organs, etc. have been harvested from my body that any other remaining parts of my remains be subsequently donated to an appropriate institution of medical learning [(Ex.) Texas Tech Medical School] for appropriate and necessary medical research purposes;

(3.) If after said institution is finished with their research with my remains and a choice is given to those I may officially designate as either a Family Representative/Interim Executor OR Head Executor/Memorial Crusade Executive Chairman {these terms will be further elaborated on in later sections of this document} and/or any living members of my family for either cremation or burial that my wishes would be to opt for cremation for the following reasons—

(A.) I figure that if the original state that my God originally created me was out of a bunch of dirt and ashes, then I might as well return this shell of a body back to its Original Owner in similar form as that of which He originally started with me;

(B.) Since funerals and memorial services are in my view primarily for the living and not the dead (and besides—I don't plan to be there with you to join you for it since I'll already be gone anyway)—I figure I might as well do everyone a favor and get them started early on the idea that I'm now gone and force all who might wish to remember me in any form at all to instead turn on the TV screens in their minds, remember what lessons and example I might have left behind for them on His behalf, and then put their focus more appropriately on praising God for what was accomplished during my lifetime and consider also going and doing likewise;

(C.) I also wish (especially if at the time of my physical demise that I might somehow be financially indigent) to help make any costs that may be incurred towards my funeral and any burdens this may place on my remaining family and loved ones as minimal and light as is possible;

(D.) I've heard that some people in the Christian world have serious problems and/or even some sort of controversy with the practice of cremation versus traditional burial. I've even heard at one time one prominent evangelical Christian leader say that the Old Testament shows that when someone was cremated that it was regarded as a curse upon the deceased.

To me, though, I don't necessarily regard this as some horrific thing. In fact, what I would be personally much more horrified over after my passing is if anything dealing with my body or the remembrance of me is used in any sort of way that might be interpreted by my God as unnecessary idolatrous worship of myself that would go against the very things my God stands for.

If I had to make a choice in this matter, I would much prefer to be considered "accursed" and have my name dragged in the mud and forced to decrease so that His name can be more fully established, published, and worshiped by all men. **In**

otherwords—let my name mean and be nothing…BUT ONLY if it will instead make my Savior and Meshiach's name more fully proclaimed to all mankind! There's NOTHING in my mortal body whatsoever in the natural that is worth any good anyway—but ONLY Christ in me…the Hope of Glory—who is able to will and do any good that I've ever done.

I also have a deeper reason best expressed in Maimonides' last two principles of his "Thirteen Principles Of Jewish Faith" that I first quoted in the last chapter—

"…Principle 12—I believe by complete faith in the coming of the Messiah, and even though he tarry in waiting—in spite of that, I will still wait expectantly for him each day that he will come…

"…Principle 13—I believe by complete faith that there will be a resurrection of the dead at the time that will be pleasing before the Creator, blessed be His name, and the remembrance of Him will be exalted forever and for all eternity…"

I figure that if the Creator and Master of the Universe was smart enough to create me out of dirt in the first place, then when it comes time for the final resurrection into His Glorious Kingdom, that He will be just as capable of putting me back together in the form that He wishes to use to present me to Himself and everyone else in His Kingdom….

(4.) That as far as my Living Will and/or DNR orders and/or the cessation of life support is concerned—should I be found gravely incapacitated in an interminable coma, etc. that the following procedures be implemented:

(A.) That no major medical decision of this kind would be made without my family first consulting with any one of the pastors of any one of the church(es) that I might be attending at the time of my passing—and that it would only be made in accordance and obedience to the wishes and the desires of the Spirit of the Lord;

(B.) That if after a certain period of time I have not otherwise naturally passed on of my own accord and if the overall consensus after appropriate consultations amongst all parties concerned {i.e.—Family representatives; medical professionals; and clergy} finds that the wisest course for all concerned is the COMPLETE cessation of all medical treatment—THEN AND ONLY THEN should the following procedures be implemented—

(1.) That after this final consensus decision is rendered, all concerned would first allow for a period of time starting from the time the decision is made until at least the next upcoming Last Great Day of the Feast of Tabernacles (i.e.—the 8th and last day of the Biblical Festival of Sukkot) has officially ended before such final cessation procedures are formally started so that the people might yet seek the Lord first one more time for my complete and total healing until this "waiting period" is completed. (The reason for this is that one of my personal requests of the Lord is that I would not die until I have at least experienced one more final Feast on this earth before I pass on.)

(2.) That if by the time the above-mentioned "waiting period" is completed and there is still absolutely no change in my medical condition, then the family, clergy, and medical professionals will be released to do what may seem good to them and the Holy Spirit to do for and to me on my behalf.

[SECTION II:] [FUNERAL/MEMORIAL SERVICES AND OPERATIONS]

To help further glorify God and do my part one final time to help bring those who have never trusted Jesus/Y'shua as their Savior and Lord, I respectfully request that the following procedures be followed as to the disposition of my remains, any memorial services, etc. on my behalf:

(1.) That I will appropriately appoint before my demise two important people that will be responsible for my final arrangements:

(A.) **Family Representative/Interim Executor**—This person within my physical family will serve as the one I officially designate as having *primary* power of attorney over all my personal matters (including legal, financial, medical, and all other concerns) in case of any sort of incapacitation or other medical, etc. situation in which I am shown to not otherwise be completely independent and of appropriate sound mind and judgment and am otherwise prevented by physical, mental, or emotional capacity of making capable and informed decisions by myself while I am still alive in some form and will also serve and act as a "de facto" interim executor over my estate in the immediate interim period immediately after my demise in accordance to the dictates and wishes stated in this will. The Family Representative/Interim Executor will liaison and coordinate closely with my appropriately designated clergy person up even until such time as the following is done...

(B.) **Chairman of the Memorial Crusade Executive Committee**—
My appropriately designated clergy WILL ALSO serve a VERY important role in any and all final arrangements—and will automatically serve as the combination FINAL Head Executor/Chairman of the Memorial Crusade Executive Committee and will work in tandem with the Family Representative/Interim Executor to insure that these final wishes are carried out:

(1.) The Head Executor/Chairman will be responsible for the recruitment, selection, and appointment of an Executive Committee for the following purposes:

(a.) Assisting the Family Representative/Interim Executor in their duties on my behalf and coordinating with the Family until such time that the Committee is fully established and able to take over the responsibility of any remaining final arrangements from the Family and the Family Representative/Interim Executor;

(b.) Family members WILL NOT be eventually responsible and liable for any financial burdens placed upon them as far as my final arrangements are concerned. Once the Executive Committee is formally established and up and running, THEY will be expected to eventually assume the reins of responsibility for believing God that HE will supernaturally take care of any remaining appropriate financial arrangements and also for directly reimbursing the Family for any expenses incurred by them prior to its formation.

(c.) Family members will NOT be required or expected to take part in ANY subsequent Memorial Crusade activities and events outside of the Private Interment Services and the FIRST night of the Crusade that they otherwise physically unable to do or are otherwise uncomfortable for whatever personal reasons they may have. Executive Committee members and others will be requested and expected to HIGHLY esteem and respect any of their personal wishes, actions, and conduct that Family members may pursue that do not otherwise contradict or unnecessarily interfere with either the written wishes of this will OR MORE IMPORTANTLY the desires, guidance, and movement of the Holy Spirit. [(Ex.) If one of the services might be too long for them to participate and a Family member feels a need to leave early for medical, religious, or any other reason—Executive Committee Members and others should not take unnecessary offense or disrespect due to such actions—but instead assist and facilitate each Family member's wishes as best as they're able to do so.]

(2.) The Family Representative and the Executive Committee Chairman will work with the Committee to ensure that no less than THREE separate services will be held in this Memorial Crusade effort:

(A.) [PRIVATE INTERMENT SERVICES:] I hereby request that two-thirds of my ashes of my remains be disposed of in two separate private interment services open ONLY to Family and/or any Executive Committee Members able to attend as follows:

(1.) One-third of my ashes will be put beneath the band director's stand that is located on the track field behind Lockney Elementary School in Lockney, TX. (This is because I spent a good amount of my youth and other parts of my life here at various times climbing this stand and having some of the most personal times with my God in my formative years literally confronting Him with some of the biggest issues I would face in life—and where some of the deepest thoughts and convictions I had of Him were first formed.)

(2.) Another third of my ashes will be poured into the Rio Grande River in Albuquerque, NM at the point where Central Ave. (Bus. 40/Rte. 66) crosses over the Rio Grande. [The reason:

Albuquerque to me will always no matter what be my 2nd adopted hometown—even though I only lived there for 8 months. It was both where I finally was forced to grow up and start working to become the man I needed to be for Him. It was also sadly the place of the biggest personal defeat I had in my life. So just in case I never get there one more time again this side of the Kingdom, I'd at least like to have a part of me go back there one more time—this time in victory.]

(B.)   [THE COY REECE HOLLEY MEMORIAL EVANGELISTIC CRUSADE:]

The primary responsibility of the Executive Committee will be to put together in lieu of a typical funeral/memorial service an interdenominational city-AND-county-wide evangelistic campaign similar to which occurred in Plainview with the Rick Gage Go Tell Crusade in Greg Sherwood Memorial Bulldog Stadium in September 2011. WHY THIS as a part of my final requests?

(1.)   It is a personal desire for myself to ploy one final grand act of revenge against the Adversary who has attempted to steal so many things in my life that I feel I am most certainly entitled and due to receive from him not only damages—but also compounding interest and fees on top of that as well. In case I'm not otherwise able to fully collect from that piddly pipsqueak cockroach before I pass on, I would wish that the universal Body of Christ where I may reside prior to my demise serve as a sort of Divine de facto collection agency on my behalf against him—and take all the booty and spoils from such collection efforts and make sure they are aptly used to see that all appropriate local ministries serving the Body of Christ in this local area are more adequately and fully funded to meet the needs of the people around them;

(2.)   One of my greatest personal desires is to do my part in helping promote unity amongst the brethren—especially across racial, socioeconomic, theological, and denominational lines. And that does NOT just mean to avoid the controversial issues that may separate them, either—but rather instead should mean that they be honest and candid with each other and humble enough to learn from each other. Let the strengths of one brother in the Body compensate for the other's weaknesses—and vice versa. And let ALL the brethren work TOGETHER in mutually beneficial causes that will not only improve the entire community surrounding them, but also see that the smiles of our Abba Father always continue over us no matter what else may happen in our world today;

(3.)   One of my biggest concerns is that after I pass on—what if there might be ONE MORE SOUL that does not finally surrender to the Master and His Will that I could have helped Him reach? I want to make bleeping sure that when my time comes that I am required to give an account for what I might have done with my life before the Master that I can somewhat be reasonably confident (even though I know for sure I definitely didn't do things perfectly) that I did as much as I was able to do before coming to stand in front of His Holy Throne.

__Therefore and to wit to insure that I can stand before Him with a clear conscience, I ask that the Chairman and the Crusade Executive Committee utilize the following guidelines and procedures to insure the success of the Crusade—__

(A.) The Chairman and the Executive Committee will conduct the crusade NO LESS than 60 to 90 days after my death to insure that adequate time and preparation is given for appropriate preparation, training of Crusade volunteers, coordination, publicity, and execution of said Crusade;

(B.) It would be especially pleasurable and beneficial to me personally if the Crusade could be held as close as possible to any of the Biblical Holy Days listed in Leviticus 23: and Deuteronomy 16: (especially if possible in the days between the Feast of Trumpets and the Day of Atonement);

(C.) The specific duration of the Crusade will be NO LESS than one week from start to finish and should be extended and allowed to last as long as the Holy Spirit may direct the Committee to do. It should also be held in the LARGEST venue possible [(Ex.) In Plainview, TX—either Bulldog Stadium or Hutchinson Center] and open to the public FREE of charge and with love offerings taken ONLY as the Spirit may guide and direct each night.

(D.) As far as participating pastors, Crusade volunteers, and churches are concerned, this again should be as truly an interracial and interdenominational effort even appropriate Sabbatarian and Messianic Jewish groups that may wish to directly participate being allowed to do so by the rest without unnecessary criticism or condemnation given either by these groups towards the rest of the Body of Messiah—or the same towards those groups by others in the Body in that particular local area.

(E.) It will be expected and even considered MANDATORY that each night's Crusade service will have an appropriate invitation time—not only for salvations or rededications—but also for pastors and trained counselors to be available to pray for the needs of the people (whether it be for Divine healing, prayers for financial prosperity, restoration of marriages, deliverance from bondages, addictions, evil spirits, etc.) as the Spirit may direct them to do so.

(F.) That the Executive Committee establish and schedule as part of the overall Crusade the following special events:

    (1.) **(FIRST NIGHT ONLY:) THE OFFICIAL PUBLIC MEMORIAL SERVICE FOR COY REECE HOLLEY**—This will be the ONLY time during the Crusade that will be allowed to serve as my official memorial service and where I'll even allow for public displays of tears, etc. over me! This will also be the ONLY Crusade service that I will expect any Family member to attend for any amount of time they feel comfortable in doing so. Any eulogies, final statements, etc. about myself from others will be said at this time.

This will also be the time where the Chairman of the Executive Committee (who will also serve as the final speaker of that particular Crusade service that night) will explain not only to the Crusade crowd that is gathered at the venue, but also to the world the purposes not only of this solemn assembly/memorial service, but for the upcoming Crusade ahead. The Chairman will then read Ps. 126: 5 & 6; the entirety of Psalm 20:, and also Numbers 30: as well as other appropriate passages that the Spirit may lead Him to utilize and explain the significance of these particular passages to the people as the Spirit may give him utterance before doing one final committal prayer over the remaining third of my ashes before spreading those ashes upon the very venue where that night's service is being conducted.

The Chairman after spreading those remaining ashes on behalf of the Executive Committee will then read what will amount to an abject declaration of spiritual WAR against Ha'Satan and, in essence, declare that local area's irrevocable secession and independence from any union of the Adversary and declare unashamedly and unabashedly their complete and total reliance of the Father who loves and cares for them.

After that, the Chairman will declare the memorial service concluded and the Crusade officially open—and will himself extend the first official invitation time of the Crusade to the public. After the invitation time is concluded, I would then request that the song "Greater Things Are Yet To Come" be sung by the worship team and the Crusade assembly as a VERY strong encouragement to the brethren assembled to get on with the work of the Crusade ahead before the closing prayer is said and the first night's service appropriately concluded as needed unless the Spirit directs the Committee to do otherwise.

(2.) At no time during the Crusade should flowers or other special gifts that are not otherwise monetary be accepted by the Committee over and above what is directly needful for the proper operation of the Crusade or what is within proper decorum and taste. In lieu of flowers, etc., it would be preferable that memorials be sent to the following ministries:

Freedom In Jesus Ministries

Crisis Center of the Plains

Restorative Justice Ministries Network of Texas [Huntsville, TX]

Loved Ones of Prisoners [Odessa, TX]

Road To Restoration Ministries

Red Life Ministries [Kansas City, MO area]

Living Water Emmaus Community

Aaron and Lily Straus Foundation (Camps Airy/Louise) [Baltimore, MD]

The Executive Committee at their discretion may also be allowed to receive memorial offerings to itself as well to not only help defray the cost of my own funeral expenses, but also of the Crusade itself.

(G.) [OTHER REQUIRED CRUSADE EVENTS AND OUTREACHES:]

(1.) One of the Crusade services/nights MUST be designated as a "Night To Honor Israel" in accordance to Genesis 12:3!

(2.) One night of the Crusade must be set aside to honor and remember those affected by my state's criminal justice system—and for Crusade attendees to reflect not only on the needs of prisoners, ex-offenders, and their families—but especially of the continuing "Krystalnacht" of suffering of those who have been victims of violent crime (especially those affected by either domestic violence and/or sexual assault).

(3.) One night of the Crusade will be set aside to honor those law enforcement officials, first responders, correctional officers, city leaders and those in authority, and all military personnel who serve us and our country every day.

(4.) During the Crusade—the Committee will especially establish and implement appropriate special direct outreach activities on behalf of the Body of Christ in the local area towards the following groups:

(a.) Prisoners and their families

(b.) Ex-offenders

(c.) Correctional officers and law enforcement

(d.) Victims of violent crime (especially those affected by domestic violence and/or sexual assault)

[Conclusion:] "…Why in the world would I desire to write my final wishes in this way?," you might ask. It's because of two things—one, a personal vision of how I might see myself when I'm called to stand before my Maker and am asked to give an account to Him for what all I did in this life…and two—a standing personal desire because of that vision to see that these final acts as well as whatever else is done and said when my name is mentioned for a final time on this earth will be the very first things the Lord Himself may decide to show me on the highlight reel when I will be required to stand before Him face-to-face in judgment for what I have done on this earth.

The vision I keep seeing about myself is this—I come before Him standing before His throne at first—but then when I finally gain a glimpse of His holiness and righteousness for myself, I find myself literally lying prostrate on the floor before Him eating carpet.…hardly even able to speak to or even dare look Him in the eye and crying absolute tears of shame and guilt for all the times I wronged and betrayed Him.

He starts the highlight reel of my life on the many TV screens showing throughout the throne room. Those scenes where He points out where I failed only add to the tears and disgust at myself over my conduct while on the earth serving as an ambassador for Him. I cry more and more—and even wail and lament pretty much like Oskar Schindler did at the end of "Schindler's List" where he goes out to the outside of his factory and looks at his possessions and constantly cries out—*"I could have done more! I could have done more! This car could have saved Jews! This watch…"*…and on and on he went. I could easily see myself bawling and squawling in similar fashion in tears and heartbreak. Scenes where He points out any good will seem like no consolation to me at that moment—for I would truly judge my past works at that time to be at best filthy rags and nothing to write home about.

Then the highlight reel stops—and my Savior and Sovereign Judge asks me to answer the questions that He will use to separate the sheep and goats—and I'm not just lying prostrate before Him—but my knees are by then knocking; I'm scared out of my wits; and I'm truly wondering if there's any hope left for me. The questions He asks are the exact same ones listed in Matthew 25:31-46. He starts going down the list—hungry? thirsty? take in strangers? By this time, it would all be a blur to me—and you might as well write me off as an emotional basketcase. My fate is truly sealed—and I'm surely doomed due to my lack of response on the previous questions on the floor.

Then He asks me the final question: "...Did you come see Me when I was in prison?" Just as I weakly attempt to explain myself, a brother dressed in a TDCJ-issued white jumpsuit comes up before my face and says to me, "...Hey, wait a minute—you came with some ministry team to my unit and counseled me about about how to receive Christ after some preacher gave an altar call. *And now I'm here today because of it! Please don't condemn Him, Lord! Have mercy on Him!*"

Another brother in TDCJ white also comes up to me and recalls, "...Yeah! I remember this guy preaching some sermon about vows...or maybe he was talking about separation...I forget exactly what it was...But I do remember that during that sermon he talked a lot about how the Jewish people viewed that subject and what it should really mean to me as a Christian as a result!"

Then the parade of prison witnesses really started coming one by one before Him rushing to give testimony to the Sovereign Judge in my defense. Before long, they were joined by correctional officers, law enforcement officers, and even victims of violent crime that I had apparently previously ministered to on His behalf, but long since forgot. As these witnesses gather around me in a circle, the scene for me becomes much more overwhelming for me to take—and I'm STILL crying and shouting in protest to the LORD continually, "...BUT I COULD HAVE DONE MORE, LORD—I COULD HAVE DONE MORE!"

At that point, I will then finally trust that my Savior/Sovereign Judge will Himself step away from the bench as the stream of tears I'm crying becomes a torrential river on my face. He then will come to me in the center of the circle surrounded by these witnesses and lovingly and tenderly say to me, "...Son, SHHH!!! Don't say anything else!!! I knew what you were truly capable of doing before you were even born—and even when you first started all of this. You may not have had very much at all to begin with—but I know now for sure that you did the best you could with what you had."

Then with the arms of some of those in that circle draped around my shoulders, keeping me steady, and helping to keep me from falling apart and collapsing—my

Meshiach I believe will then wipe away the river of tears I've been crying and continue, "…Son, look all around you—for great is your reward!" And then He will say to me the words most any believer in Him longs to hear—"…Well done, thou good and faithful servant. Enter into the joy of the Kingdom I've prepared for you. Welcome home, old soldier, back from your Siberia and Vietnam—welcome home!" Then and only then as the witnesses rejoice, shout, and clap will I probably be able to finally breathe a sigh of relief.

After I've first met with my Savior face-to-face, I'll probably after that look up at the grandstands and try to find two other special men. They'll this time for sure be a part of the cloud of witnesses that have also cheered me on for so long. Once I finally spot and see them, I hope to go up to where they are, shake hands with them, and tell them, "It's sure nice to see you both again…'"

I'll then give them back the baton they first gave me and say, "…I'm sorry I couldn't do much more that what I did. But I hopefully at least did what I could with what you both gave me and what little I had." I hope with those words and actions that they will from there let me know that they were somewhat satisfied with whatever efforts I made personally as a steward on their behalf. I will also trust that they will not feel that their own work and contributions for Him that they made were found to be entirely in vain due to anything I might have done otherwise. After that's done, then and only then will I truly feel that it's party time for me in the Kingdom from there.

[Chapter 22:] [Plainview—Part IX—North Date Street] Reflections Time: Where Do We Go From Here?]

Let's see—we've just got back in town again…but I'm not in a box of ashes yet (and don't hold your breath right now about that "memorial crusade" thing happening anytime soon. If I still have life and breath in me, Franklin Graham or Rick Gage may have to wait a good while longer before holding those altar calls…). We are, though, heading towards the home stretch of this journey in more ways than one—and we have traveled more than our share of shoe leather miles since we started. So how about going down 24th St. and head back home, ok? I think we're more than tired anyway from our recent travels—and I've got to check my mail and make sure things back at the homestead are secure.

(After a little bit, we arrive back at this book's original physical starting point—my current apartment on North Date Street. Ok---so that was an ancient Chinese secret that I didn't exactly tell you when I first started. Well, I guess the cat's out of the bag now, huh...for better or for worse?)

Be it ever so humble (so they say and sing)—there's no place like home. Seems like an eternity since we were last here. Come on back in and have a seat...**Another eviction notice on the door?** I told them I'd be gone for a little bit while I was taking you on an extended tour…Well—at least the tea in the pitcher's still full and cold. Go help yourself to some and have a seat while I head to the office and try to straighten this out and get the mail…

(After returning from both the office and the mailbox…) WHEH!!!….false alarm, thankfully…the office manager said that someone with a Star of David necklace and long flowing robes and long hair just stopped in yesterday and managed to get me caught up rentwise…PRAISE GOD!! Isn't He REALLY good? He sure does take good care of me—don't you think? (You take a drink from your glass of "iced tea" and ask me about the mail I got…) Well, much quieter in the mailbox than I thought, but it still piles up after a long trip nonetheless…hmmh…bills, bills, bills, and more bills…ministry mail…ohhh, junk, junk, junk, and more junk…don't you hate junk mail? Ah, good—I got one of my small checks and even a $25 Wal-Mart gift card that I just won in a contest. I'll need to save the gift card for later—the cupboard is getting a little bare grocerywise, you know…

Man, I'm tired—and my feet have had it. It's way past time I got back home. Nice to prop my feet on my own footstool, for sure…Now that we're getting nice and comfortable again back here at the ranch, it's time for me to put on the pair of brand-new shoes I told you about in the Introduction. Would you believe that they're actually for once HOUSE SHOES? (We both chuckle.)

You remember when I told you earlier about when I was at Camp Airy and they had "reflections time" during their Sabbath services? Well, maybe here in the comforts of my home is about as good a place as any to have our own "reflections times" over the journey that we've just traveled. There are especially some important heart-to-heart things based on the experiences of my life's journey so far that I feel my God really wants me to say to several different groups within the entirety of the Body of Christ as well as outside of it.

There will be FOR SURE certain things each group will love—but other things they may absolutely hate to the point where I might be accused of promoting outright heresy against sacred cows they might hold dear. I hope these specific groups would understand that my intent in expressing such views is not to cause offense against them and what they might specifically believe.

But I will NOT apologize for what I deeply feel is a necessary "speaking to truth in love" to each of these specific groups. Over the years, I've been through a number of rodeos of many kinds. I just want people to start learning from the mistakes I've made in my own life so they won't have to go through as many hard knocks as I did—that's all. Maybe if I put this as a bullet points style list that people can not only learn from, but also change as needed to conform to God's high standards and not ours--folks can then from there eat the meat, spit the bones, and file what they don't like into File 13. Here goes:

WHAT I WOULD SAY TO MY WCG/GCI COMRADES: (whether past or present):

(1.) I know that it's been a long, hard trail of tears for all of you. Hey—I went through it, too…and it definitely wasn't a picnic for me either. I personally lost good friends and brethren that I haven't been in contact with for years. Even now at times, I still occasionally cry tears with even the slightest mention of some of the brethren I once knew that are no longer here. It's great to go back and remember some of the good things that to me were some of the stepping stones of my faith in Him. It's hard not to think about the first two Feasts I went to in Big Sandy that I have some of my most fondest memories of—only now to realize that this particular former Ambassador College campus belongs to someone else.

But for those of you who still even after all this time have a broken heart or are holding grudges and resentments as a result of ANYTHING that might have happened to either yourself or those around you during "the changes"—can I please be allowed to do a little ministry through this particular medium of communication for about a moment or two? I hate to tell you the truth—but I found out for myself that the sun's still shining and the world hasn't stopped yet. Yes, there's a definitely a time to grieve what you've lost…because Ecclesiastes chapter 3 makes that fact plain as day. And even the Jewish people have a set time of what they call "shiva" ("mourning") over loved ones lost. But sadly, even Moses had to eventually pass on--

Joshua 1-4

New International Version (NIV)

Joshua Installed as Leader

1 After the death of Moses the servant of the LORD, the LORD said to Joshua son of Nun, Moses' aide: 2 "Moses my servant is dead. Now then, you and all these

people, get ready to cross the Jordan River into the land I am about to give to them—to the Israelites. [3] I will give you every place where you set your foot, as I promised Moses. [4] Your territory will extend from the desert to Lebanon, and from the great river, the Euphrates—all the Hittite country—to the Mediterranean Sea in the west. [5] No one will be able to stand against you all the days of your life. As I was with Moses, so I will be with you; I will never leave you nor forsake you. [6] Be strong and courageous, because you will lead these people to inherit the land I swore to their ancestors to give them.

[7] "Be strong and very courageous. Be careful to obey all the law my servant Moses gave you; do not turn from it to the right or to the left, that you may be successful wherever you go. [8] Keep this Book of the Law always on your lips; meditate on it day and night, so that you may be careful to do everything written in it. Then you will be prosperous and successful. [9] Have I not commanded you? Be strong and courageous. Do not be afraid; do not be discouraged, for the LORD your God will be with you wherever you go."

And just as Moses has already made his stage right exit, so have both Mr. Armstrong and Mr. Tkach, Sr. We can't always spend our lives in the past dwelling too much on shouldas, wouldas, ifmaybes, and couldhavebeens. If we do that, we'll never grow and be able to understand more of the wondrous things our God still has for us.

May I urge that we follow the example of the lepers in 2nd Kings chapter 7? They were between a rock and a hard place, too. But instead of sitting there on their pitypots wondering what to do, they at least had the chutzpah to attempt to get up and do something. What happened as a result? Not only did God do a miracle in their midst, but these lepers got to be the first to tell even the most prominent officials in Israel about it so that other lives could be saved. If you do nothing, guess what you'll get back…It's way past time to cry your last tear and move on.

(2.)   The Rav Shaul/Apostle Paul said this to the Romans:

Romans 13:1-7

New International Version (NIV)

Submission to Governing Authorities

13 Let everyone be subject to the governing authorities, for there is no authority except that which God has established. The authorities that exist have been

established by God. [2] Consequently, whoever rebels against the authority is rebelling against what God has instituted, and those who do so will bring judgment on themselves. [3] For rulers hold no terror for those who do right, but for those who do wrong. Do you want to be free from fear of the one in authority? Then do what is right and you will be commended. [4] For the one in authority is God's servant for your good. But if you do wrong, be afraid, for rulers do not bear the sword for no reason. They are God's servants, agents of wrath to bring punishment on the wrongdoer. [5] Therefore, it is necessary to submit to the authorities, not only because of possible punishment but also as a matter of conscience.

[6] This is also why you pay taxes, for the authorities are God's servants, who give their full time to governing. [7] Give to everyone what you owe them: If you owe taxes, pay taxes; if revenue, then revenue; if respect, then respect; if honor, then honor.

Please understand that in the course of writing this book there has been no desire on intent in any way, shape, or form to either rail or harangue the currently established GCI leadership or try to start ANY church or following of my own that is overtly contrary and disrespectful of already duly established eccleasiastical authority—and it is my hope that this book is not unnecessarily construed by GCI leaders that this work is not considered in their eyes as outside proper submission or an inappropriate challenge on my part to their legitimacy and/or their ecclesiastical authority.

In fact, I hope that our time in Amarillo during Chapter 18 made those stands clear. Let me in this public forum say it this way: As my personal spiritual journey has progressed since "the changes", so have a few parts of my personal belief system (under the inspiration of the Holy Spirit, of course) have needed to change. Some of those personal beliefs may not be in complete agreement with any current doctrinal positions that GCI now holds. But overall (essentially after all I have went through), I still after all this time will also consider GCI to be my primary church fellowship.

I very much believe that Dr. Joseph Tkach, Jr. as the current GCI President and Pastor General and his staff under him have more than shown over the years a consistent track record of continued faithfulness and have done the best reasonable job possible in doing the numerous tasks that our God has set before our denomination with the resources that have been provided and made available to them up to this point in time. I further add that the Apostle Paul told his protégé Timothy the following;

1 Timothy 5

New International Version (NIV)

[17] The elders who direct the affairs of the church well are worthy of double honor, especially those whose work is preaching and teaching. [18] For Scripture says, "Do not muzzle an ox while it is treading out the grain,"[a] and "The worker deserves his wages."[b] [19] Do not entertain an accusation against an elder unless it is brought by two or three witnesses. [20] But those elders who are sinning you are to reprove before everyone, so that the others may take warning. [21] I charge you, in the sight of God and Christ Jesus and the elect angels, to keep these instructions without partiality, and to do nothing out of favoritism.

In all that Dr. Tkach, Jr. and his staff under him may do from here, I very much ask my colleagues and brethren to cut them as much slack as is possible and allow them the freedom, liberty, and proper honor and respect necessary for them to continue to be obedient to what our God might be right now telling them to do. We individually may not always quite agree with every little thing they might do. But those of us in the rank-and-file membership regardless should not only attempt to stay informed about what's going within GCI, but more importantly do whatever parts our God desires for each of us to play. Not only will those in HQ leadership be able to live quiet and peaceable lives, holy and acceptable to Him as a result—but all of us will prosper and can truly feel that we all also had valuable roles to play in getting Kingdom business done.

(3.) NEVER EVER forget especially what Mr. Tkach, Sr. told us before he died about the damaging effects of legalism and how it can hinder our relationship with God. I don't personally think that he would have said all of this at the very risk of his own health and life as well as his long-established personal friendships and relationships for absolutely no good reason at all. He had a purpose in teaching what God led him to do. Let's remember the example he left us and not only be diligent to DO it—but also be able to teach and share what we all in GCI have personally learned with others we may have influence within our own personal worlds and spheres of influence. That way—others won't have to learn the same lessons in the same exact way that we all did—through the school of hard knocks and practical experience.

(4.) Now come two points where WCG/GCI members and pastors can certainly feel free to disagree with me on. All I ask is that YOU study what I might say here for yourself and see what the Word says about it. I'll even try to practice what I'm about to preach myself…if you, your conscience, and the Lord aren't in your eyes in complete agreement about these personal assertions I'm about to make, that's between ya'll. I won't stand in your way. But at least give appropriate room and respect for others that might be different doctrinally from you—PLEASE…with sugar on top?

(A.) Colossians 2:16-23 are Paul's reminders to us about unnecessarily waffling to doctrinal extremes. Mr. Tkach, Sr. and others rightly warned us to not judge those that had to work on Saturday and those that hold to doctrines that are most common to evangelical Christians. That to me is a right and proper teaching of HQ that should always be upheld.

But I have an equally distressing concern—that those in WCG/GCI who AFTER the split decided to abandon the Holy Days and Festivals, etc. in favor of days like Christmas and Easter could be in equal danger if they aren't careful in engaging in what I call "reverse legalism". Now DO NOT GET ME WRONG ON THIS!!! I'm NOT talking about salvation-essential issues that are non-negotiable here. I'm talking about areas of personal spiritual liberty and freedom. Remember that there are still some (at least a sizable minority that I personally know of) that would still even after all this time prefer to keep the Festivals and Holy Days in some form as Mr. Armstrong first originally taught us.

A lot of these that I know still lean towards this way couldn't leave WCG/GCI for one reason or another—but usually from what I could tell felt that they were denied appropriate opportunities to continue worshiping Him in the manner they were previously accustomed to doing while still staying loyal to HQ. In the rush of some to experience what they felt was newfound excitement over Christmas and Easter, they possibly forgot to be a bit more considerate for others still in GCI holding equally valid, but diametrically opposite views.

317

(I especially mention the above in particular in part to the way I now perceive the Biblical Festivals. To set the personal record straight, my own personal preference [in light of my past Southern Baptist background that puts a HIGH value on Christmas, Easter, and other doctrines that might best fit in with "replacement theology"] is to NOT ONLY still observe the Biblical Festivals of Leviticus 23: and Deuteronomy 16: , but also (in light of my own personal spiritual growth) to ALSO observe Hanukkah as well. I definitely DON'T expect everyone to necessarily adopt my personal doctrinal viewpoints—but I'm HIGHLY concerned that some may jump in the OPPOSITE ditch and STILL be in legalism against others that haven't grown to understand spiritual truth to the degree that they have had. Legalism can come in ANY form—regardless of whether you prefer to put ornaments on a Christmas tree or still prefer to go on a 24-hour complete fast on the Day of Atonement. Let's be smart and treat each other like we used to—as brethren giving each other true freedom and liberty to become what He wants us to be as well as grow up spiritually and otherwise in the way He might desire us to do—not man or anything else.)

(5.) Speaking of treating each other well as brethren, I hope you will once again soon take the time to reread if necessary earlier in the book about what I said about the concept of the "kehillah kedoshah" (sacred community). One thing when I first came into WCG that really fascinated me and that I very much appreciated was the numerous Feasts in the past I have been able to be personally present for.

What has been very unique to me about WCG/GCI is the WORLDWIDE/INTERNATIONAL scope and nature of our denomination. From what I see in most (not all) Evangelical denominational meetings (whether they be regional/national/etc.), it's usually ONLY the pastors, denominational leadership, and selected delegates of each association at best that are even able to some degree allowed to directly take part in any sort of "international meeting". The majority of the remaining rank-and-file members are rarely even able to get outside of their own local churches where they attend—much less, bleep forbid, another church in the same city or town they live in. It's hard most of the time for these folks to even see or conceive of a whole world of believers outside their immediate neighborhoods and city limits and/or personal circle of influence.

For us in WCG/GCI in the past until recent years, that was hardly the case in most instances. In fact, it used to be a totally opposite scenario. Sure, we had friends and brethren in our own local congregations. But I very much liked the fact (especially when we as members traveled many miles for our previous Feast of Tabernacles) that even the newest members among us (and NOT JUST PASTORS) had the potential of also developing relationships with other brethren form across the nation and even across the world. There were plenty of opportunities for even members to be able to meet leading ministers within our fellowship and possibly have more than just a quick "Hi.." with them.

If the rabbi that I mentioned in Chapter 18 would haved like to see what I might have thought was a true "kehillah kedoshah" in action and at work, I would have relished the chance to let him spend ONE day with the brethren who attended our pre-split Feasts. What he might have seen in his own life wouldn't have compared to some of the Feast experiences I had. Where else could I have been able to stay in a East Texas campground and meet young ladies from Illinois or Missouri and play miniature gold with them—or to rub shoulders with other brethren from the UK and other foreign nations on the sands of Myrtle Beach? How else could I have been able all in the place hear special music and even a sermon from some guys in Australia or be greeted by a pastor from South Africa?

Yes—there are obviously some good and necessary purposes to localization and decentralization of our local congregations. But these things have sadly come to us at a cost. I'd like to know—what happened to the true worldwide nature of our "sacred community"? This was one of our hugest advantages that other churches and denominations could only dream of and envy. We need as a denomination work to get at least some of a proper balance back between the two. We can still be decentralized in nature, but yet maintain what has been one of our biggest hallmarks and strengths. We just need to get back and seek the Lord and ask Him how we all can best do this again so that we can continue to be the shining light and example to others that He would have us be.

(6.) Two remaining major desperately needed improvements in WCG/GCI that I feel would benefit us to pursue would include the areas of evangelism and development of the "gifts of the Spirit"/"baptism of the Holy Spirit"/deliverance/spiritual warfare.

(A.) Evangelism—First, let me say that it is at least truly encouraging to me that not just HQ leadership, but also regular members have been diligent and doing their part in various locations, times, places, and functions in collaborating and coordinating with other brethren in the universal Body of Christ and alongside others from other groups and denominations in appropriate common evangelistic and humanitarian efforts that help build and strengthen our communities, states, and nations. I not only personally welcome that trend—but I very much pray and highly urge that this overall trend continue. It's a right and proper thing to pursue this goal—and I believe that the Master Himself not only take pleasure in it, but will even further bless those who are willing to take the chance and join the fight with Him.

But I do have a concern that some might have in this area based on previous WCG doctrines which I'm wondering if we have gotten a little fat and lazy when it comes to reaching those that are in possible imminent danger of spiritual destruction. I'm equally concerned over those in the Evangelical world who unnecessarily in my eyes exercise what I would consider a "…gloom-and-doom…sky's falling…you either get saved right this minute or you're toast"…but showing practically to me that they don't have enough faith that GOD HIMSELF can do a pretty good job in saving them even if we ourselves can't get there in time to do the job for them. Maybe the best way I can describe this personal conflict with me would be through a previous e-card I wrote:

Those of us, though, who are believers in Jesus/Y'shua acknowledge that there's only one true Way to get your accounts right with the Father--and that's where the concepts of salvation and repentance tend to kick in. We do this acknowledging that we simultaneously have BOTH a limited AND extended time frame to work from…limited in that we see that the end could literally come at any minute (especially at one of those that we least expect)--but yet extended because we don't know exactly WHEN that moment in time will be and therefore find ourselves seeing that time come a whole lot LATER than expected. (You know the old saying--"If Messiah comes, plant a tree.") But it's on that issue as well as many others that time and space here will not allow me to elaborate on. I hope to, though, at least, clear up a possible misunderstanding or two along the way as I am able.

The general conflict comes from what I can term no better than a battle between what I call those who are "tag-team time-limit" Christianity adherents and those of the camp of what I call "the magical Millenialists". Having once been on each side of the same overall campground they seem to occupy, I think now at this stage of my personal spiritual maturity to address this battle once and for all and to add an insight or two about how both can work together to achieve the common goal of reaching more for Him together than apart.

First, the definitions of each--
(1.) What is a "tag-term time limit" Christianity adherent? To me, it would be someone who might adopt an approach similar to that of Chicken Little of "THE SKY IS FALLING!" fame. These folks (even though outwardly they may not claim to be so) basically take the place in Scripture that says that "...today is the day of salvation..." to an extreme that I don't think even the Savior originally intended. They are constantly gripped with fear that if we don't get this person "saved", "converted", or "going to the RIGHT church" RIGHT NOW that they will forever be condemned to everlasting hellfire with no chance later to repent.

Oh--and the fear gets even worse for those who may never even hear before the time limit...they will (THE HORROR OF IT ALL!) be condemned never even having heard the "Good News" or even having ONE chance and will be judged....(sob, sob!) And oh, the guilt will be so great on OUR hands simply because we didn't get to them in time...with great wailing--all because of what they never even got a chance to say that most blessed and lovely "Sinner's Prayer" that can save their souls RIGHT NOW if they just wanted to....

You mean God is THAT bleeping unfair? They are absolutely convinced that the eternal wrestling match between our God and the Adversary is going on with a time limit--and that there's even a ghost of a chance that the ADVERSARY may yet win over God if those souls don't come to God within the time limit! Satan will therefore win and God will lose those souls forever with no chance of escape because of what WE didn't do! Oh, the sky is definitely falling, it's falling, it's falling....!!!!!!!

Now on the other side of these theological tracks come what I call the "magical Millenialists". Basically, they are the exact opposite of the "tag-team time limiters" and totally pooh-pooh the notion that the world has to be saved RIGHT NOW! In fact, they believe that now is not anywhere near the time for salvation. They instead rather rest in the hope that most everyone else that God has not otherwise called during this church era will get their chance for salvation in the Millenium to come. To them, Christ will basically wave a magic wand, instant change-o convince them that His Ways are right (which won't be too hard now that Satan has been bound for a thousand years) and as a result usher in a wonderful world indeed.

I personally think that each of these groups have both their strong points, but especially a LOT of flaws to their theology. First--what do I think about our "Chicken Littles"...ooh, sorry...I should have said "tag-team time limiters"?: **(1.)** In my humble opinion, Chicken Little needs to take a few Valiums, calm down and relax a little bit. I don't necessarily see any place in Scripture that requires our tag-team time-limiter friends to have to act as superheros to get the Work of our God's Kingdom done. There's been a number of preachers in recent years that keep wondering if the Body of Christ as a whole truly have faith enough in healing. But I'm personally wondering about something far greater than that--**do our churches today even have faith enough to believe God for what He asked us to believe for the most in the first place--a harvest of souls?**

What really burns my bacon on this whole subject is that some of the current approaches our churches are using these days are to me unnecessarily based too much on fear and a lack of proper understanding of the sovereignty of God and of a much bigger plan that HE may have for all of us than we can quickly grasp. Also, I'm very much concerned that people in the Church as a whole don't truly grasp what the role of a "witness" of the Great Commission may be in the first place. Keep in mind, for instance, that when a witness is brought into court, their job is NOT usually to be an evangelist for a particular cause, but to simply TELL the jury what they saw and experienced...nothing more and nothing less.

Now, before some people in the "fire-and-brimstone-sermon" crowd decide to close their eyes and ears to anything said here and attempt to organize a lynch mob to track me down and hang me down from the nearest tree for straying so far from their orthodoxy, I hope they'll permit me first to say this--there IS a proper role and place for the concept they espouse. And there should be times when the naked truth may need to be told in a little harsher manner in order to finally convince a sinner that he/she needs to finally sit down and stop rocking the boat. But my personal concern is this--if their approach is not properly tempered with love and compassion for the other party and a confident assurance that our God is truly who He says He is, then those attempts they may make into bringing someone into salvation will eventually end up in the toilet.

(2.) I'm also concerned that my "tag-team time limiter" friends may have forgot to read and study the essence of John 6:44--**"No one can come to me unless the Father who sent me draws him, and I will raise him up at the last day."(NIV)** You know the old saying--"A man convinced against his will is of the same opinion still." ? I'm truly worried that our "Chicken Littles" as they scream and run with their heads cut off show themselves to be the worst examples possible to those that really do need the Savior. A calm, reassuring voice that sounds steady as a rock to me will get better results in evangelistic efforts than those that succumb more to panic. It reminds me of my previous attempts at sales jobs...high-pressure salesmen can try to wrestle out the quick sale--but in my limited experience, I find that it's much better to establish relationships of trust that take LOTS of time and personal sacrifice in order to maintain things for the long haul. There is something to be said about one thing one of my college professors said in class one time-- "...perception colors viewpoint."

(3.) The "tag-team time-limit" approach to me is more naturally geared to accomplish the personal objectives of the evangelistic parties in order to make them feel good about themselves and achieve preset goals solely for THEIR personal benefit. I keep thinking to myself, " Is this an approach that the Master Himself would utilize--or would He possibly prefer to use another approach that might be more servant-oriented and much more sensitive to the needs of the other party they are attempting to serve?" As Mike Murdoch might put it, "If you'd think about that twice, you might be the genius in your family."

It's time now to turn our attention to the criticisms I might have of our "Magical Millennialist" friends:
(1.) You say to us that only a few are being called right now by Him and that most everyone else will get their chance in the Millennium. To me at times, this frankly sounds a whole lot like the doctrine of predestination to me. So I have the perfect song title for you--"WHAT'S WRONG WITH RIGHT NOW?" What if possibly right now was someone's time for salvation and they may not have another chance after this? Are you absolutely so stupid to actually close the doors to them and say, "Sorry, we're closed right now. But if you're still here when the Millennium comes, please come back to see us and you can have your shot at salvation then." STUPID,

STUPID--how really stupid of a fool can you really be? If the opportunity is staring you right in the face, why not strike when the iron is hot? DUH!!!

(2.) This is an approach that can unnecessarily lead to passivity, complacency, and exclusivity. If Christ in the Millennium is going to wave a magic wand to make everything alright, then why bother getting there in time for the Rapture in the first place? Just because we know that the ultimate victory is assured isn't necessarily an excuse to be taking a nap or even playing canasta when the Master tells you it's time to go encourage a neighbor in need or do something totally out of your comfort zone.

(3.) Just as it's insensitive for Chicken Littles to run over others, it's equally abhorrent to me why our "magical Millennialists" would much rather see Rome burn than get involved and actively find ways that they could help others in the Universal Body of our Lord more effectively accomplish their particular roles in getting the Great Commission done. The Gospel was not given to us by Y'shua/Jesus just to be kept to ourselves--but also to be shared with a hurting world. But if we don't get out of our "holy huddles" and get off our blessed assurances and "one true church" modes, not only will the cause of the Gospel be hindered, but we ourselves in the Body as a whole will be diminished in the process.

What then is the overall sum of what I'm saying here? Simply this--that when we in the Body are striving to do our best evangelistically to get the Great Commission done, we don't necessarily have to do it in fear of time limits. Our God is sovereign and can do as He pleases and has the best plan to get it done in the way He sees fit. But we don't need to be complacent or make excuses or expect someone else to do it. Instead, how about we try a radical idea--what about first listening to what the SPIRIT may want us to do (whether great or small), asking Him for the provision to get our job done for Him, then see if there's ways and common ground that we can help our fellow allies in the process?

Then from there mix in love and compassion and sensitivity. Once that's done and we've done all that we know to do on our end, then let's use our patience and stand behind others with different talents and gifts doing things that we can't do ourselves. Then maybe before you know it, before He tells us it's time to pack up from this earth and head for His Kingdom, we can have peace that we've done what we can with what He told us to do when we had the chance to do it. And we'll find that in the process that time between now and His coming will have gone sooner than we think. And we'll also see at the end of it all that He managed to get all the souls that He wanted to get inside the gates before it was all done--with or without us.

What overall I'm simply seeking is just a good simple balance between good-ol' fashioned grunt "rolling up the sleeves" evangelism work and intercession. Each of these done SEPARATELY doesn't get anyone anywhere. But done TOGETHER WITHOUT fear, but WITH true confidence and faith in Him, the two can be an unbeatable combination when He is directly involved. When we get overly into one extreme or the other, is it any wonder why we're not seeing increases in the membership of our local congregations or in available overall congregational and denominational revenues? THINK, THINK, now...

(B.) HQ and our denomination's members in our evangelism strategy needs to not forget to work towards a concentrated and organized effort to start pursuing "restorative justice" ministry worldwide— both within our own ranks and also alongside other established organizations and groups of other denominational stripes to where the wheel isn't needed to be reinvented...but that if there are needs not otherwise being filled and no other place out there seems to have the abilities to pursue a similar program, THEN and only then should we bother to attempt under the inspiration of the Holy Spirit to see about pioneer something new.

(2.) SPIRITUAL GIFTS/"BAPTISM OF THE HOLY SPIRIT"

(A.) I also feel that our historical bias against Pentecostalism and our fears about unnecessary emotionalism has sadly also kept us from being able to access certain things that I feel our God has left us so that we might be able to have the opportunity to live the victorious, overcoming lives that He would truly desire us to live. Our God IS NOT an absolute child neglector and absentee father—and He most certainly hasn't abandoned us or left us without some tools to resist the numerous things the Adversary may throw at us. I believe that if we got a better detailed understanding of the following topics, we as a global fellowship would not only be the better for it, but our individual relationships with the Father would be so much strengthened and deepened as a result. Topics that I'm referring to include:

(1.) "Baptism of the Holy Spirit"

(2.) Deliverance

(3.) Spiritual warfare

(4.) The authority of the believer in Christ/Y'shua

(5.) What Biblically-based financial prosperity should truly be

(B.)   I am also personally distressed over possibly derogatory and negative comments being expressed by many people about folks who attend "word of faith" churches or support these type of ministries as being construed as being a part of a "cult" [(Ex.) Kenneth Copeland, Oral & Richard Roberts, Kenneth Hagin] due to possibly a lack of knowledge and understanding about what they really believe—and an even more distressing unwillingness by some to look much deeper at them and their teachings than what they might hear on a 30-second TV commercial or story on the evening news. I would challenge folks to give them a very FAIR and unbiased hearing to what these ministries might claim, then decide for yourselves what you might personally do with them and what they specifically teach.

(C.)   If you REALLY want to learn what the true basic constitution and owner's manual, if you will, of what spiritual gifts truly are in accordance to Scripture, a very good DETAILED study of 1st Corinthians chapters 12 through 14 would be a good place to start so that one can not only get a good solid Word-based definition of what these things are in the first place, but more importantly how these can be advantageously used to help the believer in Christ live a victorious, overcoming life.

(D.)   Just because the hermeneutics, etc. might not exactly match up with what YOU think is orthodox doctrine DOESN'T necessarily mean that it is WRONG and FALSE! Sometimes I'm really thinking that a BIG part of the rush to judgment of our "word-of-faith" friends is the preconceived images we in our society have of televangelists have these days (especially with the deeper reason that some of us might possibly be "once bitten, twice shy" about these things). Don't judge the book by the cover so fast—until you've at least been able to skim the table of contents a little bit and read the cover story first…

(II.) WHAT I WOULD WISH TO SAY TO THOSE NOW IN THE "SPLINTER GROUPS"

[A quick author's note first to my Evangelical friends—pay VERY close attention to the definitions I give here…these in my opinion are very important to keep in mind as I discuss certain churches and groups who in some way either were started by what I must sadly term true "dissidents" from the original WCG or by pastors and ministers who at one time were involved with WCG, but who either resigned or (especially in the pre-split years when things were a lot more authoritarian in nature) were disfellowshipped by HQ for one reason or another. Please understand that this is STILL an extremely sensitive issue after all of these years for those of us who either have been a part of WCG or are still currently attending WCG/GCI—and that I'm doing my absolute best here not to label a group in this fashion UNLESS I am aware of evidence otherwise that this label is a right one to put on them.

Please also note that I tend to grade this on a bell curve and that the criteria used here is HIGHLY subjective and should therefore NOT be considered an objective and accurate basis to judge ALL of these groups. I wish to emphasize that this is a particular hard thing for me to do—putting criteria on other groups when I myself have been legalistic in the past. But I had to do the best that I could in order to help provide appropriate wisdom and discernment for all concerned.

I also want to state upfront before I go any further that under the criteria that I have put below of what I would truly consider a WCG "splinter group", I will ABSOLUTELY REFUSE to label (based on my own previous personal dealings with them and the fact that mutual respect has been shown to me by these groups and their leadership) two Texas-based groups as "splinter groups"—the Christian Church of God (pastored by Jeff Booth) in Amarillo, TX and the Huntsville Church of God (Senior Pastor—Albert Foy) in Huntsville, TX…For those two, I would urge Evangelicals to not fear reaching out to them as is feasible and work with these two groups as is possible for each to do so as long as you in the Evangelical world would appropriately extend mutual respect for them and what these two groups stand for. And I am personally right now giving them my unqualified endorsement of their legitimacy and fellowship.

I DO NOT claim to be an expert of any kind in apologetics or other Biblical study disciplines—nor are those my direct personal interests in doing so. However, like it or not—my previous WCG experiences require me to have to know something about this subject and provide a reasonable explanation as best as I can on what I might think of this. These are imperfect criteria and answers—but it was the best that I and the Holy Spirit could come up with that would truly satisfy me.]

(A.) HOW DO I DEFINE WHAT A TRUE WCG "SPLINTER GROUP" IS?

(1.)   How did they originally part with WCG Headquarters (regardless of their time of departure)—was it peaceably and in appropriate mutual agreement OR in outright disobedience and rebellion to the wishes of HQ at the time of their leaving WCG and the formation of their particular group?

(2.)   Major hallmark—They are NOT willing to work to some degree with other groups and individual Christians and willing to welcome them into their activities as fellow brethren and seekers in Christ *as they are INSTEAD OF having to become members of THEIR church FIRST!*

(3.)   Exclusivity and claims that their church is the "ONLY true Church"—and that all other Christians (EVEN those still in WCG/GCI) are STILL "Christians falsely so-called" or "harlot daughters of Babylon"—EVEN calling other splinter groups with some of these same labels

(4.)   Legalism from all indications I and/or others have seen up to this point so far is still seemingly rampant in their midst

(5.)   The group primarily attempts to "proselytize" members from mainstream WCG/GCI AND other splinter groups in order to increase their ranks with so-called "heresies" and deviations from "…the essential truths once delivered to Mr. Armstrong".

(B.) PERSONAL QUESTIONS I HAVE FOR THESE "SPLINTER GROUPS"

(1.)   *Why did you before you first split from WCG/GCI jump to conclusions and NOT hear the full matters that were concerning and directly pertaining to you and allow HQ a reasonable opportunity to explain themselves to you? What changes, etc. were you afraid of—and what did you fear losing?*

(2.) *Why through your actions and doctrinal statements are you STILL acting like Mr. Armstrong NEVER died? Why are you still in denial over this?*

(3.) *Why so legalistic? Why do you still hold to a "performance-based Christianity where jumping through doctrinal hoops is REQUIRED? (And DON'T play verbal gymnastics with me over this—I can see right through it in a heartbeat...)*

(4.) *What's so wrong with grace? (I'm NOT talking about the so-called"greasy, greasy grace" that you so vehemently cry against. I'm talking about TRUE, UNMERITED FAVOR! Wouldn't you RATHER be judged by Him in terms of His mercy INSTEAD? You fail to understand that just because someone is basically given a "mulligan" for no humanly understandable reason DOES NOT necessarily have to mean that we're allowing them to skate by without them being forced to face the consequences of their actions. NOT AT ALL!! In fact, the ideal that Scripture establishes is usually more along the lines of "...to whom much is given, much is required."*

The aim OF that grace should be that the recipient would truly appreciate that grace so much they would never ever even desire to be messed up with what previously entangled them before. But even if (bleep forbid) they do—WHY should WE as humans attempt to be their judge, jury, and executioner anyway? There is ONLY ONE just Judge of all—and His PREFERRED modus operandi IS the utilization of grace. If we attempt to stop or block grace's operation in our life—we're not only attempting to in essence step into our holy God's role Himself (which under NO circumstance should we ever think of doing), but we're also simultaneously hindering and hurting His efforts to properly discipline His kids and lead them away from that "stinkin' thinkin'" that got them into that hole in the first place.

(5.) *The way you "splinter groups" have set up your doctrinal statements, you almost set up Mr. Armstrong in the very place of*

God Himself. You claim to obey the first two of the Ten Commandments—but when you put things like "…the 18 truths that were revealed to Mr. Armstrong stand confirmed by the Board…"…and/or things along those lines that put those truths on equal or even superior par with Holy Scripture, you're coming close to the border line with outright idolatry. I believe personally that Mr. Armstrong (whom YOU revere) would be so horrified at the thought of this that I wouldn't be too surprised that if he ever came out of his grave, he would first gave a really good verbal dressing down and then slap you right in the face!

(6.) *You pooh-pooh the things of the Spirit of God and those who aren't afraid to allow them to manifest in their lives as "outright displays of Pentecostal emotionalism" and regard the Holy Spirit/Ruach Ha'Kodesh as no more than a glorified equivalent of an electric power line. You're also fearful that if such displays were allowed in your services that your meetings would become disorderly and chaotic…*

BUT YET—you bawl and squawl to the Eternal Father and go before the elders of your group and ask Him to heal you from your illnesses, deliver you out of your financial and other troubles, etc. And you STILL can't see the fact plain as day— that the Holy Spirit AIN'T a power line, but only just MAYBE the THIRD person of the Godhead. I tell you—He is HIGHLY insulted by these stout words against Him.. (AND YES---the Spirit to me IS A HE, in case you're unaware of it...)

But what REALLY grieves Him is when you call the things of His Spirit (and especially those things thereof) as "…being out of order, improper, or disorderly" just because some in the Pentecostal/Charismatic movement might have taken those things too much off the deep end due to a lack of knowledge and appropriate spiritual discipline.

The Spirit Himself would have you to know that there ARE ways that you can flow in those gifts AND STILL have some semblance of propriety and order in your worship services. A lack of understanding this has kept you from seeing that a major key to having a proper balance between the two involves who is helping to shepherd a particular meeting and discerning what those people most in tune with what the Spirit is telling them at a particular moment of a service interact and flow with both the general direction of the Spirit as well as each other.

It also involves using ONLY those people who have been specifically trained and trusted to receive, interpret, and then disseminate said info to the people as the Spirit might give them utterance. When these methods are appropriately utilized, order and propriety are still maintained, but with a marked difference—the Spirit has true freedom to reveal Himself through imperfect channels unspeakable mysteries that are inaccessible otherwise to us.

I believe He'd love to tell you that until you finally back down, give up, and at least acknowledge (even if you never choose to speak in tongues or anything like that) this Divine prerogative to move freely as He may wish or desire, the reality and truth of the Holy Spirit will never become a practical experience that is touchable and tangible in your life. And as a result, don't be too surprised if those personal prayers to Him might be hindered by your own belief system.

(III.) TO OTHERS NOW INVOLVED IN THE MESSIANIC/SABBATARIAN MOVEMENT:

(1.) Let me first say a word of praise over you—and it is this…Once upon a time when I first started in WCG, I thought we were the ONLY ones that had not kissed the knee to Ba'al. Mr. Armstrong and the message he left behind for all of us to me were forerunners to the greater things that I'm only beginning to see now. One of those great things is **_YOU!!!_** I may think like Barbara Mandrell and kid you about coming late to the party— but inside, I'm just rejoicing and tickled pink that you even decided to show up at all in the first place. It takes Divine courage and fortitude to take the bold stands you're taking for Him now. I highly encourage you to stay the course as best as He shows you how to do so and DON'T EVER lost that initial fire and zeal for Him that brought you to this dance in the first place. He had reasons to bring you to the place you are now in Him. Don't let go or get bucked off the bull—for if you'll hang on long enough, He'll more than surely give you the prize you so rightly deserve in due time.

And not JUST that—but to me personally, your presence and actions now serve as constant reminders to me that as long as you keep doing what He told you to do in the way He tells you to do it that they'll always be at least a few good things that Mr. Armstrong left behind as a legacy for all of us that will always remain. You may not have personally learned these things you know now directly from either Mr. Armstrong or WCG—but still, don't forget that he was one of those that helped set the current environment in place and set the wheels in motion for what you're now doing and in which you now benefit from as a result. The Indians have an interesting saying—"YOU are my river—without you, I cannot live." I think the same would apply to you. And if there's anything I and others that have walked these similar roads in the past might be able to do to help you walk out this new type of faith and confidence you now hold in Him, please don't be afraid to ask us.

(2.) I hope you read what I just told my current WCG/GCI colleagues in the previous two sections. If not, then I urge you to read those for yourself as well. What I told those geese are also just as good for the ganders, too. I believe that if you will also do those things—you will prosper, do well, and have good success in all you do for Him.

(C.) A particular concern and caution I have for you folks--Wherever a new movement tends to spring up, separatism and legalism sadly attempt to try to rule the day. In the effort to try to distinguish yourselves from the rest of the pack, there's a great temptation to disassociate entirely from even the good things of your past. PLEASE DON'T DO THAT entirely--for they helped make up the basic framework for the person you're now trying to become for Him. Acknowledge the GOOD things of your past as blessings from our Lord Himself to you (even if you may not right now necessarily think they are blessings). Also, since I know that a number of you are probably refugees of the Evangelical movement, please don't completely burn the bridges you once had with your former colleagues. I found out from hard experience that there might actually be times that you might need them later on. When you cut off those potential lifelines, you not only hurt yourself in the long run, but you also deny the Holy Spirit the opportunity to make through you the valuable contributions to the overall Body of Christ that He may have you to make.

(IV.) WHAT I WOULD LIKE TO SAY TO MEMBERS OF THE CHURCH OF JESUS CHRIST OF LATTER-DAY SAINTS, THE WATCHTOWER SOCIETY OF JEHOVAH'S WITNESSES, AND OTHER REMOTELY CHRISTIAN-BASED MOVEMENTS STILL CONSIDERED BY MOST "CULTS"

(A.) Before I start this section, let me qualify a few things of who I personally believe should never ever have a chance to be allowed within 100 miles vicinity of being recognized as "brothers in the Lord". I will define this as simply as I can get it for you--

(1.) If you DO NOT acknowledge Jesus Christ/Y'shua Ha'Meshiach as no less than the Son of God and the Savior of all mankind and not just a "...good moral teacher" (Read C.S. Lewis to find out more about what I specifically mean....)

(2.) If you will NOT acknowledge the basic truth of what Martin Luther taught about "...the just shall live by faith" and do not believe that salvation is really a free gift of God and His grace and not of works lest any man boast--

IF you cannot agree completely with BOTH of these principles--then don't expect any legitimate invitations to join our evangelical Christian "country club" any time soon--for it ain't going to happen!

A prime example I see in the world today (I don't care if this is politically or religiously incorrect--I've just got to tell the truth!)--You folks in Islam (FYI--go ahead and issue the fatwas now...Besides, I believe that the God I serve is both my front and rear guard--thank you very much....)...I've seen you folks out there in our prison system here in Texas. You get out there, take advantage of vulnerable and gullible men, and as my very Lord Jesus Christ said to the Pharisees, "...You make them worse hypocrites than you do!"

You claim that terrorist incidents (YES--I said the word...TER-ROR-IST...get it, love it, and live it!) and cutting off the heads of us Christians and Jewish brothers are the absolute surest way to get yourself and your family members your so-called "72 virgins in Paradise"--and yet you have no absolute guarantee or assurance that

Allah will even bother to lift a finger to save you. But MY GOD can save even to the uttermost--without YOU trying--if you will just first decide to completely switch teams, step away from the hoops and the merry-go-round, and surrender to this man named Y'shua completely and without reservation...you'd be so much better off than you are right now.

Those of you who are still in Islam should know right now that you will definitely reap what you sow. If you start telling us Christians to "...convert or die", then don't be too surprised in turn if a day will come for you when my Lord Himself won't even need to tell you "..Convert to ME or die forever!" For there WILL be a time that every knee SHALL bow and every tongue confess that Jesus/Y'shua IS THE ONLY LORD to the glory of God His Fathe. (NOTE—I DID NOT say Allah or Muhammed—but JESUS/Y'shua—get the picture?)!

And the only main difference about you trying to convert us to your stupid ways and that final Judgment Day is that YOU won't be able to stand or even say a single word in front of him (much less fight Him with a sword or other weapon of your choice). That will be due to the fact that He sure as bleep won't even give you the chance to in the first place when you have to stand before a Holy God like Him.

AND WHERE WILL YOUR SO-CALLED ALLAH BE THEN TO SNATCH YOUR DERRIERE FROM MY GOD'S HAND? HUH? ANSWER ME THAT! You'll probably be toast in a millisecond right before He gets the first two words out of His mouth if you haven't truly taken care of your necessary business with Him before that time. (YES--you will EITHER pray THAT prayer instead of your stupid so-called creed OR...) So I'm begging and pleading with you to save yourself the trouble now and get out of that insane asylum you attempt to call a religion. Then make the quality choice to make my God YOUR choice and get yourselves some true peace in your lives for once. 'Nuff said on that...

Now that I've properly ticked off about 70 to 95 percent of the rest of the world by now, let me now specifically address those of you remaining five to ten percenters that are left...ESPECIALLY those who are currently in either the LDS Church or the Watchtower Society of Jehovah's Witnesses. (Those of you who consider yourselves within the more orthodox mainstream of the Evangelical Christian movement—if you're wondering why in the world I say what I'm about to say to these LDS and Jehovah's Witnesses folks, hang on tight. I'll be chatting with you in a few minutes as well.)

I know first of all personally how it is to start out as part of a club, then be out of it, then to be finally allowed back in by the hair of my chinny-chin-chin. It's probably 10 times harder for you since you've never had the chance to be a part of the club to start with called orthodox evangelical Christianity--and you have no definite idea what it might take for you to finally be invited to join the club I just recently got back into solely by the grace of my God.

Please allow me to personally apologize on their behalf for not giving you clear guidelines on what it might take to be a member of our orthodox Evangelical Christian club. Maybe I can give you some friendly advice from this side of the Evangelical fence from personal experience and provide you with special tips that might further expedite your application to admission into our elite club and insure the favor of man as well as the favor of God come your way towards possible future acceptance as a "true brother in the Lord". But I will also be honest with you in saying that you probably right now don't even have the guts it takes to make such dramatic changes. I'm daring you to pleasantly surprise me…but I'm not holding my breath waiting on it either.

(1.) Read the previous big section I just wrote about salvation. Consider those the MINIMUM entrance requirements just to be able to APPLY for membership here. (Note that I said APPLY--this DOES NOT mean that you will be automatically accepted...Don't be too surprised if A TON more will be required from you before it's said and done.)

(2.) ALSO--Read the section of what I told the WCG "splinter groups" (ESPECIALLY the six questions)...If you can make changes in those areas, these will take you light years closer to more careful, serious consideration of said application.

(3.) Two practices you two tend to engage in MUST STOP NOW--"justified lying" and inappropriate proselytizing of other churches (regardless of whether they're Catholic, Protestant, or otherwise). These practices are HIGHLY OFFENSIVE in the nostrils of us in Evangelical Christianity. The most informed of us can see through your lies like a fruit in Saran Wrap. Quit the shell games against us--we ain't as truly stupid as you might think. TELL THE REAL TRUTH about what you REALLY believe and let US (THE PEOPLE) decide what we should believe about God and how we should go about doing it—and trust God for the results instead of trying to create them yourselves.

(4.) Also here I should by all means warn you by personal experience that should you even think of embarking on such a radical course, don't be too surprised if any or ALL of the following happen to you during the transformation process:

(a.) The conservatives/fundamentalists (or traditionalists or whatever you may end up calling them) are going to start calling your church's leadership and even those other members still loyal to them no less than traitors, heretics, or some other perjorative term. Then if they start REALLY leaving you in droves after that…well, that's all I'm going to say on that one.

(b.) BEFORE you even start this radical course, DON'T YOU EVEN DARE do this WITHOUT TONS of prayer and intercession with the Heavenly Father. If you don't, then everything you might do in this effort will be to your peril—and the wolf will definitely not survive!

(c.) Make bleeping sure you've got a very top-notch public relations, accounting, and financial team ready to hit the ground with boots running if need be. Then get them ready to put in tons and tons of overtime once you implement the changes. This team will prove to be one of the most essential and necessary tools that you will have to rely on to even have a fighting chance to make it through the subsequent storms (financial, spiritual, and otherwise) that you will most certainly be required to endure during your transition process.

(5.) ADDITIONAL BUCKET LISTS:

(A.) LDS CHURCH--Get rid of the following NOW:

(1.) Your overemphasis of Joseph Smith as a prophet over God and making him out to be your equivalent of an Islamic martyr…**Get a clue!** Look at your church history and see who he REALLY was and see what he was REALLY about…then be honest about it and change. It's probably hard to believe—but Mr. Smith and his early converts might have been, as a cursory look at U.S. history might show, a bit more of a troublemaker than you think. He, from I've read in the past, was also probably a bit legalistic in his approach and wrote the rules as it suited him at the time.

(2.) Say bye-bye to the Planet Zoloft (or however you tend to call it)…Jesus/Y'shua and Lucifer were NEVER brothers and NEVER WILL BE. Forget about space cadets and Star Trek…Scotty has decided to beam us back down to see the Kingdom of God!!

(3.) This Lamanite and Nephite war thing--GOT TO GO posthaste! There is NO such thing--and FYI--our Indian brothers are NOT Lamanites or descendants of Israel! Two words for you—REPLACEMENT THEOLOGY!!!

(4.) Ditch the Book of Mormon, Doctrine and Covenants, AND the Pearl of Great Price PDQ! They're all as fake as a million dollar bill!

(B.) JEHOVAH'S WITNESSES

(1.) Read Revelation AGAIN VERY CLOSELY about this 144,000 witnesses thing...They are JEWISH evangelists preaching in the Tribulation--NOT the total of people allowed in Heaven above. Your mathematical and geographical skills as they stand right now are QUITE fuzzy at best...

(2.) A good HONEST look at your church's history as well as getting rid of that trash you call your "New World Translation" followed by appropriate repentance, change, and PERMANENT revision of doctrines wouldn't hurt you at all, either. In fact--it'd really do you some good if you'd dared to even do it.

WHAT I NOW WISH TO SAY TO MY EVANGELICAL FRIENDS:

(1.) Put down the hatchet to my Messianic and Sabbatarian brethren and colleagues who are showing that they want to work with you. If they are truly demonstrating it and showing through their actions as well as doctrinal changes, etc.--PLEASE at least give them a decent chance to prove themselves and let them have the benefit of the doubt....**PLEASE...PRETTY PLEASE...with massive sugar, syrup, and ice cream on top?**

(2.) I'm concerned that your strategy in getting people out of groups you still consider "cults" is at best a slight bit flawed for the following reasons. [AUTHOR'S NOTE: Those family members of those suspected of being in questionable derivative movements should pay particular attention to what follows here—because I feel this would be especially useful advice for them.]

(a.) We shouldn't be trying to do things that "send these people to hell"--we instead need to do our part to send them to HIS LOVE! (That doesn't mean you can't preach things to them meant to help them avoid spiritual destruction, of course. It just means that you need to temper that talk with love as well--that's all!)

(b.) Don't compromise or capitulate what you believe--instead be so consistent in what you do with these things AND how you act around them to where THEY will want to move away from those things that aren't truly of God and turn TOWARDS Him!

(c.) Keep the door open for ANY type of relationship with them—even if THEY do not seem to want it. To be honest with you, UNLESS AND UNTIL they get in a heap of trouble over something, they will probably regard anything you say with deaf ears and not hear anything you might say. It will only be in the TOUGH times when they might be most prompted to get back in touch with them. IF AND WHEN they do, DO NOT shut them out—for it might be the open door you've been asking your God many years for. Keep your arms wide open, don't judge them for what has happened in the past, and lend them any possible assistance they might need until they can stand on their own.

[SPECIAL NOTE: I mentioned my time in "Siberia"…it was only when everything during the aftermath of "the changes" in WCG where I was literally forced to look up…and He had to finally get my attention to in turn look back down and around to those in my family who had been there all along who had patiently endured all of this with me (even though there was a good bit of the details they were not aware of most of the time). That is what it will sometimes take for those affected by these derivative movements to finally be prompted to change their ways and consider other viewpoints outside what they may have been brainwashed with in the questionable movement they've been involved in.]

(d.) ALSO--**Quit asking God for too little in terms of trying to change individuals caught up in false doctrines and questionable movements! Let's ask God for entire MOVEMENTS to change INSTEAD of simply trying to save individuals and doing things in which the effect is no more than trying to plug holes in the dyke.** Let's rediscover the true power of intercession over the leadership of these groups--because you WILL NOT get the individuals UNLESS you aim at the leadership at the top of each of these groups FIRST! The change will necessarily have to start from the top DOWN in order to even have the slightest change to take root and eventually get down to the rank-and-file. We've been so individually-focused that we've neglected to BROADEN our vision for Him!

(IV.) WHAT I NOW NEED TO PUBLICLY SAY TO MEMBERS OF MY IMMEDIATE FAMILY

There's one more group I need to address in order to feel like I have done my part to say what needs to be said (especially in case they may not necessarily hear it directly from my lips this side of the Kingdom of God). And I can probably quickly wrap that up by saying to the members of my immediate family two primary messages—"thank you"…and "I need to apologize…".

First, I hope they understand how much I have appreciated them and the various type of assistance (small and great) over the years. I know I haven't always done the greatest job in showing it in ways that you can personally grasp or understand—but please don't interpret it as me telling you that I'm not gratefully for anything done. A good number of the roads I have personally traveled in my life up to this point couldn't have been possible without your own contributions to the kitty.

Now comes the apology…Please first keep in mind that I overall do not regret my past decisions I made years ago to follow my God in the way He has led me to do. I know it sometimes seems baffling and hard to understand why I do some of the things that I do for Him—even to the point that it makes no natural sense.

But I do need to apologize and ask your forgiveness for one thing—because those things I now see are conduct that even my God and my brethren wouldn't otherwise condone themselves. That one thing is this—that I have failed to be sensitive enough to your needs and was sometimes not always considerate enough of whatever feelings, preferences, and personal agenda you might have had in regards to the things I have done in the past.

I could have done a better job in explaining myself and in doing more tangible things for you to show you that even though certain things about me have now changed, I was and still am pretty much the overall same person who you bought Christmas presents for over the years (even when I did not act like or deserve them)…I'm the same young boy you babysat at times when it probably wasn't always convenient for you and whom you probably had your own ideas of how you probably saw the way my own future should be.

For not being more sensitive to you in explaining these things a little better to your satisfaction and not going the extra mile to continue to earn and retain your trust, please forgive me and be merciful with me on these things. I've not always been the man for Him that I've needed to be (and also, by extension, you all, too)—and part of that has included my treatment at times of you all. I hope that you will overlook these past faults and be understanding of why I have had to do some of the things I've done.

But also most of all—thank you for being patient with me and enduring these challenges over the years with me (even when I didn't necessarily give you the full story of exactly everything that happened at times). You have been part of those that have helped me keep "walking…" the faith in the God that I serve that has sustained me all these years. Thank you for your help through it all.

Well—that's some of my views from my side of the fence at the homefort. You might want to start finishing up your drink and those snacks real soon—the Lord's telling me it's time to do some more walking again…I know…but He promises me this time that it'll be a ton easier. So while you're finishing, I've got to go change out of these houseshoes…Be back in a minute—ok?

[Chapter 24:] (Plainview (Part XI)—SW 3rd St.) Voices From the Grave— The Reasons I'm STILL Walking

Well, looks like we're heading towards the homestretch of this walking tour of my life. But there's still some business that I need to wrap up before we can call this tour officially complete. So let's finish our drinks here at the apartment before we get back on the road once again—ok? Yeah—I know you're tired by now—I sure am, too. We've definitely done a ton of walking during the course of this book by now. But hang on just a little while longer, please. It'll be worth it in the end—I promise you.

Ready? Let's head out the door and make our way again down Date Street/FM 400.

This time, we'll go all the way south past the light at Fifth St./US 70 and head towards Broadway Park. At the Park, we'll see a hike-and-bike trail that runs parallel to the old Running Water Draw. How about taking a walk down this trail and explore it for a little while, shall we?

As we go down this brick-pave trail, (it's sure a nice-looking one—don't you think?) we'll see some bridges cross overhead above us as we pass both Broadway and Colombia Streets.

As we continue down the bike trail, we see some covered gazebos stationed at strategic points with benches to sit on.

[The bike trail route, FYI, also runs basically parallel to a good amount of Fifth St. where we'll see a number of businesses to the north of us, but to the south, we don't see too much going on…that is until we get closer to Joliet Street.]

Along the way, we'll be able to access the place that is now called the Plainview Point Kill Site. Nearby to us will also be the recently installed and dedicated Quanah Parker Trail Marker Site (you'll know what that exactly is by seeing a HUGE arrowhead pointing down to the ground).

For you history buffs, Plainview Point was possibly one of the places on the Texas plains when buffalo was plentiful that the Comanches frequented during their dominance of the wild frontier that was once West Texas.

Now as we see Joliet in front of us, let's take a left and go south toward SW 3rd St. and one place that also holds similar personal historical significance for me—the Plainview City Cemetary…

...where my grandfather's grave (as well as the memorial plot for most of my immediate family) is located.

In case you're wondering why we're here in the first place, something about my granddad's gravesite will hopefully reveal to you what keeps me going and doing the various life missions I feel my God has called me to do. I also hope you'll see why I'm compelled to keep running the race in the way I'm doing so right now.

First, to recap the bio sketch on my granddad...As I said in Chapter 1, he was born Granvel Morris Webb on a farm in North Texas in a rural area of small towns situated between the D/FW Metroplex area on the south and the Red River/Sherman/Denison area and the Oklahoma state line on the north. "Papa", as I called him was born just prior to the Depression to a pretty large family of brothers and sisters and served in the Army in World War II as a truck driver in a tank battalion in southern France and Germany.

After he came back home form the War, he eventually married my grandmother and would become the father of 3 daughters and one son (my own mother, Lynda, being the oldest sibling of the clan). Papa never got past the 6th grade in school (mainly because he had to help his dad and family on the farm)—but he moved his family to West Texas in the 1950s and '60s and worked as a grain manager for Acco Seed (now known as Delta and Pine Land Co.) for nearly 40 years before he retired.

Papa wasn't necessarily one with whom I might have had the greatest relationship with. He and I were about the equivalent of oil and water while he was alive—he was the type who valued things like agriculture, auto mechanics, and mostly "…manual labor, manual labor…" while I tended to prefer being more of a bookworm who liked comic books and wanted to be more of an intellectual.

Of all the folks in my family who I dreaded finally telling about my decision about joining WCG, it was Papa whose reaction I feared the most. It really didn't sit too well with him when I had to tell him and the rest of the family that I wasn't going to keep Christmas anymore. And my revelation that I was not going to work on Saturday really went over like a lead balloon with him. In his view, if someone offered you a job, the ONLY valid response to the command, "JUMP!" was "..HOW HIGH???" And you'd better be willing to work ANY time they needed you—whether or not you liked it.

This seemingly continual conflict between him and I went on even until he died. And it always, in my eyes, seemed like I could never do enough to please him or could do anything that he tought was of any value. And one thing he said to me now still haunts me here as I look at his grave—"Son, I tell you that you're going to do something that you're about to regret." My granddad died the year after I finally was able to move to Plainview—and just a couple of weeks before I was to go to Hot Springs, AR for the 1997 Feast of Tabernacles. Sadly, he didn't get a chance to see some of the good things the Lord allowed me to accomplish. And I didn't get a chance ever again to respond to his harsh criticisms of myself, what I did, and what I believed.

But it isn't just my granddad's voice that speaks to me alone from the grave. There are a number of other voices that might be silent here in this cemetery—but who shout volumes to me now long after their passing. If you'd like to know what the biggest motivation might be for doing what I do, it's this—doing my part of make sure that the legacies and memories they left behind for myself and others also live well after their demise. THAT above all else is what keeps me moving on from all the pain and heartache I've face—especially in regards to being a member of WCG/GCI.

In the Introduction, for instance, remember the funeral bulletin of the lady I referenced there? I rode with her, her daughter, and her two grandsons many times for many years the distance between Plainview and Lubbock—sometimes putting up with the grandsons' constant fighting, bickering, and outright sibling rivalry while she and her daughter would talk about everything under the sun…while other times where it was just her and I alone, her unique sense of humor and optimistic attitude would always show through the many miles we went up and down I-27/US 87. She all the way until her passing, I later found out, was one of my biggest prayer warriors through the years in regards to my finding steady employment. I can still hear her say this phrase when I was able to fill her in what I might be currently doing at the time—"…Keeps you out of meanness!"

Also, I told you in the Roswell chapter about ol' Jack in the Roswell church who when I was still new to WCG could barely get around on oxygen and who eventually died sometime before I finished my studies at Eastern. His most sacrificial monetary assistance was one of the biggest things that made my very first Feast in Big Sandy a most memorable one indeed.

It's still hard for me these days to order chicken fried steak with without wanting to first call it the "Bower Wood Special". Remember in an earlier chapter when I introduced you to Bower and his mother, Lucy—who were two of the most cantankerous and interesting characters that ever graced our Lubbock WCG congregation. Bower and Lucy were elderly folks (with Bower long since confined to a wheelchair from a work accident he sustained that left him partially paralyzed and disabled) who lived in Cotton Center and in which all of us brethren who lived in the Plainview area would at various times be responsible for picking them up and taking them for church services. They had an especially equipped wheelchair accessible van or car that we might at times use to take them to church and back.

Whenever he and Lucy would go with us to a restaurant, Bower seldom ordered ANYTHING EXCEPT chicken fried steak. And Bower was legendary in our congregation for his penchant for telling horribly bad puns and jokes. But I'll definitely remember most the time I went with them and several others to the 1993 Feast in Tucson not too long after I got back home from Albuquerque (also mentioned earlier). As you hopefully saw there, the journey between home and Tucson and back was just as interesting as the entirely of the Feast itself.

I can go on and on and talk about other examples just from WCG/GCI alone about people who did some of the greatest things for me in my biggest times of personal need. But I think that I'm now finally ready to answer what Papa first said to me about regrets as I look one more time over his grave. If there might be one regret I did have about those years I've spent in WCG/GCI, it would be that I probably could in retrospect have done a much better job properly treating my family a lot better in the earlier years. I could have shown a lot more respect for proper authority and also had a better attitude in doing a number of things they might ask me to do outside of church.

But, Papa—looking back over the years, if you once thought that I would regret making the decisions I made about WCG…I hate to say this long after you've passed on—but I still believe after all this time that you were wrong….especially when so many people in so many places helped me do things that I could have never dreamed otherwise. Honestly, if you would have been able to see even a small glimpse of the good things I got out of being a WCG member, I think maybe even you might have been willing to admit the error of your ways and possibly cut me a little more slack than you did.

And it's not just your voice alone that speaks, Papa—but a great cloud of witnesses who left a lot of things behind for me that helps me keep pressing on in challenging times like these. And now for me, their sins and burdens and are now mine to carry. And for all that has been done for me—it's now my obligation to tell others the stories of who they were and what and how they contributed to the cause of Christ and the examples they left behind for others to follow.

There's a part of a song by cowboy poet and songwriter and Charlie Goodnight descendant Andy Wilkenson that encapsulizes a good bit of what I'm feeling here: "…Listen, Charlie Goodnight/there's no one left to save/When the roll is called/The answers all/Are voices from the grave". I also think a lot about the story of Quanah Parker and how he and the Comanches had to deal with the prospect of change when the survival of their tribe was on the line.

And I get a similar feeling like that when I think of my past experiences in WCG as if I were viewing things from the viewpoint of Colonel Goodnight looking out over Palo Duro Canyon and remembering what had been. Goodnight probably also had his own hardships, his highlights, his sorrows, regrets, and even people he was both angry and sore with as well as folks he remembered fondly. I feel like I'm also a kindred spirit with him in a distant way—for I feel like I've seen a lot in a very short period of time. And yet he still endured and survived—probably a lot longer than most.

Maybe this would be as good a time as any at this point of the book to further formally address a few of the audiences that I need to talk to about some stuff. To those of you who have become my friends in the evangelical community (past, present, and future)….In case you've been looking throughout all that you've read so far to give you information that might after the fact send Mr. Armstrong to hell, I think that by now you've realized that I have probably disappointed you. After all, how can I turn my back on two men who I felt served as a couple of my most important spiritual mentors in my life that helped me see my God in ways I would have never dreamed otherwise?

I hope, though, that I have done a couple of things in all that you've read so far—

(A.) That I did take as best as I could an honest look at the things (both good and bad) that from my perspective that both Mr. Armstrong and Mr. Tkach, Sr. left behind for us…

(B.) That I have not unnecessarily portrayed Mr. Armstrong and Mr. Tkach, Sr. on a pedestal high above the crowd or as prophets or religious figures that in some form must be worshiped on a level next to or even above God. INSTEAD (and I think based on even their own past writings, THEY would have even personally agreed with), I have attempted to portray them as men that did not always do things perfectly, but who nonetheless during their lifetime did what they thought in their consciences and hearts was pleasing to their God as best as they knew how. And even if they did make mistakes along the way, both of these men at least strove through their messages and examples some overall general lessons that the universal Body of Christ can learn from;

(C.) AND I have shown how over the years I have personally grown spiritually in many different ways—some of which have been totally independent of ANY preacher or denomination. There are, for instance, areas of agreement that I do have with those at WCG headquarters that I currently share and others that I now personally disagree with. The same holds true with others who have been or are still in some way personally involved in some way with WCG that are of what I might consider of a more traditionalist bent (i.e.—those that still keep the seventh-day Sabbath and Holy Days in accordance to what was traditionally taught by WCG prior to the 1994-95 doctrinal changes). And also there's areas as well with my more evangelical colleagues within what is considered "orthodox Christianity" that I now agree with as well as disagree with. My own current personal religious beliefs now are not necessarily the result of the teachings of any man or denomination—but solely as a result of personal study and examination of the Word of God, prayer, and inspiration of the Holy Spirit/Ruach Ha'Kodesh.

(D.) To those in the Universal Body of Christ/Meshiach—I wish to use this book above all else to encourage all of you to take a much closer look from a unique perspective of the subjects of legalism of ALL kinds and the heartache, pain, and devastation it can leave in its aftermath. I hope also that this work has shown and given you a very small taste of what is involved in the development of "cults", sects, and derivative Christian movements that are still considered outside what is considered by most to be "orthodox Christianity" (when sometimes even THESE folks may differ significantly about what is even orthodox or mainstream in the first place).

(E.) And most of all—to all former and current members of WCG/GCI—I trust that you have seen that it has not been my direct intention to either denigrate or disrespect the memories of either Mr. Armstrong or Mr. Tkach, Sr. or attack or try to make a name for myself or try to stand in the way of those who have been now duly placed in charged of what is now GCI. My commission from Him is NOT to try to get a following or form any type of group that wishes to replace appropriately and duly installed eccleasiastical leadership. In fact (as I stated earlier), to me from my limited viewpoint, I still feel that Dr. Joseph Tkach, Jr. and those that work under him as the current GCI leadership have even to this day done what they have felt have been policies, doctrines, etc. that have been not only beneficial for those who still remain as GCI members, but for the Body of Christ at large. PLEASE MARK THIS STATEMENT AND HAVE NO DOUBT ABOUT IT! All I'm doing from my perspective is simply tell the stories of myself and those I have personally known through my own experiences with WCG/GCI.

In short, the purpose of this book has been to present to the world some overall lessons that were left behind from all concerned that that I feel that the Holy Spirit might also wish to dissimilate a little better to the world. And it has been my personal wish here not to cause unnecessary offense in the transmission of this message to you—but instead help those of you still in WCG/GCI as well as those previously involved say things to the world that they don't normally hear.

But standing here in this graveyard, I reflect on a statement in the book "Rachel's Tears [(written by Beth Nimmo and Darrell Scott with Steve Rabey and published by Thomas Nelson Publishers; p. 174, © 2000] that best illustrates my own personal motives in bringing what to me is an extremely bittersweet and heartbreaking message that I am compelled by my Savior and Meshiach to give about the specter of legalism of ANY kind (whether it involves the day you might prefer to worship God on; special occasions you feel you must observe; the way you might do Communion/Lord's Supper; etc)—"...I write, not for the sake of glory, not for the sake of fame; not for the sake of success, but the sake of my soul...Rachel Joy..."

In that light, I feel that it is my own personal mission to do the best job that I possibly can to lend my voice to some voices within the discussion that aren't normally heard of what happened in the midst of the changes that I personally saw within the Worldwide Church of God/Grace Communion International in all the time that I have been (and I emphasize STILL...) associated with this denomination as a member. And I don't continue to try to do this just for myself—not just for the sake of myself—but on behalf of all of these voices that still speak from the grave. So many years, so many memories...may their memories be for a blessing to all of us and not be so quickly forgotten...

[Chapter 25:] [Glendora/Pasadena, CA—The Message I Never Got To Deliver To Dr. Tkach, Jr.]

Looks like the Lord reminded me of one or two final pieces of business that I still have left to do before we're finally through with this tour—and it looks like one more time the Lord's Divine transportation system is really working well for us now for this next-to-last destination on our tour. To explain what I mean, I need to first tell you yet one final travel story.

It was on another one of my planned Feast trips. As I mentioned earlier in Chapter 22, it was right after Tom and Brandy officially decided to resign from KKYN—and I was cruising the road to depression at that time. Tom had already started his new/old duties as Dean of Students at Wayland while Brandy stayed on for another month to help out with the transition. [Plus I had already put my vacation day request for this Feast trip—so Brandy graciously covered for me one more time for my vacation time before I had to finally take over the reins from them in the transition.]

The original travel plan was this—first, right before and even on the Day of Atonement, I decided to go to a prayer conference in Los Angeles sponsored by Kenneth Copeland Ministries and featuring Terri Copeland Pearsons and Patsy Cameneti as the main speakers. Then from there, I had planned to go straight from there to see a friend and his wife in Pennsylvania, then go from Pennsylvania to see my cousin in North Carolina, then back towards Huntsville, TX for the last part of the Feast of Tabernacles.

With a heavy heart over this recent turn of events at KKYN, I would up literally going all the way to California with only five bucks that I had borrowed from someone else and a one-way bus ticket to Los Angeles. (Here goes yet ANOTHER time of going on a Feast trip on my chinny-chin-chin…) I didn't AGAIN have the money for my motel once I got into LA—and it was the FIRST time I'd even been this far on the Left Coast. (In retrospect—I would obviously recommend that most people should NEVER do this in either their right OR WRONG mind…no matter what they may do otherwise).

In a way, I was VERY glad that it was ATONEMENT…because it was a good excuse to fast anyway. So I used what little money I had very sparingly on the bus going to LA and managed to have most of it available to me once I finally got in the city. I did use some of it for a city transit bus that got me part of the way until I got to (guess where?)—Bob Hope Way. From there, I had to walk the rest of the way with ALL of my luggage in tow to the hotel where the conference was. But I at least made it there (even if I didn't have any more money on my person and was going to have to sleep outside the Convention Center)…

Once upon my arrival to the hotel, I left with the folks in one of the conference booths specific letters for the main speakers and officials I had typed up and put in envelopes. But there was one letter that I had typed for someone else at someplace else in the LA area that I had also planned to stop at—but wasn't exactly able to leave with them (despite my best efforts to do so before the conference was over with). It went like this…(PLEASE NOTE: Some of the exact contents of the original letter were edited because of space limitations and also due to the fact the particular details weren't pertinent for inclusion within this book.)

Dear Dr. Tkach:

I first wish to extend my formal thanks to you and your staff for your hospitality to my visit to GCI headquarters as a part of an extended Feast of Tabernacles trip where I will literally be going from coast to coast to various destinations until time to go back home to Texas on Oct. 12th. I have never ever been able to come this way before now (either both when WCG and Ambassador was still going strong in Pasadena as well as after the split). I also extend formal greetings to yourself and your congregations out here on behalf of several churches, pastors, and ministries back home in West Texas. (Yes—there's life and activity going on past I-35!)

Noting that I may not possibly have a chance to talk to you in depth about certain matters I would hope to personally discuss with you (and also especially preferring to be one who tries to respect both your privacy and the enormous time constraints you obviously face as a minister of the Gospel), I thought it best for time's sake to make these requests in this fashion and submit them through appropriate channels while trusting my God you might personally receive these requests and consider them and even maybe if our God leads you to do so take whatever actions He may have you to do in response.

First, I ask that you take note of the enclosed prayer requests at the end of this letter and ask that you and others on your ministry staff please join in agreement with these on this list who are asking for prayer and believe with them that our God would fulfill all of these requests in accordance to Psalm 20:1-5. They run the gamut of the spectrum of needs from physical, financial, etc. The assistance of you and your ministry staff in standing in the gap and interceding with these people that my God would desire to bring to your attention would be an immense blessing to the people that are listed.

But I also have a couple of other things as well that I would like to ask of you and your ministry staff. First, I literally came to this area not just to visit you folks, but also a Kenneth Copeland Ministries Spirit-Led Conference in Burbank in absolute faith believing that my God would definitely supply all my needs according to His riches in glory. One of those is to help see that some pastors and other ministries I personally have contact with are appropriately encouraged, strengthened, and equipped to do those things that our God commissioned them to do. At present, my financial situation does not allow me to do all I would personally like to do on behalf of all the pastors and ministries concerned. But being here at this Conference does allow me to do one thing that might be the next best thing—attempt, in a sense, to speak with kings and those in authority on behalf of others back home.

...

I also come with some things that through this medium that I feel necessary to bring to your attention and trusting that you will appropriately consider and discern what is brought up here in accordance to what our God may have you to do. I do not come pretending to represent the views, opinions, etc. of others—but only bring these to your attention only on my own behalf as a member of GCI with what is said here only reflecting my own personal views alone and simply passing on nagging concerns that I have heard others express back home in Texas that are very hard to quell or die down.

I do this first with proper respect to you and the HQ staff and also with immense gratitude for being there to provide reasonable leadership and wisdom to this denomination under the leadership of our Lord since your father's death. Sir, you've definitely not had an easy job in the past 15 years...and I would not wish to see even my worst enemies deal with also seemingly impossible situations with the grace and dignity provided to you through our Savior. So it's hard to bring up some concerns and questions to someone who has faced (and is probably still facing) crossfire for all sides—and I do so with some reservations and trepidations. But I now nevertheless must do so not just for myself, but for others who I constantly hear from at home who may either never have the opportunity to ask you their questions face to face or who are too afraid to do so because they think doing so would either be totally futile or that they would be ashamed and embarrassed to ask such questions to you personally. They wish to respect the authority and nature of the position you hold as a shepherd of God's people and are not necessarily trying to bring up these concerns in an accusatory tone, but also want to let you know that even as they are in submission to leadership, they have some very serious heartfelt questions and concerns that in their eyes have never truly been addressed and answered to their satisfaction—not only through words, but especially in the place they see evidence of it at most—in the actions they see yourself and the staff at HQ do.

...

But now back to the major concerns of the brethren--there's certain issues of the heart to some that even these elders cannot completely resolve to the satisfaction of the brethren—and so as part of the denominational leadership, I feel it is necessarily incumbent on you to at least make an attempt on your end to see that these long-standing issues are at least appropriately discussed, addressed, and resolved to the satisfaction of all parties concerned. These brethren probably feel like people who reside in towns where an interstate highway may be and where a lot of traffic zips up and down the road, but not very many even think to stop by and visit them for even just a very few minutes.

As a fellow member who sometimes has to hear these things constantly from brethren, it's very hard for me in good conscience to come here to HQ and not at least attempt to say something to you personally in some way so that you can be at least aware of the situation at home. And the biggest thing that you probably need to be aware of—underneath the surface, some of the good things that have been touted in our denomination's publications have to some of the folks I know back home not necessarily been met with very much enthusiasm. In fact, there's a pretty good number of them that haven't even had the chance to completely heal and see a final resolution to the events in the Church since the doctrinal changes happened—and they would very much like an opportunity as soon as possible to have a good concentrated time with you and/or high-ranking members of HQ staff and do a PERSONAL visit out here to West Texas (especially for both members in Amarillo and Lubbock) to first truly LISTEN to their concerns without restraint and then ask you questions to which you can respond to as you feel necessary.

First, let me give you a thumbnail sketch of what happened to our churches out here since the doctrinal changes occurred. Immediately after the famous Christmas Day sermon your father gave, our churches in West Texas took a major hit. In Lubbock, for instance, when I first came into WCG/GCI in the early '90s, we had average weekly Sabbath attendance upwards of 100 or so. Then after the doctrinal changes occurred (especially after UCG formed), things went into complete nosedive for not just us—but also most of our churches back home. It wasn't uncommon to see at least 1 elder and ½ of the members of each congregation leave overnight for one reason or the other. By the time 1996 came around, our congregations back home were nowhere near the former shadow of themselves.

For example, we in Lubbock now aren't even an official GCI congregation per se…for we actually went through turmoil twice…once because of the changes, and then years later (unbeknownst to some of us that weren't able to present) were actually briefly disbanded because most of the remaining members preferred to simply start attending other churches that met on Sunday despite the objections of a few that still wanted to meet on Saturday and on the Holy Days. To those that still preferred to go on Saturday, they weren't even properly informed about the decision until it was too late and didn't feel that they had sufficient opportunity to express their concerns. A few months after the Lubbock congregation was officially disbanded, there were a few that decided to reform some sort of group that meets on Saturday that I from time to time also try to attend. Ever since, there has been a steady group that now meets for a biweekly Saturday Bible study at the very same place the disbanded congregation used to meet—most of those still pretty much preferring to have services in the traditional manner that they were accustomed to (but are now having instead to settle for a sort of Bible study format instead).

There were some in Lubbock and in West Texas after '95 that went towards the splinter groups, but there was a core that did decide to stay in spite of what happen. Some adapted to the changes, but others didn't because of firm convictions not just because Mr. Armstrong taught them, but that they also studied the Bible for themselves and (especially after the changes) found themselves convinced of a number of things still. They felt lost, confused, betrayed, and left behind not only by the fact they lost relationships that were the equivalent of family, but because certain things that you all at HQ did that caused them to lose confidence in the leadership of WCG/GCI. But they didn't know where else to go—and they didn't feel that there was truly any place else to go because of what they saw happening in other churches around them.

To give you the basic makeup of the majority of our still remaining GCI members are back home, most of the brethren I have contact with personally are much older in age than I am (above 40) with most of them able to basically qualify for senior citizen discounts at most businesses these days. Most of them are older saints—and a number of those like myself came into WCG/GCI literally knowing they could lose a lot of things in doing so. Several that I know personally either came very close (myself for example) or even actually did lose friendships and/or family relationships in order to do what they felt their God was calling them to do. Financial and other types of sacrifices were made by these folks just so they could go attend a WCG Sabbath service and/or attend a Feast of Tabernacles celebration in places far away. In general, they are very reluctant to do too much past the things that we in WCG/GCI practiced before the split. They are willing to allow others with differing opinions and focuses the liberty to do the call that their God has placed on their lives, but are simply asking in return that similar liberty be extended to them to follow their convictions as they feel led to do so while still remaining under the GCI banner.

Now over 15 years later, they see what has taken place in WCG/GCI—and frankly, what they find very much distresses and grieves them because they may not fully understand for themselves in TANGIBLE ways why what happened in GCI had to happen in the first place. A lot of them feel that they are too old to change—and in fact, feel that certain actions this denomination has taken [(Ex.) The shift to Sunday services; not fulfilling what they saw as a solemn commitment to make reasonable accommodations to do the Feast and Holy Days EXACTLY in the former manner they are accustomed to; and even the recent name change from WCG to GCI] is to them a complete repudiation of some things they cherished and held dear and has unnecessarily left them behind in the dust. They feel betrayed and disrespected and not fully respected by others in the Body of Christ because they don't truly feel that they have a place at the GCI table anymore that they can still feel somewhat comfortable with and call home as a church.

What I just said above is a very small summary of what I especially keep hearing from some of the older and more seasoned members out here in West Texas—and it highly concerns me that both sides feel that the efforts of one side are causing unnecessary division, hindrances, and dissolution of long-established, treasured, and cherished relationships with brethren they once held dear. Maybe the request to you that I'd respectfully like to make on their behalf is this—it probably has been quite a while since either yourself and/or higher-ranking ministers (such as Dan Rogers, etc.) have made a personal visit to my fellow members in West Texas (especially in Amarillo and Lubbock). The brethren would at least appreciate the opportunity to receive a visit from you folks at HQ and in particular hold an open forum at a convenient time for ALL concerned to where they could be free to ask any questions they may have of you as well as receive reliable information from the source of current happenings within the denomination NOT second-hand (most, keep in mind, usually don't even have knowledge of and/or access to the Internet and wouldn't even care to in the first place—and simply just mailing something to them just won't make the cut).

Also for various reasons, some members if an open forum was done would either feel afraid to even ask or speak their questions publicly (especially some of the women in the congregations because they may not feel it is their place in doing so—or even most of them in deference to your position would feel either uncomfortable or disrespectful to do so). So if a way that these people could use to either write down their questions to you and/or staff members to where it could be done anonymously and/or have a chance to speak to you after the service was done to ask their questions to you one-on-one, they would probably feel much more blessed, honored, and respected by HQ personnel.

The main reason I particularly would suggest doing just that is because most of these are of a generation that still prefers to receive their information **face-to-face via personal interaction**. Videos and/or other means WILL NOT communicate anything you may wish to say to them quite as adequately as a **personal face-to-face, pressing-the-flesh type visit** could provide them. They are pretty tired of receiving their info second-hand and would appreciate the respect that you and the HQ staff can give them in their service as fellow saints of God in terms they can more readily and quickly receive and understand. And it's not just words that will convince or reassure them—because a lot of them are STILL grieving over losses of many years ago of various kinds and hadn't even had a proper opportunity to find a resolution to their losses. They are also dealing with overwhelming challenges of other kinds to which the answers they are currently finding are not necessarily satisfying them.

They would not only appreciate a sympathetic and listening ear, but more importantly corresponding actions and also a message of healing, hope, and reconciliation (that would obviously need to be given first and foremost through Christ our Savior) that would tell them that they aren't just numbers or names on a fundraising list, but valued co-workers of the Gospel even if they may have differences with yourself and HQ on how certain doctrinal issues are viewed.

And may I respectfully ask that if you do decide to do this that you would do this as gently and with MUCH sensitivity as is possible—for they are still deeply, deeply hurting. They feel that certain actions and things that HQ has pursued in recent years has immensely betrayed the trust and confidence they had in WCG/GCI—and making an effort on your part to meet them right now exactly where they currently are will go a long ways in repairing what they see in their eyes as horrible breaches of trust and regaining their confidence that you and the HQ staff are truly acting in a way that is in obedience to Christ's commands instead of what they may perceive as inappropriate ulterior motives. It's been a while since you folks have been able to come our way to West Texas—they for once like to know for themselves that you as shepherds of His flock still tangibly care and that they have a purpose in the overall Works of God.

One time, we as a denomination did things in such a way at times to where even if we didn't agree completely with something HQ did, there was at least some feeling that whatever actions were done were not only done first and foremost in obedience to what Christ taught, but also for the good of the brethren. In the military, soldiers will literally risk their lives to make sure none of their brothers in battle is ever left behind. Back home, I'm sensing that some people that are in our GCI churches out here feel like they have been left behind and abandoned in a sense to the wolves.

I may not be in complete agreement personally with some things each of these folks may do—but to these older saints who helped ground and establish me in the faith of our Lord, I at least owe them a debt of honor that can only be repaid by doing everything possible on my part to seeing that those that are hurting receive some relief from their physical, mental, and spiritual afflictions. And so, I took the opportunity given to me on an extended Atonement/Tabernacles vacation to make their concerns known to you. If soldiers can risk their physical lives for their brothers, then I can at least if necessary go on complete faith to your hometown literally risking my financial welfare and having to believe my God for not only every bit of my personal needs on this trip so that brethren back home can be assured that help in their dire situations is at least on the way.

And speaking of concerns that caused me to go in faith to come here, I also wish to bring before you especially the needs of those affected by our criminal justice system [(Ex.) Currently incarcerated offenders, ex-offenders, families of prisoners, crime victims, corrections and law enforcement officials, etc.] I am very concerned that GCI has not done anywhere near enough to fulfill the Great Commission in terms of ministry to bring hope and healing to those affected by it. My God has allowed me to serve as a certified Texas Department of Criminal Justice Chaplaincy Volunteer and assist various prison ministries throughout the state of Texas in various capacities ever since the doctrinal changes occurred (even to the point where, to my knowledge, I seem to be the only one that I know of that is officially certified as a WCG/GCI volunteer).

I'm extremely curious about something--Why has GCI not seemed to have done enough (whether through our own denominational efforts and/or in coordination and cooperation with others) to see that the Gospel of our Lord has been proclaimed to these people not only through words, but more importantly with corresponding actions? Back home in West Texas alone, there's over 30 state prisons alone in a region that 50 years ago only had a handful. Our people not only here in Texas, but throughout the world need to know that there are potential mission fields literally right in their backyard or at least within reasonable driving distance. Why has HQ and GCI not done much to see that the needs of these affected by our nation's criminal justice system are appropriately addressed and taken care of? And is there a plan available to put in place that GCI and HQ can do to play a part in seeing that this type of ministry is advanced and strengthened? If so, what is it and what is involved?

…

In closing, I very much thank you in advance for your prompt and appropriate consideration of these requests. And on behalf of the West Texas brethren, we definitely extend to you and the HQ staff the very best during this Fall Festival season.

…

I tried on the Tuesday before the KCM Conference concluded to get on the LA city transit bus and attempt to go to GCI headquarters to deliver the above letter to

Headquarters staff—but I got lost in Hollywood, wound up going in circles, and eventually due to time constraints just had to go back to the hotel for the conference. And due to certain events that happened to me in LA, I wound up not only not being able to deliver this message in person to Dr. Tkach, Jr.—but I also was forced to after the Conference concluded end my entire Feast trip early and go back home. I never got to go to any other place on my planned itinerary. In fact, it was only the mercy of the Lord that I even had the money to get a one-way ticket from LA to Phoenix—much less BARELY have someone help me get from Phoenix back home. But since some of the stuff in the above letter is somewhat still valid as of this writing…I hope that Dr. Tkach, Jr. is somehow reading this and is taking note. For it's not just some stuff that I came up with—but there's a lot of others if they had the chance to talk to him personally that would wish he would also listen to these things as well…because it is somewhat reflective of the opinions that a number of WCG/GCI members still share to this day.

STANDING IN PARLIAMENT FOR THE NO-CONFIDENCE VOTE

Here in Los Angeles is also about as good a place as any to answer questions like these…Why do I walk? Why have I had to walk so many miles and endure the stares, misperceptions, and questions from people who ask me, 'Why are you walking out here today? Why can't you afford a car? Couldn't you at least get a bicycle?'…." Because this is what I feel that my God has shown me over the years based on my personal life experiences I've had to go through that I'm supposed to now be obedient to until either death or at least further notice—whichever comes first:

(1.) I'm to be a voice for those who are afraid to speak or who are humble in heart and would otherwise prefer that their God speak for them, and for those who for one reason or another can't speak at all.

(2.) I'm to be a bridge between cultures, races, traditions, socioeconomic levels, denominations, etc. so that the Work our Savior commanded us to do on this earth would be done much more efficiently, effectively, and faster.

(3.) I am to be a sort of "kinsman-redeemer" of people with broken and shattered dreams, promises, lives, etc. so that His love would be more effectively felt and published to everyone possible and draw and attract more people unto Him.

(4.) I am to do my part to pass on some of the lessons I've learned from such people as Herbert W. Armstrong and Joseph W. Tkach, Sr. and distribute them with fresh insight and revelation to new generations to come so that the personal legacies they strived to establish for the Savior and lives they both lived for Him will live on in others many years down the road—

   (a.)   [Mr. Tkach, Sr.]
- (1.) (For pastors and church leaders) "We're shepherds, NOT sheriffs!"
- (2.) Warnings about legalism (of whatever kind) and the horrible damages it can cause not only spiritually, but in every area of life
- (3.) What the REAL meaning of salvation and "grace vs. works" debate is all about

   (b.)   [Mr. Armstrong:]
- (1.) "DON'T believe me—believe your Bible!"
- (2.) "…the way of GIVE instead of the way of GET"
- (3.) Numerous lessons I've personally learned through the adventures in faith that he went through in his earlier years
- (4.) "Brethren, we have read the back of the book—and in the end, WE WIN!!!"

How will I know that I have ultimately been able to accomplish all of these above life missions that I know He has given me? Maybe the best way I can describe how I sometimes see how I feel I am judged is one that involves the activities of another government in another land that I have never set foot in.

I have had an on-and-off penchant over the years for watching CSPAN's broadcasts of "Questions Time" in the British Parliament. I've even at times jokingly have called it "my perverted substitute for pro wrestling". You see, the proceedings of even my own nation's Congress are quite tame in comparison to how the Brits do it. Seeing the Tories and Labor go into almost free-for-all verbal jousts and brawls over such issues as the National Health Service, relations with the European Union, etc. (AND especially how these folks are not bashful in making their opinions known) is at times one of my few personal guilty pleasures.

This metaphor was especially evident when I went through my original Walk to Emmaus in 2006. Once again right before I was to go on the Walk, I faced yet another eviction notice looming over my horizon. It even got to the point where even the wife of my sponsor was considering urging me to stay home. For about two weeks before the Walk, it was like the physical and spiritual battles surrounding me was the equivalent of a civil war brewing over a no-confidence vote on the government of a Prime Minister in Parliament. I had no idea how the trail would end from there—or how He'd exactly do it.

Regardless, I went on the Walk as originally planned. I did learn a few things through that time. But what really got my attention was a time before the closing service on that Sunday where we were given by the Walk team what was called "agape letters" from others in our Emmaus Community that are their unique form of well-wishes to all of us "pilgrims" on the Walk.

When I got the stack of letters, that was when I broke down in tears and lost it. Going through those was like seeing a Prime Minister stand in waiting for the results of a no-confidence vote in Parliament. Some of those came from people that I had not seen or spoken to in years. Each letter one-by-one was to me an expression of people I was not aware of taking a bold stand in SUPPORT of me. It was as if the Lord was showing me how many people over the years had been praying and thinking for me—even possibly at times I was not aware of it. And from there on in, I knew that the coalition that had taken so many years and so much effort to establish would not fall—but would still remain to fight another day.

But what cinched the deal for me was when one of those on the Walk team slipped me some money that would make the difference the next day to once again avoid the cruel eviction ax. That was the moment I knew with all certainly that the vote of no-confidence the Adversary had tried to wage against me failed miserably against me—and that I was still standing when it was all said and done.

So if you ever want to know from me how I'll know that I have succeeded in living the life that He has wanted to live? That's simple—for I'll be awaiting the results of the biggest no-confidence vote of all. But on THAT final day—there will be one marked difference. It will be the fact that just as I have shown confidence in Him, so will He even do so and more for me. And when that time comes, that's all that will matter anyway. I'll be standing before the Parliament of the Universe—and believing Him that the coalition government He has had me to help Him lead will still be standing. I'll let you know later when I find out the final results…

[Chapter 25:] [Big Sandy, TX] An Imaginary Conversation WITH And My Personal "Kaddish" Over Messrs. Armstrong and Tkach, Sr.

Hey--I just realized something while we were both in LA....hold on...it looks like we both got somehow Divinely transported completely away from West Texas. (Yep--we sure ain't in Kansas anymore, Toto!) And guess what? Remember in an earlier chapter when I told you about my first feast in Big Sandy. Guess where we wound up? Looks like we're standing right on the old grounds of what used to be Ambassador College here. We may not be in Jerusalem just yet...but I do know that we're at least east of the Trinity River here. Maybe I know why now...because I remember a vision I had years ago that in a sense helped me say goodbye to some of my past and move on to the future. Let's walk over to what used to be Lake Loma and do one more thing, ok?

[EDITORIAL DISCLAIMER:] This next-to-last chapter isn't written here either to discredit both Mr. Armstrong or Mr. Tkach, Sr. OR to conversely put them on some sort of extremely high pedestal. INSTEAD, I feel that in a sense this was truly a vision that my Lord gave me to reconcile not only my previous past in WCG/GCI, but also the current life I live now as well. One of the main themes of the Jewish ceremony called "Havdalah" that is done at the end of the Sabbath, one of the main themes involves the concept of transitions and change from one thing to another. Let's say that this chapter might serve as a sort of personal "Kaddish" or memorial service that I never got to say over these two (especially over Mr. Tkach, Sr.) after the "changes" in 1995.

To all of my brethren that are either current or former members of WCG/GCI:

I hope that you will not take what follows as blasphemy or heresy or disrespect for the memories of Mr. Armstrong and/or Mr. Tkach, Sr. Instead, I beseech you all to take this chapter as my way of personal reconciliation and healing between the spiritual roots of my past and the man that I am now. And I hope that you will prayerfully consider this as an opportunity to allow the Holy Spirit to touch your heart and help you do the same.

For those of you that are more of what I would now call a more traditional "evangelical/orthodox" Christian (or even possibly someone who has never made the quality choice to make His Son YOUR choice to be YOUR Savior

and Lord that our Abba Father intended to happen for you in the first place: I hope that for you this chapter will serve as a final synopsis of what we have discussed in this book and also especially give you some final lessons for you to remember based on what both of these gentlemen both directly and (for most of us within WCG/GCI) indirectly that I feel will be a blessing in your life today.

And especially to those of you and your family that might be a part of a church that is right now in the middle of a church split or schism of some kind, let the things that even after Mr. Armstrong's and Mr. Tkach, Sr.'s deaths still ring out, inspire, and challenge you to focus on the main things in the midst of your crisis that should matter most. I hope that you will use them as spiritual anchors given to you by God to help you navigate the rough seas ahead for all of you.

When the Lord started approaching me to write this book, I really questioned Him on how I could best communicate all of this to you, the reader, in a way you could quickly understand. I asked Him to show me the best way to paint the picture for you in words of all I have went through in WCG/GCI.

One day, He gave me His answer in the form of a vision during a time of prayer. The best way I would describe it would be to equate it like a TV news piece that maybe a prominent journalist of the stature like the late Ted Koppel might do on the program "Nightline" that would from time to time feature an interview with either a celebrity figure or politician. (This in particular probably appeals to me most primarily due to my own previous journalistic experience.) Then add some possible theme and/or background music along the lines of Madonna's "Say Goodbye" and imagine the effect that watching this news piece on TV might have on you. Then you'd probably get in a nutshell the specific feelings that I may have about Mr. Armstrong and Mr. Tkach, Sr. and the legacies they both left behind for us in WCG.

I may not exactly be able to convey in words the exact play-by-play description of this "imaginary conversation" with both of these gentlemen--but maybe I can at least convey to you the major highlights. These two men even now after their deaths still have some major influence on my own spiritual life and have served as mentors to me that pointed me to the cross of my Savior and Meshiach. But now they rest in their graves awaiting for the resurrection to come that they looked forward to all their lives.

As a result, now the obligation and burden comes to folks like me who have been involved in some way with WCG/GCI to pick up the torch and mantle that they have laid down, strive to take it even a little further down the road than they both took it, and do our best to give them voice so that you can hear a little bit about what they thought and spoke--and then (with Divine wisdom and discernment guiding you, of course) maybe urge you to take and apply those lessons in your own life as you may need to. It is a responsibility that I do not take lightly--and it will probably be a necessary burden and obligation that I'll carry with me to my death (or the Rapture...whichever may come first...)

AND NOW THE VISION:

I saw myself walking around a beach next to the Pacific Ocean (maybe around the Los Angeles, CA area...possibly even Marina Del Rey?) Hey, it's probably appropriate that I might meet these two guys here. Mr. Tkach was himself in WWII in the Navy--and I'm sure Mr. Armstrong during his lifetime may have possibly spent a little time during his children's formative years playing on the beach with his kids.

But I never thought I'd ever even see the two of them sitting on a park bench, wearing khaki shorts and Hawaiian shirts (LOL--I forgot to check to see if they were also wearing black sox and sandals....)--and of all the things I could catch them doing...FEEDING THE BIRDS! But that's where I found them--doing exactly what I never thought either of them would have the humility to do. ["Maybe, " I wondered, "... this has something to do with what the Lord said about feeding the sparrows? I don't know!"]

I saw them sitting on the park bench and recognized them right away. "Mr. Armstrong? Mr. Tkach?", I asked them. I introduced myself and we greeted each other--and the conversation began.

I first thanked them for the unique privilege of finally being able to meet them in person and the influence they both had on my life and my relationship with Christ through the teachings and legacies they both left behind. They, in turn, told me that they had heard some things about me from the Kingdom connections they had and reminded me that they as well as others that I once knew in WCG that had previously passed on were a part of the great cloud of witnesses described in

Hebrews that were cheering me on to finish the race and stay the course my God commissioned me to do.

Then the obvious question came--"...Why on earth are you two spending your time in the afterlife out here on this beach feeding a bunch of birds?"

They explained to me that this was their new and latest assignment that God the Father had put them on. Apparently, they both liked the beach so much during their lives on earth that when God handed out the job assignments and mentioned that there were some beach jobs available--well, they were the very first to raise their hands. I sure got a real chuckle out of that one..."Hmmm...ok...," I muttered after that chuckle...They also reminisced about their experiences on earth...all the lessons they learned, the trials and the triumphs, the highlights and the lowlights, etc.

Then I reported on what I had personally done and seen back on earth. I told them of all the miracles I had seen and witnessed as well as the heartbreaks and heartaches I and others not only have had, but also are still facing. I told them what I went through during the '95 split and all the H-E-double hockey sticks I and the rest of us went through during that time.

They stopped me, put their hands on my shoulders, and silently sat as I wept and cried about what happened. "...Can you please forgive us for this? We didn't mean to do this to you and put you through what you had to go through. We're sorry--can you please forgive us?" As they sat by me and wiped away the tears from my face; with a look of compassion that reflected the love the Savior has for us, I told them--"...Yes, I do. Don't worry about it. Besides, the past is behind me anyhow. And in the end, He did make it all work out for the best when everything was said and done. "

Then as I continued my report to them, I told them that "...your work wasn't completely in vain." I told them of all the things that I'm hearing from a lot more folks preaching about the Sabbath and the Holy Days in various degrees much more today than was done during their ministry--and from all places the most unexpected people and churches. I told them about the rising sun and emerging tiger that the Messianic Jewish movement in West Texas had now become. Mr. Tkach was obviously concerned about possible issues of legalism and how people can go to unnecessary extremes in what they believed--but they were both overall seemingly glad to hear that others were at least beginning to show some interest in them in some fashion.

I also told them about the revival that is happening in the prison system and how exactly God is moving mightily in those units than ever before. I also told them about all the great things my God has done for me personally over recent years-- unexpected favor, traveling mercies, financial provision, and much more.

I also told them that there's a lot more solid and balanced Biblical teaching these days from teachers in the Body of Christ that are really and truly doing their part to teach truth about how God can be their Divine Healer. I even related to them how one lady named Billye Brim was not only somewhat herself knowledgable to some degree about the Biblical Feasts, but also talked about the roots of the Pentecostal church in America--and in particular, one name that Mr. Armstrong might have been familiar with...Aimee Semple McPherson. Mr. Armstrong said with a twinkle in his eye and rubbing his chin with one of his hands: "...Yeah, I remember hearing that name at least once or twice. Come to think of it, I think that I even went to a few of her services back in my younger days..."

They both overall seemed pleased with the good reports I was giving them and had the biggest grins on their faces, smiling from ear to ear. And they seemed somewhat encouraged that at least a few people in several place had not completely bowed their knee to Baal and were at least trying to do something constructive for their Lord.

At this point, Mr. Tkach, Sr. injected a question--"How's my boy doing? How's my son doing on the job that God and I told him to do?" I responded, "From what I can tell from my limited perspective, he seems to be all right and doing what he can with the resources and help that God has given him. I did get to meet him once at church when I lived in Albuquerque. He seemed like a nice guy and easy to talk to."

I took that opportunity to tell both of them how God has blessed us all in WCG since their departures and since the '95 split. I told them the stories I knew of all the people in the evangelical Christian community and how they came alongside us while we went through the turbulent transition period. I told them of folks like Jack Hayford and other prominent figures as well as lesser-known people who've helped us out in many ways over the years.

Then they asked me, "How about YOU--how have you changed since the split? How do you see things now in WCG as opposed to when you first came in?" I first said to them that there were areas where I personally disagreed with Headquarters on--especially in regards to the issue of Sabbath and Holy Day observances. I might not be as legalistic about doing them as I once was--but I'm still more prone to keeping Passover and Tabernacles than Christmas and Easter.

They were a bit puzzled, though, to hear how I had changed spiritually in regards to "the baptism of the Holy Spirit", keeping Hanakkuh IN ADDITION TO the Holy Days, or other things such as "speaking in tongues" or what spiritual gifts really are. But after my explanation they seemed somewhat satisfied that my additional personal beliefs were based on conscience developed as a result of a detailed study of the Scriptures and were willing to tolerate these personal differences with their own past teachings.

As the conversation went on, I asked both of them if they had any regrets about what they did. Mr. Armstrong, with deep regret and sadness in his eyes, put his head in his hands and said, "I wish I had communicated to the ministers who were under me a lot better what I felt our God was trying to tell His Church. But my words got twisted; Satan used them against me; and caused the brethren I was responsible to God for to stumble. It really breaks my heart to see Christ's sheep were unnecessarily scattered due to certain things I did or said--or, even worse, what they *claimed* I said. If only I had said something just right...if only I had done things a little better...if only..." I could tell by the quivering in his voice and the sadness in his eyes as well as the deep pain of shame, guilt, and regret that Mr. Armstrong felt at that particular moment. I really felt for the poor guy...

Mr. Tkach, in contrast, when he spoke threw back a hearty laugh and piped up, "...I had the exact opposite problem. I wished that I had used a lot more wisdom and discernment when we were announcing the doctrinal changes of when NOT to speak or say anything at all. In otherwords, I regret not keeping my big fat mouth shut a little more often." We all chuckled at that remark.

By this time, I could tell that they were getting anxious to move on—but I asked them to stay a little longer and tell me something. "What would you say now to all the folks out there now? What advice would you give them? If there's anything you wish to say to them, here's your chance."

Mr. Armstrong started by telling me the following:

(1.) "...Don't believe me—believe your Bible! Don't take anything at face value what any man says about the Bible. Read the Word for yourself and be like the Bereans who '...searched the Scriptures to see whether these these things are true.'

(2.) ".....If there's anything that you believe that's contrary to the Word of God, remember that it's YOU that needs to change—NOT God or His Word! God and His Word NEVER change. You should never change Scripture to fit your doctrine. Rather, you should see that your doctrine lines up with what the Word of God says."

Mr. Tkach then added:

(1.) "...Remind the pastors of what I told them before I died about the fact that their job is to be shepherds, NOT sheriffs.

(2.) "...Remind the people that their purpose in God is not to be served, but to serve others themselves. Remind them that Christ during His lifetime came to serve and not to be served.

(3.) (referring to me personally) "...Let them know what you went through and tell them what legalism really is and what it looks like. Tell them how legalism of ANY kind (and it doesn't matter whether you believe the Sabbath is Saturday or Sunday or whatever) kills and destroys lives and shatters dreams."

M r. Armstrong then said, "There's one more thing I wanted to say to you in closing...but rather than tell you now, I'm going to let Him (referring to God Himself) tell you Himself because He's also got some things He wants to say to you after we leave." Then Mr. Armstrong looked at Mr. Tkach and said, "It's time to go."

But just as they were getting up from the park bench and preparing to leave, I stopped them for a second and said, "...But please wait a second before you go. I just want you both to know so much how I appreciate the service that both of you have given to God and His Church. Mr. Tkach, I also thank you personally as a grandson of a WWII vet for your service to your country." Mr. Tkach nodded at me when I said that.

I continued, "...But I thank you both most of all for being obedient to God and walking in the light that He gave you while you were alive. For if ya'll hadn't, I wouldn't be where I am today. And thank you both so much also for letting me have the chance to talk to you in the way we just did."

Mr. Armstrong said as he and Mr. Tkach were turning to leave, "Don't mention it. Remember that in all that you're still doing right now that we're cheering you on as you go—us and a lot of others that you both do and don't even know about. And we look forward to seeing you again soon in the Kingdom."

We bearhugged, shook hands, and then they went on their way as I stayed seated on the park bench. "Come on, Joe, " Mr. Armstrong gestured to Mr. Tkach. "…Let's see what's shaking on the other end of the beach. We've got some other birds to take care of." They walked towards the south and headed a little further down the beach to another flock of birds that was there—and I was left to myself to consider what all had just transpired.

I sat on that park bench for a little while longer pondering all of what Mr. Armstrong and Mr. Tkach had just told me. Then a man wearing a tallit (Jewish prayer shawl), long robes, and sandals started coming towards me and the park bench. I immediately recognized him and said, "…Hi, Yeshua." He greeted me with a warm smile and sat beside me on the park bench.

I then turned to Him and said, "…Thank you so much for arranging this unique opportunity to meet Mr. Armstrong and Mr. Tkach in the way I just did. I definitely had a lot to say to them—that's for sure." He nodded and looked towards the ocean. Then I asked Yeshua, "Mr. Armstrong said that You had some things to tell me?"

Yeshua responded, "Yes, I do. Tell the people when you get back home the following—tell them I died for them. Tell them that I took the stripes and punishment so that they can be healed. Tell them I was buried in the tomb for 3 days just like I said. Tell them that I rose again. Tell them that they can have everlasting life and live forever if they'll repent of their sins and believe in Me and in the Father who has sent Me."

And then with sadness in His eyes, but also with a look of compassion— "…But most of all, tell them that I love them and that I'm coming back real soon and to be ready for Me when I come. Will you tell them these things for Me?" I said to Him in response, "After what I've just heard and seen, I certainly will." Yeshua then said to me, "Thank you."

"Yeshua," I then queried Him. "…Mr. Armstrong told me that he had one more thing to tell me, but he said that You wanted to take care of that Yourself instead. What was it?"

"He wanted Me to give you this card." The card looked like one of those audiovisual greeting cards that you see a lot at places like Wal-Mart. "Open it…," He urged me. "See what's inside."

I took the card from His hands—and when I opened it, it was like I was hearing an old familiar voice from the past…in fact, it was like I was hearing a voice from the grave—and none other than Mr. Armstrong himself. But it wasn't the man I just talked to a while ago on this beach.

Instead, it sounded like Mr. Armstrong speaking as if he were in his prime…and his voice was ringing clear to me across the years as if Mr. Armstrong was giving a sermon while he was alive to either an audience of Ambassador College students or a worldwide satellite telecast during the Feast of Tabernacles, "…Brethren, we have read the back of the book. We have read the end of the story. And in the end, WE WIN!"

At hearing this, I fell apart in tears and cried on Yeshua's shoulder. Then a song came to me—

We've a story to tell to the nations,
That shall turn their hearts to the right,
A story of truth and mercy,
A story of peace and light,
A story of peace and light.

For the darkness shall turn to dawning,
And the dawning to noonday bright;
And Christ's great kingdom shall come on earth,
The kingdom of love and light.

We've a song to be sung to the nations,
That shall lift their hearts to the Lord,
A song that shall conquer evil
And shatter the spear and sword,
And shatter the spear and sword.

For the darkness shall turn to dawning,
And the dawning to noonday bright;
And Christ's great kingdom shall come on earth,
The kingdom of love and light.

We've a message to give to the nations,
That the Lord who reigns up above
Has sent us His Son to save us,
And show us that God is love,
And show us that God is love.

For the darkness shall turn to dawning,
And the dawning to noonday bright;
And Christ's great kingdom shall come on earth,
The kingdom of love and light.

We've a Savior to show to the nations,
Who the path of sorrow has trod,
That all of the world's great peoples
Might come to the truth of God,
Might come to the truth of God.

For the darkness shall turn to dawning,
And the dawning to noonday bright;
And Christ's great kingdom shall come on earth,
The kingdom of love and light.

At the last words of that old hymn, my tears melted away and my heart was once again at peace. I got up from the park bench, hugged Yeshua one last time, and headed back towards the north. After I turned to go, I went a little ways down the beach when I suddenly turned back around to look at the park bench only to find it empty again.

I had a big smile on my face for once in my life. Everything I really wanted to say to all parties concerned had finally been said. No more goodbyes, no more Havdallahs…I can go on now with the rest of my life knowing that my Savior truly loves and cares for me. I know now that it's ME and others that are still alive that these folks are counting on to get His main jobs done.

And now I also know for myself that I've got at least two powerful cheerleaders urging me to go on and move forward to the prize that's before me with boldness and confidence. And when my own work is done on this earth, these gentlemen will be among the witnesses that will greet me when I'm finally allowed to enter the joy of the Kingdom that my God will set before me. I guess it's time to get back to work then, eh? Besides a couple of older gentlemen as well as my Lord and

Savior and the very God of the universe that I don't want to disappoint. And they now expect me to carry an important message—a message that I will carry and proclaim until death.

Maybe one of the writers of the Apocrypha said it best here:

Ecclesiaticus Chapter 44

44:1 Let us now praise men of renown, and our fathers in their generation.

44:2 The Lord hath wrought great glory through his magnificence from the beginning.

44:3 Such as have borne rule in their dominions, men of great power, and endued with their wisdom, shewing forth in the prophets the dignity of prophets,

44:4 And ruling over the present people, and by the strength of wisdom instructing the people in most holy words.

44:5 Such as by their skill sought out musical tunes, and published canticles of the scriptures.

44:6 Rich men in virtue, studying beautifulness: living at peace in their houses.

44:7 All these have gained glory in their generations, and were praised in their days.

44:8 They that were born of them have left a name behind them, that their praises might be related:

44:9 And there are some, of whom there is no memorial: who are perished, as if they had never been: and are become as if they had never been born, and their children with them.

44:10 But these were men of mercy, whose godly deeds have not failed:

44:11 Good things continue with their seed,

44:12 Their posterity are a holy inheritance, and their seed hath stood in the covenants.

44:13 And their children for their sakes remain for ever: their seed and their glory shall not be forsaken.

44:14 Their bodies are buried in peace, and their name liveth unto generation and generation.

44:15 Let the people shew forth their wisdom, and the church declare their praise.

[Chapter 26: Jerusalem—At The End of The Trail]

Hey--wait a minute…I just noticed something…LOOKS LIKE WE FINALLY MADE IT—to our final home, that is! YAY!!! (And we didn't have to walk or do anything else on our own again from Big Sandy, either…isn't Divine translation and transportation a great thing?) And there's really no sense in me giving directions again, either—for even I (probably like you do) have no absolute clue how we got here in the first place, much less get around this joint. And look—the gates of the New City are right in front of us! I can't believe we're finally here—can you?

Shoot, though—that also means our most recent journey through my life—especially my life and times in WCG/GCI—must for now sadly come to an end. AWHHHH!!! It's been a fascinating trip—don't you think? Hey, look at your shoes that I gave you before we first left home? They don't look a day older than when we first started—and they sure as bleep don't look worn out! Neat—ain't it? We don't have to get you that replacement pair at Payless like we originally thought.

As we come closer to the gates of the Old City and the Jerusalem city limits and prepare to enter a place that both of us have never been before and which will now be our new permanent home, I just wanted to say that it's truly been a pleasure to have you, the reader along with me for the walk and ride every step of the way through this most recent extended trip through my life. I know that it was really a sacrifice for you to give of your time to join me for this thing—and I trust that it's been worth every mile of the trip for you in return. I also hope that through this book that you've been able to not only learn the lessons I had to learn the hard way about my time in WCG/GCI, but also the things that Mr. Armstrong and Mr. Tkach, Sr. reminded us about.

(Call comes up on my cell phone…) Yes, Lord? Yes—I just barely got in town a minute ago. In fact, I'm just coming up through the city gates right now with my travel partner and we're fixing to wrap things up and part ways…You need to see me right away as soon as I can get there? OK—show me the way…and I'll be right over….thanks, love ya, Abba…bye…(Hang up phone…)

Well, friend, it's been good to get to know you and travel all this way with you. This is sure a big city with lots to do. Once you and I get settled in here, let's do lunch again sometime, shall we? And relax—NO MORE WALKING NEXT TIME…I promise! (HA HA HA!) I think we've done more than our share of it recently anyway, don't you? Well—keep in touch, see you later—and in the meantime, shalom rubakah b'shem Y'shua Ha'Meshiach, ok? See ya! Have fun!

(Cell phone rings again…) Hello? Hey, I was just about to call ya….Listen—just barely got in town and I, uh….

(Later on after arriving in the Old City…)

Secretary: "…Sir, there's a Coy Holley is waiting to see you…"

(Door opens…)

Unknown voice: "…Coy, glad you finally got here…We've been waiting a long time to see you. Come on in…we've got a LOT to talk about…"

Chapter 27 (Jerusalem--Part II) EPILOGUE--Mourning for Javert

[At night sometime later after we each get settled in our new home and occupations in the Kingdom of God...I'm looking out over the city walls into the valley below...As I'm looking out over the New Jerusalem skyline, you suddenly appear and come towards me...]

Hey--long time, no see, friend...Good to see ya'll again...what brings you out there this time of night?...Well, I admit--I do, too. This place does look great at night indeed. Come join me in taking in this midnight view...

Man, it seems like the journey we both took together was so long ago--and yet I still remember it as if we just came into town yesterday. How are you liking your new place and job assignment?...Hmmh, a doorkeeper, eh? Not exactly what you were expecting at first? You know what the Word says about your job, do you?...if I were you, I wouldn't complain too much. Probably much easier work than what we both had to do in the past world...And the best part? No unemployment, the pay's great, and it's ETERNAL job security!! (We both laugh...)

I guess I can't complain too much, either...I'm still having to get used to this "scribe by trade" thing...not too much different than what I left behind. At least the technology's a lot better--and I don't have to deal as much with system crashes or a bunch of blankety-blank pop-up windows or slow browsers...

Yeah, life sure is good here. Definitely one of those Hallmark card moments where there's people you know back home you'd love to send those "...wish you were here" type postcards...Maybe in a sense, that's exactly what brings me out here tonight...

I just happened to be reminded earlier about what our Master said before he came back here to die in both Matthew 23:37-39 and Luke 13:34-35:

Matthew 23:37-39

The Message (MSG)

37-39 "Jerusalem! Jerusalem! Murderer of prophets! Killer of the ones who brought you God's news! How often I've ached to embrace your children, the way a hen gathers her chicks under her wings, and you wouldn't let me. And now you're so desolate, nothing but a ghost town. What is there left to say? Only this: I'm out of here soon. The next time you see me you'll say, 'Oh, God has blessed him! He's come, bringing God's rule!'"

Luke 13:34-35

The Message (MSG)

[32-35] Jesus said, "Tell that fox that I've no time for him right now. Today and tomorrow I'm busy clearing out the demons and healing the sick; the third day I'm wrapping things up. Besides, it's not proper for a prophet to come to a bad end outside Jerusalem.

Jerusalem, Jerusalem, killer of prophets,
    abuser of the messengers of God!
How often I've longed to gather your children,
    gather your children like a hen,
Her brood safe under her wings—
    but you refused and turned away!
And now it's too late: You won't see me again
    until the day you say,
    'Blessed is he
    who comes in
    the name of God.'"

You remember those, too? Don't you get the sense that when Yeshua/Jesus was looking at this city from the outside maybe He was truly crying out His heart in anguish in pure agony? I guess I do, too. I wonder if during His time, He'd given ANYTHING and EVERYTHING (oh, yeah--I almost forgot...He DID give everything, even right down to His own life, I recall...) to basically tell them THIS in Texas talk--

"MAN, what I'd give to have you truly get what I'm trying to tell you right now...to tell you how much I love you and how I only wanted to give you stuff to where you could have some hope and be able to prosper and have good success! BUT YOU WOULDN'T LET ME!!! Now I'm gonna have to go from here and head back to my Daddy in heaven--and I'm not gonna be able to be around and help you out as much as I'd like to in person! I'd like to have your back--but pretty soon I won't be able to even do THAT for you!!!

"...And now, guess what? You're gonna hurt and feel pain like you never had before! People are gonna run over you, spit on your face, mistreat ya'll, and do who knows what to you. And you're not gonna see the end of it until you FINALLY decide to (pardon the pun) have a "COME TO JESUS" type meeting with Me and finally have the horsesense to say yourself, "OK--I GIVE UP!! I SURRENDER! You're truly who You say You are! You warned us about this--and now I'm such a clumsy, stupid fool who don't have a lick of sense that You gave me in the first place! HELP--COME QUICK!! I'm in deep (bleep) trouble--and if YOU don't come help me NOW, I'm sunk!"

Would you imagine the heartbreak on the Master's face as He said that? Maybe after reading those words for myself in His Word, I'm getting a slight touch of that myself tonight...

Yeah, I know the rule...no tears allowed because we ain't supposed to cry here anymore since He's dried all our tears and taken our cares and burdens from us? But you know--all the same, it seems that the hardest part to adjusting to life out here was realizing for the first time just how many folks I once personally knew (ESPECIALLY during my time in WCG/GCI) that AREN'T here! Some of them were even pastors and others who I thought were great men and women of God that I even looked up to at one time or another. But yet, I'm here--AND THEY'RE NOT! WHY????

What kept them from coming here? What was so bad about what they thought this place might possibly be and/or even the people within it that they just had to make the stupid decision they did to totally reject Him and the things He's said to all of us? Why didn't they have a lick of sense to possibly realize that maybe coming here might be a whole lot better than going to that other place of eternal destruction where FOR SURE they'll NEVER EVER be able to change their mind ever again and possibly still repent...and turn instead towards Him and His grace?

The answers for them have been plain as day--and yet they refuse to see it! I still to this day don't understand all of that--do you?

In a sense tonight, I'm kind of like the Master in at least one way...that there's probably a few people that I'd at least like to send some "wish you were here" type postcards to if I had the chance. But now even if I did send them, they certainly wouldn't get them now considering the horrific place they're now residing. And the worst part of all--they only have themselves to blame for it.

Just like the Savior Himself said those famous words to this very city long ago, so do I at least have a couple of final impressions about how I might see this overall situation. I briefly mentioned, for instance, in Chapter 24 about the overall scene that Andy Wilkenson set in his album "The Life and Times of Charlie Goodnight" where Wilkenson paints a word and musical picture of Colonel Goodnight just before he and his wife, Molly Mary Ann, leave the JA Ranch and Palo Duro Canyon for good. The scene shows Colonel Goodnight taking a moment to reflect on all of the things he went through just to finally get to the place where at the time he thought was going to be his ultimate equivalent of Shangri-La (cowboy style, of course). And now, like it or not--it's time to go...and he'll never be able to come back.

As I look out at this Holy City's skyline, I myself tonight also feel a little bit like Colonel Goodnight once did. And what might I be seeing as I look back in my own past life similar to what Goodnight did? The answer to that lies in the eventual fate of one of the central characters of "Les Miserables"--Inspector Javert.

The contrast as you go through "Les Miz..." is very self-evident. Jean Valjean commits a petty crime in desperation to feed his family and is forced to pay an unfairly dear price to the State as a result. Valjean goes through situation after situation, rodeo after rodeo--and is forced to go through some very heartwrenching things. But at the end of his life ONLY PRIMARILY by the very grace of God, even on his deathbed, Valjean, through a confident faith and determination in the providence and wisdom of Almighty God, still manages to find a measure of peace and rest because he has decided to place his ultimate trust and hope in God that he has, despite the chains of his past, found a measure of Divine grace and favor that will allow him to truly rest in his grave inside His sovereign grace and presence.

(I struggle to hold back the tears, but they still fall regardless of anything I try to do to stop them...) But now as I look out over this city, my eyes (like the Savior's eyes were fixed on here) are firmly fixed on the eventual fate of Javert--and oh--for him and others like him especially, I'd like to do more for him that just send him a stupid "wish you were here" postcard. AND THAT"S why I'm crying--because I'm watching Javert jump off the bridge...AND I CAN'T DO A BLEEPING THING ABOUT IT!!!!

OR WAIT A MINUTE...maybe Javert HASN'T jumped off the bridge yet!!! Maybe I've still got a little time to help him out real quick and maybe give him one last chance to consider his most foolish possible decision!! In fact, maybe this would be a good time to pull a play off of Charlie Chaplin's playbook and DO SOMETHING to save him! Hurry...come with me before it's too late!!!

(Shouting to someone about to jump off the bridge below...) HEY YOU--JAVERT!!! WHY DO YOU WANT TO JUMP OFF THE BRIDGE FOR? WHAT HOLDS YOU BACK FROM RECEIVING HIS GRACE NOW? STOP--*PLEASE DON'T JUMP! PLEASE DON'T TRY TO KILL YOURSELF IN THAT RIVER...PLEASE...PLEASE...PLEASE...with major league sugar on top? You don't have to rely on this legalism thing to save you...Just because it doesn't seem fair and just and right according to your law and legalistic standards doesn't mean that His grace can't still cover you! STOP--let Him love you BEFORE it's too late!*

By the way, WHO IS this Javert fellow to me anyway? Even some of my own former brethren I once knew in WCG--but are now for one reason or another in one of the splinter groups (or one of the newest incarnations of such). In particular, this is a direct word for those NOW involved with either the United Church of God, An International Association (i.e.--Victor Kubik, James Hulme, etc.); the Restored Church of God (David Pack); the Living Church of God (Roderick Meredith); Church of God, International; the Intercontinental Church of God/Garner Ted Evangelistic Association; and other HWA-related offshoots (remember, though, my earlier mention about the Huntsville Church of God and the Christian Church of God NOT being formally considered by myself to be "splinter groups").. But Javert can also stand for ANYONE ELSE who is trapped right now in ANY form of what most in "orthodox Christianity" call cultism and/or legalism.

First, Inspector Javert--can we both have a seat and talk for a minute or two? Ok, good... Let me be straight about something. From my experience on both sides of the fence, let me give you what I generally find to be what most in what you personally might consider "Christians falsely so-called". Usually when people define a cult or a group that's totally wacko in their eyes theologically, it's usually because that THEY were raised in a certain theological tradition themselves--and to them, anything that to them is totally bizarre and unheard of IS TO THEM A

CULT--end of story. But if I try to challenge them and get THEM to tell me in detail WHAT IS a cult in the first place, I bet nine will get you ten they couldn't do it rationally. Usually instead, it's based on a fear of things that they have never heard about in the first place such as Sabbath, Holy Days, etc.

Listen, Javert--trying to get the word about about teachings like these while at the same time trying to throw rocks at them and treating them as enemies of the State if they don't completely convert to your way of theological thinking doesn't necessarily win friends or influence people. Plus saying that you're the ONLY true church--and if you aren't a part of it, you'll miss out on salvation and/or the "place of safety" in Petra or whatever...isn't any wonder why THEY might in turn decide to call you a cult?

Also--have you ever considered that during his own lifetime, even HWA himself usually refused to put himself on ANY high pedestal or say that he was anything more that just a servant of God? Do you even recall where he himself said, "I am NOT Reverend--for no one is reverend BUT GOD!"? Mr. Armstrong NEVER claimed to be God in the first place or anything bigger than a simple man of God who had many faults and mistakes. And yet YOU still put him on a pedestal regardless? I wonder how he would look at you and your claims now if he were alive during THESE times we live in? Can you please have a reality check and not put him much higher than what he actually claimed to be? And will you please lay down your spiritual and theological weapons and cease firing against the rest of Christianity?

At the same time, let me say something to my more mainstream Evangelical friends in your defense, Inspector. First to my fellow Evangelicals--have you ever truly looked back at WHY such things as the Nicene Creed was instituted by Emporer Constantine and his minions in the first place? It definitely WASN'T originally invented so that you could say some pretty things that sound good in church. Most of my Evangelical friends don't realize that the BIG reasons for the Creed's institution in the first place were primarily POLITICAL in nature at the time.

Constantine wanted to appease the pagans who wanted to keep THEIR festivals of frivolity (you don't want to know too many details about what they REALLY kept) while discriminating against those who preferred to keep the traditional Passover festival on Nisan 14 as described in Exodus. Part of the whole thing was to insure uniformity in doctrine...at the expense of what they called the "Judaisers" that didn't want to go along with the pagans and who still wanted to hold to the original doctrines Jesus' apostles REALLY taught.

(Oh--were you also aware that a good number of them whom Constantine discrimminated against were JEWISH? Somehow, that little fact tends to get left out of what we consider most of what we tend to call reliable theological sources of early "Christianity"...) In case you don't know, I've got a term for you-- "REPLACEMENT THEOLOGY"! As a result, you--my Evangelical friends haven't always been welcoming of your brethren (and YES--there ARE such things as these brethren) who prefer to go to church on Saturday or keep the traditional Jewish festivals or who don't eat things like pork, shrimp, or anything that Leviticus 11 doesn't permit). Just because they don't go to church on Sunday or keep Easter or eat a bacon cheeseburger DOES NOT necessarily mean that they can't be TRUE Christians. The way I tend to see it--you tend to treat folks like these as if they were aliens from another planet that need to be obliterated and destroyed. Give me a break--please?

BOTH lots of you in BOTH camps have seemed to have not fully understood what the Apostle Paul said to the members of the Colossian church about this very subject:

Colossians 2

New International Version (NIV)

2 I want you to know how hard I am contending for you and for those at Laodicea, and for all who have not met me personally. [2] My goal is that they may be encouraged in heart and united in love, so that they may have the full riches of complete understanding, in order that they may know the mystery of God, namely, Christ, [3] in whom are hidden all the treasures of wisdom and knowledge. [4] I tell you this so that no one may deceive you by fine-sounding arguments. [5] For though I am absent from you in body, I am present with you in spirit and delight to see how disciplined you are and how firm your faith in Christ is.

Spiritual Fullness in Christ

[6] So then, just as you received Christ Jesus as Lord, continue to live your lives in him, [7] rooted and built up in him, strengthened in the faith as you were taught, and overflowing with thankfulness.

8 See to it that no one takes you captive through hollow and deceptive philosophy, which depends on human tradition and the elemental spiritual forces[a] of this world rather than on Christ.

9 For in Christ all the fullness of the Deity lives in bodily form, 10 and in Christ you have been brought to fullness. He is the head over every power and authority. 11 In him you were also circumcised with a circumcision not performed by human hands. Your whole self ruled by the flesh[b] was put off when you were circumcised by[c] Christ, 12 having been buried with him in baptism, in which you were also raised with him through your faith in the working of God, who raised him from the dead.

13 When you were dead in your sins and in the uncircumcision of your flesh, God made you[d] alive with Christ. He forgave us all our sins, 14 having canceled the charge of our legal indebtedness, which stood against us and condemned us; he has taken it away, nailing it to the cross. 15 And having disarmed the powers and authorities, he made a public spectacle of them, triumphing over them by the cross.[e]

Freedom From Human Rules

16 Therefore do not let anyone judge you by what you eat or drink, or with regard to a religious festival, a New Moon celebration or a Sabbath day. 17 These are a shadow of the things that were to come; the reality, however, is found in Christ. 18 Do not let anyone who delights in false humility and the worship of angels disqualify you. Such a person also goes into great detail about what they have seen; they are puffed up with idle notions by their unspiritual mind. 19 They have lost connection with the head, from whom the whole body, supported and held together by its ligaments and sinews, grows as God causes it to grow.

20 Since you died with Christ to the elemental spiritual forces of this world, why, as though you still belonged to the world, do you submit to its rules: 21 "Do not handle! Do not taste! Do not touch!"? 22 These rules, which have to do with things that are all destined to perish with use, are based on merely human commands and teachings. 23 Such regulations indeed have an appearance of wisdom, with their self-imposed worship, their false humility and their harsh treatment of the body, but they lack any value in restraining sensual indulgence.

Javert, can I tell ya'll something? You say that you fail to understand why other Christians don't see things as the 10 Commandments or the other things such folks as Mr. Armstrong taught you as important. And you're afraid that if you stop keeping the laws of God that it will lead to disobedience. And what's more--I even sense that when some of my Evangelical friends might say things to you like, "But why must you keep these obsolete Jewish traditions? Didn't Christ die on the cross and make these ordinances of none effort? What's the need of them anyway?"--that's when you REALLY cringe...

And back to my Evangelical friends for a moment--do you realize that when you say things about such Scriptures such as Leviticus 23: and Deuteronomy 16: (which I bet you've never probably truly read for yourself in the first place and in which until recent times probably hasn't even been preached in our pulpits much anyway) that you might be telling folks like Javert in their eyes that "...you CAN'T and aren't ALLOWED to keep the Law AT ALL and still be a true Christian". You're intolerant of things that you don't have the foggiest clue of understanding...

Hey--maybe I've got an idea here...maybe the two of you haven't been fully introduced to each other in the first place...Ok...Inspector Javert, meet the evangelical Christian community. Evangelical Christians, here's Inspector Javert. Now can we FINALLY establish a MUTUAL framework of understanding where TOGETHER we allow the Holy Spirit to teach us and direct us who truly is either for us or against us? Now can we start to tear down the veils and begin to treat each other as fellow citizens and pilgrims within His Divine commonwealth?

Ok...first to my fellow Evangelicals...would you be willing to start treating folks like Javert and his friends not as oddball theological nuts, but instead as folks that the Holy Spirit has Divinely gifted to teach on such Old Testament subjects that most people would find complex and boring to understand? Would you be willing to consider allowing them to play a part of your universal theological dodgeball team every now and then and allow them opportunities to bless you and others that you touch? Cool beans...that might be a small start in the right direction...

Inspector--can I tell you something else about my Evangelical friends? They're NOT trying to keep you necessarily from keeping God's law, festivals, Holy Days, and other things if that is what you, your conscience, and your Father in heaven may lead you to do. What they ARE more concerned about is this--what's the state of your HEART? Are you STILL after all this time trying to get God to love you and give you His approval based on those things you've done for Him? What use is keeping the Law (which by the way--I think even the Savior Himself said could be boiled down to TWO big commandments? Remember the Shema--"...thou shalt love the Lord your God with all of your heart, all of your strength, and all your mind...And the second is like it--to love your neighbor as yourself..." Wouldn't even YOU agree that you could jump through hoops all day--but yet as Paul told the Corinthians--"...without love, I am become as nothing"?

Very soon after I went through the changes in WCG, I went through the process of applying to become a Prison Fellowship volunteer. I remember distinctly that one of the things that was required of me in order for that application to be approved was that I basically had to agree to the Nicene Creed. Well, for someone who went through a few years of the pre-split WCG, I and others like me had more than a problem or two with this Nicene Creed thing due to past doctrines that Mr. Armstrong taught. Before I could even be approved, the Prison Fellowship Area Director literally had to call my pastor in Lubbock and talk to him for over a couple of hours because even SHE had no clue what all of us in WCG have went through.

But you know what, Javert? Years later, I now find myself in at least one place reciting that same Creed periodically. Guess what's in it? I don't see ANYTHING about you having to give up Sabbath, Holy Days, etc. to be considered by other Christians as being a part of "the Universal Body of Christ". Oh, yes--there's this stuff about Jesus being born of the Virgin Mary, crucified under Pontius Pilate, and other business like that...But nowhere in creeds and beliefs like this do I see where you have to give up what some might consider a Sabbatarian/Messianic lifestyle in order to become a true follower of Christ.

Javert--what they're basically trying to tell you is that salvation is first and foremost A MATTER OF YOUR HEART! They want to see that those things that you're still currently doing CONTRIBUTE and help lead you closer to an intimate relationship with Him and NOT be a detriment. It's NOT a matter of being good enough to get His approval. It's already too late for that, anyway. Instead, HE took care of the price of salvation for you and died just for you--IN SPITE OF ALL YOU'VE ever done! You don't have to jump through legalistic hoops to earn His favor...you just need to run to Him instead and let His grace give YOU something you don't deserve...He loves you right where you are no matter where you're at.

Javert...little buddy...can you do me a little favor? Just get off that bridge and ask for His help right now! No elaborate thees and thous required...Just shout aloud and ask for His help...He wants to touch you right where you're at right now and show you how much He really loves you...no strings, no hoops to jump through, no walking journeys on your hands and knees to Rome required...I promise you--it's not all that hard. And it'll be the best choice you've ever made...

Maybe you right now are like my friend, Javert. You may not have come through legalism or what some might consider a "cult" or have been a member of a church that was once a theological outlaw, but now regardless has found grace and true favor in His sight. But that doesn't mean you don't have some of these same questions Javert has. And you don't have to go through a "walking" journey of the type of life I've personally been through to know the Abba Daddy that I serve. Stop jumping through your own hoops and stop running from Him right now...but instead COME AND RUN TO HIM! And I know for sure that you'll truly find that same grace and favor in His sight and a rest and peace that can't be earned through legalistic means, but instead is truly beyond your comprehension and understanding. If there has been one central lesson I've been forced to learn the most in my own personal "walking journey", it's been this--that except for His grace and mercy, neither I or anyone else for that matter can truly stand. But WITH HIM, I know now that I can do all things through the very Son who strengthens and helps me throughout my personal travels ahead.

If you need some help answering some of these questions for yourself, please feel free to write or email me at one of the addresses below and I'll see about doing my part to help get you started in the right way in following Him. And if there's any resources I know of that can further help you in your own spiritual journey, I'll try to make sure that you have access to them as well. To do so, I'd be honored to hear from you at one of these following addresses:

Coy Reece Holley

@ Broken and Shattered Promises Ministries

1601 N. Date, Apt. 17E

Plainview, TX 79072

Email: CoyRH_SEATCBSPM@yahoo.com

And now, my final blessing to you in the meantime is based on Psalm 20:--that He send forth help SPEEDILY from His sanctuary in your times of distress; that in the meantime as you await His ultimate deliverance, you trust NOT in chariots or horses or in any of the things of this world...but SOLELY in those things that are of Him--SO THAT when you are victorious, that we will all be able to as a result shout for joy. And may He continue to do so all of the days of your life's journey until it's time to wrap it up and go home...And yes, Javert--it can STILL be MORNING instead of mourning for you--but ONLY if you'll allow it to be so!

"...But I would not have you to be ignorant, brethren, concerning them which are asleep, that ye sorrow not, even as others which have no hope. For if we believe that Jesus died and rose again, even so them also which sleep in Jesus will God bring with Him...For this we say unto you by the word of the Lord, that we which are alive and remain unto the coming of the Lord shall not prevent them which are asleep. For the Lord himself shall descend from heaven with a shout, with the voice of the archangel, and with the trump of God: and the dead in Christ shall rise first. Then we which are alive and remain shall be caught up together with them in the clouds, to meet the Lord in the air: and so shall we ever be with the Lord. WHEREFORE COMFORT ONE ANOTHER WITH THESE WORDS..." (1st Thessalonians 5:13-18)

Maranatha, Lord...even so, come quickly...for we need You more than ever! Baruch ha'ba b'shem Adonai!

In the name of The One who keeps me walking and who has kept my foot from stumbling--and who has kept me safe thus far... B'shem Yeshua Ha'Meshiach/the Lord Jesus Christ,

Coy Reece Holley

Made in the USA
Columbia, SC
02 April 2025

56035356R00215